City of Courts
Socializing Justice in Progressive Era Chicago

What could be more "liberal" than the modern idea of social responsibility for crime – that crime is less the product of free will than of
poverty and other social forces beyond the individual's control? And
what could be more "progressive" than the belief that the law should
aim for social, not merely individual, justice? In this work of social,
cultural, and legal history, Michael Willrich uncovers the contested
origins and paradoxical consequences of these two protean concepts
in the cosmopolitan cities of industrial America at the turn of the
twentieth century. In Progressive Era Chicago, social activists, judges,
and working-class families seeking justice transformed criminal courts
into laboratories of progressive democracy. Willrich argues that this
progressive effort to "socialize" urban justice redefined American liberalism and the rule of law, laying an urban seedbed for the modern
administrative welfare state. The rhetoric of social responsibility for
crime justified new measures to improve schools and home life, industrial wages and working conditions. But socializing justice weakened
the old protections of due process and civil liberties, opening the field
of everyday life to eugenics, compulsory medical treatment, and other
coercive forms of social regulation.

Michael Willrich is Assistant Professor in the Department of History at
Brandeis University. He has received the Biennial Article Prize of the
Society for Historians of the Gilded Age and Progressive Era and the
Erwin C. Surrency Prize from the American Society for Legal History.
Other awards include a National Endowment for the Humanities
Fellowship at the Newberry Library, an American Bar Foundation Post-
doctoral Fellowship, and a National Endowment for the Humanities
Summer Stipend.

D1225680

CAMBRIDGE HISTORICAL STUDIES IN AMERICAN
LAW AND SOCIETY

SERIES EDITOR
Christopher Tomlins *American Bar Foundation*

Previously published in the series:
Barbara Young Welke, *Recasting American Liberty:
Gender, Race, Law and the Railroad Revolution, 1865–1920*
Michael Vorenberg, *Final Freedom:
The Civil War, the Abolition of Slavery, and the Thirteenth Amendment*
Robert J. Steinfeld, *Coercion, Contract,
and Free Labor in Nineteenth Century America*
David M. Rabban, *Free Speech in Its Forgotten Years*
Jenny Wahl, *The Bondsman's Burden:
An Economic Analysis of the Common Law of Southern Slavery*
Michael Grossberg, *A Judgment for Solomon:
The d'Hauteville Case and Legal Experience in the Antebellum South*

City of Courts

Socializing Justice in Progressive Era Chicago

Michael Willrich

Brandeis University

CAMBRIDGE
UNIVERSITY PRESS

CAMBRIDGE UNIVERSITY PRESS
Cambridge, New York, Melbourne, Madrid, Cape Town, Singapore, São Paulo, Delhi

Cambridge University Press
32 Avenue of the Americas, New York, NY 10013-2473, USA

www.cambridge.org
Information on this title: www.cambridge.org/9780521794039

First published 2003
Reprinted 2006, 2007

A catalog record for this publication is available from the British Library

ISBN 978-0-521-79082-6 hardback
ISBN 978-0-521-79403-9 paperback

Transferred to digital printing 2009

For my father, Mason,
and in memory of my mother, Patricia Rowe Willrich

Contents

List of Tables, Figures, and Illustrations

Tables

Figures

Illustrations

Acknowledgments

As Americans living at the turn of the twentieth century worked out the moral implications of modernity, many questioned the possibility for truly autonomous individual agency – and thus for absolute criminal responsibility – in an urban-industrial society. This book examines the progressive promise and paradoxical consequences of this new social conception of crime, as it interacted with dramatic changes in urban culture, the bureaucratization of governance, and new ways of thinking about the social function of law in the industrial city.

Whether or not turn-of-the-century social thinkers were ultimately right about the root causes of the dizzying catalogue of human behavior called "crime," their insights certainly apply to the practice of history. In historical scholarship, no one acts alone. The fortune or famine of material resources, the formative influences of family and friends, the tireless schooling of mentors, and the complicity of colleagues: all these, no less than the will and fiber of the lone historian, shape the imagining and writing of history. And although (alas) the historian cannot hold these influences accountable for the errors of fact, technique, and judgment in the work that bears his name, there is a venerable tradition that he be allowed a few last words to acknowledge and thank them.

I first got serious about history as a college senior at Yale, writing my senior essay under Bill Cronon, who as a teacher and scholar has remained a role model for me ever since. One of the best things Bill ever did for me was to nudge me toward the University of Chicago for graduate school. For six years, the university gave me an exceptionally wide-ranging, intellectually rigorous, interdisciplinary environment in which to do my work. I am immensely grateful for the University Fellowship, the Phoenix Fellowship, and the Andrew W. Mellon Dissertation-Year Fellowship, which financed my studies. This book began as a dissertation, and I owe my largest intellectual debt to my remarkable committee: Kathleen Neils Conzen, William J. Novak, Thomas C. Holt, and George Chauncey. George shared his deep insights into urban culture and social policing. Tom guided my reading in social and cultural theory and insisted that I never lose sight of the global implications of local criminal justice. My education in legal history began the day I met Bill Novak. The initial idea for this project percolated out of dawn coffee talks with Bill. His critical commentary, boundless enthusiasm, and close friendship over the years have been invaluable. No one could ask for a more dedicated, open-minded, and relentlessly inquisitive mentor than my adviser and friend, Kathy Conzen. Her extraordinary seminar in U.S. social history set the tone for my graduate studies, and her unflagging interest and support has continually revived me. Thank you all.

The extensive collections in law, history, and social science at the University of Chicago's Regenstein Library and D'Angelo Law Library – and the skilled librarians and archivists who have built those collections – made the university an excellent place to hole up and do much of my research. Over the years, many other archives and libraries have aided and abetted my work, including the Special Collections of the University of Illinois at Chicago Library, the University Archives of Northwestern University, Chicago's Municipal Reference Library, the Social Law Library in Boston, Harvard's Langdell Law Library, the Schlesinger Library of Radcliffe College, and Chicago's Newberry Library. A special thanks goes to the Chicago Historical Society and the Cook County Circuit Court Archives, where all tolled, I spent several years of my life. Archie Motley, now retired, and his fellow archivists at the historical society maintain and cultivate one of the nation's finest urban history collections. Without the prodigious efforts of Phil Costello and Jeanie Child at the Circuit Court Archives, many of my best sources would still be collecting dust in a warehouse. Thanks to them, I was the first historian ever to touch the records of criminal cases cited in my footnotes.

Workshops, seminars, and conference panels too numerous to mention here have provided testing grounds for many of the ideas in this book. I single out my colleagues in the University of Chicago's Social History Workshop and Comparative Legal History Workshop, which I attended for many years; the Newberry Library Fellows Seminar; and, most recently, the terrific working group on New Directions in American Political History, run by Meg Jacobs, Bill Novak, and Julian Zelizer. I have also benefited from presenting this work to my colleagues in the History Department at Brandeis University.

Many teachers, colleagues, and friends read chunks of the manuscript, steered me toward important sources, or offered moral support when that was what I needed most. Many thanks to Gabi Arredondo, Norma Basch, Andrew Cohen, Jane Dailey, Rob DeMillo, Gary Gerstle, Tim Gilfoyle, Mike Grossberg, Neil Harris, Harold Hyman, Barry Karl, Jim Kloppenberg, Felicia Kornbluh, Regina Kunzel, Liz Lunbeck, Ussama Makdisi, Sid Milkis, David Nord, Susan Radomsky, Leslie Reagan, Lucy Salyer, Elizabeth Sanders, Paula Sanders, Mark Schmeller, Nayan Shah, Amy Stanley, Gale Stokes, and Marty Wiener. A long overdue thanks goes to David Igler, my unindicted co-conspirator since our childhood days, who has proven the steadiest of companions in professional life, too.

I am deeply indebted to a small group of people who read the book manuscript in its entirety and gave me useful criticism and expert advice: Carl Caldwell, David Engerman, Dan Ernst, Tom Green, Dirk Hartog, Tom Haskell, David Kennedy, David Tanenhaus, and Mason Willrich. All have been mentors and accomplices in the best sense.

This book would have taken many more years to complete without the generous support of a National Endowment for the Humanities Summer Stipend, a National Endowment for the Humanities Fellowship at the Newberry Library, and research and travel support from Rice University and especially from Brandeis University. My year at the Newberry was a truly wonderful experience thanks to Jim Grossman, the library staff, and my exceptionally talented and distracting cohort of fellows.

I have inhabited not one but two extraordinary academic communities since finishing graduate school. Many warm thanks to all of my former colleagues in the History Department at Rice; I miss you all. For the past three years, Brandeis University has been an exceptionally collegial and supportive academic home. It is here that the manuscript finally came to resemble a book. I am grateful to Deans Robin Feuer Miller and Jessie Ann Owens, for securing essential research funds, and to the History Department chair, Jacqueline Jones, for her stalwart support. I extend a heartfelt thanks to all of my colleagues in the History Department, especially David Engerman, David Hackett Fischer, Jackie Jones, Jane Kamensky, and Mickey Keller.

Christopher Tomlins, my editor at Cambridge University Press, has been a wise, supportive, and stunningly efficient editor throughout. From the start, Chris saw the book I wanted to write, and he gave me the freedom and critical guidance to make it happen. Executive Editor Frank Smith has been both a decisive advocate and a determined taskmaster, insisting that I cut many, many words.

Parts of Chapter 5 appeared as "Home Slackers: Men, the State, and Welfare in Modern America," *Journal of American History* 87 (2001), and I thank the journal for granting permission to use this material.

Parts of Chapter 8 appeared as "The Two Percent Solution: Eugenic Jurisprudence and the Socialization of American Law, 1900–1930," *Law and History Review* 16 (1998), and I thank that journal for permitting me to use that material here.

The rising new class of professional social experts in early twentieth-century America attributed enormous causal potency to the family. I don't need an expert study to know that in my family I have been blessed. For their love, encouragement, and tolerance over the years, I am grateful to my siblings and their "spice": Chris and Susan, Steve and Kelly, and Kate and Erik. I am grateful also to my wonderful new family – Art, Lynne, and Dari Bookstein – for taking me in as one of their own, and especially for letting me take one of their own as my wife. I am forever thankful to my partner in crime and the love of my life, Wendy, who has lived with this project since its inception, though she promised only to live with me. As for Max, who made completing this book nearly impossible, thank you for making my life so full and for teaching me all about a father's pride. For Emily, who arrived just in time for her name to appear on this page, my gratitude grows by the minute.

And thank you, most of all, to my parents, Mason and Patricia Willrich. Exemplary teachers, scholars, and parents: to my mind they will always represent the noblest ideals of liberalism. To them this work, and much else besides, is lovingly dedicated.

Abbreviations in Notes

Archival Collections

JHO	Judge Harry Olson Papers, Northwestern University, University Archives, Evanston, Ill.
MCC	Municipal Court of Chicago Collection, 1906–1927, Chicago Historical Society, Chicago, Ill.
MCCCR	Municipal Court of Chicago Criminal Records, Cook County Circuit Court Archives, Chicago, Ill.
HODS	Harry Olson Disassembled Scrapbooks, Chicago Historical Society

Organizations

AICLC	American Institute of Criminal Law and Criminology
CAC	Citizens' Association of Chicago
CFC	Civic Federation of Chicago
CHA	Central Howard Association
JPA	Juvenile Protective Association of Chicago
VCC	Vice Commission of Chicago

Municipal Court of Chicago Annual Reports (Fiscal year begins in December of previous calender year)

MCC 1 (1907) City of Chicago, Municipal Court, *First Annual Report of the Municipal Court of Chicago: For the Year December 3rd, A.D. 1906, to November 30th, A.D. 1907, Inclusive* (Chicago, n.d.)

MCC 2 (1908) City of Chicago, Municipal Court, *Second Annual Report of the Municipal Court of Chicago: For the Year December 1, A.D. 1907, to December 6, A.D. 1908, Inclusive* (Chicago, n.d.)

MCC 5 (1911) City of Chicago, Municipal Court, *Fifth Annual Report of the Municipal Court of Chicago: For the Year December 5, A.D. 1910, to December 3, A.D. 1911, Inclusive* (Chicago, n.d.)

MCC 6 (1912) City of Chicago, Municipal Court, *Sixth Annual Report of the Municipal Court of Chicago: For the Year December 4, 1911, to November 30, 1912, Inclusive* (Chicago, n.d.)

MCC 7 (1913) City of Chicago, Municipal Court, *Seventh Annual Report of the Municipal Court of Chicago: For the Year December 2, A.D. 1912, to November 30, A.D. 1913, Inclusive* (Chicago, n.d.)

MCC 8–9 (1914–15) City of Chicago, Municipal Court, *Eighth and Ninth Annual Reports of the Municipal Court of Chicago: For the Years December 1st, A.D. 1913, to December 5th, A.D. 1915, Inclusive* (Chicago, n.d.)

MCC 10–11 (1916–17) City of Chicago, Municipal Court, *Tenth and Eleventh Annual Reports of the Municipal Court of Chicago: For the Years December 6, 1915, to December 2, 1917, Inclusive* (Chicago, n.d.)

MCC 12–14 (1918–20) City of Chicago, Municipal Court, *Twelfth, Thirteenth, and Fourteenth Annual Reports of the Municipal Court of Chicago: For the Three Years December 2, 1917, to December 5, 1920, Inclusive* (Chicago, n.d.)

MCC 15 (1921) City of Chicago, Municipal Court, *Fifteenth Annual Report of the Municipal Court of Chicago: For the Year December 6, 1920, to December 4, 1921, Inclusive* (Chicago, n.d.)

MCC 16–18 (1922–24) City of Chicago, Municipal Court, *Sixteenth, Seventeenth, and Eighteenth Annual Reports of the Municipal Court of Chicago for the Years December 4, 1921, to November 30, 1924, Inclusive* (Chicago, n.d.)

MCC 19–22 (1925–28) City of Chicago, Municipal Court, *Nineteenth, Twentieth, Twenty-First, and Twenty-Second Annual Reports of the Municipal Court of Chicago: For the Years December 1, 1924, to December 2, 1928, Inclusive* (Chicago, n.d.)

MCC 23 (1929) City of Chicago, Municipal Court, *Twenty-Third Annual Report of the Municipal Court of Chicago: For the Year December 3, 1928, to December 1, 1929, Inclusive* (Chicago, n.d.)

MCC 24–25 (1930–31) City of Chicago, Municipal Court, *Twenty-Fourth and Twenty-Fifth Annual Reports of the Municipal Court of Chicago: For the Years December 2, 1929, to December 6, 1931, Inclusive* (Chicago, n.d.)

MCC 26–27 (1932–33) City of Chicago, Municipal Court, *Twenty-Sixth and Twenty-Seventh Annual Reports of the Municipal Court of Chicago: For the Years December 7, 1931, to December 31, 1933, Inclusive* (Chicago, n.d.)

MCC 28–30 (1934–36) City of Chicago, Municipal Court, *Twenty-Eighth, Twenty-Ninth, and Thirtieth Annual Reports of the Municipal Court of Chicago: For the Years January 1, 1934, to December 31, 1936, Inclusive* (Chicago, n.d.)

Journals

AAAPSS	*Annals of the American Academy of Political and Social Science*
ABAJ	*American Bar Association Journal*
ABFRJ	*American Bar Foundation Research Journal*
AHR	*American Historical Review*
AJLH	*American Journal of Legal History*
AJS	*American Journal of Sociology*
ALR	*American Law Review*
APSR	*American Political Science Review*
CCR	*Catholic Charities Review*
CLJ	*Central Law Journal*
CLN	*Chicago Legal News*
CLQ	*Cornell Law Quarterly*
CLR	*Columbia Law Review*
HLR	*Harvard Law Review*
ILR	*Illinois Law Review*
ISR	*International Socialist Review*
JAH	*Journal of American History*
JAICLC	*Journal of the American Institute of Criminal Law and Criminology*
JAJS	*Journal of the American Judicature Society*
JSH	*Journal of Social History*
LHR	*Law and History Review*
LSI	*Law and Social Inquiry*
MLR	*Michigan Law Review*
PNQ	*Pacific Northwest Quarterly*
PSQ	*Political Science Quarterly*
RAH	*Reviews in American History*
SCLR	*Southern California Law Review*
SLR	*Stanford Law Review*
SSR	*Social Service Review*
TLR	*Texas Law Review*
VLR	*Virginia Law Review*
YJLH	*Yale Journal of Law and Humanities*
YLJ	*Yale Law Journal*

Reference Works

BOC (1905) John W. Leonard, ed., *The Book of Chicagoans: A Biographical Digest of Leading Living Men of the City of Chicago* (Chicago, 1905)

BOC (1911) Albert Nelson Marquis, ed., *The Book of Chicagoans: A Biographical Dictionary of Leading Living Men of the City of Chicago* (Chicago, 1911)

BOC (1917) Albert Nelson Marquis, ed., *Book of Chicagoans: A Biographical Dictionary of Leading Living Men of the City of Chicago* (Chicago, 1917)

BOC (1926) Albert Nelson Marquis, ed., *Who's Who in Chicago: The Book of Chicagoans: A Biographical Dictionary of Leading Living Men of the City of Chicago, 1926* (Chicago, 1926)

BOC (1931) Albert Nelson Marquis, ed., *Who's Who in Chicago and Vicinity: The Book of Chicagoans: A Biographical Dictionary of Leading Living Men and Women of the City of Chicago and Environs, 1931* (Chicago, 1931)

BOC (1936) Albert Nelson Marquis, ed., *Who's Who in Chicago and Vicinity: A Biographical Dictionary of Leading Living Men and Women of the City of Chicago and Environs Comprising Cook and DuPage Counties, 1936* (Chicago, 1936)

Preface

Thus the court becomes not merely a machine for deciding cases formally presented, but a bureau of justice.

– Roscoe Pound, 1914

For the unprecedented multitudes of Americans who lived in crowded industrial cities at the turn of the twentieth century, a modern scientific perspective on crime served as an unmistakable badge of a progressive social conscience. "Evil itself does not shock us as it once did," Jane Addams of Chicago's Hull-House social settlement boasted in 1902, "and we count only that man merciful in whom we recognize an understanding of the criminal." A progressive understanding of the criminal implied a *social* conception of crime and criminal responsibility: a recognition that much of the human behavior that society called "crime" was in fact caused by forces of biological destiny or socioeconomic circumstance beyond the individual's control. The great riddle, of course, was what to do with this new knowledge. What makes the early twentieth century so remarkable in the dreary annals of criminal justice reform is that progressive social activists, lawmakers, and judges actually tried to put this protean liberal concept of social responsibility for crime to the test in urban criminal courts. In the process of "socializing" criminal justice, urban Americans did much more than bring the treatment of criminals into line with their newfound modern sensibilities. They overturned nineteenth-century understandings of individual autonomy, liberalism, and the rule of law in America, laying an urban seedbed for the modern administrative welfare state. This bold social, cultural, and legal transformation – and its troubling consequences for human liberty – is the story at the heart of this book. Although this transformation played out in cities across America, the story here properly centers on the Midwestern metropolis of Chicago. For as contemporary observers of the urban scene often noted, the

xxi

courts of America's "Second City" led the nation in pioneering new approaches to crime and urban social governance.[1]

The years around the turn of the twentieth century constituted that anxious yet optimistic moment when Americans, in Henry Adams's suitably ambivalent phrase, realized "where they were driving." The staggering scale and pace of modern life seemed to have entirely overtaken the familiar, local ways of doing business, building communities, forming families, participating in politics, and otherwise making one's way in the world. It was the age of the "trust," the "great city," the "labor question," the "breakdown" of the patriarchal family, and the "new" immigrants with their unfamiliar tongues. It is hardly surprising that so many middle-class city-dwellers, who perceived all too acutely the ineluctable sway of impersonal forces over their own choices and chances in life, began to think differently about crime. The formal Victorian understanding of crime – as the product of the freely willed choices, flawed characters, or sinful natures of autonomous individuals – no longer passed the acid test of social experience. Even for those who did not share Jane Addams's belief that "identification with the common lot" was "the essential idea of Democracy," to understand the criminal in a social sense was to better understand one's self and one's place in the irreducibly interdependent, cosmopolitan, democratic mass of the "modern city."[2]

Social explanations of crime spilled from the pens, presses, and pulpits of America's great cities during the Progressive Era: that kinetic age of urban-industrial expansion, mass immigration, social-scientific investigation, social reform, and state formation that fell between the Depression of 1893 and the end of World War I. Genteel philanthropists and clubwomen, socialists and single-taxers, ministers and sociologists, psychiatrists and social workers, even lawyers, lawmakers, and judges engaged in free-ranging causal speculation about the handiwork of heredity and environment in making criminals. A

---

[1] Jane Addams, *Democracy and Social Ethics* (New York, 1902), 9.

[2] Henry Adams, *The Education of Henry Adams*, ed. Ernest Samuels (1918; Boston, 1973), 343; Addams, *Democracy and Social Ethics*, 11; Roscoe Pound, "The Administration of Justice in the Modern City," *HLR*, 26 (1913), 302–28. See Thomas A. Green, "Freedom and Criminal Responsibility in the Age of Pound: An Essay on Criminal Justice," *MLR*, 93 (1995), 1915–2053; Thomas L. Haskell, "A Brief Excursus on Formalism," in Thomas L. Haskell, *Objectivity Is Not Neutrality: Explanatory Schemes in History* (Baltimore, 1998), 307–17; Charles E. Rosenberg, *The Trial of the Assassin Guiteau: Psychiatry and the Law in the Gilded Age* (Chicago, 1968); David E. Ruth, *Inventing the Public Enemy: The Gangster in American Culture, 1918–1934* (Chicago, 1996), 11–23; Martin J. Wiener, *Reconstructing the Criminal: Culture, Law, and Policy in England, 1830–1914* (Cambridge, 1990).

typical catalogue of causes appeared in the 1907 report of the Central Howard Association, a Protestant agency that assisted ex-convicts in Chicago (see illustration). To be sure, mainstream opinion never wholly abandoned individual responsibility. "Indifferent deserters," like professional criminals, never moved many hearts. But the range of offenders from whom the public – and even the state – expected full responsibility appreciably narrowed. The "law in books," the stuff of state criminal codes and law treatises, continued to locate culpability in the acts and intentions of willful individuals. But the "law in action," the actual administration of justice by urban criminal courts, was enlisted in the larger culture's race to better understand and control the complex social forces that overwhelmed the modern self.[3]

It was during the early twentieth century, then, that urban crime took on the broad social and political significance that, in a muted form, it still holds for many Americans today. "The social responsibility for crime," the sociologist Albion Small called it. Crime became a proxy for investigating, theorizing, representing, debating, and ultimately governing social problems in a liberal democracy.[4]

A liberal democracy, at least as leading political theorists and jurists of the late nineteenth century understood the American version, was a polity composed of autonomous, formally equal, rights-bearing individuals and their decentralized governments. A formal boundary separated the private market realm of individual economic actors and the public sphere of politics and the state. According to the venerable liberal ideal of the rule of law, the courts were to act as impartial umpires, applying statutes and well-settled common-law principles to disputes that arose among individuals or between individuals and the state. The courts' most exalted function, bolstered in America by the distinctive institution of judicial review, was to serve as a bulwark of individual liberty against arbitrary state power.[5]

---

[3] John Peter Altgeld, *Live Questions: Including Our Penal Machinery and Its Victims* (Chicago, 1890), 168. CHA, *The Making of Men* (Chicago, 1907), 4. Roscoe Pound, "Law in Books and Law in Action," *CLN*, 42 (1909), 59. See Livingston Hall, "The Substantive Law of Crimes – 1887–1936," *HLR*, 50 (1937), 616–53; Sam B. Warner and Henry B. Cabot, "Changes in the Administration of Justice during the Past Fifty Years," ibid., 583–615.

[4] Albion W. Small, "The Social Responsibility for Crime," in Chicago Congregational Club, *The Delinquent Classes – What Shall We Do with Them: What Will They Do with Us?* (Chicago, 1900).

[5] On the rule of law in late nineteenth-century America, see Morton J. Horwitz, *The Transformation of American Law, 1870–1960: The Crisis of Legal Orthodoxy* (New York, 1992), 9–31; William J. Novak, *The People's Welfare: Law and Regulation in Nineteenth-Century America* (Chapel Hill, 1996), 235–48.

HOW CRIMINALS ARE MADE.

So long as there are bad tenements; sweatshops; brutal policemen; bad jails; child labor; dishonest and grinding employers; saloons and gambling dens; so long as boys are taught to fight and allowed to carry firearms; so long as fathers are indifferent deserters, and mothers must maintain the family by the washboard—so long crime will continue. What will you do to help this Association to prevent it?

The protean concept of social responsibility for crime emphasized the role of "social" forces – such as poverty and bad heredity – in the making of criminals. Reproduced from a 1907 report of the Central Howard Association, a Chicago-based organization that provided material assistance and moral guidance to ex-convicts. Courtesy of the Newberry Library, Chicago.

The great social and cultural changes of the late nineteenth century – the emancipation of four million slaves, the spread of Darwinism, the triumph of the wage labor system, the acceleration of urbanization and immigration – raised new doubts about individual autonomy that produced new fissures in liberal ideology. By the century's end, society had assumed an enlarged importance in American thought and moral discourse. The very word had acquired a rich double meaning. "Society" signified the collective will and moral force of the enlightened public. In the discourse of social scientists, reformers, and other interpreters of the urban scene, "the social" also referred to the realm of everyday collective life – structures, identities, needs, duties, risks – that was located, in a figurative sense, between public and private, the state and the market. Progressive social activists were especially concerned about the fragile fabric of social life among the common lot: the home life, sexuality, moral habits, health, and economic security of urban wage earners and their families. The question of how this endangered and dangerous terrain ought to be governed put enormous pressure on liberal ideology, law, and governing institutions at every level of the polity.[6]

Like Lewis Hine's poignant photographs of children who toiled in sweatshops and coal mines, the spectacle of crime in the industrial city gave a heightened focus to the era's great democratic conversation about social responsibility and the changing conditions of individual liberty. "Probably at no time in the history of criminal-law administration," the Columbia University political scientist Charles Beard noted in 1912, "has so much attention been given to the problem of preventing crime – to a study of the social and economic forces which tend to produce crime in cities." Progressive jurists, social scientists, and activists took a special interest in urban crime precisely because it seemed to implicate a host of broader public concerns that the individualistic categories and formal procedures of the law had previously kept beyond the reach of the courts. "The crime problem is not merely a question of police and courts," the Chicago City Council Committee on Crime reported in 1915. "[I]t leads to the broader problems of public sanitation, education, home care, a living wage, and industrial democracy." A social conception of crime directly challenged the

---

[6] Edward Alsworth Ross, *Social Control: A Survey of the Foundations of Order* (New York, 1901), 110–11; Amy Dru Stanley, *From Bondage to Contract: Wage Labor, Marriage, and the Market in the Age of Slave Emancipation* (Cambridge, 1998); George Steinmetz, *Regulating the Social: The Welfare State and Local Politics in Imperial Germany* (Princeton, 1993); Barbara Young Welke, *Recasting American Liberty: Gender, Race, Law, and the Railroad Revolution* (Cambridge, 2001).

old liberal pieties. It also justified a greatly enlarged role for the state, through new social welfare policies and the practices of city courts, in assisting and regulating the everyday lives of urban populations.[7]

The story told in these pages does not sit well with the conventional picture of American courts during the Progressive Era. Our standard histories and textbooks have long treated the judiciary as a monolithic, singularly conservative obstacle to progressive social and political change. But at the local level, American courts were the true laboratories of progressive democracy, flexible instruments of public welfare and social governance on a scale not matched again until the New Deal.[8]

This is necessarily a *local* story. It cannot be told by eavesdropping on congressional debates or gazing abroad for the origins of the welfare state, though national policy making and the robust transatlantic traffic in sociopolitical ideas have important roles to play. To find the state in the Progressive Era, we need to go to the local level. Until the creation of a welfare state with enlarged state and federal governmental capacities during the New Deal, progressive social reformers and policy makers assumed that local governments – local courts, in particular – would shoulder most of the burden of social governance in America. These pages center on the place where the concept of social responsibility for crime was put to its greatest test: the progressive crucible of Chicago and its widely copied effort to modernize and "socialize" its municipal court system. Since the heyday of Al Capone in the late twenties, Chicago's global reputation for crime has beat out all rivals. But during the two previous decades, the Second City enjoyed international renown as a model for new approaches to criminal justice and social governance.[9]

---

[7] Charles A. Beard, *American City Government: A Survey of Newer Tendencies* (New York, 1912), 184; City of Chicago, City Council, *Report of the City Council Committee on Crime* (Chicago, 1915), 12.

[8] For critiques of the obstructionist view of courts, see William J. Novak, "The Legal Origins of the Modern American State," American Bar Foundation Working Paper 9925 (1999); Michael Willrich, "The Case for Courts: Law and Political Development in the Progressive Era," in *Democracy in America: New Approaches to American Political History*, eds. Meg Jacobs, William J. Novak, and Julian Zelizer (forthcoming).

[9] For the transatlantic context, see James T. Kloppenberg, *Uncertain Victory: Social Democracy and Progressivism in European and American Thought, 1870–1920* (New York, 1986); Daniel T. Rodgers, *Atlantic Crossings: Social Politics in a Progressive Age* (Cambridge, Mass., 1998). For a study of early U.S. welfare policy that pays close attention to variation in the federal system, see Theda

This is also a *legal* story. It should change how we understand the historic transformation of American law during the early twentieth century. Progressive legal mandarins such as Roscoe Pound of Harvard Law School and the activist lawyer Louis Brandeis saw the reconstruction of city courts as absolutely central to the larger process of making law more responsive to modern social needs. Amid the great social struggles of their era, progressives attacked the dominant "classical" tradition of American legal thought as "mechanical" and out-of-touch, too protective of abstract individual rights to deal with the "actual conditions" of a complex capitalist economy and an interdependent society. Progressives urged judges to stop thinking like lawyers and start thinking more like social scientists, to tailor their decisions to the social context and consequences of the cases before them.[10] This new "sociological jurisprudence," as Pound called progressive legal thought, had a profound influence on judicial decision making. It legitimated new levels of administrative intervention in the economy. Ultimately, it laid the intellectual foundation for the Constitutional Revolution of 1937, when the Supreme Court effectively ratified the New Deal. Unfortunately, historians of this transformation have focused entirely on how it made regulated capitalism possible. They have thus overlooked the fact that progressive legal thinkers were also deeply interested in crime and social control. The familiar achievements of progressive jurists in the economic sphere were institutionally and conceptually tied to a burst of judicial regulation in the social sphere. When we give the social side of legal progressivism its due, the effects of the transformation look both more complicated and less completely benign. Along with the familiar landmarks of workman's compensation, factory legislation, and antitrust regulation, legal progressivism enabled the rise of eugenics and other coercive forms of social governance in America.[11]

Skocpol, *Protecting Soldiers and Mothers: The Political Origins of Social Policy in the United States* (Cambridge, Mass., 1992).
[10] Roscoe Pound, "Mechanical Jurisprudence," *CLR*, 8 (1908), 604–23; Roscoe Pound, "The End of Law as Developed in Legal Rules and Doctrines," *HLR*, 27 (1914), 197; Roscoe Pound, "Scope and Purpose of Sociological Jurisprudence," *HLR*, 24 (1911), 591–619; 25 (1912), 140–68, 489–516. Oliver Wendell Holmes, Jr., "The Path of the Law," *HLR*, 10 (1897), 457–78; Benjamin N. Cardozo, *The Nature of the Judicial Process* (New Haven, 1921).
[11] On legal progressivism, see, esp., Barbara H. Fried, *The Progressive Assault on Laissez Faire: Robert Hale and the First Law and Economics Movement* (Cambridge, Mass., 1998); Horwitz, *Transformation*, 33–63; G. Edward White, "From Sociological Jurisprudence to Realism: Jurisprudence and

Finally, this is an institutional story. It cannot be narrated by trac-
ing "deeper" social and cultural processes without giving equal billing
to the ideas, ideologies, and actions of legal thinkers, activists, and
judges, and the powerful society- and culture-shaping institutions
they made. Building on the insights of the social theorist Michel
Foucault, recent historians of urban culture have written richly textured accounts of elite efforts to police sexuality and social deviancy
in modern Europe and America. Foucault made this question interesting by insisting that the innumerable efforts of moral authorities,
social investigators, and public officials to define and discipline social
life were not simply repressive. By producing authoritative knowledge
of social life, they shaped cultural conceptions of what it meant to be a
normal, healthy, fully realized person. American historians interested
in these themes have naturally gravitated to the Progressive Era, when
urban reform organizations and professional social experts won cultural authority and public power by defining and managing a host of
new social problems, such as feeblemindedness, juvenile delinquency,
and sexual "inversion."[12]

Though indebted to Foucault's rich ideas and historical questions,
this book challenges one of the philosopher's most influential claims.
Foucault argued that ever since the birth of the prison in the early
nineteenth century, the law had withered in importance in the modern
liberal regimes of the West. Powerful new disciplines such as medicine
and psychiatry had largely displaced the law as the principal mechanisms of modern social control. In America, however, legal institutions
served as *preeminent* sites for the production of urban social knowledge
and social governance well into the twentieth century. Indeed, what
made the new city courts "modern," in addition to their novel centralized bureaucratic structures, was that they aimed not merely to punish
offenders but to assist and discipline entire urban populations: to police public health and morals, to reduce child neglect and family dependency, to correct deviant personalities, to teach immigrants good

Social Change in Early Twentieth-Century America," *VLR*, 58 (1972), 999–
1028; Michael Willrich, "The Two Percent Solution: Eugenic Jurisprudence
and the Socialization of American Law, 1900–1930," *LHR*, 16 (1998),
63–111.
[12] Michel Foucault, *Discipline and Punish: The Birth of the Prison*, trans. Alan
Sheridan (New York, 1979). See, esp., George Chauncey, *Gay New York:
Gender, Urban Culture, and the Making of the Gay Male World, 1890–1940*
(New York, 1994); Regina G. Kunzel, *Fallen Women, Problem Girls: Unmarried
Mothers and the Professionalization of Social Work, 1890–1945* (New Haven,
1993); Elizabeth Lunbeck, *The Psychiatric Persuasion: Knowledge, Gender, and
Power in Modern America* (Princeton, 1994).

citizenship, and much more. Urban court systems grew more powerful than ever during these years, partly by incorporating the therapeutic disciplinary techniques of psychiatry, medicine, and social work into everyday judicial practice. The larger institutional context of American governance, meanwhile, was undergoing profound structural changes that extended the social reach of the law. Governmental power at all levels was shifting from the particularistic and decentralized institutions characteristic of the nineteenth-century polity toward the more centralized, bureaucratic institutions of the administrative state. The new centralized municipal courts, which replaced the centuries-old system of autonomous justice of the peace courts in American cities, stood at the forefront of this process of modern state formation.[13]

Only by taking localism, legal ideologies, institutions, *and* their urban social-cultural context seriously can this story be told. At the local level, American courts were anything but reactionary bulwarks. Activists, judges, and the legal demands of ordinary people turned courts into laboratories of progressive democracy, powerful instruments of a new style of urban social governance. Merging the authority of the criminal law with the disciplinary techniques of social work, welfare administration, probation, and psychiatric testing, the new municipal courts produced authoritative social knowledge and delivered governance into the intimate details of everyday life. "Under modern metropolitan conditions a court has necessarily a profound social duty," explained Chief Justice Harry Olson, the seasoned ex-prosecutor who ran the Municipal Court of Chicago with prodigious vision, energy, and authority from 1906 to 1930. "[I]t must give a larger meaning to the word 'judicial' in an age when society is bent upon remedial action, when it is necessary to throw light into the dark corners of our civilization and procure data essential to constructive treatment of social ills." All of this implied that the courts would depart from their traditional role as neutral arbiters and intervene directly

---

[13] See Michel Foucault, *The History of Sexuality*, vol. 1: *An Introduction*, trans. Robert Hurley (New York, 1990), esp. 81–91, 144–45. For an insightful discussion of the problem of law and discipline in Foucault's work, see Laura Engelstein, "Combined Underdevelopment: Discipline and the Law in Imperial and Soviet Russia," *AHR*, 98 (1993), 338–53; Jan Goldstein, "Framing Discipline with Law: Problems and Promises of the Liberal State," ibid., 364–75; Engelstein, "Reply," ibid., 376–81. See also Daniel R. Ernst, "Law and American Political Development, 1877–1938," *RAH*, 26 (1998), 205–19; Stephen Skowronek, *Building a New American State: The Expansion of National Administrative Capacities, 1877–1920* (New York, 1982).

in the lives of criminal defendants, their families, and their urban communities.[14]

The Municipal Court of Chicago – America's first modern metropolitan court system – was invented during a transformative period in the social history of the Second City. Perched at the nexus of the nation's transportation and communications networks, Chicago epitomized to the world the wonders and dangers of the industrial city. After visiting Chicago in 1904, no less a student of modernity than the German sociologist Max Weber was moved to write that "the whole gigantic city . . . is like a man whose skin has been peeled off and whose entrails one sees at work." Decades of breakneck industrialization and labor militancy – from the massive railroad strike of 1877 to the Haymarket bombing of 1886 to the Pullman Strike of 1894 to the bloody Teamsters' Strike of 1905 – had turned Chicago into a national epicenter of industrial strife. The prospect of a better livelihood and new urban freedoms made Chicago after 1880 a major destination for three historic migration streams: unattached men and women from the hinterland, allegedly unassimilable "new" immigrants from southern and eastern Europe, and, during and after World War I, the first "Great Migration" of African-Americans from the South. Little more than a frontier outpost in 1840, by 1890 the newly anointed Second City had swelled to more than a million inhabitants. At century's turn, nearly 1.7 million people – more than three-quarters of them of foreign birth or parentage – called Chicago home. This stunningly cosmopolitan population would double again by 1930. (See Table 1.)[15]

These changes had profound – and, to some, alarming – consequences for Chicago's social and moral order. The large-scale entry of women into the wage-earning classes, for example, disrupted gender norms and traditional family economies. The infatuation of working-class girls and boys with the new commercial cultural spaces of the dance hall and nickel theater facilitated new practices of sociability and sexuality that native-born reformers and immigrant parents

---

[14] *MCC* 7 (1913), 87.
[15] Weber quoted in "Introduction: The Man and His Work," in Max Weber, *From Max Weber: Essays in Sociology*, trans. and ed. H. H. Gerth and C. Wright Mills (New York, 1946), 15; Martin Bulmer, *The Chicago School of Sociology: Institutionalization, Diversity, and the Rise of Sociological Research* (Chicago, 1984), 12–27; Lizabeth Cohen, *Making a New Deal: Industrial Workers in Chicago, 1919–1939* (Cambridge, 1990); James R. Grossman, *Land of Hope: Chicago, Black Southerners, and the Great Migration* (Chicago, 1989); Joanne Meyerowitz, *Women Adrift: Independent Wage Earners in Chicago, 1880–1930* (Chicago, 1988).

TABLE 1: Population of Chicago, 1880–1930

Year	Total population	% increase	% foreign-born white	% black
1880	503,185	68.3	12.4	1.1
1890	1,099,850	118.6	40.9	1.3
1900	1,698,575	54.4	34.4	1.9
1910	2,185,283	28.7	35.7	2.0
1920	2,701,705	23.6	29.8	4.1
1930	3,375,329	24.9	24.9	6.9

Sources: Martin Bulmer, The Chicago School of Sociology: Institutionalization, Diversity, and the Rise of Sociological Research (Chicago, 1984), 13; St. Clair Drake and Horace R. Cayton, Black Metropolis: A Study of Negro Life in a Northern City, rev. ed. (Chicago, 1993), 9; Allan H. Spear, Black Chicago: The Making of a Negro Ghetto 1890–1920 (Chicago, 1967), 12; U.S. Census Bureau, Tenth Census, 1880 (Washington, 1883), 1: 132, 540.

alike perceived as an assault on the family. The pace of immigration intensified concerns that the city population, like that of the nation, was being overrun by feeblemindedness and other hereditary mental defects that leading scientific experts held responsible for dependency and crime. A highly creative and fiercely confident generation of middle-class social activists responded to these and other social changes by using a panoply of institutions – ranging from YWCAs to social settlements to religious charities to museums – to improve physical health, provide much-needed economic assistance, and instill middle-class notions of moral order in the city's cosmopolitan working class. As an instrument of state power, the Municipal Court of Chicago occupied a privileged place among these institutions, and reformers aggressively harnessed it to their agendas.[16]

The Municipal Court of Chicago was an object of enormous interest for municipal reformers, social scientists, jurists, and journalists across the nation. Roscoe Pound, the torchbearer of progressive legal thought, made it a centerpiece of his influential essays on criminal justice and court reform, calling it "the pioneer modern judicial organization in the United States." Pound's work remains an essential resource for linking urban court reform to the broader progressive reorientation of American law and jurisprudence. But Pound was only the most distinguished of the court's long line of admirers and students. Dean John Henry Wigmore of the Northwestern University School of

[16] Steven J. Diner, A City and Its Universities: Public Policy in Chicago, 1892–1919 (Chapel Hill, 1980); Helen Lefkowitz Horowitz, Culture and the City: Cultural Philanthropy in Chicago from the 1880s to 1917 (Chicago, 1976); Meyerowitz, Women Adrift; Thomas Lee Philpott, The Slum and the Ghetto: Immigrants, Blacks, and Reformers in Chicago, 1880–1930 (Belmont, Calif., 1991).

Law dubbed the Municipal Court "the most famous city court in the world." Pioneering urban sociologists of the famous "Chicago School" at the University of Chicago dispatched graduate students to report on the court's practice. Investigators from the U.S. Children's Bureau made it the subject of densely researched studies. The Municipal Court's judges, too, had a keen sense of their place in history, and they left behind a vast untapped record of annual reports, correspondence, scrapbooks, and criminal case files.[17]

Established by an act of the Illinois General Assembly in 1906, the Municipal Court of Chicago swiftly became the national model for the modernization of urban court systems and a widely noted proving ground for the new set of concerns, assumptions, and state practices that Pound called "the socialization of law." Pound saw socialization as a "world-wide" phenomenon: the process of "adjusting the law, shaped by the individualism of the past three centuries, to the ideal of social justice of the twentieth century." For Americans, socialized law signaled a repudiation of the individualistic jurisprudence of the late nineteenth century and a new reformist role for legal institutions in directly addressing the social conditions of urban-industrial society. In large cities, where the social and political pressure for legal change was strongest, the socialization of law involved two dramatic developments in the administration of justice. The first was the structural consolidation and rationalization of urban courts. One American city after another followed Chicago's lead in converting the highly independent justice of the peace courts into centralized judicial bureaucracies with specialized branches. The second development could not have happened without the first. In the new municipal courts judicial reformers installed staffs of disciplinary personnel: psychologists, psychiatrists, physicians, social workers, and probation officers. These social experts examined offenders and advised judges on the best "individual treatment" given the offenders' mental makeup, family background, and social history. The forms of "treatment" for criminals grew far more numerous in the Progressive Era. To the conventional punitive measures of fines and incarceration, state legislatures added the far more discretionary techniques of indeterminate sentences, probation, parole, compulsory medical treatment, routine commitment to state institutions for the insane or feebleminded, and eugenical sterilization. In socialized criminal justice, the case was

---

[17] Roscoe Pound, "Organization of Courts," [1914] *JAJS*, 11 (Oct. 1927), 80; Pound, "Administration of Justice"; John H. Wigmore, "The Most Famous City Court in the World," *ILR*, 6 (1912), 591. See Appendix, "Archival Sources from the Municipal Court of Chicago."

only the starting point for a much broader set of investigations and interventions that aimed not so much to punish crime but to reform criminals and the larger social world that had produced them.[18]

In late October of 1914, as the Second City made ready for election day, Henry M. Hyde of the *Chicago Tribune* wrote a front-page column urging the voters to elect "good men" to the Municipal Court bench. By "good men," Hyde meant Republican men. But sturdy progressive that he was, the columnist had a larger public message to deliver. In the eyes of Hyde and many of his contemporaries, no local governmental institution stood taller in social importance than the Municipal Court of Chicago. Its orders and processes reached deep into the everyday life of the modern metropolis. "It is everybody's court," Hyde proclaimed.

> It is the rich man's court, for it punished 13,000 people [during the last year] for running their automobiles too fast. It is the poor man's court, for it heard the cases of 13,000 poor tenants who were brought into court for not paying their rent.
>
> It is the court of the wife, the mother, and the prostitute; of the bad boy, the big merchant, the common drunk, and the man who spits on the sidewalk. . . .
>
> One way or another this court seems to have directly affected almost every second home in Chicago during the last year. It is impossible to think of any institution which gets closer to the people; in the proper administration of which all the people must take a keener personal interest.[19]

Just as important as the extent of the court's reach was the *way* it reached. A paragon of the progressive faith that specialized knowledge and expert governmental administration could tackle the problems of social life in the modern city, the Municipal Court was a unified system of thirty-seven civil and criminal branch courts presided over by a chief justice and manned by a burgeoning bureaucracy of bailiffs and clerks. The court channeled many of its criminal defendants into special socialized branches, including a Domestic Relations Court for desertion and nonsupport proceedings, a Morals Court for prostitution and other sex offenses, and a Boys' Court for young

[18] Pound, "Organization of Courts," 72; Roscoe Pound, "End of Law," 225–34. See David J. Rothman, *Conscience and Convenience: The Asylum and Its Alternatives in Progressive America* (Boston, 1980); Andrew J. Polsky, *The Rise of the Therapeutic State* (Princeton, 1991).

[19] Henry M. Hyde, "Voter Wields Huge Power Naming Court," *Chicago Tribune*, Oct. 21, 1914. See also "The Right Sort of Judge," *Chicago Defender*, July 5, 1919.

male offenders. Each specialized branch teemed with experts: social
workers, probation officers, and a nurse or physician. Even the judges
professed expertise in the social roots of criminality. "Most striking of
all," Hyde exclaimed, was the new Psychopathic Laboratory, a criminological clinic ensconced within the Municipal Court that promised
a scientific understanding of the origins of crime in defective heredity.
Who could deny the voter's self-interest in electing qualified men to
this powerful bench – "since the court is likely to come straight into
his home at any time and summon him to its bar"?[20]

Of course, Hyde's optimistic regard for the social power of the
Municipal Court of Chicago seems impossibly Panglossian in the face
of all we think we know about crime and criminal justice in early
twentieth-century Chicago: the notorious "Levee" vice district lorded
over by aldermen "Bathhouse" John Coughlin and Michael "Hinky
Dink" Kenna; the prostitution and bootlegging rackets of Johnny
Torrio, Dion O'Banion, and Al Capone; the St. Valentine's Day Massacre. Such are the collective memories, preserved in celluloid and
pulp, of a time and place fraught with lawlessness and corruption,
where the gangsters ruled, the kegs rolled, and the politicians and
police pocketed their share of the take. But these popular images,
which helped legitimate the unprecedented federal incursion into
local law enforcement during Prohibition, have caused us to forget
the broader public relevance of criminal justice in Chicago and other
urban communities during the Progressive Era.[21]

When Americans of the Progressive Era talked about law and order,
they talked about something far more capacious than gangster rackets and crime control. As a committee of eminent progressive jurists,
including Pound and Brandeis, noted in a report on urban judicial
administration in 1914, the workaday practice of criminal justice in
the industrial city entailed the policing of countless relatively minor
breaches of public order and domestic tranquillity, such as prostitution, petty theft, assault, adultery, fornication, contributing to the dependency of children, and disorderly conduct. For these observers,
municipal courts, the ground floor of the American legal system, were
where the action was. This was not because these courts tried the most
serious felony crimes – murder, armed robbery, and the like. Many
municipal courts lacked felony jurisdiction. But they were important

[20] Hyde, "Voter Wields"; *MCC 8–9* (1914–15), 6–7.
[21] Laurence Bergreen, *Capone: The Man and the Era* (New York, 1994); Ruth,
Inventing the Public Enemy; Andrew Sinclair, *Prohibition: The Era of Excess*
(Boston, 1962); Lloyd Wendt, *Lords of the Levee: The Story of Bathhouse John
and Hinky Dink* (Indianapolis, 1944).

because they handled the vastly larger class of lesser offenses and small claims cases that involved, in the committee's apt phrase, "the everyday rights and wrongs of the great majority of an urban community."[22]

The conflicts and transgressions of the modern city kept the Municipal Court of Chicago judges busy. (See Fig. 1.) In addition to its massive civil caseload, the Municipal Court had full jurisdiction over all state misdemeanors and local ordinance violations ("quasi-crimes") committed in the city, and preliminary jurisdiction over felonies. Felonies – defined as crimes punishable by at least a year in the state penitentiary – constituted a relatively small part of the universe of crime. Every Chicago felony case had a preliminary trial in the Municipal Court; if the judge found probable cause, he was obligated to bind over the case to the Cook County Criminal Court for grand jury indictment and trial. All categories of crime grew between 1906 and 1930, as the court's caseload outstripped Chicago's population growth: The court disposed of four cases per hundred residents in 1910, seven per hundred in 1920, and almost nine per hundred in 1930. But despite the crime wave panic that overcame Chicago during the age of Prohibition, felony crimes never displaced everyday offenses as the bread and butter of the municipal judge.[23]

America's model socialized court was unmistakably a political institution, inextricably ensnared in the partisan and intensely factional politics that energized public life in early twentieth-century Chicago. The number of Municipal Court judges grew from twenty-eight in 1906 to thirty-seven by 1923 (where it remained into the 1930s). The judges, including the chief justice, who served as the court's chief administrative officer, were elected for six-year terms. Between 1906 and the triumph of Anton Cermak's Democratic party in the city elections of 1930, Republicans won about two-thirds of the openings on the Municipal Court bench. Since judicial elections coincided with the general elections in November – and given the sheer number of judicial candidates on Chicago's notorious "long ballot" – party success in Municipal Court contests tended to ebb and flow with the tides of local and national partisanship. One of the few constants on the Municipal Court bench was Chief Justice Harry Olson, who defended his post against all comers from 1906 until 1930. The voters also elected the court's chief bailiff and chief clerk, who appointed and presided over

---

[22] Charles W. Eliot, Louis D. Brandeis, Moorfield Storey, Adolph J. Rodenbeck, and Roscoe Pound, *Preliminary Report on Efficiency in the Administration of Justice* (Boston, [1914]), 29.

[23] The best guide to the court's practice is Hiram T. Gilbert, *The Municipal Court of Chicago* (Chicago, 1928).

FIGURE 1. Criminal cases disposed of in the Municipal Court of Chicago, 1908–30. (Comparable data are not available for 1907, the Municipal Court's first fiscal year.) A note of caution is in order regarding statistics from the Municipal Court. Because only a fraction of the court's case files have survived, historians must rely for general statistics on the tables provided in the court's annual reports. These are not error-free. For example, I have adjusted the data for this chart to correct a major clerical error in the comprehensive table of cases provided in *MCC 24–25* (1930–31). A clerk incorrectly tallied the number of felonies, misdemeanors, and quasi-crimes for 1920. I verified this against the original report for 1920; *MCC 12–14* (1918–20), 56. Source: *MCC 24–25* (1930–31), 35.

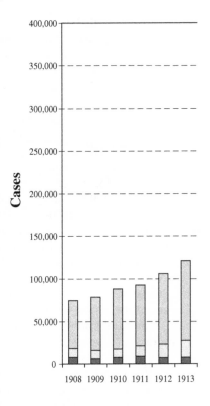

a sizable bureaucracy of deputy clerks and bailiffs – including under these titles social workers, psychologists, and nurses – that was notoriously well insulated from civil service restrictions. The euphemistically named "executive staff" of bailiffs and deputies had already exploded from 207 deputies in 1907 to 332 in 1915, when the court abruptly (and advisedly) stopped publishing their numbers in the front of annual reports.[24]

[24] *MCC 1* (1907), 3; *MCC 8–9* (1914–15), 6; *MCC 24–25* (1930–31), 8; Edward M. Martin, *The Role of the Bar in Electing the Bench in Chicago* (Chicago, 1936), 187–88, 190–91, 211. The history of Chicago politics in the early twentieth century remains to be written. But it is clear that party affiliation was not a good indicator of political ideology or even party loyalty. See Sonya Forthall, *Cogwheels of Democracy: A Study of the Precinct Captain* (1946; Westport, Conn., 1972), 18; Charles Edward Merriam, *Chicago: A More Intimate View of Urban Politics* (New York, 1929), 94–102.

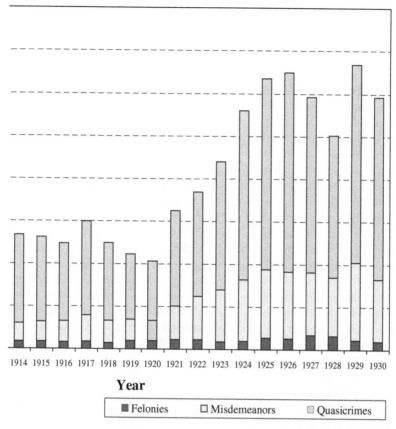

Year

■ Felonies   □ Misdemeanors   ▨ Quasicrimes

Judges and court officials from both parties embraced the rhetoric and discretionary power of socialized law. Party affiliation was not a good predictor of a judge's behavior on the bench, nor did it imply a predetermined position on the question of social responsibility for crime. But the tension between the scientific rhetoric of the court and its inevitably political nature proved a fertile source of public criticism for the court and by the late 1920s brought intense public scrutiny upon the entire project of socialized criminal justice.[25]

The municipal court movement in Chicago and other major cities during the early twentieth century was a consummate progressive reform. "Progressivism" is a much-debated term – so much so that some

---

[25] See, e.g., Raymond Moley, "The Municipal Court of Chicago," in Illinois Association of Criminal Justice, *Illinois Crime Survey* (Chicago, 1929), 393–419.

historians have thought it best to consign it to the dustbin. But many Americans who lived at the turn of the twentieth century called themselves and their times progressive, and in 1912 one of the most formidable third-party insurgencies in American history called itself the Progressive Party. In addition to the appeal of its historical authenticity, progressivism remains useful for identifying certain broad and intertwined threads of ideology and the people who put them to work in public life.[26]

In these pages, progressivism refers to two important and related developments in American political culture in the late nineteenth and early twentieth centuries: the rise of a pluralistic, issue-centered politics of social responsibility and an ideological commitment to professionalization, scientific rationalization, and administrative governance. Despite their many differences, the people I will call progressives shared a belief that only a rationally organized state, managed by nonpartisan experts, had the wherewithal to address the complex problems of a modern urban-industrial economy and society. Equally important, progressives believed that the state *should* actively manage social problems and that certain aspects of social life were too important to leave either to the market or to the initiative of private citizens. For them, "social engineering" had a positive, nonthreatening meaning. A good many of the progressives who people these pages also shared a reformist, sometimes quite radical, conviction that modern social life was irreducibly interdependent, and that to fulfill America's democratic promise the state had a legitimate and necessary role in alleviating social inequities such as unsanitary housing, family poverty, and dangerous or demoralizing working conditions.

The municipal court movement expressed progressivism's dual impulses toward administrative reform and social governance in the most multifaceted sense. Not only did the progressive reconstruction of urban courts set the agenda for a major overhaul of common law adjudication, by introducing simplified forms of pleading and record-keeping, specialized courts for specific classes of civil and criminal cases, and other procedural innovations that would serve as a model for the sweeping federal judicial reforms of the 1920s and 1930s. It also created, during the formative era of the American welfare state, the

---

[26] See Samuel P. Hays, "Preface, 1969," *Conservation and the Gospel of Efficiency: The Progressive Conservation Movement, 1890–1920* (Cambridge, Mass., 1969), vii–xiii; Richard Hofstadter, *The Age of Reform: From Bryan to F.D.R.* (New York, 1955); Daniel T. Rodgers, "In Search of Progressivism," *RAH*, 10 (1982), 113–132; Robert H. Wiebe, *The Search for Order, 1877–1920* (New York, 1967).

institutional framework for a new ideology and practice of court-based social governance in the nation's great cities, rooted in the ethos of social responsibility for crime.

It would be hard to overstate the dramatic nature of these changes in the fabric of American governance. And it would be all too easy to rush to judgment and see in them evidence that progressivism was, at its urban underbelly, a project of either "social justice" or "social control." This is an anachronistic dichotomy. It implies a clear ethical choice that the progressives themselves did not generally recognize. Roscoe Pound, who had an unusually prescient sense of the dangers of administrative justice, liked to tell the story of the time he showed an annual report of the Municipal Court of Chicago to a judge trained in the legal world of the nineteenth century. The judge cast it aside in disbelief. "But that isn't a court," the judge thundered, "that's a cross between an imperial ministry of justice and a legal aid society!" In fact, the Municipal Court had aspects of all three institutions: the court, the ministry, and the welfare agency. It is in the complex interplay between these three modes of governance – the judicial, the administrative, and the pursuit of justice for the poor – that we must look for the larger meaning that urban courts gave to the word "judicial" during the Progressive Era.[27]

---

[27] Pound, "Administration of Justice," 318.

Part I

Transformations

1

The Price of Justice

The idea that the bureau activities of the state are intrinsically different in character from the management of private economic offices
is ... totally foreign to the American way.

— Max Weber

To anyone who takes it on faith that personal gain and public duties
don't mix, the realm of local judicial administration in late nineteenth-
century America must seem a strange land. In most local communities, from the rural hamlet to the great city, the lion's share of judicial
business – civil litigation involving modest sums of money and criminal cases of the lesser grades – came to judgment before justices of
the peace. The typical justice had little or no legal training, enjoyed
a quasiproprietary control over his office, and collected most, if not
all, of his pay in the fees that he charged litigants and criminal defendants for his services. JPs were the foot soldiers of the legal order.
They had no power of judicial review, heard no appeals, and tried
no big-ticket civil cases or felony crimes. But their courts were the
judicial institutions nearest to the people. And to them fell the task
of delivering justice in the rising flood of litigation that involved the
everyday rights and wrongs of the working people in the nation's industrial cities. In the Second City, where the high-volume judicial market
enabled enterprising justices to rake in fees unimaginable in the hinterland, the working people came up with their own nickname for
the JP courts. "The justice shops," they called them. The sobriquet
ridiculed all pretensions of judicial rectitude in a court where justice
was literally for sale. It also captured, in a matter-of-fact way, the un-
apologetically entrepreneurial spirit of a set of vital legal institutions

3

that were deeply embedded in the everyday life of the urban market economy.[1]

In Chicago at the turn of the twentieth century, fifty-two justices of the peace, appointed by the governor, did a robust business out of private offices that dotted bustling, low-rent commercial strips. The typical JP disposed of nearly 2,000 civil cases and a smattering of criminal cases each year, exacting a fee, set by statute, for every service he provided – from performing a marriage to issuing a guilty verdict. From this pool of justices, the mayor selected eighteen men for a simultaneous appointment as police magistrate. In this capacity, the justices spent part of each workday trying minor criminal cases in famously seedy police-station courtrooms around the city. Only in their role as police magistrates did the justices receive a public salary, and even that did not stop them from collecting fees of various sorts in criminal cases. By legislative design and venerable custom, most justices were laymen, which meant they were unschooled in the technical niceties of common law procedure and, their critics claimed, unversed in the ethical standards of the city's increasingly self-conscious and self-policing professional bar. A trial in a JP court tended to be a highly informal affair and often proceeded without interruption from lawyers. Justices ran their police courts in a similarly personal style, while assuring that the courts served as instruments of party discipline in the political wards where they stood.[2]

In an era of social struggle and reform, the caseload of the justice courts graphically illustrated the tensions produced by a generation of unprecedented industrialization, urbanization, and immigration. Workers filed civil suits against employers for "wage theft." Landlords

[1] Aliquis, "The Injustice in our Justices [*sic*] Courts," *CLN*, March 9, 1878, 200–201. "The Injustice Courts," *Chicago Times-Herald*, Jan. 28, 1897. Bartow A. Ulrich, *How Should Chicago Be Governed?* (Chicago, 1893), 41–47. See James Willard Hurst, *The Growth of American Law: The Law Makers* (Boston, 1950), 147–52; Eric H. Steele, "The Historical Context of Small Claims Courts," *ABFRJ*, 1981 (1981), 293–376; Allen Steinberg, *The Transformation of Criminal Justice: Philadelphia, 1800–1880* (Chapel Hill, 1989).

[2] Hiram T. Gilbert, *The Municipal Court of Chicago* (Chicago, 1928), 9–10; Elijah M. Haines, *A Practical Treatise on the Powers and Duties of Justices of the Peace and Police Magistrates*, 15th rev. ed. (Chicago, 1896); *Chicago Revised Municipal Code*, 1905, ch. 50, secs. 1785–1787; "Constitution of 1870," *Illinois Revised Statutes*, 1911, art. vi, secs. 21, 28; "Law in relation to justices of the peace," approved June 26, 1895, *Illinois Revised Statutes*, 1905, ch. 79, art. i, secs. 2–5; art. ii, sec. 16; art. xviii, sec. 164; hereafter cited as 1895 JP Law; Harry Olson, "Conditions in Chicago Which Led to the Institution of the Municipal Court," *JHO*, box 3.

and tenants sued each other. Collection agencies' lawyers filed count-less suits against unrepresented working-class debtors. Wives had their husbands prosecuted for desertion. Immigrant parents filed criminal complaints against their own children for being "unruly" or failing to bring home their wages. During strikes, the police hauled in union "sluggers." No wonder New York Mayor Abram Hewitt observed of his own city's police courts in 1888 that "the position of police justice is more important to the community than that of judge of the Court of Appeals; the latter finally settles the law, but the former applies it in the first instance, in nearly all cases affecting the life, liberty, and property of the citizens." Some years later, in a speech to the Illinois Bar Association, Chicago attorney Robert McMurdy chided his peers who avoided the justice courts. At stake in routine police court cases, McMurdy said, was nothing less than "the liberty of our humble citi-zens." Those matters constituted "the really difficult puzzle of such a metropolis."[3]

For many urban civic reformers and commentators at the turn of the twentieth century, the real puzzle was why the JP system, whose roots in Anglo-American legal culture stretched back to the Middle Ages, had survived for so long. If the law was, as the sociologist Edward A. Ross aptly put it in 1901, "the most specialized and highly finished engine of control employed by society," the men in whose hands American cities had entrusted this precious mechanism seemed utterly unfit for the task. Ross mourned "the undignified and demoralizing conduct of many of our police courts, presided over by burly, vulgar-minded political henchmen." Critics everywhere faulted the JP system for qual-ities long heralded as its chief virtues: its decentralized structure, its administration by lay officials, its swift and informal style of justice. The "iniquitous fee system" lay at the heart of the controversy, as a method of compensation formerly associated with fiscal economy and administrative flexibility came to signify an inherently corrupt contract between plaintiffs and justices.[4]

[3] Hewitt in Mary Roberts Smith, "The Social Aspect of New York Police Courts," *AJS*, 5 (1899), 150; Robert McMurdy, "The Law Providing for a Municipal Court of Chicago," *Proceedings of the Illinois State Bar Association*, 1906 (Springfield, 1906), 2: 82.
[4] Edward Alsworth Ross, *Social Control: A Survey of the Foundations of Order* (New York, 1901), 106, 113–14; Edward F. Dunne, "Against Justice Court Fees" (1904), in *Dunne: Judge, Mayor, Governor*, ed. William L. Sullivan (Chicago, 1916), 83; "The Waste of Time at Court," *Nation*, March 25, 1886, pp. 253–54. See Simeon E. Baldwin, *The American Judiciary* (New York, 1905), 130–31; Charles A. Beard, *American City Government: A Survey of Newer Tendencies* (New York, 1912), 173–84.

The old West Chicago Avenue Police Court, photographed c. 1908, after it had been renamed as one of the neighborhood "criminal branches" of the new centralized Municipal Court system. Courtesy of the Chicago Historical Society (ICHi-34913).

The next chapter narrates the political struggle over local judicial administration that led to the creation of the Municipal Court of Chicago and the dozens of city courts made in its image. This chapter recovers, so far as the historical record will allow, the American way of doing justice that the municipal court movement and its rhetoric of modernity left behind. Because the justices' dockets have perished, the historian's challenge is to read through reformers' condemnations of the "antiquated" and "evil" justice shops to reveal the logic and practice of the working judicial system beneath. For progressive reformers, one of the greatest needs in American institutions was for urban courts to adopt "business methods," a phrase they associated with the organizational efficiency and hierarchical discipline of the modern business corporation. But the justice shops had always heeded business principles. The courts operated according to an older economic model of governance. This entrepreneurial model had different implications for governance and a different, though not necessarily greater, capacity for injustice than the corporate model that businessmen-reformers would fight to install in its place.[5]

The surest and shortest route to understanding the political logic and everyday practice of late nineteenth-century justices of the peace is to consider the nickname that working-class Chicagoans bestowed upon their offices, the justice shops. Brush away the odium attached since the Progressive Era to the idea of private gain in public administration – especially judicial administration. What remains is a political creature with deep roots in English and American local governance: the public officeholder as independent proprietor, with privileges and duties established by local custom and law.

English justices of the peace reached the peak of their social status and public powers between the Glorious Revolution and the Napoleonic Wars, policing and administering their counties with remarkable independence from Parliament and the central government. In contrast to the Continent, where "sovereigns entrusted magistracy to salaried functionaries," the English sovereign reserved the office of justice for members of the landed gentry, who served in lifetime (freehold) tenure and regarded the office as both an obligation and a prerogative of their standing in their communities. The justice's powers grew steadily between the fourteenth and eighteenth centuries. He acquired jurisdiction over minor criminal offenses. He met quarterly with the other justices of his county in a Court of Quarter Sessions, where they heard all but the most serious criminal cases, oversaw the workings of parish government, and exercised regulatory powers over the local market. Without general statutes that clearly defined their authority, English justices on the eve of the American Revolution possessed "a local autonomy amounting almost to anarchy."[6]

[5] See, e.g., Herbert Harley, "Business Management for the Courts: As Exemplified by the Municipal Court of Chicago," *VLR*, 5 (1917), 1–26.
[6] Norma Landau, *The Justices of the Peace, 1679–1760* (Berkeley, 1984), 1, 6–14. Sidney and Beatrice Webb, *The Development of English Local Government 1689–1835* (London, 1929, 1963), 57–67, esp. 65.

In the American states of the nineteenth century, the powers of JPs paled next to those of their English counterparts. Primarily judicial, they were limited to minor civil and criminal offenses. But the justices presided over a decentralized system of judicial administration that came to be hailed by domestic and foreign commentators as the linchpin of civil liberty and local self-government. The legal historian Willard Hurst called the American JP "the arch symbol of our emphasis on local autonomy in the organization of courts."[7]

To a remarkable degree, this local autonomy resided in the person of the justice. Freehold tenure and property qualifications were not associated with the office in the states. But like their English predecessors, American JPs effectively owned their offices for the length of their terms. A justice court was thus known to the public not by its district or jurisdiction, as were the higher courts of the states, but by the name of the justice himself. The fee system was integral to this autonomy. Unsalaried public officers, justices executed a personal bond to cover their liabilities and ensure faithful performance of their duties. At their own expense, they set up shop within their township or precinct of residence in a location likely to draw business, hired a clerk if they expected to do a large business, and levied a fee, regulated by statute, for each service they provided – from conducting an inquest ($5 in 1850 Illinois) or marriage ceremony ($12\frac{1}{2}$ cents) to summoning a jury (75 cents) or entering a guilty verdict ($12\frac{1}{2}$ cents). In exchange for conferring these governmental powers and pecuniary possibilities upon individual male citizens, Illinois and the other states (all but a few) that adopted the JP system got a flexible apparatus of minor civil and criminal judicial administration at little or no cost to the public. As a shield against inept or corrupt justices, states allowed dissatisfied litigants to appeal their cases de novo (as a new trial) to a higher county court – an empty right for litigants who could not afford legal representation. The decentralized and enterprising character of the JP system was well suited to a predominantly agrarian country in which transportation was slow and people typically lived at some distance from a county seat. As the Nebraskan Roscoe Pound sentimentally recalled, the JP's job was to "bring justice to every man's door."[8]

[7] Hurst, *Growth of American Law*, 148.
[8] Henry Asbury, *Advice Concerning the Duties of Justices of the Peace and Constables* (Quincy, Ill., 1850), 232–34; Roscoe Pound, "The Administration of Justice in the Modern City," *HLR*, 26 (1913), 304. See 1895 JP Law, art. i, sec. 9; Robert M. Ireland, *The County Courts in Antebellum Kentucky* (Lexington, 1972); *People ex rel. McDougall v. O'Toole*, 164 Ill. 344 (1896); Steele, "Small Claims Courts," 326.

The place of JPs and police magistrates within county judicial systems illustrates the patchwork quality of local governance in late nineteenth-century America. Chicago's justice courts, as both the JP offices and police courts were known, served as the neighborhood outposts of the Cook County judicial system. The county judiciary was a thicket of redundant institutions and overlapping jurisdictions, the institutional residue of earlier waves of reform. Fourteen circuit court judges and twelve superior court judges, all approved in countywide elections, possessed identical jurisdiction: original jurisdiction in all matters of law and equity (except criminal cases), as well as in condemnation proceedings, drainage matters, election contests, and proceedings regarding neglected and dependent children. Sitting judges from the circuit and superior courts rotated on and off the bench of the Cook County Criminal Court, which had jurisdiction over all criminal matters. A separate tribunal, the county court, handled probate, appointment of guardians, and tax collection proceedings.[9]

Beneath these higher-tier county courts stood the more numerous and dispersed inferior courts of the JP system. The Illinois Constitution of 1870 mandated uniformity in all of the state's county-level JP systems, except for the selection of officials, in which Cook County differed significantly. The three official personalities of the system were the JP, the police magistrate, and the constable. Magistrates and JPs, collectively referred to as justices, had identical jurisdiction in Illinois. The principal distinction was that police magistrates specialized in criminal matters and existed only in villages and cities; in rural areas, even that low level of specialization was unnecessary. Constables provided strong-arm services for a fee to JPs and magistrates. They served summonses and writs, raised juries at the request (and expense) of a litigant or defendant, and delivered prisoners to the jailer. In mocking recognition of the sheriff-like authority of the hundred constables who roamed their city, Chicagoans called them "tin stars."[10]

Justices and constables in Illinois enjoyed countywide jurisdiction. In Cook County, the state's largest, this meant that "country" justices based outside Chicago could hear cases initiated by residents of the city, and city justices exercised the same jurisdiction over

[9] Newton Bateman, Paul Selby, and J. Seymour Currey, eds., *Historical Encyclopedia of Illinois with Commemorative Biographies* (Chicago, 1925), 310–11. Orrin N. Carter, "The Early Courts of Cook County," *ILR*, 10 (1915), 80–87. "Constitution of 1870," art. vi, secs. 18, 23. Gilbert, *Municipal Court*, 1–12. Albert Lepawsky, *The Judicial System of Metropolitan Chicago* (Chicago, 1932), 19–26.

[10] Lepawsky, *Judicial System*, 146. "Constitution of 1870." 1895 JP Law.

cases brought from the country – a seemingly dry technical matter with enormous potential for abuse. The justices' criminal jurisdiction included all local ordinance violations (including the routine public order-maintaining charge of disorderly conduct); all state misdemeanors in which the punishment was by fine only (not to exceed $200); all cases of assault, assault and battery, and public affrays; and vagrancy cases. Their civil jurisdiction covered all cases where the plaintiff claimed less than $200. (The salaried judges of the county circuit and superior courts tried felonies, the more serious misdemeanors, and the higher-stakes civil actions.) In practice, magistrates did not handle civil cases. But JPs grabbed any business, civil or criminal, that came their way. The justices' criminal jurisdiction also included proceedings for the "examination, commitment and bail of persons charged with the commission of criminal offenses." If a justice found probable cause that a more serious crime had occurred – a misdemeanor or felony punishable by imprisonment – he had to bind over the case to the grand jury of Cook County Criminal Court. If the grand jury decided to indict the defendant, the case was tried in criminal court. All justice court cases could be appealed de novo to the circuit and superior courts, which exacerbated the groaning backlog of the county courts.[11]

   The justices' "inferior" jurisdiction actually gave them the vast majority of judicial business in Chicago, including nearly all of the civil business of wage earners and poor people, for whom $200 was a princely sum. In 1890, for example, Chicago police magistrates handled 62,230 cases; they bound over only 2,340 to the grand jury. Thus, more than 96 percent of the city's criminal caseload was disposed of in the justice courts. In any given year, Chicago's justice courts might try more than five times as many civil cases as the circuit, superior, and county courts combined. Newspapermen did not exaggerate when they called these tribunals "the people's courts" or, less grandly, "the poor man's courts."[12]

   To the growing number of activists interested in the legal causes of the poor, the size of the justice courts' caseload was only one measure

---

[11] Gilbert, *Municipal Court*, 10, 15–17. See *Chicago Revised Municipal Code*, 1905, ch. 50, secs. 1785–1787; "Constitution of 1870," art. vi, secs. 21, 28; 1895 JP Law, art. i, secs. 2–5; art. ii, sec. 16; art. xviii; "The Grand Jury," *Chicago Tribune*, Nov. 16, 1882.

[12] *Report of the General Superintendent of Police of the City of Chicago for the Fiscal Year Ending December 31, 1890* (Chicago, 1891), 53; McMurdy, "Municipal Court," 82; *MCC 1* (1907), 50–51; "For People's Courts of Justice," *Chicago Record-Herald*, Nov. 2, 1905; "Rescuing the Poor Man's Court," *Chicago Times-Herald*, Jan. 28, 1897.

of their social significance. The *nature* of the caseload, the types of cases and people the justices had power over, meant that the justice courts put the systemic problems of the industrial city before the public. Addressing the Illinois Bar Association in 1888, Joseph W. Errant, a Chicago lawyer who represented poor clients in the justice courts on behalf of the Protective Agency for Women and Children, noted that "a claim for $10 sometimes involves more of human justice than a claim for $100,000." The justices exercised full jurisdiction over the most common criminal offenses, including vice, petty theft, and assault, and they served as gatekeepers to the criminal justice system for defendants accused of the deadliest felonies. Nor were the penalties at the justices' disposal a small matter. A $200 fine – let alone one for $20 – could erase the slim margin between independence and dependency for defendants and their families. If a convict failed to pay his fine, he was committed to the city's House of Correction (the "Bridewell") to "work it out" at 50 cents a day. Of the 7,566 people incarcerated in the Bridewell in 1882, for example, all but 190 were imprisoned for failing to pay fines. The majority of the women prisoners identified themselves as servants, prostitutes, washwomen, and seamstresses. The men included common laborers, sailors, teamsters, railroad workers, butchers, and clerks. For John Peter Altgeld, the German-born Chicago lawyer and future Illinois governor, these figures carried a powerful social message: "*our penal machinery seems to recruit its victims from among those that are fighting an unequal fight in the struggle for existence.*" Viewed in their social context, as people such as Altgeld and Errant insisted upon viewing them, the only thing inferior about the justice courts was the wealth of the people who appeared before them.[13]

The Constitution of 1870 set the same qualifications for justice of the peace and police magistrate as for judges of the higher courts of the counties. An aspiring justice needed to be a male citizen of the United States, at least twenty-five years old, a state resident for at least five years, and a resident of the town, county, or city from which he would be selected. With the exception of Chicago's justices and magistrates, every judge in the state, from the chief justice of the Illinois Supreme Court to the lowliest country JP, was elected. (This included Cook County JPs from outside the city limits.) In Chicago, only the constables were elected. The constitution specified that JPs in Chicago "shall be appointed by the governor, by and with the advice and consent

[13] Errant, "Justice for the Poor," 77; John P. Altgeld, *Live Questions: Including Our Penal Machinery and Its Victims* (Chicago, 1890), 163, 206, esp. 168, emphasis in original.

of the senate, (but only upon the recommendation of a majority of the judges of the circuit, superior and county courts)." This appointment process reflected downstate legislators' deep-seated suspicions of participatory democracy in Chicago, but it had a loftier justification. In theory, the county judges, who heard appeals from the justice courts, would form an opinion as to the caliber and corruptibility of incumbent justices and local attorneys and would thus be in a position to recommend "fit and competent" men for the minor judiciary. In practice, this provision subjected the judges to heavy pressure from office-seekers and their patrons – aldermen, ward bosses, and party leaders. Another cloud of political influence hung over the selection of Chicago's police magistrates, who were appointed by the mayor with the consent of the City Council.[14]

In matters of compensation, the fee system ruled. In Illinois, JPs, police magistrates outside Chicago, and constables all earned their livelihood from fees, according to schedules determined by statute or ordinance. Constable fees were tacked onto the court costs paid by litigants or guilty defendants. As early as 1881, the Chicago City Council established a salary for police magistrates and forbade them to collect fees while in police court – a significant reform that, judging from many later reports, was but loosely obeyed. The magistrates also routinely fled the police courts in the afternoon to collect fees in civil and criminal cases in their JP offices. Although the General Assembly tried to check this practice in 1897, legislating that no justice of the peace could simultaneously hold the office of police magistrate, Chicago ignored this reform. The City Council of Chicago did not alter the language of its ordinance, which required that magistrates be chosen from the justices of the peace. On the eve of the Municipal Court's creation, Chicago magistrates were still earning both a city salary and fees from their own offices.[15]

---

[14] "Constitution of 1870," art. vi, sec. 28; *Chicago Revised Municipal Code*, 1905, ch. 50, sec. 1786. See Olson, "Conditions in Chicago"; *People ex rel. McDougall v. O'Toole*, at 350.

[15] *Chicago Revised Municipal Code*, 1905, ch. 50, sec. 1787; 1895 JP Law, art. 1; sec. 1; Lepawsky, *Judicial System*, 142–63; William T. Stead, *If Christ Came to Chicago! A Plea for the Union of All Who Love in the Service of All Who Suffer* (London, 1894), 3–5, 52; Ulrich, *How Should Chicago*, 42–43. I verified the existence of double-dipping justices by cross-referencing JPs listed in the 1904 "Chicago Business Directory" with justices identified as police magistrates in the local biographical digest. Of the sixteen justices listed in the digest, four were clearly identified as having served simultaneously as magistrates and JPs after passage of the statutory amendment forbidding the practice. "Chicago Business Directory," *The Lakeside Annual Directory*

The paucity of professional training, formal procedure, and centralized discipline lamented by legal professionals of the early twentieth century was lauded by an earlier generation as essential to the democratic character of the JP system. As the Illinois Supreme Court opined in 1873, "Justices of the Peace are established in every township in the State, to enable parties not acquainted with the formal requirements of law to obtain speedy trials, without pleadings, and without being compelled to employ counsel skilled in the law to assist." The justice courts provided forums where ordinary people could file their own civil suits and criminal complaints, and argue their own cases. Indeed, justices were expected to instruct litigants in how to proceed with their cases. In Chicago, immigrants often relied on the untrained counsel of fellow countrymen who were better versed than themselves in the language and folkways of the justice courts – if not of the written law.[16]

The typical justice court was no marbled hall of justice. Justices might hold court in a space they rented for the purpose or in their own homes or places of business – carpentry shops, dry goods stores, even barns. It was common for justices, especially in rural areas where their services were in limited demand, to wedge their public duties into a week filled with other kinds of work. As early as 1872, the *Chicago Legal News* vented the disapproval of an increasingly self-conscious professional bar by publishing a description of a supposedly typical justice court. "In an upper room, reached by a rickety pair of stairs, in a slimy, weatherbeaten, tumble-down frame structure, this dispenser of justice is found, dealing out law, cheap in quality and price," the article reported. "The most ludicrous spectacles are here presented. Usually as many as can gain admittance elbow each other in their efforts to draw attention, thinking their success or defeat depends on their physical exertions to obtain a prominent position in the estimation of the dirty court and its chief centre."[17]

No doubt the JP office could be a rough place. The police courts were rougher still: crowded, smoke-filled rooms, in which immigrant boys accused of stealing coal from the railroad tracks and couples arrested for fornication were herded together in the sawdust of the "bullpen" with pickpockets and prostitutes, while bondsmen and lawyers peddled their wares. But if we read through the journal's professional biases, the traces of a rich local legal culture emerge in the justice

of the City of Chicago, 1904 (Chicago, 1904); BOC (1905), 103, 113–14, 471, 504.

[16] *Bliss v. Harris,* 70 Ill. 343, 345 (1873); McMurdy, "Municipal Court," 96.

[17] Quoted in Herman Kogan, *The First Century: The Chicago Bar Association, 1874–1974* (Chicago, 1974), 32.

shop. The weatherbeaten surroundings did not dissuade a throng of people from wrestling their way into the justice court to seek an economical resolution to their problems. For the majority of a justice shop's clientele, a crowded room in a frame structure probably bore a stronger resemblance to their own homes and places of work than did the neoclassical appointments of a county courthouse. The physicality of the proceedings – the brush of elbows, the jockeying for position – also corresponded to the physical quality of everyday life among working people in a way that a more formal courtroom might not. All of this suggests an atmosphere that may have made the administration of justice seem less remote from the rest of the litigants' lives. Given the demand for the justice's services, one might have arrived at a conclusion opposite that reached by the *Chicago Legal News* – that instead of reforming or abolishing the justice courts, the state ought to have created more.[18]

The men who presided over the justice courts in Chicago were a mixed lot. Although their dockets have perished, some biographical evidence survives. The public reputation of the justices followed the lines of an 1892 Cook County grand jury report, which charged that "there are many men occupying the position of Justice of the Peace in this county who are wholly unfitted for this responsible position, both from lack of ability and want of proper comprehension of the rules of law, justice or honesty." But reformers had to concede that some justices were well qualified. Of the fourteen justices profiled by Michael L. Ahern in his celebratory *Political History of Chicago* (1886), most had received some college education – an exceptional achievement in their time. Democrats and Republicans were well represented in Ahern's selection, as were immigrants and natives. Police magistrate George Kersten, a Chicago-born Democrat, got his start in business as a cigar maker and began reading law only after his appointment as a North Side police court clerk in 1880. Three years later he accepted an appointment as a justice and then as police magistrate. "Respected by the masses to begin with, his career on the bench up to date has made prospects for him which are decidedly enviable," Ahern noted. Irish-born Peter Foote taught law at the University of Notre Dame before accepting appointments as justice and police magistrate. "He is now pushing a most flourishing justitial business on Madison near Clark Street," Ahern wrote approvingly. A few justices even possessed considerable wealth. D. Harry Hammer studied law at the University of Michigan, belonged to the Union League Club, owned

---

[18] Altgeld, *Live Questions*, 187; Errant, "Justice for the Poor," 79–81; Stead, *If Christ Came*, 301, 343–45.

"a large amount of real estate," and had "one of the finest libraries in Chicago."[19]

On the eve of their abolition in 1906, fifty-two JPs pushed a justitial business in Chicago. Sixteen made it into the elite biographical digest *The Book of Chicagoans* – not a representative sample, but illuminating nonetheless. In party affiliation, the justices listed split between seven Republicans and eight Democrats, with one unidentified. Five of the men had been born abroad (three in Ireland alone – a strong showing found throughout Chicago government), but the other eleven were native-born. Though the law stipulated no formal educational qualifications for justices, almost all had attended a college or university. Most also had experience in other lines of work. Irish-born Republican Miles Kehoe worked in a Chicago brickyard and later in the teaming business before becoming the youngest man ever elected to the state senate. Irish-born Democrat James C. Dooley served as a clerk and deputy in the Cook County sheriff's office for nineteen years before accepting appointment as a justice in the town of West Chicago. Once appointed, most justices hung on to the job. Chicago-born Democrat John K. Prindiville, one of the city's best-known justices, served continuously for twenty-seven years – ten of them at the infamous Harrison Street Police Court – before the reformers abolished his job.[20]

The commercialism of the justice shops was an integral element of a judicial system and legal culture in which, for as long as anyone could remember, many officials had gotten by on fees alone. The 1850 JP manual listed fees not only for justices and constables but also for jurors and witnesses in civil cases, and even for citizens tending jail. At the turn of the century, the unsalaried state's attorney of Cook County was still receiving $20 for each felony conviction won by his office and $5 for each misdemeanor, and he took a 10 percent cut of all forfeited bonds. Well into the twentieth century, seasoned litigants in the Cook County courts knew that a tip in the hand of the right clerk or bailiff would ensure speedier service.[21]

---

[19] Grand jury quoted in Ulrich, *How Should Chicago*, 41–42; Michael Loftus Ahern, *The Political History of Chicago* (Chicago, 1886), 149–58, esp. 149, 152, 157.

[20] "Chicago Business Directory," in *The Lakeside Annual Directory of the City of Chicago, 1906* (Chicago, 1906), 2563; *The Lakeside Annual Directory of the City of Chicago, 1905* (Chicago, 1905), 13, 78, 103, 113–14, 117, 145, 170, 193, 231, 306, 325, 396, 471, 504, 514, 580; *BOC* (1905).

[21] Asbury, *Duties of Justices*, 235–36; Ray Ginger, *Altgeld's America: The Lincoln Ideal versus Changing Realities* (Chicago, 1965), 212; Haines, *Practical Treatise*, 1093. The 1905 Municipal Court Act expressly forbade clerks and bailiffs from accepting gratuities. "An Act in relation to a municipal court in the

Even within this transaction-driven judiciary, the entrepreneurial energy of Chicago's justices of the peace – wedged between "junk dealers" and "Keystone Hair Insulators" in the *Chicago Business Directory* – was unsurpassed. Many of these state officers kept offices in the Loop and other convenient locations, favoring the 100-block of Clark Street, a section known for its saloons, gambling rooms, and dance halls. Though a location easily accessible by foot or streetcar was essential to any mercantile enterprise of the era, location took on a special significance for justice courts due to the frequent requests for a change of venue. Under Illinois law, a "venued" case went to the nearest justice court, enabling a canny justice to boost his business by setting up shop near a particularly unpopular colleague. In one case egregious enough to catch a reporter's eye, Justice Hennessy supplemented his own business with the frequent change of venue cases from Justice Hotaling's neighboring court. When Hennessy moved his office a few doors south, a third neighbor, Justice Moore, dispatched his clerk to measure the distances between the three courts. Finding that his court now stood four feet closer to Hotaling's office than did Hennessy's, he asserted his right to Hotaling's venued cases. The fast-thinking Hennessy built a long staircase that stretched from his office toward Hotaling's, and so reestablished himself as the beneficiary of Hotaling's unpopularity.[22]

Thus were the ways of the justice shop, a petty bourgeois state office that existed on the same plane of urban sociopolitical experience with the saloon keeper–precinct captain, another political creature increasingly set upon by middle-class reformers at the turn of the century. In name and in practice, the keepers of the justice shops personified everyday justice in nineteenth-century Chicago. As a new century dawned – a century whose keywords would include organization, efficiency, and professionalism – closing time loomed for the justice shops.

A cartoon is worth a thousand slurs.

In 1897, the *Chicago Daily News* blazoned page one with a cartoon that captured the growing public dissatisfaction with the city's JP system. It depicts a constable – hat cocked, cigar planted in jowl, coat pocket bursting with writs – leaning his massive frame against a justice

city of Chicago," approved May 18, 1905, *Illinois Revised Statutes*, 1911, 715. But some officers continued the practice. See Elmer E. Baldwin to Harry Olson, Nov. 26, 1915, MCC, box 4, folder 29.
[22] "Chicago Business Directory" (1904), 563; 1895 JP Law, art. iv, sec. 34; Lepawsky, *Judicial System*, 67; Grant Eugene Stevens, *Wicked City* (Chicago, 1906), 42.

JUST THE REASON.

THE JUSTICE COURT SHARK—"WHAT! THE GRAND JURY AFTER ME? WHY, I ONLY DONE WHAT THE STATOOTS OF ILLINOIS DON'T SAY I CAN'T DO."

The Chicago daily newspapers regularly ridiculed Chicago's "justice shops," as seen in this cartoon by Batchelder, "Just the Reason," which appeared in the *Chicago Daily News*, Nov. 30, 1897. Courtesy of the Chicago Historical Society.

shop counter while awaiting his next assignment. The bug-eyed, buck-toothed justice, whose resemblance to a rodent is clearly intentional, reads a newspaper with the headline: "GRAND JURY AFTER JUSTICE SHARKS." Above his desk hangs a sign that says, "*JUSTICE COURT*. NO CREDIT HERE SHELL OUT YOUR STUFF. *DONT* TALK BACK." A lone law book rests on a shelf. Retreating from the office is a citizen, his empty pockets hanging out and his back papered with summonses. In the caption the justice shark exclaims to his constable, "What! The Grand Jury after me? Why, I only done what the statoots of Illinois don't say I can't do."[23]

[23] Batchelder, "Just the Reason," *Chicago Daily News*, Nov. 30, 1897.

"Incompetent." "Corrupt." "Vicious." "Evil." "Unfit." These are but a handful of the epithets hurled upon Chicago's JPs, magistrates, and constables in the late nineteenth century. The hurlers included politicians of both parties, elite reformers, newspaper editors, lawyers, grand juries, union strikers, employers, and anyone else whose bill-fold or parlor had been emptied of its contents by the action of an unscrupulous justice. The Citizens' Association of Chicago, a reform group established by businessmen in 1874, peppered its annual reports with investigations of the JP system, which it found "antiquated and unsuited to modern methods." Criticism of the justice shops filled the minutes of the Chicago Bar Association from its inception in 1874, and the association buffeted the General Assembly with resolutions to abolish the office of justice of the peace. "So great is the odium attached to these words that few good men are willing to take the places," association member Charles E. Pope declared upon dispatching one such resolution to Springfield in 1888.[24]

The defeat of the Pope resolution, however, presaged the fate of similar efforts during the next decade and a half. The drafters of the state's Reconstruction-era constitution had thought highly enough of the JP system to enshrine it in constitutional protections. With the exception of the appointment process, the Constitution of 1870 mandated statewide uniformity in "all laws relating to the courts" and expressly forbade the General Assembly to pass "local or special laws" regulating the practice, jurisdiction, or duties of JPs, police magistrates, and constables. Strict limitations on constitutional amendment further fortified the system: The assembly had authority to propose amendments to only one article per session. Anyone seeking an amendment had to convince two-thirds of both houses that the amendment should be their top constitutional priority of the session. Time and again, proposals to reform the Chicago justice shops ran aground on these constitutional shoals. Legislators from the "downstate" districts outside Chicago could not be persuaded to commit a legislative session to the city's court problem. And many of their colleagues from Cook County had no interest in reforming a system that provided so much patronage.[25]

[24] CAC, *Annual Report of the Citizens' Association of Chicago, 1892* (Chicago, 1892), 11; Pope in Kogan, *First Century*, 47.
[25] "Constitution of 1870," art. iii, sec. 22; art. vi, sec. 29; art. xiv, sec. 2. See "Discussed by Lawyers," *Chicago Tribune*, Jan. 12, 1890; Gilbert, *Municipal Court*, 13–18; "Injustice Courts"; Kogan, *First Century*, 47, 110–16; Lepawsky, *Judicial System*, 95; "Rowe's Attack"; "To Abolish Justices."

During the three decades leading up to the 1905 Municipal Court Act, a case against the city's minor judiciary emerged. It centered on three allegations. Best substantiated was the charge that the fee system corrupted the judicial process. The second allegation was that the politicized appointment process tipped the scales of justice in favor of litigants and defendants who had influence, or "pull." The final charge, which was more inchoate than the others, increasingly framed reformer discourse: An antiquated system of judicial administration created for agrarian communities was structurally incapable of meeting the needs for conflict resolution and social control in a great metropolis.

Fears that fees might corrupt local judicial officers had an Old World precedent. Similar complaints had arisen in eighteenth-century England, as a temporary easing of property qualifications by the crown, especially in Middlesex, led to the appointment of a new class of justices who depended on fees for their livelihood. "Trading Justices," they were called, and their efforts to promote a steady business earned them the condemnation of their landed peers for "gross misconduct and unfitness." The charges were not groundless, but they reflected the landed justices' gentlemanly distaste for the lower station, limited education, and trades of their new associates.[26]

Elite lawyers in late nineteenth-century Chicago stepped forward as the toughest critics of the fee system, and their language echoed the status inflections of their English predecessors. But the Chicago lawyers' assault on the justice shops was something new. Rather than an old-guard critique of an emerging entrepreneurial style of governance, the elite bar's challenge to the justice courts was an integral part of the nationwide project of legal professionalization under way in late nineteenth- and early twentieth-century America, which simultaneously looked backward to an idealized, ethnically homogeneous bar and forward to an emerging "credentialed social order" whose hallmarks would be extended periods of professional training, unified ethical and practice standards, and discipline.[27]

First- and second-generation Americans, many of them educated in night law schools, made up the fastest-growing segment of the bar. And there is plenty of evidence that old-stock legal elites who joined local, state, and national bar associations used the cause of

---

[26] Webb and Webb, *English Local Government*, 35, 146–68.
[27] "Kill Bogus Law Mills," *Chicago Times-Herald*, Nov. 5, 1897. See Jerold S. Auerbach, *Unequal Justice: Lawyers and Social Change in Modern America* (New York, 1976); Thomas Goebel, *The Children of Athena: Chicago Professionals and the Creation of a Credentialed Social Order, 1870–1920* (Hamburg, 1996).

professionalization to make life difficult for them. In their rhetorical assault on the justice courts, Chicago professionals and newspapers used language with strong nativist resonances – describing the justices as "shysters," "ex-saloon-keepers," or simply "unfit" – suggesting that at least part of their purpose was to purge the bar and bench of ethnic working-class strivers. But Chicago legal professionals were only marginally successful in their efforts to raise the bar on immigrant lawyers due to the speed at which the bar was diversifying, the spread of night law schools, and the urban proliferation of personal injury suits, small claims cases, and criminal cases that kept many ethnic lawyers in business.[28]

However much it might have fanned the nativist fires, the assault on the fee system represented a broader set of concerns. The attack came not only from Yankee elites, but also from jurists whose compassion for immigrants and workers was beyond dispute. In an 1889 letter, John Peter Altgeld urged a member of the North Dakota Constitutional Convention not to repeat Illinois's mistake and perpetuate the fee system. "While there will be here and there one to whom the office will be incidental," he wrote, "there will be a great many who will depend largely on the fees for a living, and this leads everywhere to the same results, viz., injustice, oppression, extortion and frivolous lawsuits. . . . The courts become clogged with business, while the poor and ignorant suffer." Altgeld's sentiments were echoed by another rising Democratic pol, Edward F. Dunne, who as a Cook County Circuit Court judge in 1904 called the fee system "a fruitful source of injustice." Altgeld and Dunne were less worried about pedigrees than the harm done to the poor by profiteering in criminal justice.[29]

Heightened doubts about the fee system also reflected the new disciplinary ethos of a middle-class professional culture in which the salary was becoming the preferred mode of compensation. In contrast to the fee received for a specific service rendered, the salary was a fixed and regular payment that compensated a professional or a civil servant for a continuous period of service. Because of its very fixity and regularity, the salary supposedly freed up the professional to approach the task at hand more objectively. Reformers protested that the justices' fees were inherently corrupting and "vicious," a slur that likened the official's fees to the prostitute's "wages of sin." Like the prostitute, the justice was "absolutely dependent upon his fees," which compromised his "independence" of judgment and tarnished the "dignity" of his office. Indeed, as the British journalist the Reverend William T. Stead

[28] See Goebel, *Children of Athena.*
[29] Altgeld, *Live Questions,* 63; Dunne, "Against Justice Court Fees," 83–84.

discovered in his visit to the Harrison Street Police Court in 1893, the wages of sin and some justices' fees were one and the same. The police court was located on the edge of the infamous Levee red-light district, a neighborhood of broken-down wooden and brick buildings just south of the glittering State Street shopping corridor. Stead described the court as "the great receiving house where the police and the bailsmen and the justices temporarily pen the unfortunate women who are raided from time to time 'for revenue only,' of which they yield a goodly sum to the pockets of the administrators of 'justice.' "[30]

The justices did little to alleviate the growing public concerns about the fee system. Overcharging of fees was a common practice in the courts. Police magistrates were notorious for pocketing fees that the law required them to hand over to witnesses or the city. And fee-chasing justices tipped the scales of justice in favor of their best customers: perennial litigants and prosecutors. As a commonplace joke put it, "JP" stood for "judgment for the plaintiff."[31]

Public concerns centered on the easy conspiracy that arose between justices, constables, and the justices' most reliable plaintiffs: collection agencies. Collection agencies were ubiquitous in the industrial city. They rationalized debt collection and introduced new economies of scale into small claims litigation. The agency's bread and butter – overdue rents and bills unpaid – were sums so small that individual creditors could hardly justify the time and expense of litigating them. By pooling the debt held by many creditors – often literally buying up small debts at a fraction of their value – collection agencies were able to keep lawyers steadily at work. These same economies of scale in urban centers gave justices a strong incentive to conspire with collection agencies. Since a justice's income was a function of volume – more suits meant more fees – to disappoint a collection agency was bad business. Justice Arthur V. Lee, a Chicago JP in the 1890s and 1900s, even signed a contract with the National Investment and Security Company. The collection agency paid him 50 percent of every judgment he awarded on its behalf. Lee later claimed, in court, that he had been unaware his actions were illegal. And he knew "dozens of justices who did exactly the same thing, in fact they all did it." As businessmen themselves, court reformers empathized with the justice's market position. "Let the justice be ever so fair-minded a man, he will be subject to the continual temptation of resolving judicial questions

---

[30] Ulrich, *How Should Chicago*, 46; Errant, "Justice for the Poor," 77; Stead, *If Christ Came*, 3–5, esp. 3.
[31] Lepawsky, *Judicial System*, 152; See Aliquis, "Justices [*sic*] Courts," 2002–01; Ulrich, *How Should Chicago*, 41–44.

in favor of his customer," the *Chicago News Record* lamented in the early
1890s.[32]

Fee-driven collusion between collection agents and justices produced another common form of justice court injustice: the remote
court scam. Professional plaintiffs took advantage of the countywide
jurisdiction of the justice courts, and the exceptional size of Cook
County, to tire defendants into submission. The trick was to file suit
in the justice court least accessible to an opponent. For a collection
agency suing a Chicago debtor, for example, a country justice court
located at the outer fringes of Cook County would work beautifully.
Collection agency lawyers used the decentralized minor judiciary to
demoralize defendants into paying their bills – plus, of course, the
justice's fees. A grateful justice might waive the plaintiff's fees and
set the trial for an inconvenient hour. In one scenario, often invoked
by reformers, a country justice would call a case just before the early
morning train was scheduled to pull in from Chicago. By the time
the defendant scampered into court, the justice had found him guilty
by default. The remote court scam was particularly effective against
poor litigants, who could not afford to lose several days' wages chasing
collection agency lawyers around Cook County.[33]

Reformers' efforts to end the scam collided with a predictable obstacle. In 1881, at the instigation of the Illinois Bar Association, the
General Assembly passed a law to divide Cook County's justice of
the peace system into two districts, Chicago and the remainder of the
county. The state supreme court struck down the law, ruling that it
violated the "constitutional requirement of uniformity" in the laws.[34]

The second major allegation against the justice courts was that they
favored litigants with political pull. With no hint of irony, reformers
traced the source of influence back to the antidemocratic appointment
process peculiar to Chicago. Circuit and superior court judges, who
owed their own elective posts at least partly to the machinery of their
parties, were expected to behave as disinterested public servants while

[32] "Lee's Mill Loses Toll," *Chicago Record-Herald*, Aug. 28, 1908; *News Record*
in Ulrich, *How Should Chicago*, 42. See *Luddy v. People*, 219 Ill. 413 (1905);
"Rowe's Attack"; Steele, "Small Claims Courts," 342.
[33] Gilbert, *Municipal Court*, 16–17; "Justice Hit by a Writ," *Chicago Record-Herald*,
Jan. 4, 1905; Lepawsky, *Judicial System*, 56; New Charter Campaign Committee, *The Chicago New Charter Movement: Why the Pending Constitutional Amendment Should Be Adopted* (Chicago, 1904), 7; Olson, "Conditions in Chicago,"
3–4; B. E. Sunny, *The Proposed Amendment of the Constitution of the State of Illinois and a New Charter for Chicago*, address to Union League Club of Chicago,
April 14, 1904 (n.p.), 8.
[34] McMurdy, "Municipal Court," 85.

they designated fifty-two fit and competent men to serve in Chicago's justice courts. The demoralizing effect of this patronage power might have been anticipated: Judges were beset by influence-peddlers and office-seekers. "I think I may safely say that every judge on the bench of this county regrets that the judges are required by law to appoint justices of the peace," Judge Goggin told the *Times-Herald* in 1897. "At the last election I received 1,800 letters from candidates for justice of the peace. If I were to tell you of all the calls I received..., you would wonder when I performed my proper judicial duties."[35]

Perhaps not every judge shared Goggin's distaste for patronage power. But by the turn of the century, county judges had their reputations to worry about. A raft of newspaper articles suggested their appointments were influenced by considerations less lofty than fitness and competence. Class bias and nativism stoked this newspaper innuendo. Judges "are besieged by the most sinister influences in the politics of the slums," the *Times-Herald* charged in 1897. "Politicians of the lowest grade do not hesitate to enter the chambers of a judge and insist upon unworthy appointments." Amidst this flurry of negative publicity, judges increasingly protested that their job-doling duties compromised the neutrality of the bench – and the political legitimacy that in American democratic theory depended on it. "I am emphatically opposed," one judge declared, "to any measure which vests in the judiciary any political power."[36]

An even thicker cloud of corruption surrounded the mayor's appointment of police magistrates. In his famous first-hand account of his visit to the Second City, *If Christ Came to Chicago!* (1894), the Reverend Stead singled out the brazen partisanship of the police courts as one of the most odious features of its government. "Over and over again I have had to ask myself whether I was really in an American city or whether I had spirited away and dropped down in some Turkish pashalik, so entirely has the very conception of impartial justice died out in the police courts of Chicago," Stead reported. Harry Olson, who served as an assistant state's attorney in Cook County from 1896 until his election as chief justice of the Municipal Court of Chicago in 1906, recalled that the appointment process made the police courts "an incident to political administration," a powerful tool for enforcing party discipline. A speech written by Olson around 1910 is the most detailed surviving description of political discipline in the police courts. His account has to be regarded with caution because he wrote it more

[35] "Judges File Protest," *Chicago Times-Herald*, Dec. 22, 1897. See "Constitution of 1870," art. vi, secs. 6, 13, 18, 20, 21, 28; 1895 JP Law, art. i, sec. 1–2.
[36] "Injustice Courts"; "Judges File Protest."

to legitimate the new Municipal Court than to accurately depict the system it replaced. But unlike many critics of the police courts, as a prosecutor Olson had been in a position to know what really went on there.[37]

According to Olson, the political discipline of the police courts operated on many levels. An office-seeker angling for a magistrate's post first had to secure the backing of the two aldermen who controlled the ward in which the police court resided. A magistrate thus entered office under obligations to his sponsors. In the Levee wards, aldermen used the police courts to exact political obedience from the keepers and customers of sporting houses, cheap hotels, and saloons, institutions central to the everyday life and economy of the wards. When an alderman wished to put the keeper of a disorderly house "under obligations," he arranged for the police to raid the house. The next morning, the prostitutes and customers would be dragged from fetid police station cells into the police court, where the alderman's friends did a bustling business in bail bonds. Ultimately, upon the reaching of an understanding between the brothel-keeper and the alderman, the defendants' cases would be "dismissed upon payment of costs." The magistrate and bondsman got their fees, the chastened keeper returned to business, and the alderman tabulated the votes he had nailed down for the next election.[38]

The political discipline of the police court extended to its petty officers, the bailiffs and clerks who also had aldermen to thank for their jobs. According to Olson, bailiffs kept tabs for aldermen on every resident of their ward who appeared before the court and channeled business to the aldermen's favored bondsmen. To bailiffs also fell the task of selecting a jury if a defendant requested one, and a defendant with pull could count on a sympathetic panel. In particularly corrupt police courts, Olson said, the clerk received from an alderman each morning a list of numbers that corresponded to the magistrate's list of cases. "These numbers, in the case of a weak judge, amounted to an absolute order from the alderman either to liberate or to assess a heavy fine against the defendant in question, thus demonstrating his power in the administration of justice." Heavy fines or a term in the

---

[37] Stead, *If Christ Came*, 297–98; Olson, "Conditions in Chicago," 4. See CAC, *Annual Report of the Citizens' Association of Chicago*, 1888 (Chicago, 1888), 22–23; CAC, *Annual Report*, 1892, 10–14.

[38] Olson, "Conditions in Chicago," 4–6. See Richard C. Lindberg, *To Serve and Collect: Chicago Politics and Police Corruption from the Lager Beer Riot to the Summerdale Scandal, 1855–1960* (Carbondale, Ill., 1991), 95; Ulrich, *How Should Chicago*, 41–47.

Bridewell awaited "rebellious members of the political organization" unless they made amends with their alderman before the magistrate issued his penalty.[39]

The politicized administration of justice in the police courts was attacked from many quarters. The police protested that their hard work on the beat dissipated in the courtroom. One veteran officer, who patrolled the First Precinct near the Harrison Street Police Court, told Stead that magistrates routinely reduced charges and suspended (effectively, remitted) fines for politically connected criminals. "A fine which is imposed according to the law is taken off according to politics," the officer observed. The discretionary acts of the magistrates interfered with those of the officers themselves, the choices they made every day in the streets when they encountered lawbreakers – whether to arrest them, order them to "move along," or ignore them. Well-connected pickpockets and other criminals with pull had little to fear from the police. In 1897, one defendant went so far as to engage a substitute to appear for him in police court. "After the exposure was made," the *Times-Herald* reported, "it was explained that the bogus defendant 'had become so familiar with the ways of justice court prosecutions that he knew they amounted to nothing and therefore was willing to take his chances of punishment for a fair consideration.'"[40]

The justices were unreliable allies in the police department's frequent skirmishes with strikers. In the Stock Yards Strike of 1904, Justice Fitzgerald of the Stock Yards Police Court dismissed nearly 85 percent of the strike cases that police brought before him. During the summer of 1905, the city was paralyzed by the Teamsters' Strike, the most violent labor conflict on record in the city. Between April and August, twenty-one people died, and more than 400 suffered serious injuries. Police arrested 1,108 working men, charging most with petty assault ("slugging"), and hauled them before the police courts. In a flurry of continuances, dismissals, and small fines, the union men received a measure of justice that the *Chicago Evening Post* called "ridiculously inadequate." Former Police Chief John J. Badenoch agreed. "Fines of from one to five dollars for assaulting or beating a man to unconsciousness, and these paid by the unions, only tend to encourage this evil."[41] For many of the elite lawyers who attended the annual meeting

[39] Olson, "Conditions in Chicago," 7–11, esp. 8.
[40] Stead, *If Christ Came*, 299; "Room for Reform," *Chicago Times-Herald*, Nov. 19, 1897.
[41] *Post* in Harold Barton Myers, "The Policing of Labor Disputes in Chicago," Ph.D. diss., University of Chicago, 1929, pp. 635, 552, 557–645; Badenoch in Stevens, *Wicked City*, 49.

The violent Chicago Teamsters' Strike of 1905 paralyzed commerce and heightened public criticism of the administration of justice in the Second City. From *World's Work*, vol. 10 (1905). Courtesy of the Brandeis University Libraries.

of the Illinois Bar Association in Chicago that May, the violence in the streets outside signaled the final failure of Chicago's judicial system. Attorney William E. Church, a Civil War veteran and Republican, warned the association that "a spirit of lawlessness" was overtaking Chicago and the nation. "High and low, rich and poor, employer and laborer, men and women of mature years and children at school, are becoming infected with this dread disease, a disease which, it is not too much to say, strikes at the very foundation of our national life." Church said there was "only one remedy" for this epidemic of lawlessness: to "wipe out entirely the antiquated system under which we have been so long laboring, and substitute some new and intelligible system."[42]

Contemporaries more sympathetic to organized labor agreed that the courts needed drastic reform, but they posed the problem differently: The practice of the police courts and JP courts had undermined workers' faith in legal action. After all, police court discretion could cut both ways. During the Stock Yards Strike, police authorities secured a change of venue for strike cases from Justice Fitzgerald's court in the heart of the predominantly immigrant, working-class Stock

[42] *Proceedings of the Illinois State Bar Association, 1905* (Springfield, 1905), 54–55.

Yards neighborhood to Justice Quinn's police court in elite Hyde Park. Quinn imposed far harsher penalties on the strikers, triggering an immediate protest from the union men. Workers, whether union members or not, also had reason to complain against the justice shops. The sting of the remote court scam, for example, was felt most acutely by workers, for whom a day in court was a day off the job. Appearing before the U.S. Industrial Commission on the Chicago Labor Disputes of 1900, the social settlement leader Graham Taylor testified that "even among the more intelligent workingmen of irreproachable character," he had observed a "deep disappointment and discouragement" in the relief provided by the justice courts. "The great mass of people take their judgment of the law and its administration from these courts, and they have been notoriously incompetent and corrupt."[43]

The final charge in the reformers' case against the justice of the peace system was also the vaguest: that the decentralized system was no match for a great city. "The system of courts now prevalent in the city of Chicago was well adapted to the primitive communities which first used it, where the justice was a substantial farmer or citizen, [who] knew most of the people who had cases before him, and sat as an arbitrator of neighborhood differences," the *News Record* observed in 1893. "That it is thoroughly unadapted to a city of 1,500,000 inhabitants is clearly apparent." An explicitly theorized statement about the functional relationship between urbanization and judicial administration was still a few years in the offing. When such a statement came, in the writings of Roscoe Pound and others, it was to be a vision strongly influenced by the Municipal Court that the reformers created in Chicago. In the meantime, the Chicago court reformers seemed content to declare that a great metropolis – a city whose concentration of industry and markets and whose heterogeneous population made it a world apart from the rest of the state – had vastly different institutional needs than a nineteenth-century village. For Robert McMurdy, a reformist local lawyer who would play a critical, if ambivalent, role in the creation of the Municipal Court of Chicago, the cultural complexity of the great city tested the limits of law itself. "The population of Chicago is so heterogeneous, so restless, so virile, so diversified in the matter of previous condition, customs, manner and thought that it becomes in any case difficult to make a law to fit the whole," he said.[44]

---

[43] U.S. Industrial Commission, *Report*, 3: 539.
[44] *News Record* in Ulrich, *How Should Chicago*, 44; McMurdy, "Municipal Court," 81.

Making the law fit the whole – applying statutory language and common-law principles to the everyday conflicts and crimes of a cosmopolitan metropolis – this was the justice courts' job. By 1905, no one was disputing the reformers' claim that the justices were no longer up to it.

2

A Managerial Revolution

[B]usiness management for courts must become universal in the larger cities. As well conceive of a department store being successfully run without a manager as . . . the manifold duties involved in administering justice in the modern city being accomplished by the mere voluntary acts of unorganized judges.

– Herbert Harley, American Judicature Society, 1917

In the opening decade of the twentieth century, Chicago emerged as the vital center of a widening movement for the reform of courts, which radiated outward from the Second City, like so many railroad lines, to great cities across America. Then, as now, the "Wicked City" had an international reputation for its underworld of vice, thievery, and violent crime. Visiting businessmen stumbled through the brothels and gambling dens of the Levee district, "sporting house" guidebooks in hand. Aspiring muckrakers cut their teeth on Chicago's reliably replete police blotter. They filled national magazines with dispatches from the metropolis that Lincoln Steffens, a veteran New York City police reporter, called "first in violence, deepest in dirt, loud, lawless, unlovely, ill-smelling, irreverent, new; an overgrown gawk of a village, the 'tough' among cities, a spectacle for the nation." With no trace of irony, the same magazines praised Chicago's boldly modern Municipal Court. "Chicago is to be congratulated upon this new and efficient reconstruction of its judicial machinery," New York's *Outlook* gushed in 1908, touting the court as a model for other cities eager to abolish their police courts.[1]

---

[1] Lincoln Steffens, *The Shame of the Cities* (New York, 1904), 234; "The Chicago Municipal Court," *Outlook*, March 14, 1908, 579; Grant Eugene Stevens, *Wicked City* (Chicago, 1906). See William Cronon, *Nature's Metropolis: Chicago and the Great West* (New York, 1991), 354–55.

The municipal court movement, like so many progressive undertak-
ings, had diverse origins and served multiple purposes. The most important of these could be classified as institutional, procedural, and political. Institutionally, there was widespread consensus in Chicago and
other cities by 1900 that the prevalent arrangement of local judicial
administration – the decentralized, fee-driven JP system – had to go.
Just what would replace it was a question court reformers in Chicago
would answer decisively in the Municipal Court Act of 1905. The procedural agenda arose originally in relation to the "regular courts," the
higher local trial courts such as the Cook County Circuit and Superior
Courts. Backlogs were so deep that a suit might take years to come to
trial. Critics expressed an inchoate sense that the "uncertainty, delay
and expense" of justice in the regular courts had something to do with
the increasing complexity and contentiousness of modern economic
life. But the more proximate cause was "archaic" judicial machinery:
the technical formalism of common-law procedure, the procedural restraints state legislators placed upon trial judges, and the unruly structure of the courts. These, too, had to go. Finally, the courts had become
a political liability, widely criticized as the most regressive of American
political institutions. Labor leaders and progressives condemned the
courts for arbitrarily striking down legislation designed to control
the worst excesses of industrial capitalism. The institutional disarray,
procedural inefficiency, and political conservatism of the courts had
generated widespread "popular dissatisfaction with the administration
of justice," warned the young Nebraska law professor Roscoe Pound in
his famous 1906 speech to the American Bar Association. Champions
of direct democracy proposed that the public be given power to
remove judges and recall court decisions. Much more significant in
the long run, state and federal lawmakers were quietly handing over
pressing regulatory matters of traditionally judicial purview – such
as industrial accidents, immigration policy enforcement, and public
health – to a new kind of institution: the administrative agency.[2]

The urban cultural context of the movement was also crucial. The
Progressive Era was the heyday of a new "city sense" in Europe and
America. For a few decades around the turn of the twentieth century,

---

[2] [Herbert Harley], "Success of Organized Courts," *JAJS*, 1 (1918), 133–51;
Roscoe Pound, "The Causes of Popular Dissatisfaction with the Adminis-
tration of Justice," reprint, *JAJS*, 20 (1927), 183. See Michael R. Belknap,
*To Improve the Administration of Justice: A History of the American Judicature
Society* (Chicago, 1992); Lucy E. Salyer, *Laws Harsh as Tigers: Chinese Immi-
grants and the Shaping of Modern Immigration Law* (Chapel Hill, 1995); Eric H.
Steele, "The Historical Context of Small Claims Courts," *ABFRJ*, 1981 (1981),
313–29.

America's great cities assumed an elevated importance in progressive social politics as both the consummate modern problem and the best hope for a solution. Soot-covered centers of industrial enterprise and class strife, magnets for immigrants and country folk, public spectacles of poverty and moral danger, the cities displayed the human toll of industrialism and monopoly capitalism before the urban observer with all the realist poignancy of a streetcar running down an apple cart. For this very reason – and because they had achieved so much in so short a time – the cities seemed the ideal laboratories for bold social-political experimentation in an anxious but progressive era.[3]

The court movement reflected one of the broadest and most politically salable impulses in progressive urban reform: to consolidate and professionalize America's sprawling and particularistic city governments. The most popular urban causes of the day centered on the question of municipal "self-ownership." It was a phrase synonymous in city politics with public ownership of utilities such as street cars, waterworks, and electric power systems, and it also signified a far greater level of administrative power for city governments. Many progressives, especially businessmen and professionals of an administrative mindset, recognized that before cities could own or control even their most vital infrastructure, before they could carve out a public, or "social," piece of themselves and cordon it off from the market, they first had to own themselves in a political sense. This meant loosening the constitutional restraints on municipal self-government and seizing greater political and fiscal autonomy from state governments and party organizations, the state and local machines that had gotten hold of the institutions of city government. In the name of the public interest, the middle-class legions of structural municipal reform worked to strip public power from parties, aldermen, and bosses and place it in the hands of professional experts. Through such instruments as new city charters, civil service commissions, and city manager schemes, administrative reformers enjoyed moderate success in consolidating municipal governments into rationalized bureaucracies. Their model was the modern business corporation. Surely, it is not the least of progressivism's many ironies that the model that middle-class progressives favored most in their quest for municipal self-ownership was the very institution that so many Americans of their class and generation found threatening to their own autonomy.[4]

---

[3] On "city sense," see Daniel T. Rodgers, *Atlantic Crossings: Social Politics in a Progressive Age* (Cambridge, Mass., 1998), 112–208.

[4] Lincoln Steffens, *The Struggle for Self-Government* (New York, 1906). See Martin J. Schiesl, *The Politics of Efficiency: Municipal Administration and Reform*

The municipal court movement, one of the most far-reaching episodes of urban reform in this progressive age of city sense, has important implications for how we think about the "organizational revolution" of the twentieth century, the bureaucratization of economic and political life. Historians have long been aware that the progressive drive for administrative efficiency involved high costs to participatory democracy. But in this narrative of expert authority versus popular power, something fascinating has slipped under historians' radar: the extraordinary disciplinary capacities of the corporate model.[5]

The institutional design of the Municipal Court of Chicago – a centralized system of functionally specific branch courts presided over by a managerial hierarchy – was a revealing product of this historical moment. In their search for an administrative solution, court reformers embraced the ascendant organizational model of their day: the businsss corporation, with its visible accountability and operational efficiency, its rational structure and facility for breaking down complex problems into discrete tasks. What organizational form could better address the multiple purposes of court reform? "Business management for courts" – a slogan of the municipal court movement – promised to streamline civil procedure, a boon for business interests demanding a more predictable system of debt collection and commercial litigation. It promised to make courts more socially responsive, restoring popular faith in American institutions against the claims of socialism and political radicalism. Above all, the managerial model seemed well equipped to carry out the double-edged disciplinary project of court reform: to provide a more efficient machinery of social regulation in a great city and to police the behavior of judicial officials themselves.[6]

Criticism of Chicago's JP system might have rumbled on as it had for decades had municipal reformers in the opening years of the new

in America, 1880–1920 (Berkeley, 1977); Robert H. Wiebe, *Businessmen and Reform: A Study of the Progressive Movement* (Cambridge, Mass., 1962); Robert H. Wiebe, *The Search for Order, 1877–1920* (New York, 1967); Olivier Zunz, *Making America Corporate 1870–1920* (Chicago, 1990), 66, 202.

5 Louis Galambos, "The Emerging Organizational Synthesis in Modern American History," in *Men and Organizations: The American Economy in the Twentieth Century*, ed. Edwin J. Perkins (New York, 1977), 3–15. Samuel Haber, *Efficiency and Uplift: Scientific Management in the Progressive Era 1890–1920* (Chicago, 1964); Samuel P. Hays, "The Politics of Municipal Government in the Progressive Era," *PNQ*, 55 (1964), 157–69; Schiesl, *Politics of Efficiency.*

6 Herbert Harley, "Business Management for the Courts: As Exemplified by the Municipal Court of Chicago," *VLR*, 5 (1917), 1–26.

century not tied court reform to a larger cause: the broad-based movement to win a new home-rule charter for the Second City. The political momentum of this larger struggle for local autonomy enabled
court reformers finally to leap over the constitutional hurdles that
had long blocked their efforts and to usher in a self-consciously modern era of urban judicial administration. Charter reformers viewed
court reform as only one phase of a larger plan to consolidate the
political power, secure the fiscal footing, and rationalize the governmental machinery of their great city. Charter delegate Robert
McMurdy called court reform the "tail to the consolidation kite." But
as events played out, the tail soared, while the kite itself crashed to the
ground.[7]

The Chicago charter campaign was a classic exercise in administrative progressivism. Dominated by businessmen and professionals
(most of them Republican), steeped in the rhetoric of public interest
and efficiency, and generally unresponsive to working-class demands
for more direct popular control of government, the campaign aimed
to solve a wide array of social and institutional problems by centralizing
administrative power and revenue-raising authority in the municipal
government.[8]

The New Charter Convention met in the fall of 1902 in the chambers
of the Chicago City Council. The cast of delegates included several
aldermen, two representatives of the Chicago Federation of Labor,
and a throng of businessmen and professionals representing elite organizations such as the Chicago Bar Association, the Civic Federation,
and the Illinois Manufacturers' Association. Charles Merriam and
Ernst Freund, professors of political science and law, respectively, at
the University of Chicago, provided the convention with expert advice. The convention's stated goal was "a more simplified, compact
and scientific plan of local government, adapted to the situation and
wants of this great and growing city." The program stood upon three
legs: "an adequate municipal revenue system," "an adequate municipal judicial system for police cases and minor civil cases," and local
self-government "with respect to all matters of local concern." This
last demand paid tribute to the rising political power of Continental
European immigrants in Chicago, who resisted the General Assembly's

---

[7] Robert McMurdy, "The Law Providing for a Municipal Court of Chicago,"
Proceedings of the Illinois State Bar Association, 1906 (Springfield, 1906),
2: 86.
[8] See Maureen A. Flanagan, *Charter Reform in Chicago* (Carbondale, Ill., 1987);
Thomas R. Pegram, *Partisans and Progressives: Private Interest and Public Policy
in Illinois, 1870–1920* (Urbana, 1992), 87–120.

efforts to regulate public drinking in the city. But for mainstream charter reformers, the essence of home rule was political consolidation.[9]

The stakes of consolidation were high. Like other major cities,
Chicago's ability to respond swiftly to the crises triggered by its rapid
growth and industrialization – housing shortages, overburdened public services, epidemics – was hindered by constitutional restraints and
an unsympathetic state legislature. The Constitution of 1870, drafted
when Illinois was still an agrarian state of two and a half million people, mandated uniformity in the incorporation of municipalities. It
expressly forbade the General Assembly to enact special laws to in-
corporate municipalities or amend their charters. Under the 1872
Cities and Villages Act, Chicago had the same administrative structure and meager revenue-raising powers as all other cities of 1,000 or
more residents. By 1900, Chicago was a global economic force with a
cosmopolitan population approaching two million. As Merriam later
recalled, "the City was still unable to grant a concession for checking
hats or selling pop-corn on the new municipal pier without a special act of the Legislature, to say nothing of powers adequate to deal
with the complicated questions of transportation and communication
in a growing city." Any tinkering with the city's administrative design
required a constitutional amendment. The result was thirty years of
patchwork governance in Chicago: eight separate governing bodies
with taxing authority, five police forces, and a collective headache for
the citizens every time election day rolled around or taxes came due.[10]

By 1904 there was public support for a constitutional amendment
that would clear the way for municipal court reform and a new charter.
The Civic Federation, an elite progressive group organized during
the Reverend Stead's 1893 visit to Chicago, drafted the amendment.

---

9 Chicago New Charter Convention, *Proceedings of the Chicago New Charter Con-
   vention* (n.p., 1902), 4–5. United Societies for Local Self-Government, *Home
   Rule: The Truth about the Sunday Question,* bulletin, 5 January 1907.
10 Charles Edward Merriam, *Chicago: A More Intimate View of Urban Politics* (New
   York, 1929), 14; "Constitution of 1870," *Illinois Revised Statutes,* 1911, art.
   iv, sec. 22; New Charter Campaign Committee, *The Chicago New Charter
   Movement: Why the Pending Constitutional Amendment Should Be Adopted*
   (Chicago, 1904), 2. See Steven J. Diner, *A City and Its Universities: Public Policy
   in Chicago, 1892–1919* (Chapel Hill, 1980), 155–61; Milton J. Foreman,
   "Chicago New Charter Movement – Its Relation to Municipal Ownership,"
   AAAPSS, 31 (1908), 640–41; Hugo S. Grosser, "Municipal Problems of
   Chicago," *AAAPSS,* 23 (1904), 281–96; Pegram, *Partisans and Progressives,* 92;
   B. E. Sunny, *The Proposed Amendment of the Constitution of the State of Illinois
   and a New Charter for Chicago,* speech to Union League Club of Chicago,
   April 14, 1904 (n.p.).

It authorized the legislature to pass a new charter for Chicago that would consolidate the powers of all those rival local governments, to raise the city's limit of bonded indebtedness, to levy and collect taxes for corporate purposes, and, "in case the General Assembly shall create municipal courts in the city," to "abolish the offices of Justices of the Peace, Police Magistrates and Constables." No law based upon the amendment could take effect without the approval of Chicago's voters. The amendment did not meet everyone's definition of home rule. Judge Edward F. Dunne and the Chicago Federation of Labor had urged that it include provisions for the initiative, the referendum, and municipal ownership of utilities. But the convention delegates balked. With the City Council's blessing, the amendment passed in Chicago by a landslide and prevailed in the state as a whole.[11]

Reform of the inferior courts fit neatly into the progressive rhetoric and institutional aims of the charter campaign. Chicago's JP system was the consolidation problem writ small: designed with an agrarian community in mind, decentralized, and overseen by political amateurs. The justice courts, like the old charter itself, seemed to reformers such as attorney Wallace Heckman totally inadequate to the governmental needs of "a mighty city – the center of intricate and diversified activities and occupations, the source of unmeasured political energy, as well as weakness and danger." The association of court reform with the charter movement sharpened the contours of the court critique and made a radical solution seem inevitable: the abolition of the JP system and the creation of a consolidated municipal court.[12]

Exactly what the new court would look like was still an open question. The charter delegates might have drafted a bill that simply eliminated the fee system, made all the justices salaried officials, and required all cases arising in Chicago to be tried by justices within the city limits. Only a decade earlier, reformers would have been elated at such a prospect. But these were heady days in Chicago politics. The convention ultimately went for something grander.

Soon after the amendment's ratification, the convention appointed a blue-ribbon committee to draft a court bill. The bipartisan committee consisted of men of impeccable elite credentials and records of public service, the sort of men who might see the advantage of a court run according to modern business principles: Carter H. Harrison II, a Yale Law School graduate and mayor's son completing his own fourth

---

[11] "Constitution of 1870," art. iv, sec. 34; Foreman, "Charter Movement," 640; Pegram, *Partisans and Progressives*, 99–100.

[12] Wallace Heckman, *The Extent of Necessary Constitutional Amendment*, address to Chicago Law Club, March 29, 1901 (Chicago, 1901), 5.

term as Democratic mayor; Circuit Court Judge Murray F. Tuley, a former Democratic corporation counsel; attorney John S. Miller, a Republican former corporation counsel who now represented Standard Oil Company; attorney John P. Wilson, a specialist in corporation law; Civic Federation president Bernard E. Sunny, a Republican and the western manager of General Electric Company; and merchant Bernard A. Eckhart, a former Republican state senator. In the progressive fashion, the committee hired an expert to draft the bill, a Democratic attorney named Hiram T. Gilbert. A gentleman legal scholar with a cultivated interest in ancient Roman law, Gilbert had published a tome entitled *The Railroads and the Courts*. His vision, more than any other, gave shape to America's first modern municipal court.[13]

In early January of 1905, this august committee gathered at the elite Union League Club to hammer out revisions of Gilbert's draft bill. As Gilbert conceded – and his critics protested – the bill represented "a radical departure from previous long-standing court practice." His proposed scheme would have dismantled the judicial class structure of "inferior jurisprudence," which he described as the "universal custom" in common-law countries to assign cases involving "small amounts of money or property" to judges "inferior in learning, ability and social standing." His bill provided for the abolition of JPs, magistrates, and constables in Chicago. A new, fully unified municipal court would have unlimited original jurisdiction to hear civil and criminal cases in the entire county, with the sole exception of suits in equity. Structurally, it would consist of a "common pleas court," possessing this full jurisdiction and outfitted with a grand jury for felony cases, plus five territorially based "city courts," whose jurisdiction mirrored the old justice court jurisdiction (with a higher limit on the value of property recovered or fines imposed). Twenty-four judges, elected for six-year terms, would take turns presiding over the common pleas court and the city courts, rotating from one to the other at the command of the Municipal Court's elected chief justice.[14]

Just as innovative as the wide jurisdiction envisioned by the Gilbert bill was its plan to impose a professionalized bureaucratic structure

---

[13] *BOC* (1905), 181, 232, 266, 411, 559, 577, 621–22; "A Court That Runs like a Business Corporation," *New York Tribune*, Jan. 16, 1910; Hiram T. Gilbert, *The Municipal Court of Chicago* (Chicago, 1928), 19–26; Hiram T. Gilbert, *The Railroads and the Courts* (Ottawa, Ill., 1885); see Herman Kogan, *The First Century: The Chicago Bar Association, 1874–1974* (Chicago, 1974), 113.

[14] Gilbert, *Municipal Court*, 405–40; Hiram T. Gilbert, *New Municipal Court System*, address before Union League Club of Chicago, April 10, 1906 (n.p.), 4.

upon the local judiciary. No longer would justice be administered by
fee-compensated laypeople: Aspiring judges had to be at least thirty
years of age (five years older than the entry age for JPs), to be U.S. citizens and Chicago residents, and to have at least five years' experience
as an attorney or judicial officer in Cook County. The judges would
receive their entire pay in a fixed public salary. They would appoint
a chief clerk and chief bailiff for the entire court, who would in turn
appoint staffs of deputies, to be hired in strict accordance with the
Illinois Civil Service Act of 1895. No longer would the halls of justice
open and close at the convenience of a single justice. The Municipal
Court would "be always open for the transaction of business," six days
a week, the whole year round.[15]

Perhaps it was Gilbert's deep knowledge of the law of railroads,
America's first modern business corporations, that inspired his vision
of a court "so organized that its business could and would be conducted
with some regard to good business principles." The body of judges,
whom Gilbert envisioned as a board of directors, would hold monthly
meetings. They would review the performance of bailiffs and clerks,
devise economical methods of record-keeping and accounting, and
"bring into use a modern and sensible system of practice." The bill
empowered the chief justice – a figure Gilbert fashioned in the image
of a corporate manager – to set the trial calendar, establish specialized
branch courts, assign associate judges to specific branches, and require
them to submit monthly written reports on their work. For Gilbert, the
unique disciplinary powers of the chief justice were vital to prevent the
court from becoming a new trough of patronage. "What corporation,"
he asked an audience of Union League Club men, "paying annually to
its . . . employees in salaries a million dollars, would permit its business
to be carried on without a general manager or superintendent?" This
was a court designed not merely to provide efficient social regulation
in a modern city, but also to bring court officials under heel.[16]

The New Charter Convention's court committee approved Gilbert's
bill with few significant changes. Most troublesome to Gilbert was the
committee's insistence that municipal judges receive a salary lower
than that of the circuit and superior court judges, thus maintaining a
status hierarchy that Gilbert (correctly) predicted would draw judicial
talent away from the city. (The committee's motives are unclear; fiscal
conservatism is the likeliest explanation.) The committee also rejected
Gilbert's proposal that the Municipal Court have county-wide jurisdiction with the sound reasoning that this would not pass constitutional

[15] Gilbert, *Municipal Court,* 416, 410–17.
[16] Ibid., 21, 408–9; Gilbert, *New Municipal Court,* 8.

muster. Otherwise, the bill that the Chicago Republicans Senator
Joseph F. Haas and Representative Robert E. Pendarvis introduced
in the General Assembly on January 24, 1905, and which presently slid
into the mailboxes of hundreds of members of the Chicago bar, bore
the distinctive design of Hiram T. Gilbert.[17]

The Gilbert bill met with swift opposition from unexpected quarters.
There was surprisingly little resistance to the wholesale destruction of
Chicago's JP system. No one seized the assembly floor to defend the
honor of the justice courts. Perhaps the momentum toward abolition
was so strong that even the men who had controlled patronage in
the JP system could see that their time would be best spent creating
an opening for patronage power in the new municipal court. The
opposition came instead from within the Chicago bar itself, led by
Robert McMurdy and a faction of charter delegates. Three weeks after
Gilbert's bill hit the assembly floor, a counter bill appeared, presented
with a letter written by McMurdy and signed by seventy-two prominent members of the Chicago bar and bench (including five future
Municipal Court judges). The dissenting bill preserved almost all of
the administrative features of the Gilbert bill. The chief point of con-
tention was the scope of the new court. The McMurdy bill followed
Gilbert's plan for city courts but scrapped the common pleas court
entirely. The effect, the *Chicago Tribune* explained, was to shrink the
Municipal Court's jurisdiction to that of "a dignified sort of justice
court," leaving the rest of the field to the county courts.[18]

McMurdy's letter explained the dissenters' opposition to a fully consolidated municipal court in rhetoric that mixed professional conservatism with urban populism. It reminded the General Assembly of the
political importance of Chicago's inferior courts as institutions that
mediated the conflicts of immigrants, wage earners, and their families. "The disposition of this vast business, so intimately concerning
the life of the people of this city, is and must be a specialty." Gilbert's
scheme would not dissolve the judicial class structure, the letter insisted; municipal judges would now maneuver for positions on the
common pleas court, leaving the city courts and "the cases of the poor
people" to the least qualified among them. Shifting from the populist mode, the letter made a lawyerly case for gradualism. "Radical
legislation requiring radical changes of procedure either by courts or
municipal bodies, is sure to cause much litigation construing the new
laws," the letter cautioned. "The wise course to follow for the new

[17] Gilbert, *Municipal Court*, 19–20, 27.
[18] Ibid., 441–60; "Has a New Courts Bill," *Chicago Tribune*, Feb. 17, 1905; Robert
S. Iles, "Municipal Courts," *CLN*, March 4, 1905, 235–36.

court . . . is to provide for this court salaried officials, and then make as few changes in justice of the peace procedure as possible, so that the great body of decisions and law that has been in force for generations in this state will still apply and control litigation in the new courts."[19]

What followed was, in Gilbert's words, "a very bitter contest in the General Assembly." The final Municipal Court bill illustrates the sorts of political compromises that progressives everywhere had to swallow to get legislation enacted. The act was faithful to Gilbert's design, and it embodied his progressive ideals of centralization and professionalism. But the legislative struggle had bent those ideals to political imperatives. The impact of McMurdy's charter faction was evident in the way the legislators narrowed Gilbert's vision of a truly unified Municipal Court with a jurisdiction equal to the circuit and superior courts. The Municipal Court's jurisdiction, however, far exceeded that of the old JP system. The court had full jurisdiction over civil cases, except when a plaintiff sought an equitable remedy such as an injunction. The court's criminal jurisdiction covered all criminal cases below the grade of felony: city ordinance violations (quasicrimes) and all state misdemeanors punishable by a fine or imprisonment for less than one year in the Chicago House of Correction or Cook County Jail. In felony cases, the court had the same preliminary jurisdiction as the old police courts; if the judge found probable cause, he had to bind over the case to the Cook County Criminal Court. A Municipal Court decision was as authoritative as that of any county court; only an appellate court could reverse it. There would be no more de novo appeals in Chicago, a fact that provided instant relief to the county courts.[20]

The other significant amendments to Gilbert's bill were blatantly political. They originated in the assembly, the handiwork of the dominant faction of the Cook County Republicans. A centralized Municipal Court implied a new bureaucracy and hundreds of new political jobs. Recognizing this, both the Gilbert and McMurdy bills had specified that the judges appoint the chief clerk and chief bailiff, and that those officers appoint their deputies in accordance with the Civil Service Act. The final Municipal Court Act made the chief clerk and chief bailiff citywide elective positions, effectively reserving the positions for men

---

[19] Gilbert, *Municipal Court*, 442, 444.
[20] Ibid., 27. For the legislative record (without debates), see *Journal of the House of Representatives of the 44th General Assembly of the State of Illinois* (Springfield, 1905), 111, 317, 424, 451–52, 458, 461–62, 525–46, 809–30, 893–96; *Journal of the Senate of the 44th General Assembly of the State of Illinois* (Springfield, 1905), 274–75, 379, 380, 440, 498, 724–46; "Act in relation to a municipal court," chs. 265, 282.

sponsored by the major party factions. Their deputies would be among the few municipal officeholders *not* regulated by the civil service law. Gilbert credited similar partisan motives for the insertion of a provision that judges be elected in the November general elections, rather than the less crowded spring municipal elections. The predictable effect was that many voters, faced with Chicago's already daunting "long ballot," would vote the straight ticket, miring the municipal bench in party politics. The legislation, charged McMurdy, created a "powerful and uncontrolled political machine and, most unfortunately, a judicial machine."[21]

On May 18, 1905, Governor Charles S. Deneen signed the Municipal Court Act. To take effect, it still had to pass muster with the voters. The *Record-Herald*, a progressive daily, urged the city's voters to do their duty and put an end to "the anomalies, the injustice, the oppression, the shame of the so-called justice shops." On November 7, 1905, the enfranchised men of Chicago voted overwhelmingly to abolish the city's justice of the peace system and establish in its place America's first modern municipal court. The Illinois Supreme Court found the act constitutional the following year.[22]

Notwithstanding all the jerry-rigging in the General Assembly, the Municipal Court Act *was* a radical measure that launched a managerial revolution in judicial administration. The justice of the peace – a fixture of local government in England and America since the late Middle Ages – had survived revolutions and civil wars, constitution-making and codification campaigns, only to perish on the rails of industrialization and urbanization. Out with the keepers of the justice shops went a decentralized system of judicial administration, in which justices effectively owned their offices, drummed up their own "justitial business," and passed judgment on the conflicts and crimes of the ordinary people in language the ordinary people could understand. Within only a few months of the court's creation, newspapers and magazines across America were trumpeting Chicago's great experiment as a national model. Perhaps the greatest symbolic victory came when the *American Review of Reviews*, the American edition of the Reverend Stead's London-based magazine, published a glowing tribute to the Municipal Court. The court, the *Review* announced, "has made a clean, wholesome, American atmosphere in the judicial strata lying next to the ground in Chicago." During the next two decades,

---

[21] McMurdy, "Municipal Court," 98. For the bills and final act, see Gilbert, *Municipal Court*, 28, 409–10, 412–15, 448–53, 466–71.

[22] "For People's Courts of Justice," *Chicago Record-Herald*, Nov. 2, 1905; *City of Chicago v. Reeves*, 220 Ill. 274 (1906).

some forty American cities would recapitulate the judicial revolution begun in the Second City, as businessmen and bar association lawyers persuaded state lawmakers to centralize judicial administration into accountable professional bureaucracies after the fashion of the Municipal Court of Chicago.[23]

Addressing the Illinois Bar Association a few months after the act's passage, Robert McMurdy articulated a principled – and, as it turned out, *prescient* – ambivalence about this judicial transformation. The court act, he noted, far exceeded the 1904 amendment's mandate to abolish the evils of the inferior courts. But to create a more dignified local judiciary, the act had discarded all that was good about the JP system – its informality, affordability, and accessibility to "humble citizens." For years, immigrants had been represented in justice courts, often for free, by "non-professional friends" who were "more familiar with our language and institutions than they are, and at all events very much more familiar with the proceedings in the justice court." The new court would be a court of record, which meant its judges could refuse to recognize any counselor not certified to practice before the Illinois Supreme Court. The new office of the chief justice, McMurdy warned, concentrated judicial power in the hands of a judicial "monarch." "It would seem that the court is a contrivance for the benefit of the legal profession, but it is nothing to be rejoiced at," he concluded. "Our profession cannot be exalted through the medium of a dignified court by hardships imposed upon the man with the dinner pail and the woman with the needle."[24]

McMurdy's populist rhetoric points up the absence of any organized opposition from below to the Municipal Court Act. The attorney did not take his case to the humble citizens; he made it in the public but elite fora of the assembly floor and bar association meeting. But if he had reached out to a broader public, would the humble citizens – the immigrant with a legal problem, the workingman with his dinner pail, the seamstress with her needle – would they have responded to his call? The answer is somewhat different depending on whether one imagines McMurdy's humble citizens as workers or immigrants. A large proportion of Chicago's workingmen were immigrants (and vice versa), but

---

[23] Stanley Waterloo, "The Revolution in Chicago's Judicial System," *American Monthly Review of Reviews*, April 1907, p. 455; Frederic B. Crossley, "Chief Justice Harry Olson and His Court,"*JAICLC*, 3 (1912), 346; "Editorial," *JAJS*, *1* (1918), 131–32; Roscoe Pound, "Organization of Courts," [1914], *JAJS*, *11* (1927), 69–83.

[24] McMurdy, "Municipal Court," 82, 96, 98, 97.

in their identities as workers or immigrants, they had a different historical relationship to the courts and to the politics of consolidation.
(As for the seamstress, women could not vote in Chicago elections
until 1913. Middle-class women did play a major role in socializing the
courts before winning the ballot – a story we'll return to.)

Few Americans workers would have disputed Chicago labor leader
T. P. Quinn's bitter assessment: "The greatest handicap to progress
and the development of justice is the judiciary." But workers knew "the
judiciary" was no monolith. Their legal experience varied, depending
on the level of court with which they had to deal. Federal and state
appellate courts in the period frequently (though by no means always)
wielded their powers of judicial review to eviscerate hard-won pieces
of labor legislation that regulated hours, wages, and working conditions. This experience with judicial review, historian William Forbath
argues, drove labor leaders such as Samuel Gompers to "abandon
broad ambitions for reform in the public political sphere in favor of
a more thorough reliance on economic action, strikes, and collective
bargaining." Even at the higher court level, however, labor leaders dis-
criminated between federal judges – appointed, tenured-for-life, and
predominantly Republican – and elected state judges, who were less
insulated from popular politics and somewhat more sympathetic to
labor. Courts below the appellate level were responsible for the hated
regime of "government by injunction." Federal, state, and local courts
reinvented the injunction, an old remedy in equity that allowed courts
to forbid specific actions before the fact, and used its powers broadly to
outlaw strikes and boycotts. The sweeping language of some labor in-
junctions, posted like royal decrees at worksites and in neighborhoods,
imposed judge-made criminal codes on entire communities of workers
in Chicago and other cities. At the level of the local criminal courts, the
great bane of organized workers was the grand jury. The Cook County
grand jury was routinely packed with business executives, who could be
counted on to issue indictments in labor cases. A "tool of the corporations," Chicago Federation of Labor Secretary E. M. Nockels called it.[25]

As for the inferior local courts, worker sentiments were justifiably
mixed. This became clear as the U.S. Industrial Commission heard
testimony from workingmen and employers on the Chicago Labor

---

[25] "Grand Jury Decried," *Chicago Record-Herald*, Dec. 12, 1903; William E.
Forbath, *Law and the Shaping of the American Labor Movement* (Cambridge,
Mass., 1989), 59, 37–127; "Union Denounces Grand Jury," *Chicago Record-
Herald*, Feb. 1, 1904; "Workingmen and the Courts," *ISR*, Nov. 1908, 383–85.
See Ray Ginger, *Altgeld's America: The Lincoln Ideal versus Changing Realities*
(Chicago, 1965), 213.

Disputes of 1900. The power wielded by the police courts and justice shops – administrative power over everyday rights and wrongs – was a much more diffuse form of power than the power to review legislation or issue injuctions. Its abuse tended to be experienced in the particular case, not as a collective injustice. It was common knowledge that many police magistrates favored light punishments for strikers arrested in slugging bouts with strike-breakers. But wage earners involved in civil cases were the worst victims of inefficiency and corruption in the justice shops. "A working man, if his wages were due, could go into the courts and be there a year before he could recover it," James Brennock of the Building Trades Council told the commission. One group of aggrieved Chicagoans, describing themselves as "poor laboring folks," actually won an injunction against a justice who appeared to be conspiring with a collection agency.[26]

In retrospect, then, it should not have surprised McMurdy that a workingman might set down his dinner pail to vote for a law that would abolish the fee system and make city judges directly answerable to the electorate. From the vantage point of the immigrant, the problem sized up differently. To understand the lack of organized immigrant opposition to judicial reform, it is useful to recall the fate of the "consolidation kite," the new charter that was finally lofted before the electorate in September 1907. The defeat of the charter shows how diverse ethnic groups could form a popular front against consolidation, *if* they perceived it as a threat to cultural values and personal liberties they valued in common.

The "Continental Sunday" – immigrants' cherished tradition of public drinking on the day of rest in beer gardens, at fraternal society picnics, and at other gatherings – was one of the oldest and most divisive issues in Chicago cultural politics. In 1841, the General Assembly outlawed the sale of liquor on Sunday. Ever since, attempts to enforce that law in Chicago had met fierce opposition. At the very moment the Charter Convention was about to reconvene, the Anti-Saloon League stepped up pressure on Mayor Edward F. Dunne and State's Attorney John J. Healy to enforce Sunday closing. It also demanded that the City Council stop issuing special permits that allowed private

---

[26] U.S. Industrial Commission on the Chicago Labor Disputes of 1900, *Report of the Industrial Commission on the Chicago Labor Disputes of 1900* (Washington, 1901), 8: xxix, 9, 16, 249–52, 373, 519–22, 539, esp. 467; "Justice Hit by a Writ," *Chicago Record-Herald*, Jan. 4, 1905. See "The Injustice Courts," *Chicago Times-Herald*, Jan. 29, 1897; Harold Barton Myers, "The Policing of Labor Disputes in Chicago," Ph.D. diss., University of Chicago, 1929, pp. 552, 557–645.

ethnic clubs to serve alcohol on an occasional basis without a costly saloon license. Continental Chicagoans responded by organizing mass demonstrations in the streets and forming the United Societies for Local Self-Government, a coalition of ethnic societies that claimed to represent more than 90,000 voters. Under the inspired leadership of the Bohemian American Anton J. Cermak, a Democratic assemblyman, the United Societies made clear demands on the charter delegates. The societies would oppose any charter that failed to give the City Council full powers over Sunday observance and to issue special bar permits.[27]

The charter delegates tried to meet the United Societies's demands while preserving their own definition of local self-government. The draft charter the convention sent to the General Assembly in March 1907 centralized the authority of the various local governing bodies in the municipal government. It gave the city ample taxing powers and a higher ceiling of bonded indebtedness. It restructured the ward system. And it gave the city clearer lines of regulatory authority with a broad police power clause. The draft also attempted to repair the defects of the new Municipal Court by placing its employees under the civil service law; the delegates sent down separate bills providing for judicial elections in April and giving judges power to dismiss the chief clerk and bailiff. Finally, to meet the United Societies' demands, the delegates sent down separate bills concerning Sunday regulation and special bar permits.[28]

The charter sent to Springfield was not the one returned to Chicago for a vote. The assembly discarded the court reforms, killed the liquor bills, and cut provisions to establish direct primaries. Unlike the tampering with the Municipal Court Act two years before, legislative revision of the charter proved fatal. A loose anticharter alliance formed between the United Societies, the Chicago Federation of Labor, the Democratic party, and the Independence League, a group sponsored by newspaperman William Randolph Hearst. Charter reformers maintained that the charter, in Merriam's words, lay "a foundation for efficient democratic government." But to the United Societies,

[27] "Home Rule Features of the New Charter," *City Club Bulletin*, March 13, 1907, 152–56; United Societies, *Home Rule*. See Robin L. Einhorn, *Property Rules: Political Economy in Chicago, 1833–1872* (Chicago, 1991), 161–64; Flanagan, *Charter Reform*, 33–35, 86–91, 113–16; Pegram, *Partisans and Progressives*, 105–12.

[28] Chicago Charter Convention, *Bill for an Act to Provide a Charter for the City of Chicago...* (Chicago, n.d.) 90. See Diner, *City and Its Universities*, 159; Flanagan, *Charter Reform*, 105–7; Pegram, *Partisans and Progressives*, 102–5, 111–13.

consolidation without the guarantee of personal liberty, as Continental immigrants understood it, was not self-government. A spokesman told an audience at the City Club that the supporters of the Continental Sunday were better off without the new charter: The police power clause might make city officials more directly liable for enforcing Sunday closings. Chicago "is a cosmopolitan city of continental habits, manners and customs," he declared. "This charter would enforce puritanical ideas upon men who have acquired for generations certain ideas and customs that are dearer to them than the power of the council to sell more bonds."[29]

In September 1907, Chicago voters defeated the charter by a vote of 121,935 to 59,786. Governmental regulation of liquor and public drinking would continue to be a potent cultural and political issue in the city until the end of Prohibition.[30]

It would be interesting to know whether Robert McMurdy ever thought about the implications of the charter defeat for his own populist concerns about the Municipal Court. McMurdy worried that the new court would be less solicitous than the justice courts of the liberties of humble citizens. The charter defeat showed that the progressives' agenda of consolidation and professionalization could generate decisive popular opposition if these goals were interpreted as a substantive threat to collectively valued personal liberties. Though part of the same progressive agenda as the charter, court organization remained too diffuse an issue, too purely procedural in appearance to be perceived as such a threat. Had Continental immigrants believed the Municipal Court Act endangered their personal liberties – or that the new judges would be under greater obligations than the magistrates to enforce Sunday closings – they might well have rallied against it. But they did not. As a Chicago representative to the General Assembly in 1905, Anton Cermak must have been familiar with McMurdy's arguments. Cermak voted for the court act. Good for him that he did. In 1912, this champion of Continental personal liberties would win control of 150 patronage jobs in the Municipal Court as its second chief bailiff.[31]

The Municipal Court of Chicago opened for business on December 3, 1906. The inaugural bench of twenty-eight elected judges – clad in

---

[29] "Home Rule Features," 151, 155. See Flanagan, *Charter Reform*, 98–109, 119–23; Gilbert, *Municipal Court*, 267, 270; Pegram, *Partisans and Progressives*, 113–14.

[30] Pegram, *Partisans and Progressives*, 117–18. See Lizabeth Cohen, *Making a New Deal: Industrial Workers in Chicago, 1919–1939* (Cambridge, 1990).

[31] *Journal of the House of Representatives*, 1905, p. 896; *MCC* 7 (1913), 5.

In 1911, the Municipal Court of Chicago moved into new quarters that symbolized its growing stature in the city's public life. Seen here in an architect's
rendering is Chicago's new courthouse and City Hall, designed by the prestigious firm of Holabird and Roche. Photo courtesy of the Chicago Historical
Society, (ICHi-34914).

business suits, all men, all but one a Republican – assumed the seats
assigned them by their new chief justice, the veteran county prosecutor,
Harry Olson. The judges had to make do with some preexisting political infrastructure – most regrettably, the blighted police station courtrooms now housed most of the court's criminal branches. But despite
elements of continuity, the new institution lived up to its official billing
as something "unique in the development of American courts and jurisprudence." Organized "on modern business lines," as its widely dis-
seminated *First Annual Report* boasted, the court was in many ways a
paragon of the historical process of bureaucratic rationalization that
the German sociologist Max Weber, writing his monumental treatise
on *Economy and Society* during this same era, considered so indispensable to modern capitalism (and to modernity in general). Just as the
justice shops had become something of a caricature of the nineteenth-
century entrepreneurial economy, the new Municipal Court claimed
for itself the managerial mastery of corporate capitalist enterprise.[32]

[32] *MCC 1* (1907), 5, 8; "Court That Runs"; Max Weber, "Bureaucracy," in Max
Weber, *Economy and Society*, ed. Guenther Roth and Claus Wittich (Berkeley,
1978), 2: 956–1005; Max Weber, "The Types of Legitimate Domination,"
ibid., 223–26.

The *First Annual Report* teemed with impressive results, which Olson's executive summary attributed to "strict economy in administration." In a single year, the Municipal Court had disposed of nearly 31,000 civil cases and more than 58,000 criminal and quasicriminal cases. Its enlarged jurisdiction, compared with the justice courts, and the greater finality of its judgments had reduced both the civil and criminal caseloads of the county courts by one-third. Capitalizing on a timely dip in Chicago's arrest rate, the report claimed the Municipal Court's guarantee of swift and certain justice had already reduced "crime" (including spurious arrests) by one-third. The court had even turned a profit: balancing receipts against expenditures, the institution netted a surplus of $8,115. Perhaps conscious of the irony – after all, this court had been created to eliminate profiteering in judicial administration – Olson couched this achievement in a rhetoric of fiscal responsibility. "The court," he said, "has not been a burden upon the taxpayer."[33]

No one better personified the business-like image of the new Municipal Court than its first chief justice, the thirty-nine-year-old former prosecutor who would preside over the municipal bench without interruption for the next quarter-century. At six feet, 200 pounds, with deep-set blue eyes and an imposing bald dome, Harry Olson cut an unmistakable figure in Chicago politics – part Taylorite efficiency expert, part family man, part crime-fighter. The *Tribune* said he had "the face of an honest man.... His clear, ruddy face and bright blue eyes tell their own story of his clean, abstemious life, and they also tell of the hardy Swedish stock from which he is sprung."[34]

Olson was born in 1867 to Swedish immigrants in Goose Island, a hardscrabble section on Chicago's North Side. He was three when his family moved to rural Kansas. His father, a stonemason, died when Harry was only twelve, leaving him as the family's chief breadwinner. He sawed wood, painted barns, and trained for a trade as a carriage painter. But like many an immigrant's son, he created personal opportunity through education. He attended St. Mary's College and taught primary school, becoming the youngest principal in Kansas – his first administrative post. He attended Washburn College in Topeka for two years, but departed for Chicago without a degree when his money ran out. By teaching night school, Olson put himself through Chicago's Union College of Law (later renamed Northwestern University School of Law). Upon earning his LL.B. in 1891, he launched a practice as an examiner of real estate titles in Chicago. After serving as an

[33] *MCC 1* (1907), 20, 25, 50.
[34] Edward F. Roberts, "Municipal Court Judge Harry Olson, Whose Chief Amusement Is Just Work," *Chicago Tribune,* Aug. 16, 1908.

Former prosecutor Harry Olson, pictured here c. 1915, served as the visionary Chief Justice of the Municipal Court of Chicago from its founding in 1906 until 1930. Courtesy of the Chicago Historical Society (ICHi-34917).

appointed special prosecutor in a sensational murder trial, he clinched a job in 1896 in the Cook County state's attorney's office, where he hitched his political fortunes to the rising star of the Republican State's Attorney Charles S. Deneen, a future governor and U.S. senator. During his decade in the state's attorney's office, Olson led high-profile prosecutions against bank presidents, the "Maxwell Street Gang," and more murderers than he cared to remember. On several occasions, he pressed judges to impose the ultimate penalty; all told, he sent seven men to the gallows. Many years later, when Olson had distinguished himself as one of America's leading propagandists for eugenics, he would conclude that all but one of those men had suffered from a hereditary mental defect; they should have been eugenically sterilized and institutionalized rather than executed. Like nearly all Swedish-Americans of his day, Olson was a life-long Republican. A man whose political ambitions surpassed the local judiciary, he sought his party's nomination for mayor in 1915 and 1919. Despite the support of

Deneen and Chicago's progressive reform community, the consummate technocrat lost both bids to a boisterous coalition-builder, who played the city's racial politics better than Olson ever could: William Hale "Big Bill" Thompson.[35]

Olson was in one sense an odd pick for chief justice. He had signed McMurdy's letter protesting the "radical" nature of Gilbert's Municipal Court bill. But Governor Deneen, whose Republican faction ruled Cook County in 1906, secured the nomination for his former protégé. "Your Court is to be a great experimental station in regard to the practice of the law," Deneen told Olson in a letter congratulating him on his easy victory at the polls. As the court's executive officer, Olson was a perfectionist and ardent disciplinarian, using the ample powers of his office to rein in maverick judges and maintain a semblance of order in the burgeoning court bureaucracy. Within just a few years, Harry Olson's name would be familiar to American readers of law reviews, political science and criminology journals, magazines, and city newspapers from Lewiston, Maine, to San Francisco. He carried his three-part gospel of court organization, procedural reform, and scientific criminology to local bar associations, businessmen's clubs, creditmen's associations, civic groups, and women's clubs from coast to coast. He served on the boards of local and national associations concerned with crime and social reform, including Chicago's Juvenile Protective Association, the Chicago Vice Commission, and the American Institute of Criminal Law and Criminology at Northwestern University. When the American Judicature Society was established in Chicago in 1913, as a national clearinghouse and advocacy group for court reform, Olson was the natural choice for chairman. Many of Olson's peers on the municipal bench shared his views and supported his efforts. But more than any other individual, Harry Olson, the former school principal from Kansas, was responsible for turning the Municipal Court of Chicago into a nationally renowned experimental station for new

---

[35] BOC (1926), 660; Herbert Harley, A Modern Experiment in Judicial Administration: The Municipal Court of Chicago, address to Louisiana Bar Association, May 8, 1915 (Chicago, n.p.), 5–9; "Harry Olson," CLN, Dec. 8, 1906, 139; Harry Olson, "Crime and Heredity," in City of Chicago, Municipal Court, Research Studies of Crime as Related to Heredity (Chicago, 1925), 9–29; Roberts, "Municipal Court Judge"; Harold J. Rust, ed., "Illinois Judicial Who's Who," ILR, 14 (1920), 442. See Douglas Bukowski, "Big Bill Thompson: The 'Model' Politician," in The Mayors: The Chicago Political Tradition, ed. Paul M. Green and Melvin G. Holli, rev. ed. (Carbondale, Ill., 1995), 62, 70; Edward R. Kantowicz, Polish-American Politics in Chicago, 1888–1940 (Chicago, 1975), 137–40; Ernst W. Olson, The Swedish Element in Illinois: Survey of the Past Seven Decades (Chicago, 1917), 113, 343.

sociological approaches to crime and dependency, which would extend the court's power deeper into the social life of the Second City
than its creators could have possibly imagined.[36]

At least according to contemporary accounts, Olson and his peers
on the Municipal Court bench were a cut above their justice-court
predecessors. Few could match the elite pedigree of Judge Stephen A.
Foster, a Vermont native and former *Harvard Law Review* editor who
had fifteen years' experience as an attorney in Boston and Chicago.
Still, more than half of the judges had attended college, the vast majority had a law degree, and all had logged at least five years as an
attorney or judicial officer in Cook County.[37] The Republicans had so
broadly prevailed in the city elections that it was little surprise that,
with but one exception, they swept in the court as well. But the press
attributed Republican dominance in the court contest to the Deneen
organization's decision to ban all former justices from the ticket.
(In fact, the organization had let Olson and a small committee hand-
pick the judicial slate.) The Democratic ticket, headed by Hiram
Gilbert himself as the nominee for chief justice, had included nine
former justices and five alderman. The sole victorious Democrat was an
attorney named Thomas B. Lantry, who had the backing of the Chicago
Bar Association and no political background whatsoever. Even Lantry's
victory reportedly had less to do with his own qualifications than with
the political handicap of the Republican he defeated. F. L. Barnett was
the sole African-American candidate for municipal judge – a post no
black man would win until 1924. Gradually, a handful of old justices
would make their way into the new system: John Caverly and James
Martin in 1910, John Prindiville and John Mahoney in 1912, John
Richardson in 1916, and Asa Adams in 1920. But they would have to
adjust to the folkways of a new legal order.[38]

[36] Deneen to Olson, Aug. 18, 1907, MCC, box 1, folder 6. Belknap, *Administration of Justice,* 14–15. On Olson as national spokesman, see, e.g., "Courts
of the People," *Buffalo Express,* Feb. 6, 1909; "Municipal Court Would Eradicate Many Evils," *Cleveland Press,* March 2, 1910; "Chicago's Police Court Explained by Judge Olson," *Springfield (Mass.) Daily Republican,* April 28, 1910;
"Judge Olson Will Speak on Reform," *Atlanta Constitution,* March 22, 1912;
"Court Reform," *Colorado Springs Gazette,* July 14, 1912.
[37] I compiled biographical information by cross-listing the judges from *MCC 1*
(1907) with their listings in *BOC* (1911) and *BOC* (1917). Data were available for twenty-three of the twenty-eight judges.
[38] *BOC* (1911), 3, 126, 462, 551; *BOC* (1917), 569; Harley, "Business Management," 7; Edward M. Martin, *The Role of the Bar in Electing the Bench in Chicago*
(Chicago, 1936), 58–74, 154–56; *BOC* (1917), 404. Albert George, the
only black man to serve on the municipal bench between 1906 and 1936,

The Municipal Court was a well-ordered system of functionally specific branch courts. The Municipal Court Act divided the city into five districts, each of which was to have at least one civil and criminal branch. Within a year, the judges streamlined the system and set up the basic framework that would survive for several decades. They cleaved the city into two districts. The First District covered all of Chicago north of 71st Street plus the area south of 71st Street and west of Cottage Grove Avenue. The First District had a population of 2,306,000 in 1907. The Second District – its existence a testament to the limits that Chicago's sprawling size placed upon governmental consolidation – comprised the rest of South Chicago, an area with only 59,000 residents. The First District had seventeen civil branch courts, all located in a single building in the heart of the Loop, and thirteen criminal branches. Two criminal branches were located in the Loop in a Criminal Courts building; the rest convened in police stations around the city. The outlying Second District had but one branch court, the only court in the system to handle both civil and criminal cases. As judicial business grew during the next quarter-century, the judges would add new branch courts to the system, increasing their number from thirty-one in 1907 to thirty-nine in 1931.[39]

A hierarchically organized bureaucracy presided over this centralized court system, which operated on a budget fixed by the City Council. The judges, the *First Annual Report* boasted, acted "as the board of directors of a corporation." They fixed salaries of court personnel, crafted new rules of civil procedure, and even drafted legislation. In their own courtrooms, the judges could hear cases more or less as they saw fit, as long as they acted in accordance with the common law and the statutes of Illinois. But the judges were disciplined, with varying degrees of success, by the court's bureaucratic design. The fact that they received their compensation in a fixed salary was in itself a form of discipline that Weber considered crucial to the development of modern bureaucracy. Compensation in fees or in-kind payments, a common feature of traditional political offices, implied a level of autonomy ill-suited to modern bureaucratic rationality. Precisely like a salaried manager or a wage earner in a modern capitalist economy, the bureaucrat worked "entirely separated from ownership of the means of administration and without appropriation of his position."

ran for the office five times and won once (in 1924); *BOC* (1931), 357. The *Chicago Defender*, the city's leading African-American newspaper, often protested the lack of black judges on the municipal bench. See, e.g.,"Our Race Needs Judge," March 31, 1917.
[39] *MCC 1* (1907), 12–13.

Municipal Court judges were also constrained by more obvious forms of discipline. The full body of judges had authority to publicly investigate an errant fellow judge and take "such steps as they deem necessary or proper" against him. The annual reports provided a forum for public shaming: A chart actually toted up the average number of hours per day that each judge spent in court! As if all this weren't enough, Olson let it be known that he kept a scrapbook in his chambers, into which he mercilessly pasted every newspaper clipping – no matter how unflattering – about the court and its officers.[40]

In 1900, Chicago's mail-order giant, Montgomery Ward and Company, adorned the cover of its catalogue with an unforgettable image: an illustrated sectional view of its massive Michigan Avenue warehouse, its exterior walls stripped away. Entitled "A Busy Bee-Hive," the image revealed the meticulously honeycombed corporate hierarchy that buzzed away, unceasing and unseen, behind the warehouse walls. Just a few blocks north on Michigan Avenue, the offices of the Municipal Court's chief clerk and bailiff were organized on much the same principle. The offices were organized into specialized departments (Accounting, Criminal Records, and so on) and equipped with "modern appliances": adding machines, "neostyles," tabulating typewriters, electric time stamps. The deputy clerks and bailiffs, in contrast to the virtually untouchable constables, were minor bureaucrats. They served at the pleasure of their chiefs and could be removed by a vote of the judges.[41]

Addressing a Chicago audience in 1909, President William H. Taft called the reform of civil and criminal procedure "the greatest need in American institutions." The site of Taft's proclamation was appropriate. In procedural reform, Chicago's Municipal Court was already riding the crest of a long wave of innovation that led from Roscoe Pound's 1906 American Bar Association address to the adoption of the Federal Rules of Civil Procedure in 1938. Chief Justice Olson and his associates turned the Municipal Court into a proving ground for procedural reform and new administrative strategies for the massive caseload of a centralized urban judicial system. The court's first

[40] Ibid., 9, 19, 22; Weber, "Legitimate Domination," *Economy and Society*, 1: 221, 222; Max Weber, "Patriarchalism and Patrimonialism," ibid., 2: 1031–38. "Act in relation to a municipal court," secs. 271–280; *MCC* 24–25 (1930–31), 8; "Scrapbook to Warn Judges," *Chicago Tribune*, Sept. 3, 1908. Olson's disassembled scrapbooks (hereafter cited as HODS) are held by the Chicago Historical Society.

[41] *MCC 1* (1907), 18; "A Busy Bee-Hive," reproduced in Cronon, *Nature's Metropolis*, nonnumbered page. For cases of judges removing bailiffs, see Harry Olson to William E. Tousley, March 29, 1910, MCC, box 3, folder 16.

administrative innovations appeared first in the chiefly economic realm of civil cases. But the success of these new techniques gradually shaped the way judges thought about and administered to the social side of their jurisdiction in criminal cases.[42]

Criticism of excessively technical procedural rules – the formal ground rules of pleading and court practice in civil litigation – was one of the oldest complaints in the annals of American court reform. Since the early nineteenth century, businessmen and merchants in commercially advanced states had called for a more orderly and predictable alternative to the cumbersome and verbose forms of common-law pleading. Substituting clear and economical codes of procedure for the common-law forms was one of the more successful phases of the larger mid-nineteenth-century movement to codify American law. Although New York's famous 1848 "Field Code" of civil procedure had been adopted in modified form by many states by 1900, Taft and Pound represented an army of lesser-known critics who found the "archaic" state of civil procedure in America to be wholly inadequate to a modern urban-industrial economy and society. Procedural reform again became a cause célèbre, as court reformers tried to restore the public legitimacy and political viability of the courts as instruments of governance. The situation was especially dire in Illinois, one of the few states that still practiced old-fashioned common-law pleading, which England itself had radically reformed in 1873.[43]

American progressives often gazed searchingly across the Atlantic for political solutions to their domestic problems. In judicial matters, they looked first to England, the birthplace of the common law. But looking to England was an inevitably dispiriting exercise. Without a federal system, the English faced far fewer constitutional obstacles to unifying their laws and institutions. In the late nineteenth century, the English had been quicker than Americans to centralize their courts and, though impressed with the Field Code, had done a much more thorough job of simplifying civil procedure. In the English Judicature Act of 1873, Parliament consolidated most of the nation's historically independent tribunals into a single Supreme Court of Judicature, setting a standard of court unification that American progressives could only dream about. And dream they did, filling pages of law reviews

---

[42] Taft quoted in William Bayard Hale, "A Court That Does Its Job," *World's Work*, March 1910, p. 12695.

[43] Thomas M. Cooley, "The Administration of Justice in the United States of America in Civil Cases," *Michigan Law Journal*, 2 (1893), 341–53; Lawrence M. Friedman, *A History of American Law*, 2d ed. (New York, 1985), 391–98; Steele, "Small Claims Courts," 303–5, 320–26.

and bar association speeches with paeans to the idea of "one great court."[44]

American court reformers also wanted to remove the power to make civil procedure from legislatures and hand it over to judges themselves. The democratic theory behind legislature-made procedure was that it would provide an important check upon the extraordinary power that judges wielded over the citizen. But to many progressives, this rule-making power was woefully misplaced. It left rule making in the inexpert hands of legislators and made judges less accountable for their judicial product. Equally galling, legislature-made procedure had consigned American judges to a narrowly restricted role in civil contests. In contrast to their free-wheeling English counterparts, who interrupted court proceedings at will and conducted their own interrogations from the bench, American judges were supposed to serve as impartial umpires in contests between adversarial litigants. As George W. Alger observed in a 1909 article for the *Atlantic Monthly*, "In England everything is done which can be done to make the first trial a conquest of substantial justice.... [T]he judge has free play. He is fettered with no technical rules."[45]

The Municipal Court Act of 1905 broke with American tradition by giving the judges as a body power to make the court's procedural rules. The judges rose to the occasion. They championed the court as a laboratory for a historic experiment in simplified civil procedure, which they hoped would be replicated by the General Assembly in a general practice act for the state. Soon after the court opened, the judges dispatched Judge Foster on a transatlantic fact-finding mission to study organization and procedure in England's Supreme Court of Judicature. Upon Foster's return, the judges abolished common-law pleading in civil cases and introduced a simplified system of affidavits modeled on contemporary English practice. In the older common-law forms of pleading, litigants stated all of the material facts involved in a case. In the Municipal Court, plaintiffs filed an affidavit of claim, a

---

[44] Felix Frankfurter and James M. Landis, *The Business of the Supreme Court: A Study in the Federal Judicial System* (New York, 1927), 223, n. 18. On the English Judicature Act of 1873 as a model for American reform, see J.W.G., "Judicial Efficiency in Chicago and England Compared," *JAICLC*, 1 (1910), 120–22; Jesse Macy, "The Efficiency of English Courts: An Example for America," *McClure's*, Sept. 1909, pp. 552–57; Pound, "Popular Dissatisfaction," 183–87; Henry Upson Sims, "The Problem of Reforming Judicial Administration in America," *VLR*, 3 (1916), 598–621. See Rodgers, *Atlantic Crossings*.

[45] Alger in Steele, "Small Claims Courts," 325; [Harley], "Organized Courts," 133; Nathan William MacChesney, "Efficient Administration of Justice," *ILR*, 15 (1920), 15.

written statement that laid out only the substantive facts of the claim in language "as brief as the nature of the case will permit." A claim that under the common-law system might have run to a dozen pages could be distilled into a few sentences in an affidavit. A Municipal Court defendant was not entitled to the common-law response of filing a general denial, which denied the overall charge without addressing the specific facts alleged. Instead, the defendant had to file an affidavit of merits, which responded directly to the facts in the plaintiff's affidavit; any facts not disputed were taken by the court as admitted. Both affidavits were submitted under oath, under penalty of perjury. And so, as the judges expected, thousands of cases were disposed of administratively each year in a judgment by default, when defendants failed to respond to the claims made against them. "In other Illinois courts," one admirer of the court observed, "these actions would clog the calendars for months and years."[46]

The Municipal Court's system of abbreviated record-keeping could have been invented by Frederick W. Taylor, the engineer and zealous publicist whose infamous time studies and principles of "scientific management" were just beginning to have an impact in the American workplace. Engineering argot was second only to business jargon in the court reformers' bag of metaphors: Court reformers were not redesigning judicial architecture, they were reconstructing judicial "machinery." The Taylorist engineering mindset prized simplification, standardization, and system in its secularized quest for human perfectibilty. Judicial record keeping in America at the turn of the century lacked all of these qualities.[47]

Unlike the old justice courts, the new Municipal Court was a court of record. This meant it had the power to punish offenders by imprisonment, and in recognition of this power, it was required by law to maintain exact records of its proceedings. In a court that disposed of 90,000 cases in its first year alone, finding the most time-efficient form of record keeping in civil and criminal cases was a worthy obsession. The ancient method of judicial record keeping – writing out

---

[46] Harley, "Business Management," 8; Stephen A. Foster, *The Municipal Court of Chicago*, 2d ed. (Chicago, 1912), 186–99; Hiram T. Gilbert, "Legal Tactics Series: II. Practice in the Municipal Court of Chicago," *ILR*, 1 (1906), 94–105; Harry Olson, "The Proper Organization and Procedure of a Municipal Court," reprinted from *Proceedings of the American Political Science Association*, 1910, 88–89; *MCC 10–11* (1916–17), 25. See R. S. Saby, "Simplified Procedure in Municipal Courts," *APSR*, 18 (1924), 760–72.

[47] "Improving Judicial Machinery," *New York Evening Post*, March 17, 1909; Belknap, *Administration of Justice*, 26; Daniel T. Rodgers, *The Work Ethic in Industrial America, 1850–1920* (Chicago, 1974), 53–57.

orders in longhand, in all their glorious verbiage, into a docket book
was not going to work. Chief Justice Olson introduced a standardized method of record keeping that systematized the orders of the
court by breaking them down into their most common components,
like interchangeable parts on an assembly line. The court produced
a two-volume authoritative order book that contained the full texts of
2,449 standard orders, typed out in the baroque language approved by
judicial precedent. These authoritative orders were then broken down
into 154 components – the standard units of legal language that, in
one combination or another, could be reassembled to produce all
2,449 orders. A slim volume containing these 154 items, paired with
a simple abbreviation for each, was distributed to the minute clerks,
the deputies assigned to record orders in the branch courts. When a
judge issued an order, the minute clerk simply entered the necessary
chain of abbreviations on a standardized case record form – called
the half-sheet. Unusual orders not found in the clerks' order books
could always be written out. If a litigant requested a transcript, a copyist
would simply refer to the larger volume of amplified orders and type
up the transcript. Olson delighted in the "mathematical accuracy" and
irrefutable efficiency of his system.[48]

The most striking managerial innovations of the Municipal Court's
early years occurred when Chief Justice Olson started to make use of
his power to create specialized branch courts, which would handle
specific classes of cases for the entire First District (virtually the entire
city). Praised as a sterling example of business management in the
courts, the ability of judges to create specialized courts was a wholly
unique power at the time. In most states, including Illinois outside
the Chicago limits, creating a new specialized branch still required an
act of the legislature. This had been one reason why social reformers
needed to agitate for years to get America's first Juvenile Court created
in Cook County in 1899. In the Municipal Court, a specialized branch
could be created with a stroke of the chief justice's pen. Of course,
a dizzying multiplicity of courts was as old as the common law, and it
was one of the things the municipal courts were designed to abolish.
But specialized *branch* courts, as departments within one big beehive
of a court – first at the level of the great city, and someday, perhaps,
servicing the entire state – was something palpably modern, a product
of the progressive quest for rationalization and expertise in judicial
administration.[49]

---

[48] Olson, "Proper Organization," 92, 90–91; *MCC* 2 (1908), 25. See Gilbert,
"Legal Tactics," 104.
[49] Harley, "Business Management," 10–15.

The theory of specialized courts was that judges assigned to them would become experts in handling specific kinds of cases, and the wheels of justice would spin more swiftly. Within a short time, the practice of these courts – particularly in criminal cases – would make the theory seem much too modest, as judges and urban social reformers imagined ever wider applications of specialized judicial administration to the social governance of a modern city. Chief Justice Olson's first experiments with specialized courts involved classes of civil cases, but he would soon apply the organizational innovation to classes of criminal cases – clear evidence of the many forgotten ways in which new styles of economic and social regulation in the early twentieth century grew out of the same set of administrative impulses.

The Municipal Court's first specialized tribunal was the Attachment, Garnishment and Replevin Branch. Its jurisdiction covered three common forms of civil action in which plaintiffs sued to recover or seize through judicial order property possessed by or, in the case of garnishment, owed by the defendant. A second specialized court handled all civil actions seeking the recovery or repossession of a specific kind of property: real estate. In the early 1910s, Olson would use his court-making power in criminal as well as civil cases, creating the Court of Domestic Relations (1911), the Morals Court (1913), the Speeders' Court (1913), the Boys' Court (1914), and the Small Claims Branch (1915) – all either the first or among the first of their kind in America. Other major cities – and even many smaller ones – soon had their own specialized courts. Many were consciously modeled after the Municipal Court of Chicago, others were more purely the product of local political movements and urban legal cultures in transition. Along with innovations in court organization, civil procedure, and record-keeping, specialized courts soon became expected fixtures of urban governance. As Herbert Harley, secretary of the American Judicature Society, observed in 1915, "In a short time the sensation of today will be a convention as natural as the star on the bailiff's coat."[50]

Within just a few years after its creation, the Municipal Court of Chicago was well established as the embodiment of America's judicial future. No one said the court was perfect. In Weberian terms, many features of patrimonial governance persisted in this judicial bureaucracy. It was still a political machine as well as a judicial one, and the court's hundreds of patronage jobs were distributed to party faithful; the

[50] Herbert Harley, "The Small Claims Branch of the Municipal Court of Chicago," American Judicature Society Bulletin, 8 (1915), 25–49, esp. 34; MCC 7 (1913), 79–88; MCC 24–25 (1930–31), 11.

number of court clerks who doubled as precinct captains suggested that pull had not been altogether routed from the judicial system. Absent complete felony jurisdiction, the dream of one great urban court was not yet realized. Without this, and without a new Chicago charter, political consolidation – so central to the progressives' city sense and their ideal of the self-owned city – was incompletely realized in Chicago. But none of this prevented court reformers, progressive legal scholars, political observers, and the mainstream press from insisting that something wonderfully modern had transpired in the organization of courts in America's Second City.[51]

The Municipal Court's quarters in the new City Hall at Washington Boulevard and LaSalle Street, completed in 1911, reflected the ambitions of this enterprise. The stately neoclassical edifice, designed by the prestigious firm of Holabird and Roche, would house all of the First District's civil branches in addition to the offices of the Municipal Court's bureaucracy: the offices of the chief justice, chief bailiff, and chief clerk. Noting that centralization and specialization went hand-in-hand in modern administration, Chief Justice Olson chose to locate all of the specialized branches at the heart of the system – and the seat of municipal power – in City Hall. This assured also that these experimental branches would enjoy exceptional public visibility and exert an especially strong influence on public conceptions of the Municipal Court's role in Chicago's social life.[52]

Something interesting happened at this very moment. Moral reformers and social activists, including members of women's organizations and the Hull-House social settlement community, began to see in this new judicial machinery its enormous potential for social governance in a modern city. As the administrative reformers – the businessmen, bar association attorneys, and professionals who dominated the New Charter Convention and created the Municipal Court – turned their attention elsewhere, these social activists took up the baton of court reform in Chicago. Inspired by two relatively new constellations of social ideas – a widening sense of society's responsibility for crime and new ways of thinking about the social function of law – these activists would work together with Municipal Court judges to extend the institution's administrative reach into the everyday life of their great city. That they chose the unlikely instrument of the criminal law to do so would make all the difference.

[51] "Self-owed city" comes from Rodgers, *Atlantic Crossings*, ch. 4; "Court That Runs."

[52] Olson to Holabird and Roche, Architects, Aug. 6, 1907, MCC, box 1, folder 6.

3

Rethinking Responsibility for a Social Age

The circumstances of city life and the modern feeling that law is a product of conscious and determinate human will put a larger burden upon the law, and hence upon the agencies that administer the law, than either has been prepared to bear.

— Roscoe Pound, 1913

Between the collapse of Reconstruction and the height of the New Deal, the role of law in American life underwent a halting but decisive transformation. The common-law polity of nineteenth-century America – organized around core principles of local self-government, individual liberty and responsibility, and the supremacy of law – gave way to the increasingly centralized, pluralistic, and administrative political framework of the modern liberal state. A new interventionist rhetoric of "social facts" and "social interests," forged in the social-political struggles and intellectual revolts against laissez-faire that engulfed the western industrial nations around the turn of the century, gradually displaced the autonomous individual from the center of American liberal ideology and jurisprudence. New administrative agencies at the local, state, and federal levels took on much of the regulatory business hitherto handled by common-law courts and carried their "executive justice" into new fields of social and economic intervention, from setting electricity rates to insuring workingmen and their families against industrial accidents. But the common-law courts did not crumble in significance as the administrative state grew up around them. From the lowliest city tribunal to the federal judiciary, the courts themselves assumed a more administrative function. No longer content to play the role of neutral umpires adjudicating private disputes, criminal cases, or constitutional issues, judges now more openly weighed the social interests at stake in the cases before them. In many areas of the law, from probation in criminal cases to equity receivership in bankruptcy, judges even crafted administrative remedies that, unlike the traditional verdict or ruling, required ongoing judicial supervision. Although Americans did not see the full effects of this historic shift until 1937, the tipping point was reached in the first two decades of the twentieth century.[1]

The new municipal courts of the Progressive Era played a vital role in the creation of the modern American state. Picking up on the pungent antijudicial theme in the era's political discourse, some historians have outdone Theodore Roosevelt in portraying "the" American judiciary, from the U.S. Supreme Court on down, as a monolithic, singularly reactionary bulwark against social reform. But the epigram above from Roscoe Pound, the most influential progressive legal thinker, plots out a more compelling narrative. Viewing the legal order from the bottom up, as Pound did in his essays on "the administration of justice in the modern city," yields a richer perspective on the law's relationship to political development than the starkly laissez-faire appellate court opinions that dominate historical memory of the era. Much of the pressure for legal change came from the cities, where local courts, buckling under huge civil and criminal caseloads, began to reach beyond individual defendants in order to address the root social causes of crime. Social activists and judges championed new approaches to criminality and dependency, turning city courts into flexible, administrative instruments of social governance. It was the Municipal Court of Chicago, not some appellate court or public-service commission far from the urban scene, that Pound singled out as America's "pioneer modern judicial organization."[2]

---

[1] David S. Clark, "Adjudication to Administration: A Statistical Analysis of Federal District Courts in the Twentieth Century," *SCLR*, 55 (1981), 65–145; John Dickinson, *Administrative Justice and the Supremacy of Law in the United States* (Cambridge, Mass., 1927); Daniel R. Ernst, "Law and American Political Development, 1877–1938," *RAH*, 26 (1998), 205–19; Morton J. Horwitz, *The Transformation of American Law, 1870–1960* (New York, 1992); James T. Kloppenberg, *Uncertain Victory: Social Democracy and Progressivism in European and American Thought, 1870–1920* (New York, 1986); William J. Novak, "The Legal Origins of the Modern American State," American Bar Foundation Working Paper 9925 (1999).

[2] Roscoe Pound, "The Administration of Justice in the Modern City," *HLR*, 26 (1913), 302–28; Roscoe Pound, "Organization of Courts," [1914], *JAJS*, 11 (1927), 80. Landmark statements of "laissez-faire constitutionalism" include *In re Jacobs*, 98 N.Y. 98 (1885); *Lochner v. New York*, 198 U.S. 45 (1905). See Louis D. Brandeis, "The Living Law," *ILR*, 10 (1916), 463–64; William F. Dodd, "Social Legislation and the Courts," *PSQ*, 28 (1913), 1–17; Melvin I. Urofsky, "State Courts and Protective Legislation during the Progressive Era: A Reevaluation," *JAH*, 72 (1985), 63–91.

Pound's reference to the law's social "burden" hints at the awkward, contested process by which urban courts came to administer a wider sphere of everyday life, including intimate moral terrain once entrusted to the governance of households, religious organizations, and private charities. To the minds of many administrative reformers, the real work of court reform was done when cities such as Chicago razed their justice-of-the-peace systems and raised modern municipal courts in their place. The bureaucratic design of the new courts did provide a more rational and efficient framework for the adjudication of private disputes and criminal cases. But the early successes of the new courts in fulfilling these traditional judicial duties presented the possibility that they might be harnessed for broader social purposes. To understand how and why municipal courts became interventionist instruments of social governance, especially in criminal cases, we need to look closely at the local debates over the public significance and just treatment of urban crime. And we need to look beyond the courts themselves to the larger crisis of liberalism in America at the turn of the twentieth century.

The problem of crime in the modern city raised two far-reaching social questions, which could not be resolved within the cultural and legal framework of late nineteenth-century, Victorian liberalism. The first was how far one could trace the actual autonomy, personal agency, and moral responsibility of the individual self in an "interdependent" urban-industrial society. The second question, intimately related to the first, was what role the courts, the workhorses of nineteenth-century governance, should play in the regulation of a complex economy and society. This chapter and the next take up these questions in turn. This one traces the ideological origins of the progressive concept of social responsibility for crime. The explosive local debate over Municipal Court Judge McKenzie Cleland shows how hard it was to put this controversial notion into practice in the courtroom. The next chapter examines the progressive idea of socialized law, which made urban court reform so integral to American legal and political development during the early twentieth century. How Americans in the Progressive Era debated these two great issues of their day illuminates the momentous upheaval in cultural perception and liberal ideology under way in their lifetimes. The outcome was an unprecedented expansion of governmental power, through the criminal courts, into the everyday social life of American cities.[3]

---

[3] I am indebted to Thomas Haskell's brilliant work on changing conceptions of personal agency and moral responsibility in American history. See, esp., Thomas L. Haskell, "A Brief Excursus on Formalism," in Thomas L. Haskell,

The Municipal Court of Chicago had barely opened for business when it became embroiled in a public debate over a judge's power to intervene in the social world beyond the individual criminal defendant. Standing improbably at the center of this nationally publicized controversy was the diminutive figure of Judge McKenzie Cleland, an evangelical Protestant who believed a judge had a duty to deliver justice in an unjust world. In 1907, he created his own free-standing probation system in the Municipal Court's criminal branch at Maxwell Street, in one of the city's poorest immigrant neighborhoods. Like so many middle-class reformers of his day, Cleland stood astride two cultural eras, which had yet to become distinct. He was part Victorian moralist, part progressive. The Victorian (and the evangelist) in him looked reflexively to individual character as the pure causal origin of social ills, and thus the proper site of moral reform. The progressive in him could overlook neither the "social" causes of crime – the influence of heredity and environment upon human action – nor the social consequences of punishment. Like so many similarly situated contemporaries, Cleland eagerly harnessed governmental power to his cause. The debate that raged around him illuminates a system of criminal justice at a moment of ambivalent but profound transition.[4]

A low-slung brick building at the corner of Maxwell and Morgan Streets, the Maxwell Street Criminal Branch stood amidst the pushcarts and food stalls of the West Side, less than a mile from the factories that rose from the banks of the Chicago River's South Branch, where many of the area's residents earned their daily wages. Home to a Russian Jewish ghetto that predated the Great Fire of 1871, the Maxwell Street area provided crowded, unsanitary housing in wood-framed tenements and boarding houses to tens of thousands of southern and eastern

---

Objectivity Is Not Neutrality: Explanatory Schemes in History (Baltimore, 1998), 307–17; Thomas L. Haskell, "Persons as Uncaused Causes: John Stuart Mill, the Spirit of Capitalism, and the 'Invention' of Formalism," in ibid., 318–67. For an introduction to the literature on liberalism, see James T. Kloppenberg, *The Virtues of Liberalism* (New York, 1998).

[4] *BOC* (1917), 138; McKenzie Cleland, "The New Gospel in Criminology," unpaginated draft, MCC, box 2, folder 12. The Cleland controversy is reconstructed from correspondence, newspaper accounts, the report of the Municipal Court committee created in January 1909 to investigate him, and his own accounts. See William E. Barton, "Judge Cleland and Chicago's Four Hundred," *Independent*, Jan. 2, 1908, pp. 141–47; McKenzie Cleland, "The New Gospel in Criminology," *McClure's*, July 1908, pp. 358–62; and the untitled, undated committee report, MCC, box 2, folder 12, hereafter cited as Cleland Committee Report.

European immigrants who arrived in Chicago during the decades before World War I. One of the city's poorest sections, it also served as
a laboratory of social investigation and humanitarian intervention for
the well-educated and well-heeled residents of Jane Addams's world-
famous Hull-House social settlement, ensconced amidst Italian and
Greek neighborhoods a few blocks to the north on Halsted Street.[5]

Thanks partly to its proximity to Hull-House, the point of embarka-
tion for many a muckraker's foray into the city wilderness, the Maxwell
Street area acquired something of a national reputation as a breeding
ground of criminals. One Chicago newspaper, quoted for a national
audience in *McClure's Magazine*, painted a horrific tableau. "In this
territory murderers, robbers and thieves of the worst kind are born,
reared and grown to maturity in numbers which exceed the record
of any similar district anywhere on the face of the globe; murders by
the score, shootings and stabbings by the hundred, assaults, burglaries
and robberies by the thousand – such is the crime record each year
for this festering place of evil which lies a scant mile from the heart
of Chicago." In fact, Maxwell Street was not the most criminally active
district in Chicago (let alone on the globe), but its ramshackle homes
and filth-strewn streets did see more than their share of lawbreaking.
The Maxwell Street Criminal Branch was the Municipal Court's fourth
busiest. It disposed of 8,464 cases in 1908 (compared with 10,815 at
the top-ranked Desplaines Street Criminal Branch). The typical defendant, neither murderer nor thief of the worst kind, was one of the
100,000 workingmen who lived in the neighborhood. His legal troubles often began with a trip to one of the area's 400 saloons. The
docket teemed with cases of public drunkenness, petty larceny, disorderly conduct or assault and battery (either might signify domestic
violence), and other crimes punishable by a fine or a term, up to one
year, in the House of Correction.[6]

To this overtaxed outpost of the municipal legal order, Chief Justice
Olson assigned McKenzie Cleland in January 1907. In his wire-rimmed
spectacles, stiff collars, and dark suits, Cleland looked the part of
the urban missionary. By his own accounting, the forty-six-year-old

---

[5] Edith Abbott, *The Tenements of Chicago, 1908–1935* (Chicago, 1936), 10, 86–
87; Jane Addams, *Forty Years at Hull-House: Being "Twenty Years at Hull-House"
and "The Second Twenty Years at Hull-House" in One Volume* (New York, 1935),
97–101.

[6] *McClure's* in Cleland, "New Gospel," draft; *MCC* 2 (1908), 63 (this was the
first report to list statistics by branch); unsigned notes of Harry Olson's visit
to Maxwell Street Criminal Branch, Jan. 24, 1908, MCC, box 2, folder 8.
See McKenzie Cleland, undated, unpaginated memo to Harry Olson, MCC,
box 1, folder 7, hereafter cited as Cleland Memo.

To his supporters, Judge McKenzie Cleland was a great Christian humanitarian, "the little father of the parole system." To his immigrant detractors, his court at Maxwell Street was a "Temperance Vaudeville." This campaign poster, from Cleland's failed bid for the Circuit Court in 1909, reprised the maverick judge's own favorite theme: A wise judge could reclaim criminals as worthy breadwinners and thus save their families from ruin. Courtesy of the Chicago Historical Society (ICHi-34912).

Republican attorney had "very little experience" in the criminal law before his election to the bench in 1906. Born in the vicinity of New York's
Burned-Over District, where the cinders of antebellum revivalism still
smoldered in 1860, Cleland carried forth a long tradition of Protestant
activism in "charities and corrections." But unlike many men in that
tradition, including the University of Chicago sociologist and chaplain Charles R. Henderson, Cleland did not shed the older language
of benevolence for the scientific argot of penology. Henderson once
remarked that "to assist us in the difficult task of adjustment to new
situations God has providentially wrought for us the social sciences."
For Cleland, the Bible remained a reliable guide to human nature. In
an era when claims to scientific expertise came dressed in masculine
rhetoric, Cleland's appeal to an older ethics of benevolence exposed
him to charges of womanly sentimentality.[7]

But Cleland's judicial world view departed from the benevolent tradition in its emphasis on the social environment of crime. The judge
laid out his judicial philosophy in a 1908 article for *McClure's*, suitably titled "The New Gospel in Criminology." Like so many manifestos
of urban moral reform during the early twentieth century, the "New
Gospel" was an ideological hybrid. It joined the enterprise of individual character-building, which evangelical Protestantism and Victorian
liberal ideology had brought to nineteenth-century penal reform, to
a more modern, twentieth-century perspective on the social causes
and consequences of crime. "The key-words of every successful enterprise in these days are economy and humanity," he wrote. "There is
no economy that will compare with that economy which will take a
worthless member of society, such as a convicted criminal now is, – a
man who is of no benefit to himself or society – or to his family – and
make him a useful, industrious, honored member of a community,
and there is no humanity that will compare with that which will take
his wife and children from the wash-tub and the sweat-shops and restore to them their inalienable rights." Cleland's brief experience at
Maxwell Street convinced him that the true riddle of criminal justice
was neither retribution nor deterrence nor rehabilitation per se; it
was dependency. Usher before him a workingman arrested for disorderly conduct, and he saw a web of economic relations: a breadwinner
whose wife, children, and perhaps parents depended on his wages for

7 Cleland, "New Gospel," draft; Henderson quoted in Steven J. Diner, *A City
and Its Universities: Public Policy in Chicago, 1892–1919* (Chapel Hill, 1980),
32; *BOC* (1911), 140; *BOC* (1917), 138; "Obey the Law," *Chicago Tribune*,
Jan. 23, 1909. See James Gilbert, *Perfect Cities: Chicago's Utopias of 1893*
(Chicago, 1991), 37–38.

support. This social perspective made it hard for Cleland to square punishment with justice. It was impossible to fine or jail a workingman without also punishing his dependents, depriving them of "necessities" and "their means of support."[8]

Judge Cleland devised an alternative to the fine and workhouse that placed enormous discretionary power in his own hands. He ran his "parole docket," as he called his probation system, entirely on his own terms – without the blessing of his judicial brethren, the authority of a statute, or a whisper of common law to guide him. As Cleland heard a case – a summary process with no jury present and little intrusion from prosecutors or defense attorneys – he confidently sized up the defendant's prospects for reform. He alone decided who was "reclaimable," a dispensation he reserved almost exclusively for breadwinners who had been arrested while drunk, "or as the result of some other special cause which could be removed." To add a defendant to his parole docket, Cleland imposed a heavy fine, often the stiffest penalty allowed by law, then vacated his own judgment until a later date. In the interim, he ordered the defendant to stay sober, support his family, and report monthly to a special session of the court. Cleland held this session at night, so the men would not miss work, and he required them to bring along their wives "to vouch for their good behavior." Pity the man who broke Cleland's rules. If Cleland reinstated his judgment, the defendant had to pay his fine on the spot, or stand committed to the House of Correction to "work it off" at fifty cents a day. Such was the unexceptional fate of George Gregory, whom Cleland found guilty of disorderly conduct in March 1907, fined $100, and paroled. When Cleland learned that Gregory had shirked his duties, he reinstated the fine. Gregory failed to produce the $100 – a sum few workingmen had in pocket – and Cleland sent him to the House of Correction, where he spent more than five months working off his fine.[9]

What started as an experiment with a few men soon evolved into a full-blown system of social policing. Within a year, Cleland had "paroled" 1,200 defendants. The judge preached his gospel of criminology to respectable residents of the Maxwell Street area. Local merchants signed on as volunteer probation officers, visiting defendants in their homes and reporting to Cleland on their compliance. Claiming that a "lack of thrift and economy was responsible for much of the dissipation and disorder among the foreigners," Cleland persuaded two local banks to offer savings accounts to men on his parole docket. As

---

[8] Cleland, "New Gospel," draft; "Cleland Memo"; VCC, *The Social Evil in Chicago: A Study of Existing Conditions* (Chicago, 1911).
[9] "Cleland Memo"; "Cleland Committee Report," 6.

an incentive, the bank put up the first five dollars, which the defendant could not withdraw unless he deposited two dollars each month, kept sober, and supported his family for a full year. In a brazenly impolitic gesture, Cleland "invited" the saloon-keepers of Maxwell Street to a meeting in his courtroom, and ordered those who showed up not to sell liquor to men on the docket. When one saloon-keeper defied his order, Cleland fined him $50 for contempt.[10]

Judge Cleland's activities at Maxwell Street soon aroused public debate. Some ministers, clubwomen, and businessmen praised the little judge as a hero. But saloon-keepers and political representatives of the many Continental European immigrants in the area, steeled by their recent success in defeating the Chicago charter, protested Cleland's temperance rule as an unconstitutional interference with personal liberties. At first, Cleland's peers on the bench were not quite sure what to make of him; many supported the general idea of probation, if not Cleland's particular version of it, and they were reluctant in any case to interfere with the independence of a fellow judge. But the Municipal Court Act made the judges accountable for each other's behavior. When Maxwell Street made the front pages, and Justice Orrin Carter of the Illinois Supreme Court publicly questioned the legality of Cleland's practices, the judges acted quickly. In January 1908, Chief Justice Olson transferred Cleland to a civil court, pending a full investigation of his parole system by a committee of his fellow judges.[11]

The debate over McKenzie Cleland's authority to release and regulate criminals as he saw fit raised issues much broader than the personal mission of one city court judge. Since the late 1870s, American penal reformers had been reconsidering the meaning of criminal responsibility in an increasingly interdependent, urban-industrial society, raising new doubts about the economy and humanity of punishment. Addressing the prisoners of Cook County Jail in 1902, the defense attorney Clarence Darrow had memorably declared, "I do not believe that people are in jail because they deserve to be. They are in jail simply because they cannot avoid it on account of circumstances which are entirely beyond their control and for which they are in no way responsible." As usual, Darrow's sentiment ran at the margins of public opinion – even one of the prisoners told a guard the speech was "too radical." Still, it was suggestive of a broader line of critical thinking about the social causes of crime and the social consequences of punishment, with which lawmakers and judges had to contend. The new doubts about criminal responsibility contributed to growing public

[10] Olson to Cleland, Oct. 29, 1907, MCC, box 1, folder 6; "Cleland Memo."
[11] Barton, "Judge Cleland"; "Cleland Committee Report."

dissatisfaction over the failure of legal institutions to respond positively
to popular demands for social justice. So as Cleland's peers reviewed
the legality of his parole docket, their deliberations implicated larger
concerns about the social facts of crime in the modern city, and the
ability of the courts to address them.[12]

Speculation about the hold of nature and nurture (not to mention oth-
erworldly forces) on the criminal is likely as old as crime itself. Since
the dawn of the American Republic, moral authorities have decried the
demoralizing effect of urban disorder on the personal virtue essential
to republican citizenship. But Americans at the turn of the twentieth
century talked about the "cause and cure of crime" with a new urgency.
They unsettled Victorian conventions of causal attribution and left no
corner of the criminal justice system untouched. Crime took on an enlarged public significance as a proxy for the full spectrum of modern
social problems – from the inequities of wage labor to the weaken-
ing of traditional gender roles. Progressives turned crime talk into a
graphic language for defining and mapping the social itself as a realm
of collective structures, identities, risks, and needs that lay between the
market and the state. Born of the eruption of industrial capitalism, urbanization, and mass immigration in the late nineteenth century, this
new realm of collective life inspired a rich field of investigation, philosophy, and politics: socialism, social ethics, social Christianity, social
democracy, sociology, social law. Crime talk was a tangible way of expressing the growing perception that the conditions of everyday life
in the industrial city had a moral claim upon the public, opening up
new vistas for state intervention.[13]

Understanding the criminal used to be a less far-flung affair. In
nineteenth-century England and America, Victorian conceptions of
the criminal, like the larger legal cultures in which they were embedded, expressed a broad ideological commitment to the formal equality,
causal potency, and unshakable liability of the individual. The cultural
ideal and legal norm of the moral free agent had ideological roots
running deep into the soil of Anglo-American culture: in the classical
Christian doctrine of free will, in the common law, and, most recently,
in liberal political thought. When it came to assigning guilt and meting
out punishment for crime, few people felt compelled to look beyond

---

[12] Clarence Darrow, *Attorney for the Damned*, ed. Arthur Weinberg (New York,
1957), 3–4, 15.
[13] See Jonathan Simon, "Law after Society," *LSI*, 24 (1999), 143–94; George
Steinmetz, *Regulating the Social: The Welfare State and Local Politics in Imperial
Germany* (Princeton, 1993).

the individual will and its internal moral governor, character. For entire classes of Americans – slaves, Indians, married women, and children – the legal norm of the moral free agent was a hollow fiction (or, at best, a status deferred). But it was a fiction upon which the narrative of American law during the nineteenth century increasingly turned.

Leading American treatise-writers and judges of the late nineteenth century described law as a body of timeless principles – and a set of rules devised from them – that governed relations between individuals (the chief concern of what we now call private law, including torts, contracts, and property), and between each individual and the state (a central issue of public law, including constitutional law and criminal law). Through the measures of lawmakers and especially the decisions of the courts, "classical" legal thinkers professed, the rule of law policed boundaries, settled conflicts, protected the rights and liberties of autonomous individuals, and kept state power in check. For the origins of law itself, many commentators invoked the classical liberal theory that society originated in a state of nature: To more safely pursue their self-interest and foster the common good, individuals ceded some of their liberty to government in exchange for legal protection. In the standard late nineteenth-century treatise on *Criminal Law*, first published in 1865, Joel Prentiss Bishop defined law as the "rules of association" that enabled individuals to coexist. Bound inextricably to these rules was punishment, the "penal sanction" that gave them teeth. Law is "not merely the precept, but the penalty also," Bishop averred. "Indeed, law, without punishment for its violation, is in the nature of things impossible. It is as though we were to speak of an earth without matter, an atmosphere without air, an existence without existence."[14]

As the spread of popular sovereignty and a market capitalist economy had transformed American law between 1787 and the Civil War, virtually every area of public and private law (with the exception of equity) presumed – and *enforced* – a robust conception of individual autonomy and responsibility. The will theory of contracts represented legal agreements as a "meeting of the minds" between "reasonable men," whom the courts would hold answerable to the terms of contract with little regard for disparities of power between the parties. In the law of sales, judges imposed an enlarged expectation of foresight and self-sufficiency upon buyers; old standards of implied warranty and a just price receded before the unblinkingly individualist doctrine of caveat emptor. In the emerging field of torts, judges and jurists enshrined the moral free agent in the doctrinal inventions of assumption

---

[14] Joel Prentiss Bishop, *Bishop on Criminal Law*, 9th ed., ed. John M. Zane and Carl Zollmann (Chicago, 1923), 1: 3; Horwitz, *Transformation* (1992), 9–31.

of risk, contributory negligence, and the principle of fault itself. Even in family law, where patriarchy continued to govern, women's legal and political action prodded judges and lawmakers to extend greater recognition that wives and children had interests of their own.[15]

The individualism of nineteenth-century law is often mistakenly remembered as the legal handmaiden to political laissez-faire. But until the late nineteenth century, the human liberty guaranteed by the common law was "civil or regulated liberty": the conditional freedom of a person living, in association with other individuals, within a well-ordered, self-governing local community. The moral free agent was a cultural ideal and a legal norm. In the hands of different judges and lawmakers, the norm served different purposes: to release economic energies, to discipline workers, to teach Americans to be forward-thinking market actors, and to sometimes legitimate, and sometimes condemn, the concentration of wealth and power. It was an age of great faith in the didactic power of the law. In an 1838 speech Abraham Lincoln declared, "Let reverence for the laws . . . be taught in schools in seminaries, and in colleges; let it be written in Primmers, spelling books, and in Almanacs; – let it be preached from the pulpit, proclaimed in legislative halls, and enforced in courts of justice. . . . [I]n short, let it become the *political religion* of the nation." Many Americans believed that treating individuals as fully free and responsible in the law was the surest way to make them more self-governing in fact.[16]

In no area of the law did the norm of the moral free agent carry a larger ideological burden – or greater implications for force – than in criminal law. The norm undergirded the definition of crime and the procedural rights that each defendant possessed under the common law. A crime had to have two elements: an act expressly forbidden

---

[15] *M'Farland v. Newman*, 9 Watts 55 (Pa., 1839); *Farwell v. Boston & Worcester Railroad Corporation*, 45 Mass. 49 (1842). See Michael Grossberg, *Governing the Hearth: Law and the Family in Nineteenth-Century America* (Chapel Hill, 1985); James Willard Hurst, *Law and the Conditions of Freedom in the Nineteenth-Century United States* (Madison, 1956); Morton J. Horwitz, *The Transformation of American Law, 1780–1860* (Cambridge, Mass., 1977); G. Edward White, *Tort Law in America: An Intellectual History* (New York, 1985), 3–62.

[16] William J. Novak, *The People's Welfare: Law and Regulation in Nineteenth-Century America* (Chapel Hill, 1996), 11; Hurst, *Law and the Conditions of Freedom*, 5; David Montgomery, *Citizen Worker: The Experience of Workers in the United States with Democracy and the Free Market during the Nineteenth Century* (Cambridge, 1993); Abraham Lincoln, "Address before the Young Men's Lyceum of Springfield, Illinois" (1838), in *The Collected Works of Abraham Lincoln*, ed. Roy P. Basler (New Brunswick, N.J., 1953), vol. 1, p. 112; emphasis in original.

by law and an intent to do wrong. Lacking either, an act might be morally wrong, but not a crime. Most states in the nineteenth century replaced common-law crimes with criminal codes, and violation of the positive law of a statute – the action itself – carried a strong legal presumption of intent. The voluntarist premise of the intent standard required exceptions for individuals deemed constitutionally incapable of having the guilty mind (*mens rea*) necessary to form intent: young children or anyone too insane to know right from wrong. "Neither in philosophical speculation, nor in religious or moral sentiment, would any people in any age allow that a man should be deemed guilty unless his mind was so," Bishop explained.[17]

A strong presumption of free will and responsibility was also the common coin of the secular and religious rationales for punishment that shaped the nineteenth-century penitentiary system. In the late eighteenth and early nineteenth centuries, enlightenment thinkers rejected theological conceptions of criminals as sinners, and humanitarian reformers led campaigns for the abolition of torture and public executions. Classical criminology – a disparate body of writings on punishment by political thinkers such as Cesare Beccaria and Jeremy Bentham – conceived of the lawbreaker as an autonomous individual, like any other, who by his nature possessed free will and thus full responsibility for his actions. The causal script of criminology was utilitarian: Self-interested individuals chose to break the law, because they made a hedonistic calculus that doing so would minimize their own pain and maximize their pleasure. For all their differences, the evangelical Protestants and utilitarians who set the terms of antebellum penal discourse agreed that criminals suffered from a deficit of character, the moral fiber of self-governing individuals. The utility of punishment followed from this universalistic causal script. To build character and give individuals a reliable guide to their own self-interest, punishments must be uniform, certain, and determinate. Punishment must be calibrated to fit the crime, Bentham advised, so the cost of an offense outweighed the "profit" of committing it. Thus deterred, the individual would steer his self-interest into less harmful pursuits. "Punishments," Beccaria wrote, "prevent the fatal effects of private interest, without destroying the impelling cause, which is that sensibility inseparable from man."[18]

---

[17] Bishop, *Bishop on Criminal Law*, 192, 135–38; Hurst, *Law and the Conditions of Freedom*, 19; Christopher G. Tiedeman, "Police Control of Dangerous Classes, Other Than by Criminal Prosecutions," *ALR*, 19 (1885), 547–70.

[18] Jeremy Bentham, *An Introduction to the Principles of Morals and Legislation*, (1780; London, 1823), II: 15; Cesare Bonesana, marchesi di Beccaria,

To be sure, deterministic ideas of various kinds circulated in nineteenth-century penal discourse. Classical criminology itself stressed the force upon the will of pain and pleasure – mankind's "two sovereign masters," Bentham called them. But these were forces internal to, constitutive of, the self. The humanitarian reformers who made the penitentiary the preeminent site of penal discipline in Jacksonian America argued that removing the offender from a disordered social environment was the first step to regenerating moral character. Phrenology and other scientific inquiries into the body and mind of the criminal implied a determinism rooted deep in the criminal's nature. But despite all of these determinist rumblings, until the late nineteenth century, the criminal law remained wedded to the concept of the moral free agent. And criminal justice remained an unmistakably legal process. A physician or alienist might appear in court to size up the mental state of a defendant, but the law, legal officials, and the jury possessed unrivaled authority to represent, judge, and punish criminality.[19]

The formal individualism of the nineteenth-century criminal law did not create an equitable criminal justice system. The workaday policing and punishing of lawbreakers was a local affair shaped by local relations of power. In urban communities, the enterprise of character-building through law – an agenda to make *all* citizens forward-thinking, sober, and responsible – had a particular force on the lives of working people. Historians have argued that as the capitalist economy and popular sovereignty spread during the early nineteenth century, the criminal justice system became a vital piece of social machinery, whose most important function was to discipline the working class into lawful and sober citizen workers. This argument has strong evidence behind it: the invention of the first uniformed municipal police forces in the 1840s and 1850s in response to urban rioting and disorder, the decline of the popular tradition of private prosecution by ordinary citizens and the introduction of public prosecutors who cooperated with the police and represented the state, and the enforcement of laws, such as vagrancy acts, that targeted the most marginal elements of society.

An Essay on Crimes and Punishments, trans. M. De Voltaire (Edinburgh, 1778), 27; Harry E. Barnes, "Criminology," in *Encyclopaedia of the Social Sciences*, ed. Edwin R. A. Seligman (New York, 1931), 4: 584–92. See Michel Foucault, *Discipline and Punish: The Birth of the Prison*, trans. Alan Sheridan (New York, 1979); David Garland, *Punishment and Welfare: A History of Penal Strategies* (Brookfield, Vt., 1985), 6–18; Wiener, *Reconstructing the Criminal*.
[19] Bentham, *Introduction*, I: 1. See Adam Jay Hirsch, *The Rise of the Penitentiary: Prisons and Punishment in Early America* (New Haven, 1992); David J. Rothman, *The Discovery of the Asylum: Social Order and Disorder in the New Republic* (Boston, 1971).

The common-law tradition of police power – the right of self-governing communities to restrain individual liberty for the benefit of the health, safety, morals, and welfare of the people – provided an additional legal rationale for policing the "dangerous classes." Police regulations authorized the apprehension and involuntary confinement of the insane, habitual drunkards, and people carrying contagious diseases. In rapidly industrializing states, governments gave quasipolice powers to private charitable associations to enter and police the home lives of dependent families. And in the city police courts and jails of the Gilded Age, the fee system fostered an entrepreneurial legal culture that favored better-off offenders. In the New York City "Tombs," America's most notorious jail, money could buy a swifter trial, better food, a private cell, protection from abuse, even the privilege to come and go.[20]

But within the wide and inequitable field of urban social policing that flourished by the 1870s, the common law and state constitutions did set important procedural limits on governmental interference with liberty. In the higher criminal courts, due process rights were honored with greater regularity than in the police courts. And as modern criminologists increasingly warned of biologically determined "born criminals" in the urban population, they noted with frustration that the procedural protections of the "unscientific" law forbid the state to apprehend such "presumptive criminals" *before* they committed a criminal act.[21]

Even in the heyday of the moral free agent in American law, the criminal justice system did recognize one class of offenders as partially exempt from the full penal sanction of the law. During the early nineteenth century, childhood took on an enlarged cultural significance as a critical stage in the development of self-governing republican citizens. Particularly in middle-class families, a protected childhood symbolized the ideal of a home life safely removed from the market. The new cultural conceptions of childhood had its most decisive impact on family law. Judges adopted the "best interests of the child" as a new standard for deciding child custody cases. The new sentiment also altered public perceptions of children born into urban

[20] Timothy J. Gilfoyle, *A Pickpocket's Tale: George Appo and the Urban Underworlds of Nineteeth-Century America* (forthcoming); Montgomery, *Citizen Worker*, 52–114; *Novak, People's Welfare;* Allen Steinberg, *The Transformation of Criminal Justice: Philadelphia, 1800–1880* (Chapel Hill, 1989).

[21] Henry M. Boies, *The Science of Penology: The Defense of Society Against Crime* (New York, 1901), 20, 59–60, 91–92; Tiedeman, "Police Control of Dangerous Classes."

poverty, who were far more likely than affluent children to fall into the rough hands of the criminal justice system.[22]

Under the common law, children under seven were presumed incapable of the "guilty knowledge" necessary to willfully commit a crime. To children between seven and fourteen, the common law granted a prima facie presumption of incapacity: the state had to prove that the defendant had understood that he or she was committing a crime. A fourteen-year-old was as liable as a man of forty. As the states codified the criminal law in the nineteenth century, they showed little inclination to let children off the hook. The Illinois code of 1845 set the floor of criminal responsibility at ten. But as early as the 1820s and 1830s, philanthropists in major eastern cities successfully campaigned for special treatment of youth offenders. Boston, New York, and Philadelphia founded houses of refuge for children convicted of petty crimes, homeless "streets arabs," and intractable youths committed by their parents. Part school, part jail, houses of refuge reflected contemporary beliefs that children were both less responsible and more reformable than adults. After the Civil War, many state legislatures authorized courts to commit dependent and delinquent children to private "industrial schools." Chicago had four industrial schools by 1887, operated by Catholic and Protestant organizations for children of their faith. The existence of these institutions, however, did not diminish the formal legal responsibility of youths. In fin-de-siècle Chicago, children were still detained in filthy police station lockups, tried in police courts, and committed with "hardened" adults to the Chicago House of Correction and Cook County Jail.[23]

Amidst the social struggles of late nineteenth- and early twentieth-century America, the classical liberal conception of law as rules of association that mediated relations between individuals and between individuals and the state gradually gave way to a progressive conception of law as a purposeful and penetrating instrument of social justice and control. This emergent conception of law came early to criminal justice. Decades before there was serious talk of "socializing the law"

---

[22] See Grossberg, *Governing the Hearth*.

[23] Bishop, *Bishop on Criminal Law*, 1: 259, 261, 260–64; William Blackstone, *Commentaries on the Laws of England*, annotated by Thomas M. Cooley, 4th ed. by James DeWitt Andrews (Chicago, 1899), 1: 400; *Illinois Revised Statutes*, 1911, ch. 38, sec. 283; James Kent, *Commentaries on American Law*, 12th ed. by Oliver Wendell Holmes, Jr., 13th ed. by Charles M. Barnes (Boston, 1884), II: 236–80, 301–19; *Regina v. Smith*, 1 Cox, C. C. 260 (1845), in Frances Bowes Sayre, *A Selection of Cases on Criminal Law* (Rochester, N.Y., 1927), 465, 464–68; Lawrence M. Friedman, *Crime and Punishment in American History* (New York, 1993), 99–101, 163–66; Rothman, *Discovery of the Asylum*, 206–36; Walker, *Popular Justice*, 99–101.

to facilitate direct state regulation of the industrial economy, Protestant benevolent reformers in the institutional world of charities and corrections started to question the classical liberal notion of criminal responsibility. In this long period of flux in American legal culture, penal reformers began to develop a social conception of crime and to imagine the possibility of penality without punishment, an atmosphere without air.

Criminal justice reform seems always to occur in a context of crisis. The famous penal reforms introduced in many states between 1876 and 1900 – reformatories for adult first offenders, indeterminate sentencing and parole, and punitive sentencing laws for "habitual criminals" – were no exception. Prisons had fallen into a state of overcrowding and disrepair after the Civil War, eviscerating the Jacksonian ideal of the penitentiary as an orderly asylum for character building. When Protestant reformers such as Zebulon Brockway and the Reverend Enoch C. Wines met with fellow prison officials and penologists in the National Prison Association, they took up the torch of their antebellum predecessors and attempted to revitalize the penitentiary as a useful site of moral regeneration. But the influence of the natural sciences and evolutionary determinism on understandings of the criminal complicated this agenda. Reformers insisted that the "treatment" of prisoners ought to be designed with an eye to the forces of heredity and environment that, they now believed, lay at the root of criminality. The penal crisis also had a political dimension. Convict labor, the chief form of inmate discipline in penitentiaries, was drawing heavy criticism from organized labor in the industrial states. Many states placed new limits or bans on contract labor and industrial labor in prisons. So the new penology arrived with new disciplinary techniques at precisely the moment that prison officials needed new ways to control inmates.[24]

The new penology broke with the universalistic tenets of classical criminology by stressing the scientific differentiation of criminal types and causes. Classification would produce the intimate knowledge necessary to design an effective and humane "individual treatment" for each offender. The progressive criminologist Harry Elmer Barnes, drawing an analogy to Herbert Spencer's evolutionary theory, described the late nineteenth-century penal reforms as "a passage from a crude and undifferentiated homogeneity to a differentiated and specialized heterogeneity." Incarceration could be made into a

---

[24] Friedman, *Crime and Punishment,* 155–63; Jonathan Simon, *Poor Discipline: Parole and the Social Control of the Underclass, 1890–1990* (Chicago, 1993), 15–38.

better instrument of moral regeneration by segregating reformable first offenders from "incorrigible" criminals. Prison wardens gained wide authority to investigate each prisoner's background and personal makeup; to classify them according to their personal characteristics, offense, and behavior while in prison; and to reward well-behaved prisoners with improved conditions and early release.[25]

Indeterminate sentencing and parole laws applied the principal of prisoner classification to a wide range of adult offenders, by taking sentencing discretion from judges and giving it to prison officials and state parole boards. The Illinois Indeterminate Sentencing and Parole Act of 1899 required judges in felony cases – with the exceptions of treason, rape, murder, and kidnapping – to impose an indeterminate sentence: from one year to the maximum allowed by the criminal code. The law empowered a three-member state board to grant the early release of prisoners. In sizing up a prisoner's prospects for parole, the board heard a report from the penitentiary warden detailing the prisoner's "constitutional and acquired defects and tendencies." Paroled convicts remained in the legal custody of the warden and could be returned to the penitentiary at any time for a parole violation. They were required to find work, stay in the county, report monthly to a sheriff, and "continuously remain a law-abiding citizen of industrious and temperate habits." In theory, parole extended prison officials' powers of surveillance into the community. In practice, the power to grant early release gave wardens a new carrot with which to keep inmates in line. Once parolees left the penitentiary, penal reformers expected the struggle for subsistence in the private labor market, rather than an expensive and impracticable system of state surveillance, to discipline the offender.[26]

Despite its affinity for industrial discipline, the new penology subtly undermined the universalistic premises of Victorian liberal ideology, creating an opening for more radical commentary on crime and punishment. The conspicuous link between penality and the industrial working class attracted to penal reform nonspecialists with broad agendas of social justice. The most penetrating nineteenth-century critic of the Illinois penal system – in fact, of *any* state penal system – was John Peter Altgeld of Chicago, the German-born lawyer and future

[25] Harry Elmer Barnes, *The Evolution of Penology in Pennsylvania: A Study in American Social History* (Indianapolis, 1927), 3.
[26] "An act to revise the law in relation to the sentence and commitment of persons convicted of crime . . . ," approved April 21, 1899, *Illinois Revised Statutes*, 1911, ch. 38, sec. 501, secs. 498–509; Friedman, *Crime and Punishment*, 161; Simon, *Poor Discipline*, 34–37; Walker, *Popular Justice*, 95–96.

During the 1880s, John Peter Altgeld, a German immigrant lawyer and future Illinois governor, published a passionate indictment of America's "penal
machinery" in which he challenged the conventional Victorian conception of
crime as a product of individual free will. His radical claim that "social" conditions such as heredity and environment drove individuals to commit crimes
would become progressive orthodoxy by the turn of the twentieth century.
Courtesy of the Chicago Historical Society (ICHi-09404).

governor. (Altgeld would win national notoriety for pardoning the
four surviving Haymarket anarchists in 1893.) In 1884, Altgeld published *Our Penal Machinery and Its Victims*, an incendiary little book
that described the American penal system as a burgeoning complex of
institutions whose officials extracted their living from "the shortcom-
ings and transgressions of their fellow-men." For Altgeld, the Chicago
justice shops were only one egregious example of this larger injustice.
The penal system, by failing to distinguish between minor and serious offenders, turned impoverished workers, perhaps guilty only of
stealing food for their families, into hardened criminals.[27]

---

[27] John P. Altgeld, *Live Questions: Including Our Penal Machinery and Its Victims*
(Chicago, 1890), 159; Ray Ginger, *Altgeld's America: The Lincoln Ideal versus
Changing Realities*, paperback ed. (Chicago, 1958, 1965), 209–33.

A changing account of crime causation informed Gilded Age penal reform. Altgeld challenged the liberal tenet of the moral free agent in terms that revealed the growing influence of Darwinism and the natural sciences on conceptions of criminality: the logic of determinism, the need to classify people in order to understand them. "The subject of *crime-producing conditions* has received but little attention in the past," he wrote.

> It has always been assumed, in our treatment of offenders, that all had the strength, regardless of training and surroundings, to go out into the world and do absolutely right if they wished, and that if any one did wrong it was because he chose to depart from good and to do evil. Only recently have we begun to recognize the fact that every man is to a great extent what his heredity and early environment have made him, and that the law of cause and effect applies here as well as in nature.

Altgeld located the causes of crime outside the will of the individual. Equally important, punishment had consequences beyond the lone prisoner. Raising a theme that would soon become a commonplace of criminal justice reform, Altgeld noted that every male prisoner had family members dependent on him for support. These, too, were the penal machinery's "victims." In an era of little public provision, he estimated that there were at least five people dependent on "every man who is wearing striped clothing and responding to a number in a State prison" or "breathing the corridor air of the county jail." As crime and dependency became intertwined in public discourse, so did criticism of the government policies and agencies supposed to address these problems of criminal justice and public welfare.[28]

Even radical critics of the criminal justice system such as Altgeld believed the law should make a sharp distinction between the reformable first offender – often represented as a breadwinner driven to petty theft by poverty – and the "vicious and hardened criminal" arrested for a "heinous crime" like highway robbery. A central aim of penal reform was to sort out a population that had long been treated as one undifferentiated "dangerous class." The motives for making such distinctions varied, however. For progressives such as Altgeld or Jane Addams, the aim was social justice for the poor: to conserve the lives and families of working men and women driven to crime by poverty or personal weakness. For a penologist such as Brockway, classifying criminals meant discovering the criminal nature and restoring purpose to the penitentiary. Whatever the motive, distinctions between reformable and

[28] Altgeld, *Live Questions*, 168–69, 157–58, emphasis in original.

incorrigible offenders reinforced the invidious lines that charity officials were drawing among urban working people in Victorian America:
the lines between the "respectable" and the "rough," the "deserving"
and the "undeserving" poor.[29]

Late nineteenth-century criminal justice reform focused on individ-
ualizing the treatment of offenders already within the grip of penal
institutions. Penitentiaries were centralized institutions, much easier
targets than police forces or urban courts for a campaign to reform
the treatment of criminals. Deterministic ideas about prisoners, people
already set apart from society as deviant "others," were also less threatening to the values of individual freedom and responsibility than they
would have been in the apprehension and trial phases of the criminal
justice system. But despite the political success of the new penology,
faith in the penitentiary continued to wane. "The belief gains ground
that the penitentiary system, like all the abandoned devices for the
suppression of crime, will undoubtedly prove a disappointment," the
former secretary of the Illinois Board of Public Charities, Frederick H.
Wines, observed in 1905. "It accomplishes none of its avowed aims. As
punishment, term imprisonment is inequitable and unjust. As a deter-
rent, its influence is inappreciable. As a reformatory agent, conducted
as most prisons have been and still are[,] it is on the whole a failure."
As the search for flexible, case-by-case alternatives to incarceration became the guiding aim of progressive criminal justice reform, the site
of reform moved from prisons to the courts, the far more public sites
where responsibility for crime was first assigned.[30]

The invention of the world's first juvenile court in Chicago in 1899
marked the first important step in this shift. The Illinois General Assembly established the Cook County Juvenile Court to hear all cases of
delinquency and dependency involving boys and girls aged sixteen and
under. The statute authorized the circuit court judges to appoint one
of their number to preside over this specialized branch of their court.
By design, the Cook County Juvenile Court was not supposed to be a
criminal court at all. Instead, judges followed the more flexible procedure of a chancery court. In an extension of the common-law doctrine
of parens patriae (which conceived of the state as the guardian, or parent, to people with legal disabilities), the court heard cases informally,
without the adversarial format, or the attention to due process rights,

---

[29] Ibid., 188. See Garland, *Punishment and Welfare*, 37–40; Karen Sawislak,
Smoldering City: Chicagoans and the Great Fire, 1871–1874 (Chicago, 1995),
69–119.
[30] Frederick Howard Wines, "The New Criminology," in CHA, *A New Chance*
(Chicago, 1905), 20; Rothman, *Conscience and Convenience*, esp. 43.

of an ordinary criminal proceeding. The judge still had the power to
commit juveniles to a private institution or sentence them to the House
of Correction, where the Board of Education had established the John
Worthy School for boys in 1897. But now he could also release them,
under the supervision of a probation officer.[31]

The juvenile court campaign had presented the public with a broad
indictment of Chicago's criminal justice system – especially its police
courts. Until 1899, children arrested in Chicago appeared before police court justices and in Cook County Criminal Court, awaited trial in
the county jail and police station lockups, and if convicted, did time
with adult criminals. It's not hard to see why the presence of juvenile
delinquents in the police courts and lockups invoked public sympathy
and moral outrage: ill-educated, scantily clad, thrown into the bottom
of the labor market at an early age, they were the children of the industrial city. In 1898, nearly 600 youths aged sixteen or under spent
time in the Cook County Jail. Another 2,000 did time in the House
of Correction during a twenty-month period in 1897 and 1898. Their
crimes included disorderly conduct, petty theft, stealing rides on railroad cars, and fighting. Fully a quarter of them were charged with
truancy. Adopting the new rhetoric of preventive medicine, reformers
protested that the police courts were incapable of expert "treatment,"
and they charged that impressionable young offenders were being
morally "contaminated" through their contact with older criminals.[32]

The rhetoric of the juvenile court campaign illustrates the strong
connection between social conceptions of crime and the emerging
progressive politics of needs. "The fundamental idea of the law," said
Cook County prosecutor Albert C. Barnes, "is that the state must step
in and exercise guardianship over a child found under such adverse
social or individual conditions as develop crime." This evocative image
of the state stepping in, through the agency of a court, to the social
world of crime shows how quickly courts were being reconceived in
public discourse as flexible tools of social amelioration and control.
The mandate announced in the Juvenile Court Act's full title – "to regulate the treatment and control of dependent, neglected and delinquent children" – reveals the vast complex of "social or individual conditions" that reformers hoped to "treat" and "control" through local
courts: not only crime, but also dependency, neglect, and youth itself.

[31] David S. Tanenhaus, "Policing the Child: Juvenile Justice in Chicago, 1870–
1925," Ph.D. diss., University of Chicago, 1997.
[32] Lathrop, "Background of the Juvenile Court," 290, 292; Timothy D. Hurley,
"Origin of the Illinois Juvenile Court Law," in *The Child, the Clinic and the
Court* (New York, 1925), 321.

This broad mandate opened up the home lives of dependent and delinquent children to the scrutiny of court officials and the public. It exposed to public view the effects of structural factors such as unhealthy housing and low wages, while also generating greater concern about the personal failings of delinquent parents who failed to make suitable homes for their children. In the juvenile court, crime and dependency blurred into one another until they were almost indistinguishable.[33]

The juvenile court campaign had set a new standard for the leadership of private associations in progressive court reform. The statute was the culmination of nearly two decades of agitation by the Catholic Visitation and Aid Society, the Hull-House social settlement, and the Chicago Woman's Club – "a body of women, many of unusual cultivation and public spirit," as Julia Lathrop of Hull-House remembered them. The Chicago Bar Association provided expert aid in drafting the measure, assuring that it passed constitutional muster. Every phase of progressive court reform raised problems of institutional capacity in an age of deep suspicion of public spending and patronage. The problems were often resolved by associational arrangements between the state and civil society. In the Juvenile Court's early years, the unfunded job of probation officer was usually filled by police officers and volunteers from Hull-House, the Visitation and Aid Society, and other private associations. The widening institutional success of social conceptions of crime owed a great deal to the cast of women reformers on the Juvenile Court Committee at Hull-House, who managed, over many years, to persuade an all-male legislature, bench, and legal profession to take dramatic steps on behalf of the rights and needs of poor women and children. In 1909, many of these same women reformers would come together in a new group, based at Hull-House, called the Juvenile Protective Association.[34]

Catholic activists were also instrumental in the creation of the juvenile court. Visitation and Aid Society president Timothy Hurley, a Chicago police magistrate and key figure in the campaign, praised the court as an "acknowledgment by the State of its relationship as the parent to every child within its borders." These are startling words

---

[33] Barnes in Herman Kogan, *The First Century: The Chicago Bar Association, 1874–1974* (Chicago, 1974), 102; "An act to regulate the treatment and control of dependent, neglected and delinquent children," approved April 21, 1899, *Illinois Revised Statutes*, 1911, ch. 23, secs. 169–190.

[34] Julia C. Lathrop, "The Background of the Juvenile Court in Illinois," in *Child, the Clinic and the Court*, 291; U.S. Department of Labor, Children's Bureau, *The Chicago Juvenile Court*, by Helen Rankin Jeter (Washington, 1922); Allen F. Davis, *American Heroine: The Life and Legend of Jane Addams* (New York, 1973), 149–56; Walker, *Popular Justice*, 99–101.

from an American Catholic official. The international Catholic ideal
was indeed a paternalist state. But this ideal had to be tempered wher-
ever the state was secular or Protestant in its composition and ideology.
For decades, the Archdiocese of Chicago had resisted the encroachment of the "soulless state" into charity and education in Illinois, which
church leaders saw as a threat to their own charitable institutions and
the bonds they created between parishoners and the church. Most
Catholic officials, moreover, did not share the increasingly secular
world view and social democratic agenda of Hull-House; Catholic charity work aimed at individual redemption, not "social reform." Despite
these reservations, the Archdiocese already had a close relationship
with the courts. Catholics operated two of Chicago's four industrial
schools, which received dependent Catholic children committed by
the courts. After the Juvenile Court opened, the Visitation and Aid
Society placed three volunteer probation officers there. By 1906 the
society was filing half of the court's dependency cases. Other Catholic
charitable institutions also received wards from the Chicago courts, including St. Vincent's Infant Asylum, St. Mary's Training School, and the
House of Good Shepherd, a shelter for wayward girls and prostitutes.
The Archdiocese depended on the courts for help in reaching the
city's poorest Catholics, and the church benefited from the state sub-
sidies and recognition that came from this relationship. The church,
in turn, gave the courts greater legitimacy in a city heavily populated
by Catholic immigrants.[35]

In the widening variety of literature on crime in turn-of-the-century
America, the "modern city" was the ultimate emblem of the social.
From popular true-crime books to criminology treatises to progressive
reform tracts, writers represented city life as exerting an irresistible
influence on behavior – not just of criminals but of all who called
the modern city home. Realist fictional accounts of urban life often
opened by recounting the experience of a lone individual, just arrived by train from the country, overwhelmed by the prostrating social
force of the great city. Theodore Dreiser's *Sister Carrie* described the

---

[35] Hurley in Friedman, *Crime and Punishment,* 165; Hurley, "Origin of the
Illinois Juvenile Court Law," 320–30; Charles H. Shanabruch, "The Catholic
Church's Role in the Americanization of Chicago's Immigrants, 1833–
1928," Ph.D. diss., University of Chicago, 1975, pp. 346, 114–55, 330–70.
See Edward R. Kantowicz, *Corporation Sole: Cardinal Mundelein and Chicago
Catholicism* (Notre Dame, 1983), 22–32, 130; James W. Sanders, *The Education of an Urban Minority: Catholics in Chicago, 1833–1965* (New York, 1977),
33–34; John Patrick Walsh, "The Catholic Church in Chicago and Problems
of an Urban Society: 1893–1915," Ph.D. diss., University of Chicago, 1948,
pp. 95–118.

particular sexual dangers that greeted the single woman migrating alone from the hinterland to Chicago. Franc B. Wilkie's lesser-known work, *The Gambler: A Story of Chicago Life* (1888) recounted the moral downfall of a country boy, lured into the city's masculine subculture of gambling, drink, and vice. The "wicked city" genre of true-crime literature exposed the evils of urban life for the reading public. In a dark mirror image of nineteenth-century urban boosterism, these sensational books toted up crime statistics and guided the reader into gambling dens and sporting houses. Authors alternately condemned and delighted in the disorderly underworld that lurked beneath the surface of the capitalist dynamo of the central business district. The literature's heady mix of prurience, horror, and moral outrage suggests a middle-class audience similarly conflicted about the heightened eroticism, personal danger, and social responsibility it felt in the vicarious presence of the city's wicked others.[36]

In the literatures of social reform and academic social science, the modern city was a problematic but promising historical development. The city signified industrialization, the cultural pluralism spawned by decades of high immigration, the corruption of machine politics, and the immoral influences of commercial amusements, and urbanism created new obstacles and opportunities for social control. By "social control," progressives did not mean simply top-down policing of working-class behavior. They used the term, in the spirit of Edward A. Ross's influential 1901 treatise of the same name, to talk about a broad array of state and nonstate interventions that adjusted the actual relations among individuals, the market, and the state. Following Ross, progressives such as Jane Addams argued that modern urban life was characterized by social atomism: the substitution (in the Chicago sociologist Louis Wirth's famous phrase) of "secondary" social contacts for the "primary" contacts of the small town. As Addams observed in her 1912 book on prostitution, "[t]he social relationships in a modern city are so hastily made and often so superficial, that the old human restraints of public opinion, long sustained in smaller communities, have also broken down." But the modern city also created new commitments beyond the self and new mechanisms of control. "Fortunately the same crowded city conditions which make moral isolation possible constantly tend to develop a new restraint founded upon the mutual dependencies of city life," Addams wrote. "The city itself socialized the very instruments that constitute the

---

[36] Theodore Dreiser, *Sister Carrie* (1900; New York, 1987). Franc B. Wilkie, *The Gambler: A Story of Chicago Life* (Chicago, 1888); Samuel Paynter Wilson, *"Chicago" and Its Cess-Pools of Infamy*, 4th ed. (Chicago, 1910).

apparatus of social control – Law, Publicity, Literature, Education and Religion."[37]

This common perception – that beneath the atomization of city life, modern society was growing ever more "interdependent" – was one of the many cultural strands that tied progressive court reform to the contemporary "revolt against formalism" in American social thought. Thomas Haskell has argued that between 1880 and 1920, Americans experienced an upheaval in their cultural conventions of causal attribution, the taken-for-granted explanatory schemes that governed how people interpreted human events. In Victorian culture, the adult self was "an uncaused cause, a pure point of origin . . . , in which purposeful activity arose out of nothing and surged into the world." This robust conception of the self receded as Americans, living in a more secular age, came to terms with the undeniable interdependence of social life in a mature capitalist economy of national markets, large corporations, massive factories, immigrant cities, and violent clashes between labor and capital. Social scientists were among the first intellectuals to think seriously about the implications of interdependence, and the cultural authority of their disciplines depended on their ability to explain and mediate interdependence for educated Americans and policy makers. The very concept of the social sciences, like the statistical evidence on which many social scientists relied, implied the weakened autonomy of the individual in the face of impersonal forces. By the turn of the century, this causal sensibility pervaded American culture. As historian Willard Hurst observed, ordinary Americans showed "a new inclination to think in matter-of-fact terms about cause and effect in social relations and to cast up balance sheets of profit and loss in terms of community-wide effect."[38]

The discovery of interdependence had profound implications for the way Americans thought about criminal responsibility. The doctrine

[37] Edward Alsworth Ross, *Social Control: A Survey of the Foundations of Order* (New York, 1901); Louis Wirth, "Urbanism as a Way of Life," *AJS*, 44 (July 1938), 21; Jane Addams, *A New Conscience and an Ancient Evil* (New York, 1912), 104, 210. See Jane Addams, *The Spirit of Youth and the City Streets* (New York, 1909); Paul Boyer, *Urban Masses and Moral Order in America, 1820–1920* (Cambridge, Mass., 1978), 162–283.

[38] Morton White, *Social Thought in America: The Revolt against Formalism* (Boston, 1957); Haskell, "Brief Excursus," 307–17, esp. 309; Hurst, *Law and the Conditions of Freedom*, 73. See Thomas L. Haskell, *The Emergence of Professional Social Science: The American Social Science Association and the Nineteenth-Century Crisis of Authority* (Urbana, 1977); Arthur McEvoy, "The Triangle Shirtwaist Factory Fire of 1911: Social Change, Industrial Accidents, and the Evolution of Common-Sense Causality," *LSI*, 20 (1995), 621–51.

of free will, liberalism's inheritance from classical Christian ethics, had long held that where personal agency went, moral responsibility followed. As cultural conceptions of criminality widened to account for social causes beyond the will, criminal responsibility lost its mooring in the self. The University of Chicago sociologist Albion Small raised this issue in a 1900 address to the Chicago Congregational Club, entitled "The Social Responsibility for Crime." The son of a New England minister, Small understood his subject would make his audience flinch. "Now, gentlemen, do not think that anybody who talks about 'social responsibility for crime' has gone back upon the fundamental notion of personal responsibility," he assured his listeners. But his assurances were tentative. In an interdependent age, society itself could not escape a measure of responsibility for crime. "We are making or maintaining the conditions that will predispose people to be better or worse," Small cautioned. "Our cities are vast machines for producing conditions favorable to crime." The social responsibility for crime placed an affirmative obligation on "we," the enlightened public, to improve conditions of housing, employment, and public health.[39]

No single factor emerged in public discourse to replace individual willfulness as the overwhelming, independent explanatory variable in producing crime. Hereditarian and environmentalist explanations of human behavior were surprisingly permeable in the early twentieth century. Both rejected the formalist conception of the autonomous individual – freely acting and fully responsible – taken for granted in Christian ethics, liberal ideology, and the common law. Even the most ardent eugenicists tempered their enthusiasm for hereditary explanations with grudging references to a social world replete with accessory causes. In a thick treatise on the state of criminological research in 1901, Pennsylvania charity official Henry M. Boies announced that "the searching investigations of scientists into the physical and psychical conditions of the criminal" had repeatedly turned up bad heredity as the common causal denominator in criminality. But the scientists, Boies conceded, were left with an environmental remainder too large to ignore: drunkenness, parental neglect, poor education, weakened religious values, and "social conditions producing a superstimulated desire for indulgences honestly unattainable." Commentators committed to materialist explanations of social problems were similarly left with a residue of hereditary evidence. The Chicago socialist editor

---

[39] Albion W. Small, "The Social Responsibility for Crime," in Chicago Congregational Club, *The Delinquent Classes – What Shall We Do with Them: What Will They Do with Us?*, pamphlet from meeting in Chicago, March 19, 1900 (n.p.), 4, 8–9. See Haskell, *Professional Social Science*, 241–42.

Algie M. Simons blamed "the hellish conditions of the modern competitive system" for the city's crime problem. But he added that "long years of capitalism have developed a class of mental, moral and physical cripples, degenerates and insane, whose instincts are wholly anti-social." Most urban commentators did yet not feel compelled to choose between heredity and environment – or even, with any finality, between individual and social responsibility.[40]

The concept of social responsibility for crime grew increasingly pervasive in the Progressive Era, as social scientists and activists pointed to crime as a symptom of a much broader set of social ills that government had a duty to cure. Crime became a proxy for the collected social problems and needs of the modern city and a banner for state action to address them. Few took the argument as far as Clarence Darrow, who called monopoly capitalists such as John D. Rockefeller the true born criminals. "It's easy to see how to do away with what we call crime," Darrow told the prisoners at Cook County Jail. "Make fair conditions of life." By this he meant destroying monopolies, abolishing the right of private ownership of land, and making workers equal partners in production. But even the most moderate progressives expressed hope that, with the right combination of environmental and eugenic reforms, urban governments might dramatically reduce or even eliminate crime within a generation or two.[41]

Still, there remained the thorny issue of how social explanations of crime ought to affect the way the courts handled adult offenders. Social responsibility for crime was a highly protean concept. Notwithstanding the wealth of social science knowledge that progressives marshaled behind this concept, the cultural politics of the moment and the legal traditions of the past shaped even the most rigorous understanding of the criminal. Given cultural anxieties about changing gender roles, for example, would reformers apply the same sympathetic standard of social causation to a male breadwinner, arrested for deserting his family, as to a prostitute hauled into court from the Levee? Was society equally responsible in each case? The concept of social responsibility also raised issues of a more recognizably legal nature. If an individual could not be held fully responsible for a criminal act, how should social responsibility actually register in the legal process? Who decided what portion of the blame rightfully belonged to society and what to the individual criminal – and how? What implications did the new doubts

---

[40] Boies, *Science of Penology*, 12, 27; A. M. Simons, *What the Socialists Would Do If They Won in This City* (Chicago, 1901), 21–22.
[41] Darrow, *Attorney for the Damned*, 9, 14–15; Charles A. Beard, *American City Government: A Survey of Newer Tendencies* (New York, 1912), 186.

about personal agency hold for defendants' procedural rights, which were firmly grounded in the liberal legal conception of the moral free agent?

Judge McKenzie Cleland put these legal questions squarely before his fellow Municipal Court judges, the press, and the public. He had created his parole docket to reconcile the judicial role of assigning blame and punishment to individual offenders with his perception that crime often had social causes and punishment social consequences. In doing so, Cleland stepped outside the formal boundaries of the law and into a mode of magisterial discretion that Roscoe Pound called "justice without law." Pound argued that whenever the law lagged too far behind the moral opinion of the age, a period of lawless justice ensued, which temporarily severed the legal tethers on arbitrary power until the law caught up with the times. The Court of Star Chamber in sixteenth-century England was Pound's favorite example. But the Court of McKenzie Cleland at Maxwell Street would have served him just as well.[42]

The public reaction to Cleland's removal from the court illuminates the cultural politics of law and order in early twentieth-century Chicago. Ministers, attorneys, merchants, and a few manufacturers from the Maxwell Street area protested the ouster, urging Chief Justice Olson to restore Cleland to his "great and noble work" for "the reclamation of the criminal classes." An official of the Henry Booth House Settlement praised Cleland as a missionary of justice who had worked to "redeem the fallen" in one of Chicago's "vilest and most notorious" sections. But Continental immigrants who called that place home celebrated Cleland's departure and his replacement by Isidore Himes, a former city prosecutor with more conventional notions of penality. "Maxwell street station has ceased to be the stomping ground of Reverend Ministers and Sunday school pupils," a Bohemian newspaper, *Denni Hlasatel,* announced. "It has become what it should be, a *court room.*" The paper chided Cleland for turning his court into a "Temperance Vaudeville" where "temperance grandmothers" interfered with the "liberty" of workingmen as breadwinners and saloon patrons.[43]

---

[42] Pound, "Organization of Courts," 71; Roscoe Pound, "Justice According to Law," *CLR,* 13 (1913), 696–713; 14 (1914), 1–26, 103–21.

[43] John P. Lenox to Harry Olson, Jan. 14, 1908, MCC, box 2, folder 8; Samuel W. Packard to Harry Olson, Jan. 14, 1908, MCC, box 2, folder 8; C. W. Diehl to Harry Olson, Jan. 10, 1908, MCC, box 2, folder 8; *BOC* (1917), 327. The quotes come from two translated versions of *Denni Hlasatel* articles. One is an undated report labeled "Judge Cleland and His Parole System," MCC,

The committee investigating Cleland's parole docket stuck to the more narrowly legal issues. Those were complicated enough. For as the judges soon learned (if they did not already know), Cleland's practices were only an extreme example of a quietly growing trend. Even before the Municipal Court opened, local judges had tinkered with alternatives to punishment. Police magistrates were notorious for using their courts for extralegal forms of political discipline. Less well publicized was the fact that some of them, including Justice Timothy Hurley, the Catholic activist, had an informal practice of vacating their own judgments, in particularly desperate cases, and assigning defendants a penance with an eye to their reformation. Judges on the Cook County Criminal Court were also engaging in acts of human reclamation at the margins of formal criminal procedure – even in felony cases. Thanks to one prisoner's complaint, the Illinois Supreme Court, located far downstate in Springfield, had begun to take interest in the informal handling of criminal cases in Chicago.[44]

In the 1903 case of *People ex rel. Boenert v. Barrett*, the supreme court reviewed the habeas corpus petition of Anton Boenert, who had been convicted of grand larceny in the Cook County Criminal Court three years earlier. The record showed that the trial judge had released Boenert on his own recognizance, pending his motion for a new trial, and let two and half years pass before overruling the defendant's motion and sentencing him to the penitentiary. The criminal court's backlog did not explain the delay, the justices concluded; the judge had given the defendant a chance to reform, and Boenert had disappointed him. The supreme court ordered the criminal court to discharge Boenert. Justice Orrin Carter's opinion made a powerful defense of due process rights. A trial court was a forum for determining innocence or guilt, not for judicial speculation about a defendant's personal circumstances and prospects for reform:

> The rendering of judgment and the final sentencing of the defendant cannot be made a mere matter of discretion with the judge or the public prosecutor, nor to depend upon the subsequent conduct of the convicted person. If it were so, what subsequent conduct would demand or justify the pronouncing or the withholding of the sentence? And who would determine its character? Such conduct might be innocent in itself yet offensive to those in whom the power to

box 2, folder 12. The other, untitled, is dated Jan. 25, 1908, MCC, box 2, folder 8. See "Cleland Defiant Paroles Forty-Six," *Chicago Examiner*, Jan. 23, 1909; "Cleland Resumes Former Methods," *Chicago Tribune*, Jan. 23, 1909.
44 T. D. Hurley, "Adult Probation," in CHA, *A Friend in Need* (Chicago, 1906), 11–14.

apprehend or to punish resided. The liberty of the citizen cannot in a free country be made to depend for its security on the arbitrary will of any public officer; it can be taken from him by due process of law only.[45]

Barrett was still good law as the committee reviewed Cleland's practices. But the committee also knew that the procedural formality that *Barrett* symbolized was everywhere loosening. Contrary to Cleland's claims, he did not invent probation. It was one of the fastest spreading innovations in criminal justice. The technique was first used widely in juvenile justice: By 1907, twenty-five states, including Illinois, had statutes allowing probation for juvenile delinquents. The technique was making inroads with adult offenders – particularly first offenders accused of run-of-the-mill crimes – as lawmakers in many states arrived at much the same conclusion as Cleland: Incarceration and fines took breadwinners and scarce resources from fragile working-class families, which turned to private charities and meagerly funded county welfare offices for support. In 1900, only Massachusetts had a statutory system of adult probation. By 1907, seven states, including Illinois, had enacted statutes that authorized court-supervised probation for adults found guilty of desertion and nonsupport. Nine states had extended probation more generally to adult offenders. In 1907, Municipal Court of Chicago Judge Stephen Foster had gone on a scouting mission to Boston to see adult probation in action in that city's court system; he had returned full of enthusiasm, and had already begun to draft a statute for Illinois when the Cleland controversy erupted. As Foster noted, probation would help Municipal Court judges deal more intelligently with their overwhelming responsibilities. A conscientious judge, inundated with between fifty and a hundred minor criminal cases every day, would welcome whatever light a probation officer could shed upon a defendant's background and family, to help the judge "determine what should be the proper disposition of the case."[46]

Cleland made the investigating committee's job easier than it might have been. The committee unearthed a record of irregularities that attested to the dangers of magisterial discretion unrestrained by law. By the measure of conventional penality – fines and imprisonment – the parole docket was a good deal for defendants. Cleland discharged nearly 80 percent of the defendants who appeared before

---

[45] *People ex rel. Boenert v. Barrett*, 202 Ill. 287, 290–91, 300 (1903).
[46] Judge Stephen A. Foster, "An Adult Probation Law," in CHA, *Men Who Make Good* (Chicago, 1908), 17, 15–18; Walker, *Popular Justice*, 155.

him, compared with an average discharge rate of 55 percent in the
Municipal Court's criminal branches. But Cleland was not a conventional judge. Tallied among his discharges were all of his paroled defendants and the many men jailed overnight on his orders. When Cleland
lost faith in a defendant's character, he came down hard. The committee charged that Cleland had violated defendants' constitutional
rights by imposing excessive bails and sending defendants to jail without the option of bail on minor charges. (Cleland's defense: Jail was
a good place for drunks to dry out.) He had fined defendants twice
for the same offense. He had placed defendants in double jeopardy by
changing his own rulings from not guilty to guilty. And he had ordered
police to apprehend men on his docket for the crime of "violation of
parole," though no such crime existed.[47]

The committee's final report, read to the full body of Municipal
Court judges on February 19, 1909, was a forceful public statement
that reasserted the authority of the rule of law over magisterial discretion. The report expressed support for a well-safeguarded system
of probation, "if legislation securing it can be secured in this state."
But the judges accused Cleland of "serious violations of the rights of
individuals as guaranteed by the constitution and laws of this state."
Chief Justice Olson confronted Cleland in the presence of reporters.
"[Y]ou have usurped rights of citizenship that are as old as the Magna
[C]harta," he declared. "You have overridden the rights of the poor
and the ignorant, who knew nothing of a writ of habeas corpus or an
appeal to the Supreme Court." The Chicago press cast the Cleland controversy as a Manichean struggle between liberal legal principles and
arbitrary magisterial discretion. The *Tribune* called Cleland a "fuddle
headed sentimentalist" who had perpetrated "the gravest evil known
to a civilized society – arbitrary, personal judgment." On the editorial
pages, if not in the actual practice of the courts, law was still a body
of timeless principles and rules. The purpose of law was to protect
individual rights and liberties. The role of the judge was to know these
rules and faithfully apply them.[48]

[47] "Cleland Committee Report," 10–18; "Cleland Plan Target," *Chicago Daily
News,* Nov. 1, 1911; *MCC* 2 (1908), 46–47, 70.
[48] "Cleland Committee Report," 9; "Cleland Flayed; Record Exposed," *Chicago
Tribune,* Feb. 20, 1909; "Cleland Reign Ends; Judges Pass the Lie," *Chicago
Record-Herald,* Feb. 20, 1909; "Obey the Law." See also "The Case of
Judge Cleland," *Chicago Record-Herald,* Feb. 23, 1909; "Parole and the Law,"
Chicago Tribune, Feb. 22, 1909; "End Cleland Parole Work," *Chicago Journal,*
Feb. 20, 1909; "Reach Liar Stage in Cleland War," *Chicago Tribune,* Feb. 22,
1909.

Cleland drew on the same deep-rooted rhetorical traditions to denounce the report – the work of a "Star Chamber," he called it – and to assert his independence against the centralized authority of the Municipal Court. In a letter to the judges, Cleland said that only an appellate court could pass judgment upon his orders; Olson had overstepped his authority. "He is not *my* general superintendent, and will not be during the remainder of my term in office," Cleland declared. "I am perfectly willing to take any assignment, but I will continue to be in the future, as in the past, the only judge in the branch court over which I preside."[49]

But the power of assignment was power enough for Olson to close the books on Cleland's parole docket, and to assure he never again presided over a criminal trial.[50]

The debate over adult probation raged on. Between 1909 and 1911, the debate shifted from Chicago to Springfield, where the General Assembly considered rival probation bills put forth by Cleland and the Civic Federation of Chicago. In social clout and political power, Cleland was outclassed. Backed by ministers, clubwomen from the well-to-do suburb of Oak Park, and a few merchants and manufacturers from Maxwell Street, Cleland vied with an organization whose membership included leading Chicago lawyers, bankers, financiers, and corporate executives. The Civic Federation had many prominent allies in social reform circles, including Louise de Koven Bowen and Jane Addams of Hull-House. A driving force in the charter campaign and the creation of the Municipal Court, the federation had remained active in criminal justice reform. Prominent experts in welfare and criminal justice – Charles R. Henderson, Harry Olson, Graham Taylor of the Chicago Commons, and Superintendent John L. Whitman of the House of Corrections – served on the federation's Committee on Indeterminate Sentence and Parole. The Municipal Court's own Judge Foster drafted the federation's conservative probation bill. The federation quickly marginalized Cleland, casting the innovative judge as a cautionary symbol of the dangers of excessive "sentimentality" toward lawbreakers and excessive discretion on the bench.[51]

Ironically, the Civic Federation's propaganda for its probation bill could have been written by Cleland. Federation literature said the bill

---

[49] Cleland's written response to the Cleland committee, submitted Feb. 19, 1909, MCC, box 2, folder 12.

[50] Harry Olson to McKenzie Cleland, Feb. 20, 1909, MCC, box 2, folder 12.

[51] CFC, *Legislative Report* (1911), 4–5; *BOC* (1911), 245; Albion W. Small, "The Civic Federation of Chicago: A Study in Social Dynamics," *AJS*, 1 (July 1895), 79–103.

aimed "to give first offenders an opportunity to reform while following their regular employment instead of locking them up with hardened criminals while those dependent upon them become objects of
charity." Like Cleland, the federation and its progressive allies aimed
to refocus the agenda of criminal justice from an exclusive concern
with individual offenders to a broader program of social regulation
that would address the needs of working-class families and, not incidentally, reduce the burden on private charities and county welfare
agencies. But the contrast between the Foster and Cleland bills reveals the principled disagreements about the proper bounds of judicial power that attended the era's debates over adult probation. Under
Cleland's system, *anyone* (including repeat offenders) convicted of a
noncapital crime was eligible for probation. The bill set no time limit;
a judge simply entered the maximum statutory penalty for the crime
and suspended the sentence indefinitely. Foster's bill applied only to
ordinance violations, misdemeanors, and a much more limited class
of felonies. Ordinance violations and state misdemeanors carried a
maximum term of one year on probation; felonies, a three-year term.
As the *Chicago Daily News* put it, Cleland's bill threw open the doors of
the courthouse to "well-nigh unlimited adult probation," while Foster's
laid out "a well-safeguarded system."[52]

It's not hard to see why an organization of conservative but reform-
minded lawyers and businessmen would favor the Foster bill, with its
tighter eligibility requirements and clear procedural restraints. In ways
less obvious, the bill also suited the federation's class orientation. During the same legislative session that it was pushing the adult probation
bill, the Civic Federation was aggressively helping to kill what it called
a "dangerous" resolution to amend the state constitution and provide
voters with the initiative and referendum. The struggle between capital
and labor, federation literature opposing the resolution declared, created an urgent need for the "fair-minded men and women of character
of the commonwealth" to generate "a wise, conservative solution" to
the problems before the public. Viewed in this light, the federation's
support for Foster's probation bill can be read as a strategic attempt
to deal with an obvious cause of dependency in Chicago, while head-
ing off more radical measures such as Cleland's. A federation bulletin
boasted that the bill's scope was "more limited than that of any other
law in the country."[53]

[52] CFC, *Legislative Report* (1911), 2; "In Aid of First Offenders," *Chicago Daily
News,* Feb. 25, 1909.
[53] CFC, *Legislative Report* (1911), 8; CFC, *Bulletin No. 6: Biennial Report, October
1911* (Chicago, 1911), 4–5; CFC, *Legislative Report* (1911), 5.

Neither Cleland nor the Civic Federation had the power to impose their visions of justice on the Second City – especially in a city where, thanks largely to Cleland, the word "probation" sounded so much like "prohibition." The Cleland and Foster bills both ran into immediate opposition in the General Assembly from lawmakers who represented districts with large immigrant populations, who feared a statewide replication of the "Temperance Vaudeville" at Maxwell Street. Civic Federation literature blamed Cleland for alienating the "foreign element": "[R]epresentatives of these districts in the legislature opposed anything that bore the name of Adult Probation." Effectively mobilized by Anton Cermak of the United Societies for Local Self-Government, now an alderman on the City Council, lawmakers served their Continental constituents by defeating the Foster bill twice in the house, and helping to kill Cleland's bill in the House Judiciary Committee. Once again, the "personal liberty" forces had mobilized and placed limits on a Civic Federation reform. The Foster bill was amended to place tighter limits on judges' discretionary powers over probationers. A strict construction of the measure would prohibit judges from making sobriety a condition of probation. Governor Deneen signed the revised measure into law on June 10, 1911.[54]

The title of the Adult Probation Act promised a system of penality "without punishment." The act gave criminal courts discretionary power to released convicted lawbreakers if they agreed to comply with a system of state surveillance. McKenzie Cleland, quick to claim the law as a product of his own ideas if not of his pen, captured its essence: "The law makes the court, instead of the prison, the reformatory agent." The act applied to first offenders found guilty of ordinance violations and misdemeanors, and it covered several classes of felonies, including larceny, embezzlement, and malicious mischief. A defendant had to apply to be considered for probation, and the judge decided whether there was "reasonable ground to expect that the defendant may be reformed and the interests of society will be subserved." To grant probation, a judge entered an order continuing the case for a definite period – six months for an ordinance violation, one year for a misdemeanor or felony – and ordered a probation regimen. All probationers were required to enter into a recognizance bond; if convicted of a felony or misdemeanor, they were forbidden to leave the state without the court's permission. The statute authorized the court (at its discretion) to require the offender to make restitution to the injured party and

---

[54] CFC, *Legislative Report* (1911), 2–3; "An act providing for a system of probation...," approved June 10, 1911, *Illinois Revised Statutes*, 1911, ch. 38, secs. 509a–q, hereafter cited as Adult Probation Law.

to contribute to the support of his own wife and children "subject to the supervision of the court." Any defendant who violated the terms of probation was subject to arrest and to a full sentence for the offense.[55]

The most novel feature of the system was the new agent of state power it introduced. The court assigned each case to a probation officer, a county officer appointed by the circuit court who might be a police officer or any "reputable private person" of "good character." Probationers had to make monthly reports to their officers, keeping them apprised of their "whereabouts, conduct and employment." The officers had broad authority to investigate the probationer's "personal characteristics, habits, associations and previous conduct" and "the names, relationships, ages and conditions of those dependent upon him for support, maintenance and education." To keep the system from becoming a trough of patronage, the assembly placed a tight limit on the number of officers – one per 50,000 residents, capped at twenty for any single county. In Chicago this fiscal conservatism imposed serious limits on the ability of probation officers to keep close watch over their charges.[56]

The Cleland controversy and the probation debate had kept the Municipal Court in the public eye for two years. Chief Justice Olson emerged from the conflict with his centralized authority vindicated, his court on sound constitutional ground, and his public image as an innovative but cautious reformer – a progressive – firmly established. Olson and his peers on the bench also came out of the battle far more persuaded by Cleland's general point of view. Many of them now believed that the interdependence of urban life made criminal responsibility a relative matter and that legal justice should take social conditions into account. In a speech that touted the new Adult Probation Act as an outgrowth of the "modern thought of penologists," Olson set an ideological and programmatic course that would guide him through his next two decades as steward of the Municipal Court. Crime was no longer understood as something that could be attributed solely to the individual will. "[I]t is recognized that heredity, environment and accident have so much to do with the making of the criminal that he is in a measure entitled to the special protection of the State in overcoming his delinquency," Olson declared. "To this end, he is given only such measure of punishment as is deemed necessary for the protection of

---

55 "Judge Cleland Likes New Probation Law," *Chicago Daily Journal*, May 16, 1911; Adult Probation Law, secs. 509b–d.

56 Adult Probation Law, sec. 509i–n; "Adult Probation and Parole," *JAICLC*, 1 (May 1910), 126–27; CFC, *Bulletin No. 12: Legislative Report of the Civic Federation of Chicago, 1915* (Chicago, 1915), 14; MCC 7 (1913), 107.

society. However else he may be treated after conviction of crime, such treatment is considered not to be punishment but treatment for his benefit." The public meaning of crime and the legal response to it were shifting. The category of the irresponsible offender, once reserved for children and the mentally incapacitated, now applied, in varying degrees, to *all* offenders. This created a new sphere of entitlement: the lawbreaker entitled to treatment rather than subject to punishment for purposes of deterrence or vengeance. Olson did not acknowledge that this entitlement, penality without punishment, implied new forms of state power over the individual.[57]

The modern age in criminal justice had no room for the likes of McKenzie Cleland. For Olson, the Civic Federation, and many other criminal justice reformers who thought of themselves as progressives, Cleland had served as a useful foil. They denounced him as an antimodern – a sentimentalist, a maverick, a religious zealot, and a despot with no respect for due process. The record shows that Cleland was guilty on all counts. But reformers used the figure of Cleland to represent the centralized structure of the new Municipal Court, and the highly discretionary methods they were beginning to implement there, as scientific, modern, well safe-guarded, and in line with American legal traditions. Only time would tell whether the version of socialized justice that carried the day in the Municipal Court would in fact be so different from Cleland's maverick practices. Cleland would not be around for the comparison. After his Municipal Court term expired in 1910, the self-styled "little father of the parole system" made an unsuccessful run for the superior court. After that, Cleland remained a prominent figure in Illinois welfare reform. But he did so from his new position as director of the fundamentalist Moody Bible Institute, not as a member of the municipal bench, with a judge's power to fuse personal notions of social justice with concrete motions of state power.[58]

[57] Harry Olson, "The New Adult Probation Law (Old Speech)," [1912], JHO, box 3.
[58] "Cleland and Parole Plan Get Slap at Bar Primary," *Chicago Examiner*, April 4, 1909; "Cleland Makes Reply," *Chicago Daily News*, Oct. 31, 1911; "Cleland Reign Ends." See H. M. Fullerton to Harry Olson, Nov. 21, 1910, MCC, box 3, folder 19. After 1910, Cleland became a prominent advocate of state assistance to poor families. He claimed authorship of the 1911 Illinois Funds to Parents Act, a landmark in the movement for "mothers' pensions." But Louise Bowen of the JPA fiercely disputed this claim; *BOC* (1917), 138. "'Work of Enemies,' Cleland's Assertion," *Chicago Record-Herald*, Feb. 1, 1912; "Mrs. Bowen Answers Cleland Statement," *Record-Herald*, Feb. 2, 1912. See Joanne L. Goodwin, *Gender and the Politics of Welfare Reform: Mothers' Pensions in Chicago, 1911–1929* (Chicago, 1997).

4

Socializing the Law

When we recognize that legal rules [and] decisions themselves are
not ... born of pre-existing legal principles but are social events with
social causes and consequences, then we are ready for the serious
business of appraising law and legal institutions in terms of some
standard of human values.

– Felix S. Cohen, 1935

The emergence of a distinctively modern rationale and practice of
court-based social governance in early twentieth-century America is
an urban story. But it is a *national* urban story. Until Prohibition got
the federal government into crime control and the New Deal created
new federal responsibilities for social insurance and public assistance,
the power to police and provide for citizens in the name of the public welfare resided chiefly in state and local governments. In contrast
to Edwardian England, no national policy-making elite orchestrated
criminal justice reform in America; local activists, voluntary associations, and judges set the agenda. The pace and extent of urban court
reform varied from city to city, as far as local political cultures and
legal traditions allowed. And yet the waves of court reform cresting
over Chicago, Philadelphia, New York, Boston, Detroit, Birmingham,
Atlanta, Cleveland, Buffalo, Kansas City, and other modern cities between 1900 and 1930 were not isolated incidents. The juvenile court
became the national standard for handling young offenders. At least
forty American cities redesigned their local judiciaries into centralized municipal court systems, modeled after the Municipal Court of
Chicago. Cities from Charlottesville, Virginia, to San Francisco created specialized courts to deal with specific classes of civil and criminal cases: small claims courts, landlord-tenant courts, family courts,
morals courts, women's courts, traffic courts, and courts for adolescent
offenders. Chicago's judges and reformers had a sense of their starring

role in a national drama: a broad-based progressive movement for the "organization of courts" and the "socialization of law."[1]

Late nineteenth-century penal reformers had shaken the individualistic moorings of the criminal law by pointing out the complicated causal origins of crime in an interdependent society. At the turn of the twentieth century, a rising generation of progressive legal academics, swept up in the transatlantic revolt against formalism in social and political thought, launched a much broader assault upon the individualistic, rights-based framework of American law and jurisprudence. By the early 1910s, the progressive rhetoric of socialized law had spilled over from the pages of law reviews and social science journals into mainstream public discourse. It gave court reformers, clergymen, legal aid activists, social workers, psychiatrists, psychologists, and welfare activists, working in different urban contexts across America, a common and compelling rationale for innovative new governmental approaches to managing urban populations. For legal scholars and social scientists, the new municipal courts served as experimental stations of socialized law.[2]

<hr/>

[1] Roscoe Pound, "Organization of Courts," [1914], *JAJS*, 11 (1927), 69–83. See Michael R. Belknap, *To Improve the Administration of Justice: A History of the American Judicature Society* (Chicago, 1992); Frederic B. Crossley, "Chief Justice Harry Olson and His Court,"*JAICLC*, 3 (1912), 346; "Editorial,"*JAJS*, 1 (1918), 131–32; Felix Frankfurter and James M. Landis, *The Business of the Supreme Court: A Study in the Federal Judicial System* (New York, 1927), 226–27; "Former Judge Harry Olson, Municipal Court Chief, Dies," *Chicago Daily News*, Aug. 1, 1935; "Harry Olson, Former Chief Justice, Dies," *Chicago Tribune*, Aug. 2, 1935; Herbert Harley, "Business Management for the Courts: As Exemplified by the Municipal Court of Chicago," *VLR*, 5 (1917), 1–26; [Herbert Harley], "Success of Organized Courts," *JAJS*, 1 (1918), 133–51; "To Reform Courts of Inferior Jurisdiction," *Survey*, 4 (1910), 177–79. For local press accounts, see, e.g., "Bar Would Abolish All Minor Courts," *St. Louis Republic*, Feb. 6, 1909; "Chicago's Municipal Court," *Birmingham Age-Herald*, March 24, 1912; "A Court That Runs like a Business Corporation," *New-York Daily Tribune*, Jan. 16, 1910; "Courts of the People," *Buffalo Express*, Feb. 6, 1909; "Reform of the Inferior Courts," *Boston Evening Transcript*, Feb. 21, 1912. And see the letters Olson received from reformers in other cities, MCC, boxes 2–3, and JHO, box 3.

[2] James Harrington Boyd, "Socialization of the Law," *AJS*, 22 (1917), 822–37; "How Far Can Court Procedure Be Socialized without Impairing Individual Rights?" in U.S. Department of Labor, Children's Bureau, *Proceedings of the Conference on Juvenile Court Standards* (Washington, 1922), 55–74; Benjamin N. Cardozo, *The Nature of the Judicial Process* (New Haven, 1921); Urban A. Lavery, "Some Tendencies of Social Legislation," *ILR*, 9 (1914), 24–31; Peter Alexander Speek, "The Need of a Socialized Jurisprudence," *AJS*, 22 (1917), 503–18. See Francois Ewald, "A Concept of Social Law," in *Dilemmas*

The progressive legal revolt was so fundamental and lasting as to constitute a new rationality of social governance, a new way of articulating the relationship between state and society and how that relationship ought to be governed. Socialized law, with its overt allusion to social justice, was a richly evocative name in an era that seemed intent on socializing everything. On its face, the phrase has the ring of a tautology. Isn't all law social, in the sense that all human interactions, whether more or less formalized, are social? But in early twentieth-century Europe and America, social law meant something more specific. For legal thinkers from Max Weber in Germany to Leon Duguit in France to Roscoe Pound in the United States, it meant law that purposefully reshaped society by directly addressing concrete problems of social life, such as legislation regulating the hours and wages of industrial workers, regulatory measures to inspect housing and police the milk supply, and social insurance systems. In America, where courts had the peculiar power to review and strike down legislation, the socialization of law also entailed a new "sociological jurisprudence": new conventions of legal reasoning that would force judges to explicitly consider the "social facts" and "social interests" – the actual contexts and consequences – of their decisions. Progressive critics of the American judiciary, such as Theodore Roosevelt and the political scientist Charles Beard, tended to exaggerate the laissez-faire leanings of appellate judges. But they were right that the liberal rule of law ideal at the heart of turn-of-the-century legal thought was inherently resistant to the sort of direct, discretionary, and continuous administration that a mature capitalist economy and pluralistic society seemed to demand. More than many progressives, Roscoe Pound, whose stature in American jurisprudence grew to exceed that of most Supreme Court justices, had a deep and prescient sense of the dangers that administrative power posed for human freedom. For him, court reform offered a way out of a difficult modern dilemma: how to reconcile the rule of law with social justice and control.[3]

of Law in the Welfare State, ed. Gunther Teubner (Berlin, 1986), 40–75; Barbara H. Fried, *The Progressive Assault on Laissez Faire: Robert Hale and the First Law and Economics Movement* (Cambridge, Mass., 1998); Morton J. Horwitz, *The Transformation of American Law, 1870–1960: The Crisis of Legal Orthodoxy* (New York, 1992); Edward A. Purcell, Jr., *The Crisis of Democratic Theory: Scientific Naturalism and the Problem of Value* (Lexington, Ky., 1973), 74–94; G. Edward White, "From Sociological Jurisprudence to Realism: Jurisprudence and Social Change in Early Twentieth-Century America," *VLR*, 58 (1972), 999–1028; Morton White, *Social Thought in America: The Revolt against Formalism* (Boston, 1957), 94–106.
3 Michel Foucault developed his idea of "governmental rationality" during a series of lectures in the 1970s. The concept is useful because it suggests

American and European reform writing of the late nineteenth and early twentieth centuries teems with references to "social law," "socialized law," and "sociological jurisprudence." Jurists and social scientists grew sharply critical of the "conceptualist" mode of late nineteenth-century legal science, which abstracted law from its social context and consequences and thus disguised law's political function in addressing competing claims to economic and political power. As early as 1872, the German legal philosopher Rudolph von Jhering rejected the premises of conceptualist jurisprudence, calling law an "uninterrupted labor" of "struggle," the dynamic outcome of "restless striving and working of a whole nation, afforded by its activity in the domain of economic and intellectual production." Max Weber criticized the widening gap between "the ideal 'legal order' of legal theory" and the "world of real economic conduct." In America, advocates of a socially conscious jurisprudence found a hero in Oliver Wendell Holmes, Jr. In his famous introduction to *The Common Law* (1881), Holmes asserted, "The life of the law has not been logic: it has been experience." The problem was that most judges did not give serious thought to how experience ought to shape the law. In his 1897 essay "The Path of the Law," Holmes urged judges to "consider more definitely and explicitly the social advantage on which the rule they lay down must be justified." Roscoe Pound defined the purposes of "sociological jurisprudence," a phrase he himself coined, in the boldest terms: "The main problem to which sociological jurists are addressing themselves to-day is to enable and to compel lawmaking, and also interpretation and application of legal rules, to take more account, and more intelligent account, of the social facts upon which law must proceed and to which it is to be applied." The intelligent accounting of social facts would need to take place at every level of the American legal order: in legislative law making, in judicial interpretation, and in the application of legal rules in courts and administrative agencies.[4]

the mutually constitutive processes of governance as ways of thinking and as practice. As Colin Gordon has explained, "A rationality of government will thus mean a way or system of thinking about the nature or the practice of government (who can govern; what governing is; what or who is governed), capable of making some form of that activity thinkable and practicable both to its practitioners and to those upon whom it is practiced." "Introduction," *The Foucault Effect: Studies in Governmentality*, ed. Graham Burchell, Colin Gordon, and Peter Miller (Chicago, 1991), 3.
[4] Jhering quoted in Boyd, "Socialization of the Law," 824–25; Max Weber, "The Economy and Social Norms," in Weber, *Economy and Society*, ed. Guenther Roth and Claus Wittich (Berkeley, 1978), 1: 312; Oliver Wendell Holmes, Jr.,

Throughout the industrializing western world in an age of violent class struggle, critical legal thinkers insisted that law was a social, historical, and political production; judges who sacrificed social legislation on the altar of abstract rights were a threat to social stability and an obstacle to progress. "The propertyless masses especially are not served by a formal 'equality before the law' and a 'calculable' adjudication and administration, as demanded by 'bourgeois' interests," Max Weber explained. "Naturally, in their eyes justice and administration should serve to compensate for their economic and social life-opportunities in the face of the propertied classes. Justice and administration can fulfill this function only if they assume an informal character to a far-reaching extent." Cleaving to the ideological course charted by progressives in America and social democrats in Europe, legal progressives helped forge a *via media* between socialism and classical liberalism that would widen the permissible scope of state intervention in the economy and society without effecting a wholesale redistribution of wealth and power. American progressives warned that the hostility of the courts to social legislation handed political dynamite to radicals. Even the *Chicago Tribune*, a stalwart defender of capital against organized labor, supported the general idea of socialized law. "If our judges were more aware of this broad current of tendency and more in sympathy with it," the paper editorialized in 1913, "radical attacks upon the courts would be fewer and less fundamentally just; radical legislation would be less frequent and less potent; radical feeling would be less poignant, concentrated, and pervasive."[5]

Despite its appeal in some quarters as a reformist alternative to socialism, socialized law was in fact a radical departure from the liberal assumptions taken on faith by much of the bar, bench, and legal academy at the turn of the century. The liberal ideal of a rule of law – "a government of laws, not men" – was a pillar of America's constitutional tradition and a core tenet of classical legal thought. The rule of law

The Common Law (Boston, 1946), 1; Oliver Wendell Holmes, Jr., "The Path of the Law," *HLR*, 10 (1897), 468; Roscoe Pound, "Scope and Purpose of Sociological Jurisprudence," *HLR*, 25 (1912), 512–13. See James E. Herget, "The Influence of German Thought on American Jurisprudence, 1880–1918," in *The Reception of Continental Ideas in the Common Law World 1820–1920*, ed. Mathias Reimann (Berlin, 1993), 203–28.

5 Max Weber, "Bureaucracy," in *From Max Weber: Essays in Sociology*, trans. and ed. H. H. Gerth and C. Wright Mills (New York, 1946), 221; "A Wise and Timely Warning," *Chicago Tribune*, March 1913, date illeg., HODS, box 1, "Municipal Court" file. See James T. Kloppenberg, *Uncertain Victory: Social Democracy and Progressivism in European and American Thought, 1870–1920* (New York, 1986).

expressed a vision of state power harnessed in universal legal restraints: Law must consist only of formal, generally applicable rules, rather than single out specific individuals or classes; retroactive legislation was forbidden; strict rules of procedure, spelled out in advance, must govern all legal activities. In a nation with a strong tradition of civil liberty, individual responsibility, and local self-government, the rule of law was never merely an expression of possessive individualism or laissez-faire. But in post–Civil War America, the rule of law ideal did take on a more formalized and individualistic meaning in constitutional law and legal science. In an explosive period of judicial review, state and federal appellate courts drew sharper lines between private and public, the individual and the state. And as legal scholars, caught up in the Gilded Age romance with the natural sciences, set out to discover and classify the generative principles of public and private law, the categories of the law grew even more formal and absolute.[6]

The thinly procedural conception of the rule of law in classical legal thought meshed well with the formalist way in which many judges of the era imagined, or at least represented, their rapidly changing society. Even judges in the most industrialized states conceived of the economy as a decentralized market – the neutral, self-regulating distributor of justly earned rewards. Their decisions expressed an idealized image of the individual as a rights-bearing, formally equal, moral free agent, whose freedom depended on the ingenious decentralized structure of the nation's political institutions: federalism, the tripartite separation of powers at every level of government, the distinctive American practice of judicial review. Although the Fourteenth Amendment radically reconfigured the place of the federal government and the American citizen in the constitutional order, state and federal judges vigorously defended the dual sovereignty of federalism, the ideal of separate powers, and the rights of local communities and state governments to classify and discriminate against their citizens on the basis of race. In reviewing particular kinds of legislation – most notably, measures to improve the wages and working conditions of industrial workers – they actually imposed new restraints on state police power. Although progressive critics exaggerated the extent of the American judiciary's deference to big business, many judges did indeed approximate the progressives' stereotype of the formalist judge: individualistic and conservative in their world view, precedent-bound and deductive in their style of legal reasoning, and aggressively

---

[6] Horwitz, *Transformation*, 9–31; William J. Novak, *The People's Welfare: Law and Regulation in Nineteenth-Century America* (Chapel Hill, 1996); White, "Sociological Jurisprudence."

apolitical in their self-representation, even as their decisions protected capitalist enterprise against legislation to regulate monopoly capital and the conditions of industrial labor. For progressive social thinkers, such legal formalism all too perfectly exemplified the head-in-the-sand attitudes and glaring contradictions of classical liberal individualism in a mass industrial society. They called for a fundamental reorientation of American jurisprudence to make the law a more historicist, pragmatic, realistic, social scientific enterprise. As John Dewey put it some years later, "[F]ailure to recognize that general legal rules and principles are working hypotheses, needing to be constantly tested by the way in which they work out in application to concrete situations, explains the otherwise paradoxical fact that the slogans of the liberalism of one period often become the bulwarks of reaction in a subsequent era."[7]

The infamous decision of the U.S. Supreme Court in *Lochner v. New York* (1905) was both the high-water mark of classical legal thought and a critical moment in the emergence of legal progressivism. The case involved a constitutional challenge to a New York statute, which set a maximum ten-hour workday for bakers. The statute was typical of the raft of "social legislation" that state legislatures enacted at the turn of the century to address the worst effects of industrialization. Among other public health purposes, the bakers' statute aimed to reduce respiratory disease caused by excessive exposure to flour dust. The Court struck down the statute. Writing for a slim five-to-four majority, Justice Rufus Peckham expressed the issue before the Court as a straightforward question of "which of two powers or rights shall prevail – the power of the State to legislate or the right of the individual to liberty of person and freedom of contract." The New York law, Peckham wrote, was like many statutes enacted in recent years that constituted "meddlesome interferences with the rights of the individual." The concept of "the individual," in Peckham's authoritative language, applied equally to the baker and his boss; each possessed an equal right to freely contract with one another and to set mutually advantageous terms of employment through a meeting of their individual wills. This "liberty of contract," the Court ruled, trumped the state's police power. This was how the rule of law, in classical legal theory, was supposed to work.[8]

The dissenting opinions in this narrowly decided case reveal a dramatic shift in the style and substance of judicial reasoning. Defending the statute's legitimacy as a public health measure, the dissenting

---

[7] Dewey quoted in Gerald E. Frug, *City Making: Building Communities without Building Walls* (Princeton, 1999), 4; Horwitz, *Transformation*, 4, 9–63.

[8] *Lochner v. New York*, 198 U.S. 45, 56, 61 (1905).

Justices Harlan, White, and Day countered the abstract logic of "liberty of contract" with social science data that documented the harmful health effects of bakers' long work days. The dissenters' reliance on concrete "social facts" put a new spin on the trope of legal science: Rather than model itself after the natural sciences, the law should now be a pragmatic, empirical, inductive discipline in the spirit of the social sciences. The dissenters' language implied an expanded field of administrative governance for the state, a field not to be tightly confined by formalist abstractions such as "liberty of contract" and "equality before the law." As Justice Holmes thundered in his famous separate dissent: "General propositions do not decide concrete cases." No single sentence could have more directly disputed the epistemological premises of classical legal thought. Exactly how a system of law without general propositions ought to work on the ground was a question the dissenters left to administrators and lower court judges to sort out, on a case-by-case basis.⁹

The sharpest critique of *Lochner* came from the pen of a rising progressive legal scholar at the University of Chicago named Roscoe Pound. In an acid-soaked essay for the *Yale Law Journal* in 1909, Pound exposed the recent vintage of the doctrine of "liberty of contract." No mention of "liberty of contract" could be found in political science classics such as Francis Lieber's *Civil Liberty and Self-Government* (1853) or John W. Burgess's *Political Science and Constitutional Law* (1890), and no decision had turned on this supposedly timeless doctrine until 1886. Since then, state and federal judges had brandished the doctrine to strike down social legislation that limited the hours of female factory workers, banned payment of wages in scrip, and outlawed "yellow dog" contracts (which forbade employees to join a union). "Why do so many [courts] force upon legislation an academic theory of equality in the face of practical conditions of inequality?" Pound asked. Why do the courts insist upon treating employers and laborers in industrial enterprises "as if the parties were individuals – as if they were farmers haggling over the sale of a horse? Why is the legal conception of the relation of employer and employee so at variance with the common knowledge of mankind?"¹⁰

⁹ *Lochner v. New York*, 198 U.S. 45, 65–74, 76 (1905).
¹⁰ Roscoe Pound, "Liberty of Contract," *YLJ*, 18 (May 1909), 454–87, esp. 454. See *Ritchie v. People*, 155 Ill. 98, 103 (1895); *Godcharles & Co. v. Wigeman*, 113 Pa. St. 431 (1886); *Adair v. U.S.*, 208 U.S. 161 (1908). Pound's historical reputation as a legal conservative does not do justice to the critical tone and reformist vision of his early work. See, e.g., Morton J. Horwitz, "The Conservative Tradition in the Writing of American Legal History," *AJLH*,

Pound's answer to his own query set the agenda for the style of legal reasoning he called "sociological jurisprudence." Liberty of contract, he argued, was a typical product of "mechanical jurisprudence," which he defined as "the rigorous logical deduction from predetermined conceptions in disregard of and often in the teeth of the actual facts." In their slavish adherence to "dead precedents" and abstract notions of individual rights, judges papered over glaring inequalities of economic and political power. The scholar called upon judges and jurists to adopt a new sociological jurisprudence and make their decisions reflect an explicit accounting of the social context and consequences of law. It was no coincidence that the publication of Pound's "Liberty of Contract" came so close on the heels of William James's *Pragmatism* (1907). Pound acknowledged the debt, defining sociological jurisprudence as "the movement for pragmatism as a philosophy of law, the movement for the adjustment of principles and doctrines to the human conditions they are to govern rather than to assumed first principles, the movement for putting the human factor in the central place and relegating logic to its true position as an instrument." Pound's work constituted a frontal assault on the epistemological basis and avowedly apolitical rhetoric of American law.[11]

Roscoe Pound (1870–1964) is well known today as a leading progressive legal thinker, the formidable dean of Harvard Law School (1916–36), and the founder of sociological jurisprudence, a movement remembered for the crucial ideological support it gave to progressive criticism of the courts and to the expansion of state intervention in the economy. Far less well known is Pound's complementary role as a critical intellectual figure in the history of urban

17 (1973), 275–94, which portrays Pound as emblematic of a "conservative tradition" in legal history writing that uses history to justify the existing legal order. With *Transformation of American Law* (1992), Horwitz softens this critique. Richard Hofstadter correctly noted many years ago that "for all his formal conservatism," Pound belongs among the roll call of "the distinguished social scientists of the Progressive era" who were "prominent in their criticism of vested interests or in their support for reform causes"; *The Age of Reform: From Bryan to F. D. R.* (New York, 1955), 154. Despite his enthusiasm for professional expertise and his desire to defend the political legitimacy of courts, Pound described legislation as "the most direct and accurate expression of the general will." Roscoe Pound, "Common Law and Legislation," *HLR*, 21 (1908), 407. See N. E. H. Hull, *Roscoe Pound and Karl Llewellyn: Searching for an American Jurisprudence* (Chicago, 1997).

[11] Pound, "Liberty of Contract," 462, 464; Roscoe Pound, "Mechanical Jurisprudence," *CLR*, 8 (1908), 604–23; William James, *Pragmatism*, ed. Bruce Kuklick (1907; Indianapolis, 1981).

Roscoe Pound as a rising young law professor at the University of Chicago, c. 1909, the year his brilliant article "Liberty of Contract" sounded his call for a new "sociological jurisprudence" and established him as the leading thinker of legal progressivism. Courtesy of the Special Collections Research Center, the University of Chicago Library.

judicial administration. Pound was one of the few legal scholars of his day to work through the implications of legal socialization for the everyday practice of local courts. His work bridged the gap between the everyday practices of urban courts and the theoretical issues at the center of socialized law. His speeches, articles, and books on judicial "organization" (centralization and bureaucratization) and legal "socialization" (making the law more responsive to "social interests") were widely influential, not only in American legal discourse, but also in social policy circles. Although written from his law school perches at Northwestern (1907–9), the University of Chicago (1909–10), and Harvard (1910–47), Pound's writings had a palpable influence on the shape and pace of court reform. For professionals working on criminal justice and welfare policy in the two decades before the New Deal, his writings on the socialization of law provided an ideological framework for understanding – and accelerating – the historic transformation under way in the law. Finally, Pound made a major institutional contribution as a founder of the American Institute of Criminal Law and Criminology at Northwestern in 1910. The institute's *Journal of Criminal Law and Criminology* was the leading forum for expert discussion of criminal justice issues in the 1910s and 1920s. With the strong support of Northwestern School of Law Dean John Henry Wigmore, the journal's pages brought together the voices of lawyers and judges with those of experts in the disciplines of social science, medicine, psychiatry, psychology, and social work, serving as a site of production for expert discourse on the causes of crime and the relationship between law and the disciplines in modern social regulation.[12]

Pound's ideas are uniquely and reciprocally intertwined with the history of the Municipal Court of Chicago, which he called "a thoroughly organized modern court with power to make the law an effective instrument of justice." The court provided him with an endless source of empirical evidence and intellectual inspiration.[13] Pound lived in Chicago during the Municipal Court's early years, and he remained an avid reader of the court's annual reports. "I have made it a point for many years to study these reports carefully and find them full of meat for my purposes," he told Chief Justice Olson in a 1918 letter.[14] As one might expect, Harry Olson did not shrug off the attentions of one of America's best-known jurists. Like many progressive court reformers, he used Pound's language to explain and justify socialized law to the public. Olson's own copious articles and speeches on court reform, socialized judicial administration, and eugenics bore the visible impress of the scholar's ideas, and it is clear that he found in Pound's scholarship a wealth of insight and, to be sure, legitimation. For a time, the

---

[12] James W. Garner, "The American Institute of Criminal Law and Criminology," *JAICLC*, 1 (May 1910), 2–5; James W. Garner, "Plan of the Journal," ibid., 5–7. U.S. Department of Labor, Children's Bureau, *The Child, the Family, and the Court: A Study of the Administration of Justice in the Field of Domestic Relations*, part I: *General Findings and Recommendations*, by Bernard Flexner, Reuben Oppenheimer, and Katharine F. Lenroot (Washington, 1929), 2–5. See Paul D. Carrington, "The Missionary Diocese of Chicago," *Journal of Legal Education*, 44 (1993), 507; Thomas A. Green, "Freedom and Criminal Responsibility in the Age of Pound: An Essay on Criminal Justice," *MLR*, 93 (1995), esp. 1951–58.

[13] Pound, "Organization of Courts," 80, 79–83; Roscoe Pound, "The Administration of Justice in the Modern City," *HLR*, 26 (1913), 315, 313, n. 29; 314–19, 326; Roscoe Pound, *The Spirit of the Common Law* (Boston, 1921), xii–xiii.

[14] Roscoe Pound to Harry Olson, Dec. 9, 1918, Roscoe Pound Papers, Harvard Law Library, box 76, folder 1. See also the letters from Pound to Olson in JHO, box 7.

judge and the jurist were affiliated institutionally. Olson served on a committee of the American Institute for Criminal Law and Criminology in 1909. In 1913, the men helped found the American Judicature Society, a Chicago-based association that spread the gospel of court organization to cities and states across the nation.[15]

Roscoe Pound stormed the national stage of legal reform in 1906. A native of Lincoln, Nebraska, with a free-ranging intellect – in 1897, he earned the University of Nebraska's first Ph.D., in botany, of all things – Pound was still the largely unknown dean of the Nebraska law school when the American Bar Association invited him to speak at its annual meeting in St. Paul. Addressing a profession acquainted with legal history largely as an exercise in self-legitimation, Dean Pound held forth on "The Causes of Popular Dissatisfaction with the Administration of Justice." He inveighed against the "sporting theory of justice" that reduced every courtroom to an arena of conflict. He called American courts "archaic," their procedure woefully "behind the times." Just as anachronistic as the forms and institutions of the law, he declared, was the "individualist spirit of our common law, which agrees ill with a collectivist age." Dean Wigmore of the Northwestern University School of Law later recalled that "the conservative hearers sat in dumb dismay and hostile horror at the deliverances of the daring iconoclast." Soon after the meeting, Wigmore invited Pound to Northwestern.[16]

Surely, it is no coincidence that Pound's conception of the historic direction of American society from a homogeneous nation of towns and farms to a modern urban-industrial society resembled his own journey from the Lincoln of his birth to the Second City in the early twentieth century. Chicago was the leading center of progressive legal scholarship in the 1900s, home to such notable scholar-activists

[15] The chief justice even borrowed a speech title directly from Pound. See Harry Olson, "The Administration of Justice in the Modern City," undated speech typescript, JHO, box 3. In 1913, Olson ordered from the *Harvard Law Review* fifty copies of Pound's article of the same name, which praised the Municipal Court. W. S. Warfield III to Harry Olson, Feb. 18, 1913, JHO, box 7; Garner, "American Institute"; "Bulletins of the American Institute of Criminal Law and Criminology," Bulletin No. 1, July 1909, *JAICLC*, 118–121; Henry M. Hyde, "Chicago Bureau Leads Fight for Judicial Reform," *Chicago Tribune*, Oct. 30, 1913.

[16] Roscoe Pound, "The Causes of Popular Dissatisfaction with the Administration of Justice," reprinted in *JAJS*, 20 (1927), 178–87, esp. 182, 183, 181; John H. Wigmore, "Roscoe Pound's St. Paul Address of 1906," *JAJS*, 177; Carrington, "Missionary Diocese," 507. See Hull, *Roscoe Pound and Karl Llewellyn*; Paul Sayre, *The Life of Roscoe Pound* (Iowa City, 1948); David Wigdor, *Roscoe Pound, Philosopher of Law* (Westport, Conn., 1974).

as Pound, Wigmore, and Ernst Freund, and it served as the site for
many legal progressives' imaginative encounters with the modern city.
Pound's encounters ran deeper than most. Edith Abbott, a former
student from Lincoln and now a pioneer of scientific social work at
the Chicago School of Civics and Philanthropy, introduced him to the
community of activist intellectuals who congregated at Hull-House,
including political scientist Charles Edward Merriam and philosopher
George Herbert Mead. Pound served for a time with Freund and Jane
Addams on the settlement's Juvenile Court Committee, the direct pre-
cursor to the Juvenile Protective Association, which would play a leading role in socializing the Municipal Court of Chicago during the teens.
The committee assisted in the Cook County Juvenile Court's day-to-
day operations, raising funds to pay probation officers and founding a
detention home for defendants awaiting a hearing. Through the University of Chicago's Social Science Club, Pound became acquainted
with more of the era's leading social scientists, including Albion Small,
who gave Pound a forum in the *American Journal of Sociology*. Pound's
move to the University of Chicago School of Law in 1909 could have
only strengthened his ties to these South Side reform communities.[17]

Legal progressivism involved a fertile encounter of law with social
science – especially the empirical sciences of economics, statistics, and
sociology. (In the 1920s, a rising movement of law school academics,
dubbed "legal realists," would carry forth this progressive struggle to
transform law into a social science.) As a colleague of leading sociologists such as Small and Edward A. Ross, and as a prolific contributor to and eager consumer of the burgeoning literature of sociology,
Pound noted with embarrassment the wide gap between the rulings
of the courts and the findings of social science. "To economists and
sociologists," he wrote in 1908, "judicial attempts to force Benthamite
conceptions of freedom of contract and common law conceptions of
individualism upon the public of today are no less amusing – or even
irritating – than legislative attempts to do away with or get away from
these conceptions are to bench and bar."[18]

For Pound, the pressing question of law's role in modern society boiled down to two intertwined problems: "socialization" – the
"world-wide" movement for reforming law to meet popular demands
for "social justice" – and "organization" – the administrative imperative to consolidate the decentralized legal institutions inherited from
the nineteenth century and make them more efficient instruments

[17] Carrington, "Missionary Diocese," 508–11; Lela B. Costin, *Two Sisters for
Social Justice: A Biography of Grace and Edith Abbott* (Urbana, Ill., 1983), 18–19.
[18] Pound, "Common Law and Legislation," 384.

of social management. Pound's understanding of these two broad legal problems, socialization and organization, formed his perspective on urban judicial reform. Description and prescription merged in Pound's writings. Like many progressives, he viewed American history through the prism of present political concerns, which led him, at times, to exaggerate the individualism of nineteenth-century law and the homogeneity and liberal consensus of nineteenth-century society. In Pound's narrative of legal history, socialization and organization appeared both as inevitable legal-historical processes and as urgent directions for reform.

Following Jhering, Pound argued that legal socialization required abandoning individual rights as the sine qua non of legal philosophy and refocusing jurisprudence on the interplay of competing "social interests." In his 1872 volume *Der Kampf ums Recht* (*The Struggle for Law*) and other works, Jhering had rejected the conceptualist premise that law existed to protect an abstract individual will through a system of rights. Instead, he viewed law in more pluralistic terms as the dynamic outcome of struggles between individuals and groups advancing competing interests. Rights were not timeless concepts but interests that had successfully claimed the protection of law.[19] As Pound saw it, once "social interests" were recognized as "the ultimate idea behind rights," the function of law changed. Law no longer existed to protect timeless individual rights but, rather, to balance the time-bound interests against other interests. "When natural rights are put in this form," he wrote, "it becomes evident that these individual interests are at most on no higher plane than social interests, and, indeed, for the most part get their significance for jurisprudence from a social interest in giving effect to them." The "social interest in the individual life" was not inherently superior to other social interests, such as those in the "general security," in the "general progress," or in the conservation of resources.[20]

Pound's theory of "social interests" was an evocative way of representing a shift from individualism to pluralism in American political culture more generally: a reconceptualization of the purpose of law and governance in progressive politics from the protection of abstract

[19] Boyd, "Socialization of the Law," 824–26; Herget, "Influence of German Thought," 205–7; Max Weber, "The Formal Qualities of Modern Law," *Economy and Society*, 2: 882–89, 897–98, n. 20.

[20] Roscoe Pound, "The End of Law as Developed in Legal Rules and Doctrines," *HLR*, 27 (1914), 225–26. He presented his typology of interests in a series of lectures on criminal justice in 1923, later published as Roscoe Pound, *Criminal Justice in America* (New York, 1930), 5–9.

individual rights to the satisfaction of human "needs." Rather than
the essentially negative social role of defending a bundle of individual
rights – policing boundaries among individuals and between individuals and the state – the essentially positive purpose of socialized law was
to balance and manage competing social interests, including "the social interest in the full moral and social life of every individual." "Such
a movement is taking place palpably in the law of all countries today,"
Pound wrote. "Its watchword is the satisfaction of human wants, and
it seems to put as the end of law the satisfaction of as many human
demands as we can with the least sacrifice to other demands. This new
state of legal development may be called the socialization of law."[21]

Pound's conception of the "social interest in the individual life" was
vague but important. It represented his sense that individuals living in
modern society had acquired certain positive rights, secured through
the social interest in those rights. These attributes of a new social citizenship included "individual free self-assertion, physical, mental, and
economic"; "individual opportunity... that all individuals shall have
fair opportunities, political, physical, social, and economic"; and the
social interest dictating "that each individual shall have secured to him
the conditions of at least a minimum human life under the circumstances of life in the time and place." But when the "social interest in
the individual life" conflicted with other social interests, socialized law
might not come down on the side of individual freedom. In his 1915
essays on the "Interests of Personality," written as war raged in Europe
and dissent grew at home, Pound couched his discussion of the affirmative social interest in the individual "personality," including the
"free exercise of one's mental and spiritual faculties," with a warning
about the limits of free expression:

> The social interest in the free development of the individual
> must be weighed with the social interest in the state as a social
> institution.... Where men live congested in large cities, especially
> where there are great numbers subjected to severe economic pres-
> sure who are more or less ignorant of the local political institutions
> and more or less ignorant of the language in which the law is ex-
> pressed, the danger of mobs, which are controlled by suggestion,
> may require confining of free expression of political opinions on cer-
> tain subjects to times and places where such things may be discussed
> without grave danger of violence and disorder.

[21] Pound, "End of Law," 229, 226; Walter Lippmann, *A Preface to Politics* (1914;
Ann Arbor, 1962). On the politics of needs, see Philip J. Ethington, *The
Public City: The Political Construction of Urban Life in San Francisco, 1850–1900*
(Cambridge, 1994), 345–407.

The danger of urban immigrant mobs tipped the scales of interest in favor of state security.[22]

Pound's portrayal of law's function as a balancing act, the weighing of competing interests, reflected a significant trend in the law. This was the rise of "balancing tests" in many areas of the law after 1910, including the "rule of reason" test in antitrust and the "clear and present danger" test for free speech. The emergence of the balancing test signaled a more administrative and managerial role for legal institutions, a trend that posed the second major problem of Pound's jurisprudence: "organization."[23]

Legal history, Pound argued, was marked by pendulum swings from periods in which common-law courts dominated the business of dispensing justice ("legal justice") to eras in which administrative bodies superseded the courts' role ("justice without law"). In sixteenth-century England, three centuries of dominance by the common-law courts had given way to an era of administrative governance in the Court of Star Chamber and other tribunals where summary procedure reigned. In Pound's cyclical narrative, swings toward "justice without law" occurred when law had lagged too far behind "the moral sense of the community." But these necessary corrections must never be allowed to become permanent; the "legal yoke" must be thrown back upon executive justice to defend the people against the arbitrary discretion of administrators. "For executive justice is an evil, even if sometimes a necessary evil," Pound cautioned. "It has always been, and in the long run it always will be, crude and as variable as the personalities of officials."[24]

In late nineteenth-century America the pendulum had once again swung violently in the direction of discretionary administrative justice. Pound blamed the explosion of judicial review in state and federal courts after the Civil War, and the particular hostility of the courts to social legislation, for setting the pendulum in motion. Lawmakers responded by handing over pressing governmental business to administrative agencies that were more insulated than courts and legislatures from judicial review. Administrative bodies ruled on water rights

---

[22] Roscoe Pound, "Interests of Personality," *HLR*, 28 (1915), 343–65, 445–56, esp. 453, 455. See David M. Rabban, "Free Speech in Progressive Social Thought," *TLR*, 74 (1996), 951–1038. Rabban argues that Pound exhibited greater sympathy for free political expression after witnessing the federal government's repression of political dissent during and after World War I. Ibid., 1014–17.

[23] Horwitz, *Transformation*, 18.

[24] Pound, "Organization of Courts," 71, 73.

in the western states. Commissions investigated and regulated public utilities, unhampered by legal rules of evidence. Workman's compensation acts transferred a growing class of tort litigation from courts to administrative bodies. Even in the criminal law – "par excellence the domain of the common law" – parole boards had seized discretionary sentencing powers. "Truly there is danger that, whereas but yesterday the courts played the chief role in the practical conduct of affairs, tomorrow there will be nothing of any real moment left to them," Pound mused. Herbert Harley, the secretary of the American Judicature Society, echoed Pound's concerns about the growing public reliance on administrative agencies to "adjudicate the living issues of modern law." Harley warned, "We might easily forecast a day not far distant when our courts, still dignified and ritualistic, would be holding an empty bag, good for nothing but spanking delinquent juveniles, keeping books for dead men, sorting out crazy folk, marrying couples, and collecting bills for the grocer and the butcher."[25]

Much of Roscoe Pound's prodigious output can be read in precisely this spirit (though, alas, without Harley's flair for the picturesque): as an attempt to save common law courts from the jurisdictional imperialism of the modern administrative state. The legal realists who claimed to be stunned by Pound's hostility toward the New Deal in the late 1930s and the historians who have speculated about the motives for Pound's supposed "about-face" on the administrative state have overlooked this bright thread in his work. Saving the law by reforming it was the chief motive behind Pound's advocacy of both the "socialization of law" and the "organization" of the nation's courts, which he hoped would make the courts more competitive with administrative agencies.[26]

Pound argued that America's decentralized system of courts, designed for a society of farming communities and small towns, was no match for the demands made upon it by a population exploding in numbers and diversity. His solution was to unify state court systems on a bureaucratic model and establish specialized branch courts, so that judges might become specialists in a field of litigation. He advocated modern record-keeping and the careful supervision of administrative personnel by judges. "If ... we meet the movement away from law by modernizing the legal and judicial machinery which will enable it to meet more effectively the demands of the present," he wrote, "we may

---

[25] Ibid., 71, 69–70; Herbert Harley, "Business Management for the Courts: As Exemplified by the Municipal Court of Chicago," *VLR*, 5 (1917), 24–25.

[26] Pound, "Organization of Courts," 82; Horwitz, *Transformation*, 217–20. See Afterword.

be confident that now, as in Tudor and Stuart England, the law will prevail."[27]

The problems of organization and socialization took on an added urgency in the industrial cities of the United States. Pound laid out his concerns and program in an influential 1913 article in the *Harvard Law Review* entitled "The Administration of Justice in the Modern City." He argued that the "common law polity" of the nineteenth century – with its particularistic courts, cumbersome procedural protections, and reliance upon traditional social controls – had created more bedlam than order in the modern city. The structure of American legal institutions presupposed an Anglo-Saxon country of farms and villages, but decades of industrialization, immigration, and urban growth had created the modern city, which Pound portrayed as "a heterogeneous community, divided into classes with divergent interests, which understand each other none too well; containing elements ignorant of our institutions." Pointing to the Municipal Court of Chicago as a model, he urged that urban courts be organized and their scope of administration broadened to include social and moral jurisdictions once policed by family, church, and community. The simultaneous expansion of state power and attenuation of procedural rights were necessary means to the end of socialized law: to "secure the social interest in the moral and social life of every individual under the circumstances of the modern city."[28]

The social interest in the individual life had a complicated, double-edged meaning in the modern city with its heterogeneous populations. It imposed an affirmative duty upon local courts, as instruments of the state, to satisfy basic human wants and needs, to provide swift and cheap justice in minor civil cases, and to assist the individual in self-actualization by creating opportunity and providing the conditions necessary to a "minimum human life." The social interest also justified a new role for courts in investigating and ameliorating the "social facts" that underlay criminality in an urban-industrial community. These

---

[27] Pound, "Organization of Courts," 73.
[28] Pound, "Administration of Justice," 311, 310, 302–28. Pound's theory rested on assumptions about "modernization" shared by many of his contemporaries in social science, including his University of Nebraska colleague E. A. Ross. Edward Alsworth Ross, *Social Control: A Survey of the Foundations of Order* (New York, 1901). "Chicago School" sociologists posited that modernization (accelerated industrialization, immigration, and urbanization) fostered social "disorganization" (the breakdown of family and community relationships), which rendered obsolete the traditional social controls of home, church, and community. Robert E. Park, Ernest W. Burgess, and Roderick D. McKenzie, *The City* (Chicago, 1925).

social facts included structural factors such as unjust wages and working conditions, unsanitary housing, and poor educational systems. But they also included a range of more personal factors. Defendants' "home life," habits, and mental makeup became "social facts," not just in Pound's writing but in the exploding social science and reform literatures on urban crime. In eugenics-tinged language reminiscent of the writings of his friend Edward A. Ross, Pound noted the challenge of administering "punitive justice in a community where the defective, the degenerate of decadent stocks, and the ignorant or enfeebled victim of severe economic pressure are exposed to temptations and afforded opportunities beyond anything our fathers could have conceived." Pound and other progressives endorsed a diverse range of experimental techniques for addressing these social facts: the expansion of summary justice (trial by judges only) in misdemeanor and quasicriminal cases, psychological examination of defendants in court-based clinics, and the new state surveillance of probation. The same rationale later justified compulsory medical treatment of accused prostitutes for venereal disease. Under the circumstances of city life, the social interest in the individual life was both affirmative and coercive.[29]

The double-edged implications of socialized law in the modern city would achieve their fullest realization not in the pages of law reviews but in the everyday practice of city courts. While he was pulling together the Municipal Court of Chicago's *Seventh Annual Report* in 1913, Chief Justice Harry Olson paused to reflect on the court's rapid transformation into a modern "socialized court." The mere fact of this annual report – a 150-page compendium of policy statements, budget charts, and criminological statistics – showcased the superior efficiency of America's model organized court. A bureaucracy of more than 300 clerks and bailiffs processed the 180,000 demands for justice that police officers, social workers, and aggrieved citizens laid at the doorstep of the Municipal Court in 1913, and channeled them into thirty branch courts, including two specialized criminal branches: the Domestic Relations Court and the Morals Court. Olson announced that he would soon open a third socialized branch for young male offenders. Each new branch embodied the ideals of legal socialization and the social conception of crime within the rationalized design of an organized court. The chief justice mused,

> The development of branch courts with resulting specialization, expertness, equipment for meeting current needs, [and] opportunity for adopting constructive policies, has proved that a city court can be

[29] Pound, "Administration of Justice," 311.

much more than was deemed possible only a few years ago. It proved also what few understood, that the court is one most significant social factor; it is the gateway through which must pass all those who need the counsel and assistance, as well as the restraint of their fellow men.

Olson's description of the Municipal Court of Chicago as a "gateway" is suggestive but also a little deceptive. The court did serve as a major point of confluence between urban society and the local state. But gateway is too passive a metaphor. Through the agencies of the police, probation officers, social workers, and voluntary associations, the court *reached out* into society. Combining therapeutic ideologies of social intervention and individual treatment with eugenic techniques for population management and racial betterment, the Municipal Court governed everyday life in Chicago.[30]

As Roscoe Pound's deeply thoughtful (and, at times, deeply troubling) writings attest, striking a just and effective balance between the rule of law and administrative power, even in the law-bound setting of an organized court, was a delicate matter. European and American jurists and social theorists continue to puzzle over this dilemma today. Pound expressed confidence that rationally organized courts, presided over by well-trained judges assisted by professional social experts, would deliver socialized law to the heterogeneous populations of the modern city and restore faith in the law by bringing it back into sync with "the moral sense of the community." Investing a new scope of social governance in the courts, he insisted, would quell popular dissatisfaction with the law without letting the pendulum swing too far in the direction of magisterial discretion and "executive justice." Whether Pound intended them to or not, his writings thus provide a historically situated and pragmatic ethical framework with which to assess the complex human consequences of socialized law in action. For Pound's work raised a question that only the passage of time could answer: By making legal power more bureaucratic and administrative, did legal socialization enable courts to respond more effectively to human needs, without letting them tread too hard on that venerable commitment to human freedom, which, after all, lay at the heart of the liberal rule of law ideal?[31]

---

[30] *MCC* 7 (1913), 87.
[31] William E. Scheuerman, ed., *The Rule of Law under Siege: Selected Essays of Franz L. Neumann and Otto Kirchheimer* (Berkeley, 1996), esp. 1–25; Jurgen Habermas, *Between Facts and Norms: Contributions to a Discourse Theory of Law and Democracy*, trans. William Rehg (Cambridge, Mass., 1996).

Part II

Practices

Interlude: Socialized Law in Action

The paradoxical quality of socialized law – the tension between its progressive promise of social justice and its darker implications for social control – received little serious attention at the level of legal theory. To be sure, for many progressive legal thinkers there was no paradox to ponder. The stability of a complex capitalist economy and urban-industrial society required purposeful state intervention. The only questions worth debating were what form this "social control" should take. Should it be primarily private or public in character, legal or administrative? And how far should it penetrate specific areas of social and economic life? For Roscoe Pound, making American courts more bureaucratic, professional, and flexible instruments of social governance was the best way to assure the survival of legal authority in an age of social-political movements, monopoly capitalism, industrial cities, and polyglot populations. Socialization would restore the viability of the courts as the sentinels of human liberty against arbitrary executive power, while compelling judges to take notice of the quintessential social fact: that the inescapable interdependence of modern life had profoundly and irreversibly altered the meaning of liberty itself.

As the scope and vigor of individual free will and responsibility diminished in the progressive imagination, and as new cultural conventions of causal attribution ascribed ever greater significance to impersonal social forces, liberty acquired a new meaning as "the satisfaction of human wants." The new liberty was both more dependent on affirmative governmental power and more contingent in light of the clashing interests of a pluralistic social order. For progressive jurists, social scientists, and activists, sociological jurisprudence provided an authoritative yet flexible legal language for articulating this changing relationship between the liberal state and its citizens. As the constitutional historian Henry Steele Commager once observed, progressive

119

jurists "saw law not primarily as a concise body of principles regulating
the relationship between the individual and his government but as a
sprawling body of practices conditioning the conduct of the individual
in his society." The consequences of socialized law for the citizens of a
democratic society could be known only at the level of those sprawling
practices.[1]

The four chapters in Part II examine the concrete embodiment and
application of socialized law in one particularly influential set of local state practices: the criminal jurisdiction of the Municipal Court
of Chicago. During the early 1910s, the high tide of progressivism in
American political life, the Municipal Court emerged as a national
exemplar of socialized law in action. Building upon the court's international reputation as a widely replicated model of rational judicial
organization and procedural reform, Chief Justice Harry Olson and
local social activists took on the even more ambitious task of changing
the way the court handled criminal cases. In the everyday operations
of the Municipal Court, socialized law joined criminal legal authority
to the disciplinary power of probation officers, psychiatrists, and professional social workers, including those placed in the courts by local
voluntary associations and charities. Socialized law made headway in
all of the court's criminal branches. All of them, for example, relied
upon the court's new staff of salaried probation officers to investigate
the home life and work histories of defendants, to advise judges on
the best individual treatment for each case, and to keep offenders
in line during probation. But socialized law had its greatest effect on
those particular classes of offenders for whom Olson created special
socialized branch courts.[2]

After the fashion of the Cook County Juvenile Court, each of the
socialized branch courts originated in a cooperative effort of judges
and voluntary associations active in criminal justice, moral reform, and
public welfare in Chicago. Each court addressed an area of pressing
public concern and moral anxiety by turning it into a distinct criminal
jurisdiction.

In 1911, as the General Assembly put the final touches on the adult
probation law, Olson collaborated with the Juvenile Protective Association (JPA), the women-led voluntary association based at Hull-House,
to establish the Court of Domestic Relations. At a time of serious public

[1] Henry Steele Commager, *The American Mind: An Interpretation of American Thought and Character since the 1880's* (New Haven, 1950), 380.
[2] See Harry Olson, "The Municipal Court of Chicago: A Tribunal of Proce-
dural Reform and Social Service," reprinted from the *San Francisco Recorder*,
May 12, 1916.

concern about the instability of working-class families and the consequent demands for public assistance, Olson and the JPA designed the Court of Domestic Relations to enforce more efficiently and humanely the Progressive Era criminal statutes against desertion and nonsupport. Most of the court's defendants were workingmen arrested for shirking their legal duty to support their families. But the court's social staff worked intensively with defendants' wives and children as well.

Olson had served in 1910 on the famous Chicago Vice Commission, a blue-ribbon body of private citizens, church leaders, businessmen, law enforcement officials, and social scientists commissioned by Mayor Fred A. Busse to investigate the Second City's spectacularly open and extensive market in women's "bodies and souls." The commission's nationally publicized report, *The Social Evil in Chicago* (1911), called for a special tribunal to handle all of the city's criminal cases related to prostitution. In 1913, Olson created the Morals Court for that purpose. Almost all of the defendants tried and "treated" there were women. The court served as a public forum for exposing and policing the root causes of prostitution and for interpreting the changing place of women in urban society.[3]

In 1914, the JPA waged a new public campaign. In a well-publicized expose of the local jails, JPA president Louise de Koven Bowen protested that young male offenders, still in the throes of adolescence and only a year or two above juvenile court age, were routinely jailed and tried with hardened criminals. The association again collaborated with Olson to create America's first specialized criminal court for young men between the ages of seventeen and twenty-one. The effort of Boys' Court judges to apply the concept of social responsibility for crime and the socialized techniques of juvenile justice to young men in the prime of their "criminal careers," many of whom were charged with serious felonies, was perhaps the Progressive Era's most daring test of the idea that no one is fully responsible for his criminal acts.[4]

That same year, Olson opened the Psychopathic Laboratory, a criminological clinic that serviced all of the Municipal Court's criminal branches. The laboratory was the central institution in the court's extensive eugenics program. The laboratory tested defendants for hereditary "mental defects" and developed scientific profiles of criminal personality. The Municipal Court judges used the laboratory not only to control urban crime but also govern the urban

---

[3] VCC, *The Social Evil in Chicago: A Study of Existing Conditions* (Chicago, 1911).
[4] Louise de Koven Bowen, *Boys in the County Jail: Their Needs* (Chicago, 1913).

population at large. The most extreme example of socialized law's authoritarian potential, court-based eugenics addressed the fears of a nation deeply concerned about its own biological and racial destiny. For all of the cultural freight it carried, however, eugenic jurisprudence was decidedly a product of mainstream progressive legal ideology.[5]

"It is a maxim of legal history," a U.S. Children's Bureau report on socialized courts observed in 1928, "that it is easier to effect a change in the substantive law than it is to effect a change in procedure." In common-law countries, where procedural restraints on state power have an almost mythic status as the ramparts of human freedom, this maxim has often seemed to have the wisdom of the ages behind it. But it was in precisely this area that Progressive Era court reform made its most decisive break with the common law.[6]

The reform of criminal procedure in the Municipal Court resembled the earlier innovations in the administration of economic disputes in civil cases. Judges specialized in a distinct field of cases. Whether their jurisdiction consisted of small claims or prostitution cases, specialization emboldened judges to think of themselves as experts and makers of social policy, rather than as impartial umpires in an adversarial contest. Formal strictures of common-law procedure were loosened to allow for a more direct, "inquisitorial" style of judging that contemporary observers described as more in line with Continental traditions of judging than the conventional practice of common-law courts. In both civil and criminal cases, parties typically waived their rights to jury trials – rights exercised at a cost of six dollars in the Municipal Court – leaving all questions of fact and law to judges. The court published statistics that totaled up, for the interested public, the caseload of each branch court, fines levied and sentences served, and demographic profiles of criminal defendants. Olson provided space in the court's annual reports for judges presiding in the specialized criminal branches to describe their work; the judges threw themselves in to the task, composing miniature treatises on socialized law in action. All of the Municipal Court's thirty civil and criminal branches handled cases that originated outside the court itself, in the troubled social and economic relations

---

[5] Michael Willrich, "The Two Percent Solution: Eugenic Jurisprudence and the Socialization of American Law, 1900–1930," *LHR*, 16 (1998), 63–111.

[6] U.S. Department of Labor, Children's Bureau, *The Child, the Family, and the Court: A Study of the Administration of Justice in the Field of Domestic Relations*, part I: *General Findings and Recommendations*, by Bernard Flexner, Reuben Oppenheimer, and Katharine F. Lenroot (Washington, 1929), 18.

of everyday life in the industrial city. Criminal proceedings were initiated by relatives, neighbors, and social reformers in addition to the police. But in the specialized criminal courts, which had their own staffs of social personnel, the case itself was only the starting point, the point of entry for a broader range of interventions that included probing personal interviews, visits to defendants' homes, assistance in finding new employment, referrals to charitable agencies, and compulsory psychiatric and medical examinations. Across urban America, a rising class of professional social experts found in socialized law a means of expanding their cultural authority and public power. As trained professionals in the rich new field of social knowledge and personality adjustment – the "personal problems jurisdiction," in sociologist Andrew Abbott's apt phrase – the experts quickly established themselves as indispensable personnel of urban socialized courts.[7]

It was no accident that the socialized branch courts dealt most aggressively with issues of domestic life, adolescent criminality, and sexual norms. The rhetoric and administrative logic of socialized law required the construction of a recognizable social jurisdiction that could not be adequately addressed by previous legal structures. The progressives' well-documented alarm over the "breakdown" of the family in urban-industrial society and the revolution in morals and manners taking place among young working-class men and women provided sturdy ideological timber for this project. The involvement of women's reform groups such as the JPA and the Chicago Women's Club as creators and promoters of socialized courts also assured a focus on domestic relations, a gendered field of investigation and intervention that women benevolent reformers had carved out for themselves in the nineteenth century and which female social workers were aggressively taking over in the twentieth. The very word "social," when placed opposite "law" in reform literature, connoted both the modern and the scientific techniques of individual treatment and the jurisdiction of the domestic. The 1913 *Handbook for the Women Voters of Illinois*, published on the occasion of women winning the right to vote for local offices in the state, noted the significance of the Municipal Court to the causes of newly enfranchised women: "As a local court it is largely important because of its attempt to treat the cases before it from a social as well as from a legal point of view." Judges of the socialized branches appealed directly to progressive women in their reelection

---

[7] Andrew Abbott, *The System of Professions: An Essay on the Division of Expert Labor* (Chicago, 1988), 280–314. See Judge Willis B. Perkins, "Family Courts," *JAJS*, 3 (1919), 19–21.

campaigns. "WOMEN CAN VOTE FOR THIS OFFICE," announced a 1914
campaign poster for Judge Charles N. Goodnow, "Originator and First
Judge of 'The Court of Domestic Relations.'"[8]
The 1928 Children's Bureau report was produced by two male
lawyers and a female social worker – a gendered division of labor characteristic of socialized law. The report summed up the procedural
revolution of the previous two decades:

> The distinction between the new procedure and the old common-
> law ways cannot be overemphasized. The old courts relied upon the
> learning of lawyers; the new courts depend more upon psychiatrists
> and social workers. The evidence before the old courts was brought
> by the parties; most of the evidence before the new courts is obtained
> by the courts themselves. The old courts relied upon precedents; the
> new courts have few to follow.... The judgments of the old courts
> were final, save for appeal; in the new courts, appeals are infrequent,
> and the judgment of the court is often only the beginning of the
> treatment of the case. In the old courts the jury was a vital factor;
> in the new courts, in practice, the jury is discarded. The system of
> the old courts was based upon checks and balances; the actual power
> of the new courts is practically unlimited. Justice in the old courts
> was based on legal science; in the new courts it is based on social
> engineering.

The authors did warn, somewhat as an afterthought, that socialized
procedure carried within it the "danger of all magisterial justice." But,
they insisted, "the theory of the new procedure is sound because it is
adapted to modern conditions."[9]
Each of the next four chapters retraces the path of socialized law as it
moved into a new domain of the criminal universe that was particularly
vulnerable to social thinking about criminal responsibility and to socialized strategies of criminal justice: the delinquency of working-class
families (the Court of Domestic Relations), prostitution and pandering (the Morals Court), the full range of crimes committed by young

[8] Alice Greenacre, *A Handbook for the Women Voters of Illinois*, ed. Sophonisba
P. Breckinridge (Chicago, 1913), 46. The poster can be found in Chicago
Municipal Court, "Miscellaneous Pamphlets," Chicago Historical Society.
See Regina G. Kunzel, *Fallen Women, Problem Girls: Unmarried Mothers and the
Professionalization of Social Work, 1890–1945* (New Haven, 1993); Elizabeth
Lunbeck, *The Psychiatric Persuasion: Knowledge, Gender, and Power in Modern
America* (Princeton, 1994), 23–45; Kathryn Kish Sklar, *Florence Kelley and the
Nation's Work: The Rise of Women's Political Culture, 1830–1900* (New Haven,
1995), 69–90.
[9] Children's Bureau, *Child, the Family, and the Court*, 21–22.

men above juvenile court age (the Boys' Court), and, finally, hereditary mental defectiveness (the Psychopathic Laboratory). The chapters recount the cultural, legal, and political origins of each institution, the actual exercise of socialized law in each court, and the factors that enabled or constrained this exercise – including residual notions of individual responsibility, the tethers of legal tradition, the fiscal conservatism of early U.S. welfare policies, and the unpredictable effects of cultural assumptions about race, class, gender, and age.

Examining the practice of socialized criminal law in the Municipal Court of Chicago raises issues of broad significance for the history of law and political development in early twentieth-century America. The socialization of urban judicial administration was the leading edge of a broad legal and political transformation that extended state power into both large-scale structural processes and the intimate detail of everyday life. In the first three decades of the twentieth century, appellate courts authorized local, state, or federal governments to police industrial working conditions, in order to protect the safety of working men and conserve the good morals and reproductive capacities of working women; to regulate the socially harmful concentration of economic power in "trusts"; to restrain political speech in the interests of national security; to sterilize mental defectives in order to reduce crime and dependency and improve the nation's racial stock; and to quarantine and treat suspected prostitutes, against their will, for venereal disease. The experience of urban courts during this period serves as a much-needed reminder that the progressive transformation of American law altered legal power in ways both liberating and repressive.[10]

This double-edged quality of socialized law revealed itself in each new jurisdiction of the Municipal Court. It surfaced in the inherent tension between the notion of social responsibility for crime – which called attention to structural causes such as poverty – and the imperative of individual treatment, which focused expert disciplinary power on offenders and their immediate families. At the level of social policy, this dualism appeared in the tight ideological and institutional linkages between punishment and welfare, for example, between new criminal statutes against delinquent husbands and the administration of public assistance to single mothers. Perhaps most startling, the dualism of socialized law was manifest in the surprising compatibility of environmentalism and eugenics in professional criminology, progressive social reform, and actual judicial practice during the 1910s and early 1920s.

---

[10] See *Muller v. Oregon*; *Standard Oil Company v. United States*, 221 U.S. 1 (1911); *Schenck v. United States*, 249 U.S. 47 (1919); *Buck v. Bell*, 274 U.S. 200 (1927).

Socialized law flourished in a context of extraordinary cooperation between government and the voluntary associations of civil society. Historians of political development in the modern United States have called attention to the distinctive "associational" aspect of American liberalism during the 1920s and early New Deal era. Building on the wartime experience with price and production controls, federal agencies worked with trade associations, farmers, labor organizations, and professional societies to introduce new levels of coordination to the market without greatly increasing the scale of government. But well before trade associations assumed such an important role in the governance of the American economy, local voluntary associations and charitable organizations cooperated with municipal courts in the governance of urban social life. Not only did private associations such as the JPA help establish specialized criminal courts, but they helped *run* them. Along with representatives from church organizations, Jewish charitable societies, and local charities, the JPA's professional "protective officers" filed criminal complaints in the courts, investigated cases for the courts, and did follow-up work with offenders and their families. In an era when fiscal conservatism continually threatened the ability of progressive institutions to live up to their billing, voluntary associations bolstered the institutional capacities of criminal courts. The socialization of city courts would have quickly run aground without such deep reserves of private reform energy.[11]

There is no mistaking the powerful cultural effect of these legal institutions, as they mapped for the public gaze the social landscapes of the modern city. Progressive reformers and judges fully intended that urban criminal courts would become laboratories for the production and dissemination of authoritative social knowledge. The sociologist Pierre Bourdieu has insightfully described the power judges wield to interpret and, in effect, to constitute social reality through their official acts of judgment. "The judgment represents the quintessential form of authorized, public, official speech which is spoken in the name of and to everyone," he writes. The "performative utterances" of a court, Bourdieu continues, "are magical acts which succeed because they have the power to make themselves universally recognized. They succeed in creating a situation in which no one can refuse or ignore the point of view, the vision, which they impose." Judges and social personnel in the Municipal Court worked, often with great earnestness and

[11] Alan Brinkley, *The End of Reform: New Deal Liberalism in Recession and War* (New York, 1995), 5, 34–37, 44–47; Ellis W. Hawley, "Herbert Hoover, the Commerce Secretariat, and the Vision of an 'Associative State,' 1921–1928," *JAH*, 61 (1974), 116–40.

compassion, to scientifically understand the social environment, psychological dimensions, and racial origins of criminality. But they had a much larger hand than they acknowledged in inventing the facts of social life in the modern city. Court officers applied their own particularized cultural assumptions to the populations they were charged to manage in the name of an objectified, scientific conception of social order. And their public reports had a large and influential audience. Sociologists studied the courts' reports with great interest. Newspapers found in the courts' daily deluge of humanity a ready supply of narrative subjects for their public stories of moral danger and social reform. To the social workers of the U.S. Children's Bureau, a federal agency created in 1912 and staffed with many veterans of Chicago women's reform organizations, the courts were a rich fund of data and experience as they developed welfare policy ideas for the nation. But it was the ordinary people who came before these new socialized tribunals – as citizens filing criminal complaints, defendants on trial, or family members of the accused – who found the courts' point of view on modern social life hardest to refuse.[12]

[12] Pierre Bourdieu, "The Force of Law: Toward a Sociology of the Juridical Field," trans. Richard Terdiman, *Hastings Law Journal*, 38 (1987), 838; Christopher L. Tomlins, *Law, Labor, and Ideology in the Early American Republic* (New York, 1993), 16. See Children's Bureau, *Child, the Family, and the Court*; U.S. Children's Bureau, *Youth and Crime: A Study of the Prevalence and Treatment of Delinquency among Boys over Juvenile-Court Age in Chicago*, by Dorothy Williams Burke (Washington, 1930); Robyn Muncy, *Creating a Female Dominion in American Reform, 1890–1935* (New York, 1991).

5

"Keep Sober, Work, and Support His Family":
The Court of Domestic Relations

Our courts are becoming domesticated.

– Chicago Tribune, 1913

In March 1914, Judge Joseph Z. Uhlir of the Chicago Court of Domestic Relations issued a warrant for the arrest of Frank Bumba. A thirty-three-year-old teamster, Bumba was a native-born American, a husband, and the father of two young children: all in all, not the sort of fellow one expected to find in the rough hands of the criminal law. But like most defendants in this socialized branch of the Municipal Court, Bumba was a failed breadwinner, a workingman who shirked his "natural and legal duty," in the words of the United States Supreme Court, to support and maintain the dependent members of his household: his wife and children. By the measure of contemporary epithets, as often hurled by a judge from the bench as by a minister from the pulpit, he was a "delinquent husband," a "shiftless and lazy drunk," a "worthless man," a "married vagabond," a "home slacker."[1]

The thin file that survives from *The People of Illinois v. Frank Bumba* illuminates the new punitive, coercive, and therapeutic powers that early twentieth-century criminal statutes against desertion and nonsupport

---

[1] *People v. Frank Bumba*, Case 105502, March 9, 1914, MCCCR; *Audubon v. Shufeldt*, 181 U.S. 575, 577 (1901). See "Errant Fathers Face Jail," *Chicago Tribune*, April 4, 1911; William N. Gemmill, "Chicago Court of Domestic Relations," *AAAPSS*, 52 (1914), 118; Mary E. Richmond, *Friendly Visiting among the Poor* (1899; New York, 1918), 47. See John Stelk, *1917 Report of the Domestic Relations Branch of the Municipal Court of Chicago: With a Special Report on Its Organization and Operation, with Suggestions and Recommendations of Needed Legislative and Administrative Measures to Increase Its Value and Efficiency* (Chicago, 1917). I examined 1,000 surviving cases from the court: 500 consecutive cases (105501–106000) from March 9 to April 23, 1914, and 500 consecutive cases (413001–413500) from April 12 to June 12, 1923.

and the new machinery of a socialized court placed in the hands of a judge and his officers. In the progressive rhetoric of socialized law, the identity of the family as the "social unit" of the state – the engine of racial reproduction, the wellspring of life's necessities, the nursery of child welfare – created a social interest in the family that trumped the interests of its individual members. In a time of grave public concern about the ability of wage-earning men and women to provide healthy, moral, and self-sustaining home lives for their children, that social interest justified bold new policies to insure, police, and provide material aid to working-class families in America's great cities. Between 1890 and 1915, every state in the union enacted new laws that made a husband's desertion or failure to support his wife or children a crime, punishable in many locales by imprisonment at hard labor. To administer the statutes more efficiently and humanely, cities across the nation during the 1910s and 1920s rolled out a new piece of judicial machinery, the socialized family court, which united the old-fashioned legal authority of a criminal court with the modern techniques of social work, probation, and scientific charity. The Chicago court used those powers to the fullest, not only to police husbands – the actual defendants in most cases – but to regulate entire working-class families. As Judge John Stelk, who presided over the court in 1917, put it, "Why not do all of the family washing in the same tub?"[2]

The social interest in the family asked a lot of American legal institutions. The Boston legal aid activist Reginald Heber Smith understood this burden well. He explained:

> Here the law, even at its best, labors under a heavy disadvantage in trying to work out justice because the controversies are peculiarly intimate in nature and because they are produced by causes as variable and elusive as human nature itself. . . . Yet in precisely this

---

[2] Stelk, *1917 Report*, 25; William H. Baldwin, *Family Desertion and Non-Support Laws: A Study of the Laws of the Various States Made in Connection with the Associated Charities, Washington, D.C.* (Washington, 1904); William H. Baldwin, "The Present Status of Family Desertion and Non-Support Laws," delivered at National Conference of Charities and Corrections, Boston, June 10, 1911 (n. p.); U.S. Department of Labor, Children's Bureau, *The Child, the Family, and the Court: A Study of the Administration of Justice in the Field of Domestic Relations*, part I: *General Findings and Recommendations* (Washington, 1929). See Anna Rachel Igra, "Other Men's Wives and Children: Anti-Desertion Reform in New York, 1900–1935," Ph.D. diss., Rutgers University, 1996; Martha May, "The 'Problem of Duty': The Regulation of Male Breadwinning and Desertion in the Progressive Era," University of Wisconsin – Madison Law School, Institute for Legal Studies, *Legal History Program Working Papers*, ser. 1: 3 (Feb. 1986).

field the law is increasingly being urged to put forth its supreme effort, its sphere is being widened, [and] new complementary administrative agencies are being added to it, because in all these controversies is involved the security of the home, on which the existing state is founded, and the welfare of children, on whom the future state depends.

Until the creation of a modern "welfare state" during the New Deal, progressive jurists and child welfare activists assumed local governments would have to handle this burden. Under the poor law tradition, county governments and private charities had responsibility for poor relief when families could no longer take care of their own. Given the entrenched fiscal conservatism and patronage politics of Chicago and other urban centers, activists had learned the hard way not to expect too much from county relief offices. But in an era of municipal court reform, judiciaries seemed a more promising venue for social justice. Progressives called upon local courts to make productive citizens of juvenile delinquents, to administer new state programs of aid to mother-headed families, to institutionalize hereditary mental defectives, and, not least, to compel errant husbands to support their families.[3]

Judge Uhlir's warrant charged Bumba with contributing to the dependency of children, a misdemeanor punishable by a $200 fine and a year busting rocks in the House of Correction. The file does not detail the conditions of dependency that Bumba had allowed to settle into his home on Alexander Street, a few blocks east (which is to say, downwind) of the Chicago River's puffing chimneys on the South Side. The essence of the offense, which the General Assembly had added to the Illinois Criminal Code just nine years earlier, was to let one's own legal dependents slip into such a state of destitution that they became dependent on others: relatives, neighbors, private charities, or, worst of all, the public. That Bumba's wife, Mary, had to neglect her motherly duties and take in "occasional scrubbing" – a fact noted

---

[3] Reginald Heber Smith, *Justice and the Poor: A Study of the Present Denial of Justice to the Poor and of the Agencies Making More Equal Their Position before the Law with Particular Reference to Legal Aid Work in the United States* (New York, 1919), 73. See Joanne L. Goodwin, *Gender and the Politics of Welfare Reform: Mothers' Pensions in Chicago, 1911–1929* (Chicago, 1997); Michael Willrich, "The Two Percent Solution: Eugenic Jurisprudence and the Socialization of American Law, 1900–1930," *LHR*, 16 (1998), 63–111. The notable exception was workman's compensation legislation, which created state commissions to administer cases of work accidents, previously adjudicated in common-law courts.

by one of the court's social workers during a routine interview with her – would have been viewed by the court as evidence of dependency in the Bumba home.[4]

According to standard procedure in the court, Bumba would have first received a letter from the court's Social Service Department, asking him to come in for a "conference" with his wife. In this session, a trained female social worker would have attempted to reconcile the spouses and "adjust" the family situation. If the defendant failed to appear, if prospects for reconciliation looked dim, or if the social worker deemed the case an emergency, she would have advised the judge to take legal action. Bumba's file does not say which scenario led to the warrant. But it does suggest that such judicial interventions were already a fact of life in his household. As a personal reference, he named "Miss Schaffer – Juvenile Court."[5]

The police acted swiftly on the warrant (since Bumba still lived with his family, he was easy to find), and in two days' time they hauled him into court. If Bumba's experience fit one judge's description of a typical arraignment in the court, he arrived there in shackles after a night spent in the company of drunkards and thieves in a putrid police station cell. He was "paraded past a room full of spectators and locked up in the 'bull pen.'" When the bailiff called his case, he stood before the court "in his working clothes, unshaven and unkempt." There he faced his wife, who had a public prosecutor and "the People of Illinois" on her side. The defendant "must shift for himself, as far as counsel is concerned."[6]

A clerk's pen records that on March 11, 1914, Judge Uhlir found Bumba guilty and placed him on probation for one year. Bumba got off easy. Roughly one-sixth of the men tried by the court served time. Bumba signed a $500 bond to guarantee compliance with the court-ordered conditions of his probation: "Keep sober work and support his family." So common was this phrase upon the records of the court that the clerk didn't bother with commas.[7]

Spring and summer came and went, and the Bumbas managed to stay out of court. But in late November, as the widening national

---

[4] *People v. Bumba.* "An Act to provide for the punishment of persons responsible for or directly promoting, or contributing to, the conditions that render a child dependent, neglected or delinquent...," approved May 13, 1905, *Illinois Revised Statutes*, 1911, ch. 38, sec. 42hb. "An Act relating to children who are now or may hereafter become dependent, neglected or delinquent...," approved June 4, 1907, ibid., ch. 23, sec. 169.

[5] *MCC 12–14* (1918–20), 160; *People v. Bumba.*

[6] Stelk, *1917 Report*, 28.

[7] *People v. Bumba.*

financial depression and the tightening of markets in war-torn Europe
precipitated an unemployment crisis in Chicago, Frank's probation
officer reported that he had violated the conditions of his freedom:
"Wont work, comes home drunk and abuses wife and children." The
presiding judge issued another warrant. The police again dragged
Bumba into court. This time, the judge ordered him to pay the clerk
of the Municipal Court four dollars a week for the duration of his
probation term. Frank apparently made these payments, and each
week Mary collected the money from the clerk's office in City Hall,
where she may have compared experiences with other wives waiting
in line for their support payments. At another public building downtown, another line of poor women formed outside the office of the
Cook County Agent, which controlled distribution of poor relief in
Chicago. These women, whose husbands were not home slackers but
were either dead or permanently disabled, had been approved by the
Juvenile Court to collect tightly regulated cash "pensions" under the
state's Mother's Aid law, a controversial new program of public assistance for mother-headed families. A well-maintained legal barrier
stood between those two lines of poor women, but their histories
were intertwined. Their fates would remain so during the next two
decades, as the fledgling American welfare state rose up around
them.[8]

In March 1915, Bumba's probation officer recommended that
he be discharged as "improved." Judge Uhlir released him from
surveillance. The officer closed his file.[9]

The Court of Domestic Relations enjoyed pride of place as the first
fully socialized criminal branch of the Municipal Court, the first space
in that modern organized court where the protean ideologies of social
responsibility for crime and socialized law converged in practice. Part
criminal court, part "social agency," the Court of Domestic Relations
bustled with social workers, probation officers, interpreters, and
agents from women's organizations and private charities, in addition
to the usual cast of judges, bailiffs, clerks, prosecutors, and the odd
defense attorney. Only one-fifth of the men tried there had legal
representation.[10]

---

[8] Charles Ashleigh, "The Job War in Chicago," *ISR*, 15 (1914), 262–67; U.S.
Department of Labor, Children's Bureau, *The Administration of the Aid-to-
Mothers Law in Illinois*, by Edith Abbott and Sophonisba P. Breckinridge
(Washington, 1921).
[9] *People v. Bumba.*
[10] Stelk, *1917 Report*, 24; Gemmill, "Chicago Court," 121.

Like all specialized courts, this one was defined by its jurisdiction, the legally constituted field of social life it called its own: "all cases involving wrongs against women or children." This was not meant to be taken too literally. A purse-snatcher could be tried just as well in a regular criminal branch, and a rapist, like any accused felon who received a preliminary hearing in the Municipal Court, had to be bound over to Cook County Criminal Court if a judge found the state had sufficient evidence to proceed. The Court of Domestic Relations specialized in a more routine class of misdemeanors and ordinance violations that in recent years had taken on enlarged public significance – offenses that caused injustice to women and minors *in their prescribed domestic roles* as wives, mothers, and children. Most of the cases – fully 84 percent of the 4,578 warrants issued in 1917 – originated in complaints signed by wives, social workers, charity officials, and other parties against husbands under criminal statutes enacted since 1900: abandonment and nonsupport of wife and/or child (1903), contributing to dependency or delinquency (1905), and simple nonsupport (1915). The court also tried bastardy cases – another form of male nonsupport – as well as cases of child abduction; selling cigarettes, liquor, or weapons to minors; and admitting minors to dance halls that sold liquor. Some offenses committed by minors themselves fell within the court's purview – gambling in saloons, leaping onto moving cars, truancy violations – the sort of youthful infractions that in a small town could be entrusted to parental discipline. And each year the state prosecuted a few dozen mothers there for contributing to the dependency or delinquency of their own children. But the court's chief purpose was to compel wage-earning husbands to do their manly duties – to keep sober, work, and support their families – thus keeping their families intact and, not incidentally, off the welfare rolls.[11]

Municipal judges and middle-class women activists from Hull-House had invented the Court of Domestic Relations less than four years before Bumba's trial, in an extraordinary series of closed-door meetings in Harry Olson's chambers. Present at the creation were the chief justice, several associate judges, State's Attorney John E. W. Wayman, and three women from the Juvenile Protective Association (JPA): president Louise de Koven Bowen, the wife of a banker and a member of the Hull-House inner circle; Gertrude Howe Britton, a social worker and longtime resident of the settlement; and Jane Addams herself. No records of the proceedings were published. No one consulted the General Assembly or City Council. No reporters witnessed the event.

[11] *MCC* 5 (1911), 68–73, esp. 68; *MCC* 7 (1913), 79–80; Stelk, *1917 Report*, 112.

Women activists from the Hull-House social settlement collaborated with municipal judges to create the Chicago Court of Domestic Relations. This photo from the court's opening day, April 3, 1911, features three of the founders: from left, Jane Addams, Judge Charles N. Goodnow, and Gertrude Howe Britton of the Juvenile Protective Association. Photo by the *Chicago Daily News* (DN-009072). Courtesy of the Chicago Historical Society.

The Municipal Court Act empowered the chief justice to create specialized courts as he saw fit, and these women, seasoned champions of feminist social politics in the Second City, had ignited Harry Olson's moral imagination.[12]

No group of people better exemplified the ideology of social responsibility for crime than the JPA, and no one made a stronger moral case that the criminal courts had to be socialized in order to protect the welfare of poor women and children. Established in 1909,

[12] Harry Olson to Edward A. Dicker, Dec. 16, 1910, MCC, box 3, folder 19; Harry Olson, "The Municipal Court of Chicago: A Tribunal of Procedural Reform and Social Service," reprinted from *The Recorder* (San Francisco), May 12, 1916, 8; Stelk, *1917 Report*, 70.

the JPA grew out of the Juvenile Court Committee at Hull-House (the same women-led organization that Roscoe Pound had joined as a Chicago law professor). The JPA was headquartered at the settlement, just across Halsted Street from the Juvenile Court, and had access to the community's ample legal, philanthropic, and political resources. The JPA's corporate donors included the Armour and Swift meat-packing firms. Its board included Olson, Juvenile Court Judge Merritt W. Pinckney, and Mrs. Julius Rosenwald, the wife of the city's leading Jewish philanthropist and president of Sears, Roebuck and Company. The JPA's official mission was to stem the tide of 10,000 minors who passed through the city's courts each year: "to get at the child before he goes down, to influence his parents to raise the standard of the home, to remove temptations, to better conditions in his neighborhood . . . to use formative rather than reformative measures." This mission led in two directions: out into the urban cultural world of bright lights and commercial amusements and into the dimly lit interior of the working-class home.[13]

The JPA's professional "protective officers," based in districts around the city, policed the dance halls, cheap theaters, and other spaces where working-class boys and girls congregated. The association made headlines with its shocking investigative reports, usually authored by Bowen, under titles such as *The Road to Destruction Made Easy in Chicago.* The reports were not just moralistic screeds; they were well-documented sociological briefs replete with specific recommendations for legal reform. JPA officers visited the homes of Juvenile Court defendants and discovered that desertion, nonsupport, and the need for mothers to work for wages were major causes of dependency and delinquency. (Hull-House veterans Sophonisba Breckinridge and Edith Abbott backed up this argument with social scientific data in their classic 1912 study, *The Delinquent Child and the Home.*) The JPA kept the courts busy with criminal complaints against dance hall proprietors, brothel keepers, and unfit parents. Between October 1909 and October 1910, JPA officers handled 4,305 criminal complaints. More than half were for abandonment or contributing to the dependency or delinquency of children. Protective officers made more than 2,600 visits to local courts, including 1,910 to the Municipal Court, and persuaded judges to issue nearly 450 warrants. Already, the JPA's mission centered less on the Juvenile Court, just across the street, than on the Municipal Court, with its thirteen criminal branches dispersed around the city. "It was found that the various judges had no concerted plan of treatment," Bowen recalled. "One man would perhaps be sent

[13] JPA, untitled annual report (Chicago, 1910), esp. 12.

to the city prison and another, guilty of the same offense, would be put on probation, and still another dismissed with a reprimand." Bowen approached Olson and persuaded him to appoint a committee to create a specialized branch, where one expert judge, assisted by capable female social workers with the combined resources of the Chicago's private social agencies behind them, could hear all of the city's domestic relations cases and develop a plan of treatment for troubled working-class home life.[14]

In Olson's chambers, the women activists and judges designed the court's jurisdiction, crafted flexible rules of procedure, and agreed to appoint a JPA officer as the court's first "social secretary." Bowen told the Association of Commerce it was her belief that the "niceties of legal procedure" should not be "observed with the care that is taken in other courts." By December 1910, the headlines started to appear. "WOMAN'S COURT NOW A CERTAINTY." "LAZY HUSBAND PUT IN DESERTER CLASS." The *Chicago Tribune* found the case for a domestic relations court "beyond argument. There is no question that the unity of the family is threatened among the poor by many circumstances not involved in the problems of the well to do, and in such cases a wise paternalism, guided by special knowledge of the social, economic, and physical factors out of which these special difficulties grow, cannot but bring better results than now are possible."[15]

When the court opened on April 3, 1911, Jane Addams delivered the keynote address. She spoke from the bench to the crowd of reporters, social workers, and white-gloved clubwomen, who had come to view the procession of poor wives, shawls on shoulders and babes in arms, receiving justice against their husbands. Done up in jonquils and roses, the domesticated courtroom on the ninth floor of City Hall was a world apart from the smoke-filled, saloon-like atmosphere of the typical criminal branch. The voluntary associations represented in the audience – including the Jewish Bureau of Social Service, the United Charities, and the St. Vincent de Paul Society – attested to the court's diverse constituency in civil society. "Many of us who for years have seen

[14] Louise de Koven Bowen, *Safeguards for City Youth: At Work and at Play* (New York, 1914), 128; JPA, annual report, 1910, pp. 15–17; Louise de Koven Bowen, *The Road to Destruction Made Easy in Chicago* (Chicago, 1916); Sophonisba P. Breckinridge and Edith Abbott, *The Delinquent Child and the Home* (New York, 1912).

[15] *MCC* 5 (1911), 72; "Lone Woman Pleads Cause of City Youth," *Chicago Daily News*, Dec. 21, 1910; "The Court of Sorrows," *Chicago Tribune*, Dec. 3, 1910. See "Woman's Court Now a Certainty," *Chicago Tribune*, Dec. 2, 1910; "Give Heart Suits to Cupid Court," *Chicago Tribune*, Dec. 23, 1910; "Lazy Husband Put in Deserter Class," *Chicago Examiner*, Dec. 23, 1910.

The view from the bench in the Chicago Court of Domestic Relations on opening day, April 3, 1911. The women on the viewer's left, wearing fashionable
floral hats, represent the many women's organizations and charitable societies
interested in the court. The women sitting on the right, wearing shawls, appear to be the complainants; they have filed criminal complaints against their
husbands for desertion or nonsupport. The men seated behind them, wearing
workingmen's clothing, appear to be defendants. Photo by the *Chicago Daily
News* (DN-009080). Courtesy of the Chicago Historical Society.

children in poverty and degradation welcome the opening of this court
in a manner that we can hardly express," Addams said. "We have long
felt that crimes against property are consistently punished, but those
wherein little children are made to suffer are lightly dealt with." Some-
where in the crowd, perhaps finding some vindication in Addams's
words, sat the former judge McKenzie Cleland, who just two years earlier had been accused of sullying the Magna Charta at Maxwell Street
by ordering men to keep sober, work, and support their families.[16]

It makes sense that the Court of Domestic Relations was the Municipal Court's first socialized branch. Progressive Era crime talk – public
discourse about the social causes of crime and the social consequences
of punishment in the modern city – had long been preoccupied with

[16] Addams in "Heart Court in First Act Unites Broken Family," *Chicago Evening
American*, April 3, 1911. See "Errant Fathers Face Jail"; "Family Jar Court
Begins with a Rush," *Chicago Inter Ocean*, April 4, 1911; "Joy in Family Court,"
Chicago Daily News, April 3, 1911.

working-class home life. For this very reason, the "Court of Sorrows," as Harry Olson liked to call it, had a delicate task before it: to strike a balance between those two perspectives: the family as cause and as consequence. Middle-class reformers and social scientists viewed working-class home life as a breeding ground for criminality, especially in families deprived of the support of the normal, male breadwinner due to death, desertion, or drunken indifference. Eugenicists warned that the inferior racial stock of working-class families (especially those of recent, non–Anglo-Saxon immigrant origin) produced the mental defects at the root of almost all criminality. The environmentalist view assumed that the insecurity of the wage labor market and the ignorance of parents caused instability and inevitable delinquency in the home. Both ways of understanding the social etiology of crime were accepted, with varying degrees of commitment, by JPA leaders and most other people involved in progressive court reform during the teens. As the JPA's very existence shows, the invention of the juvenile court had intensified interest in the home life of delinquent and dependent children, creating pressure to punish unfit parents such as Frank Bumba. But the legislative debates on adult probation, still under way in Springfield in the spring of 1911, expressed a new consensus that conventional forms of punishment posed their own hazard to home life by removing the chief breadwinner. All of this meant that the unstable boundaries between individual and social responsibility, criminality and dependency, and punishment and welfare would be even less certain in judicial practice than in the rhetoric of social responsibility.[17]

If the court's domestic jurisdiction required its judges and social personnel to maintain a kind of ideological double-vision, this was especially true with regard to its defendants: adult, able-bodied men who failed, "without good cause," to provide shelter, food, and clothing for their families. Although the court used the criminal complaint as a point of entry to regulate entire families, it had to make a legal decision about the individual before the bar – even if that decision was not to prosecute. In the gallery of criminal types, only adult men who committed extreme acts of violence or major property crimes were a harder case for social responsibility than home slackers. The new modes of social explanation did color official representations of delinquent husbands. To some judges, they were less than fully competent adults – and less than fully men – weaklings produced by the struggle for survival in the industrial labor market, excessive drink, or their own degenerate constitutions. During economic downturns such as the depression of 1914–15, the court's social workers handled a higher proportion of cases without seeking a warrant, explaining in their reports that a tight labor market made it hard for even good men to do their duty. In better times, though, it was hard to look past "indifferent" men and assign responsibility to forces beyond their control.[18]

These tensions at the heart of the court's practice were amplified by the vital political role that socialized family courts played in the development of the welfare state. The American welfare state was a modest affair compared with those built by other western nations in the early twentieth century. It owed much of its minimalist logic and design neither to objective economic criteria nor to a liberal constitutionalism that prized individual liberty over social equality but to morally freighted gender norms. Prescriptive cultural assumptions, with deep roots in English and American law, defined the proper roles of men and women as workers, husbands, wives, fathers, and mothers. The policing of home-slacker husbands was the most punitive element of a new complex of gendered welfare policies, established at the state level during the 1910s, that included state-administered social insurance systems for injured workingmen and their families (workmen's compensation) and state-funded payments to mother-headed households (mothers' pensions). Despite diverse origins and constituencies, those policies expressed a common set of gendered values and expectations for breadwinners and their families. Together, they aimed to provide working families with greater security from modern risks, without undermining the family as an institution and work as a duty or allowing responsibility for women's and children's poverty to fall entirely upon the public.[19]

Since the colonial period, the most elemental relations of home and hearth had always been the subject – indeed, the *creation* – of law. The husband's duties to "support and maintain" his wife and children had long traditions in the systems of common law and equity that all but a few American states adopted from England. The common law treated a husband's failure in those duties as a violation of

---

[18] Stelk, *1917 Report*, 13; CHA, *The Making of Men* (Chicago, 1907), 4; MCC 8–9 (1914–15), 59.

[19] There is a large literature on gender and welfare. See Linda Gordon, ed., *Women, the State, and Welfare* (Madison, 1990); Seth Koven and Sonya Michel, eds., *Mothers of a New World: Maternalist Politics and the Origins of Welfare States* (New York, 1993). For a discussion of the implications of breadwinner regulation for this literature, see Michael Willrich, "Home Slackers: Men, the State, and Welfare in Modern America," *JAH*, 87 (2000), 460–89.

private right – a breach of the reciprocal obligations of protection and
dependency that existed between husband and wife, parent and child –
not as an offense against the public. The common law bound the
husband to provide his wife with those things essential to her survival
and well-being and to repay third parties for credit they extended to
her for such "necessaries." Every man had a further obligation "to provide for those descended from his loins." Each of those patriarchal
duties came with a reciprocal, though hardly symmetrical, obligation
of obedience on the part of his dependents. As the South Carolina
Supreme Court put it in 1858, "[t]he obligation imposed on the husband to provide for their wants and protection, makes it necessary
that he should exercise a power of control over all members of his
household."[20]

Under the systems of common law and equity, there were two ways
a delinquent nineteenth-century husband could end up in court. If
he failed to repay a merchant for credit extended to his wife for
necessaries, the creditor could sue him. What made for a necessary
purchase was a matter of judicial interpretation. The answer – whether
a loaf of bread or a fur tippet – rested upon a male judge's perception
of the wife's "station in life" and her husband's ability to provide. A
husband who deserted or abused his wife might also be called before
a court of equity, to answer to his wife's demand that he provide her
with a "separate maintenance" in a home apart from him. To prevail
in a separate maintenance suit, a wife had to prove she had good cause
(such as desertion or cruelty) to live apart from her husband. In either
form of action, a necessaries suit or a maintenance case, a private individual – not a police officer, prosecutor, or other agent of the state –
had to initiate the case.[21]

[20] William Blackstone, *Commentaries on the Laws of England*, ed. James DeWitt
Andrews, 4th ed., 2 vols., 1765–1769 (Chicago, 1899), I: 448, 433–60. *Ex
parte Hewitt*, 11 Rich. 326, 329 (1858), quoted in Peter W. Bardaglio, *Reconstructing the Household: Families, Sex, and the Law in the Nineteenth-Century
South* (Chapel Hill, 1995), 40; Joel Prentiss Bishop, *Commentaries on the Law
of Married Women under the Statutes of the Several States, and at Common Law
and in Equity*, 2 vols. (Boston, 1873), I: 680; James Kent, *Commentaries on
American Law*, ed. Charles M. Barnes, 13th ed., 4 vols. (Boston, 1884), II:
146–49, 190–95. See Michael Grossberg, *Governing the Hearth: Law and the
Family in Nineteenth-Century America* (Chapel Hill, 1985); Hendrik Hartog,
Man and Wife in America: A History (Cambridge, Mass., 2000).
[21] Equity emerged in thirteenth-century England as a distinct body of principles and remedies that mitigated the rigidity of the common law. Equity
gave magistrates wide discretion, especially in cases involving classes of people deemed less than fully competent juridical subjects: minors, idiots, the

In his capacity as father, the husband had to answer to a third legal tradition: the poor law. For three centuries since the Elizabethan Poor Law of 1601, the poor laws of England and America had tightly regulated poor relief by holding three generations of family members – "the father and grandfather, and the mother and grandmother, and the children," in the words of the Elizabethan statute – liable for the support of a pauper. State poor laws still on the books in America during the New Deal era reserved relief for paupers who were physically unable to work and had no family to support them. The laws provided for the prosecution of relatives unable or unwilling to contribute. Illinois was unique in that in 1833, its lawmakers added siblings to the list of liable family members. Under normal circumstances, married women were exempt from this regime of family responsibility. In a nod to coverture and to the common-law regime of support duties, the Illinois pauper laws stipulated that married women, "whilst their husbands live, shall not be liable to a suit."[22]

As a final prod for hard-up husbands, Illinois and some other states allowed men who deserted their wives and children "without suitable means of subsistence" to be prosecuted as vagrants. Like the poor law, Illinois's 1819 vagrancy statute was designed to keep women and children from becoming public charges. If the family of a vagrant resided in the county where he was tried, the court could release him on bond to return home and maintain them. Otherwise, the statute authorized the sheriff to hire out the vagrant to the highest bidder for up to nine months, during which time his earnings would be paid to his wife. If no one hired the vagrant, the court might order him whipped (not to exceed thirty-nine lashes). Illinois lawmakers did not end the system of forcibly hiring out vagrants until 1874, nine years after the Thirteenth Amendment abolished slavery. Thereafter, vagrants worked out their terms in a county jail or house of correction. With later revisions that

---

insane, and married women. By the nineteenth century, equity had become a source of new legal rights for married women; Norma Basch, *In the Eyes of the Law: Women, Marriage, and Property in Nineteenth-Century New York* (Ithaca, NY, 1982), 21, 70–112; John Norton Pomeroy, *A Treatise on Equity Jurisprudence as Administered in the United States of America* (1881; San Francisco, 1907).

[22] Elizabethan statute quoted in June Axinn and Herman Levin, *Social Welfare: A History of the American Response to Need* (New York, 1997), 10; Illinois pauper law in William P. Quigley, "The Quicksands of the Poor Law: Poor Relief Legislation in a Growing Nation, 1790–1820," *Northern Illinois University Law Review*, 18 (Fall 1997), 38. See Edith Abbott, *Public Assistance*, vol. 1: *American Principles and Policies* (1940; New York, 1996), 155–79; Sophonisba P. Breckinridge, *The Illinois Poor Law and its Administration* (Chicago, 1939); *People v. Hill*, 163 Ill. 186 (1896).

widened the statutory definition of vagrancy, this law remained in effect
at least until the 1930s.[23]

Men who fathered children outside the sanctity of a marriage contract were liable to state charges of bastardy. In recognition of bastardy's ambiguous status at the borderland of civil and criminal law,
nineteenth-century bastardy laws commonly allowed for hybrid judicial proceedings that anticipated the later desertion and nonsupport
statutes. "We find it distinctly provided," Ernst Freund explained in
a review of bastardy legislation, "that while the prosecution shall be
in the name of the State, the rules of evidence and of competency of
witnesses, and the trial shall be governed by the law regulating civil
suits." The court's orders had the muscle of criminal law – defendants
were arrested instead of summoned – but the proceedings adhered to
the more flexible style and lower evidentiary standards of a civil case.
Under Illinois's 1872 statute, which remained on the books through
the Progressive Era, a man found guilty of bastardy had two options for
supporting his child: He could pay an amount fixed by the court – not
to exceed $100 for the first year and $50 each for the next nine years –
or settle with the mother for a one-time payment of $400. Failure to
pay constituted contempt of court, an offense punishable by jail.[24]

So home and hearth had never guaranteed a safe haven from
government interference in America. As U.S. Supreme Court Justice
Stephen Field explained in 1888, the presumption of regulation
was what made marriage contracts unique. "Other contracts may
be modified, restricted, or enlarged, or entirely released upon the
consent of the parties," he observed. "Not so with marriage. The
relation once formed, the law steps in and holds the parties to various
obligations and liabilities." Paramount among these obligations was
the one that Field's brother on the bench, Justice Horace Gray,
described in 1901 as "the natural and legal duty of the husband to
support the wife."[25]

The marriage contract was unique for another reason: Only the marriage contract created an explicitly unequal relation of status. Paired
with the husband's obligations of support and protection was the wife's
dependence and legal subordination. In the latter decades of the
nineteenth century, the rapid industrial expansion produced social

[23] Breckinridge, *Illinois Poor Law,* 528–30.
[24] U.S. Department of Labor, Children's Bureau, *Illegitimacy Laws of the United States and Certain Foreign Countries,* by Ernst Freund (Washington, 1919), 47–48, 128–132, esp. 26; *MCC 12–14* (1918–20), 156.
[25] *Maynard v. Hill,* 125 U.S. 190, 211 (1888); *Audubon v. Shufeldt,* at 577.

conditions that made this status relation increasingly difficult to justify in the old terms of male support.

The modern social problem of the delinquent breadwinner first surfaced in this emerging social context, soon after the Civil War. As Amy Dru Stanley has insightfully argued, the ascendance of the wage labor system in those years "disrupted the fundamental premise of the marriage bond: the relation of male protection and female dependency." The notion of a "natural wage," high enough for a workingman to maintain his dependents, had long been a tenet of liberal political economy, antislavery ideology, and labor politics. In the era of slave emancipation, this manly right to a home life outside the market occupied a preferred, but visibly endangered, position in the expansive liberal ideology of contract. Already in the 1870s, public authorities in the most heavily industrialized states were remarking upon the disturbing discovery that many workingmen could not support their families on their wages alone. The Massachusetts Bureau of Labor Statistics warned of "the desperate need of extra work from wife and children," which reduced workers' homes to "mere crowds of lodgers, the family robbed of mother's care." More shocking still were reports of dissolute husbands who defiled their marriage contracts by squandering their wages on drink. "In our large cities thousands of women toil to support families, including often their indolent and inebriate husbands," the sociologist Lester Ward wrote in 1883. "How false is the assertion that men perform the labor of support, while women confine themselves to maternal and domestic duties."[26]

Those discoveries precipitated a moral and political dilemma. If married women assumed male economic roles, and married men failed at them, what, then, of the family? Feminist activists in Chicago and other communities petitioned their state legislatures for measures that would acknowledge the reality of married women's wage work and give wives the right to protect themselves from the hazards of unreliable male support. State legislators responded by passing two new kinds of laws. Earnings statutes gave married women a new property right in their own wages, protecting scarce family resources from shiftless husbands. And "separate maintenance" statutes made it easier for deserted wives to sue their husbands for support in any civil court. Well ahead of the curve, Illinois enacted its maintenance statute in 1867 and an

---

[26] Amy Dru Stanley, "Conjugal Bonds and Wage Labor: Rights of Contract in the Age of Emancipation," *JAH*, 75 (1988), 491–92; Massachusetts Bureau of Labor Statistics quoted in ibid., 489; Ward quoted in ibid., 491; Amy Dru Stanley, *From Bondage to Contract: Wage Labor, Marriage, and the Market in the Age of Slave Emancipation* (Cambridge, 1998), 138–74.

earnings law two years later. While the earnings statutes implied a new level of independence for wage-earning wives – an implication swiftly narrowed by judicial interpretation – the maintenance statutes announced that the uncertainties of the wage labor system had not freed husbands from their common-law duties as breadwinners. The public debates surrounding both kinds of statutes were filled with discussion of "worthless men" who shirked their duties of support. Feminists used the image of the unfit husband to strengthen their case for married women's emancipation. Male lawmakers and judges used the same negative image to reinforce the legal norm of the male breadwinner and demand that workingmen live up to this standard of manliness. Skilled workingmen themselves valorized the husband's duties as an attribute of manly independence. The laboring man "is and should be head of his own department, in the management of his business for the support of his family," the Chicago *Workingman's Advocate* declared in 1869. But workingmen did not have much of a hand in defining the social problem of the delinquent husband, and they certainly did not invite greater state interference with their home lives.[27]

At the turn of the twentieth century, dispatches from the field of urban charity work led to a renewed public interest in the social problem of the errant husband and triggered a new wave of legislation. The feminist arguments that a few decades earlier had linked male irresponsibility to female legal emancipation had quieted. Middle-class officials of private charities led the turn-of-the-century legislative campaigns. They emphasized the public costs of desertion and nonsupport and called upon state lawmakers to use the criminal law to enforce the duty of male support.

Beginning in the 1870s, public authorities in many states had gradually ceded much of the jurisdiction of poor relief to "organized" private charities. In Chicago, the Cook County government never relinquished control, but a strong organized network of private charities rivaled the public system of relief. Secular in outlook, middle-class "charity workers" aspired to make relief a more professional and scientific undertaking. Opposed to sentimentalism in all its guises, they tended to attribute poverty to the personal failings of the poor. But they also insisted that only through a detailed knowledge of social conditions, rather than indiscriminate almsgiving, could relief agencies hope to reduce dependency. Local charity organization societies and associated charities, operating in a hundred cities by the 1890s, kept detailed records on the people who sought their aid. The New York

---

[27] *Workingman's Advocate,* quoted in Stanley, "Conjugal Bonds," 486, 485; Stanley, *Bondage to Contract,* 175–217.

Charity Organization Society alone amassed data on 170,000 individuals and families.[28]

Charity officials perceived and represented the "dependent classes" in gendered terms. Even during the terrible crisis precipitated by the great Chicago fire of 1871, relief officials withheld aid from many able-bodied men, lest their temporary dependency turn into a permanent condition. Officials ministered more freely to the needs of widows, children, and the elderly or infirm – the recognizably deserving poor, who were not expected to be entirely self-sufficient in the best of times. In the 1890s, private charities began to screen out widows from deserted wives among their cases, in order to withhold relief from the families, however needy, of able-bodied men. In the name of male responsibility (and to protect their own turf from state encroachment), charity workers adamantly opposed the new proposals to provide public assistance to single mothers. Charity Organization Society officials helped kill an early New York mothers' aid bill in 1897 by tarring it as a "Shiftless Fathers Bill."[29]

By 1900, shiftless men were high on the agendas of the National Conference of Charities and Corrections and the General Conference of Associated Charities. During the next five years, urban charity societies conducted the first systematic surveys of desertion. As the organizations pooled their data, they found that deserted families made up roughly 10 percent of relief cases in U.S. cities. The figures ranged from 7 percent in Washington, D.C., to 13 percent in Seattle. Public welfare officials, who private charity workers claimed were slower to discriminate between widows and deserted women, would soon make similar discoveries. The Cook County Agent provided clothing, food, and other noncash relief to 67,213 families between 1909 and 1915 (excluding 1914, for which the county published no report). Some 13 percent of those families (8,957) had been deserted. By any accounting, desertion was a major cause of women's and children's poverty.[30]

---

[28] Paul Boyer, *Urban Masses and Moral Order in America, 1820–1920* (Cambridge, Mass., 1992), 143–61, esp. 150.

[29] Karen Sawislak, *Smoldering City: Chicagoans and the Great Fire, 1871–1874* (Chicago, 1995), 69–119, esp. 87; "History of United Charities" (1937), United Charities Papers, Chicago Historical Society, box 9, folder 3. See Brandt, *Five Hundred and Seventy-Four Deserters*, 7; Gordon, *Pitied but Not Entitled*, 41; Mark H. Leff, "Consensus for Reform: The Mothers'-Pension Movement in the Progressive Era," *SSR*, 47 (1973), 402–4.

[30] See Rev. E. P. Savage, "Desertion by Parents," *Proceedings of the National Conference of Charities and Correction at the Twenty-fourth Annual Session Held in Toronto, Ontario, July 7–14, 1897*, ed. Isabel C. Barrows (Boston, 1898),

Because of its provenance in the case files of the charity societies –
and, after the turn of the century, in the files of the new juvenile courts –
the social problem of desertion and nonsupport was cast as an urban,
working-class phenomenon. It was only when their wives turned to
relief agencies or their children turned to crime that deserters left a
paper trail. The experts condescendingly dubbed desertion "the poor
man's divorce." The phrase had a certain logic. To the poor, a legal
divorce was a prohibitively costly proposition; to devout Catholics, it
was no option at all. Still, most deserters never intended, or at least
never made, a permanent break; they returned home, if only to walk
out again. Sociologists also made the culturally biased and plainly in-
accurate claim that lax moral standards in immigrant, working-class
communities fostered desertion. As James R. Barrett has shown, many
immigrant families in early twentieth-century Chicago made extraordinary efforts to stay together and off relief. Given the dispropor-
tionate representation of women and children among applicants for
relief, desertion was inevitably defined as a male act. Of more than
9,000 desertion cases handled by the United Charities of Chicago, the
city's largest private relief organization, from 1909 to 1915, only eleven
involved deserting women.[31]

Despite the definition of desertion and nonsupport as a working-
class problem, scientific charity workers, who tended to be far more
conservative than the residents of social settlements such as Hull-
House, steadfastly denied any significant causal connection to the
industrial economy. Social scientists at the turn of the century increasingly blamed societal ills on the socioeconomic environment. But
charity officials emphasized the "moral defects" of "shiftless" men.
The New York charity worker Mary Richmond offered a sketch of
one deserter that was gentler than most. "One good woman, whose
husband had left her for the second time more than a year ago, declared often and emphatically that she would never let him come

317–28; Zilpha D. Smith, *Deserted Wives and Deserting Husbands: A Study of
234 Families Based on the Experience of the District Committees and Agents of the
Associated Charities of Boston* (Boston, 1901), 3. See Baldwin, *Family Desertion
and Non-Support Laws*, 5–8; Brandt, *Five Hundred and Seventy-Four Deserters*,
7–10; Edward T. Devine, *The Practice of Charity: Individual, Associated and
Organized* (1901; New York, 1907), 133; Eubank, *Study of Family Desertion*, 6,
15–16.
[31] Brandt, *Five Hundred and Seventy-Four Deserters*, 7; Joanna C. Colcord, *Broken
Homes: A Study of Family Desertion and Its Social Treatment* (New York, 1919),
7; Eubank, *Study of Family Desertion*, 8, n. 1, 14–15, 19; James R. Barrett,
Work and Community in the Jungle: Chicago's Packinghouse Workers, 1894–1922
(Urbana, 1987), 90–107.

back," Richmond recalled in an 1899 report. "We rescued her furniture from the landlord, found her work, furnished relief, and befriended the children; but the drunken and lazy husband returned the other day, and is sitting in the chairs we rescued, while he warms his hands at the fire that we have kept burning." It was moments like these, Richmond wrote, that galvanized charity workers to demand stiffer nonsupport laws. By 1901, Edward T. Devine, head of the New York Charity Organization Society, had made prosecution of delinquent husbands an "elemental principle" in his popular handbook for charity workers.[32]

The case for criminalization centered on the social interest in husbands as economic providers. "The chief value of a good law, well enforced," the New York charity worker Lilian Brandt observed in 1905, "is that it expresses the estimation in which society holds men who shirk their obligations to their families, and that it relieves society of the necessity of assuming their responsibilities." The feminist rhetoric that had previously paired the default of "worthless men" to the emancipation of their wives was absent from charity officials' legal arguments. William H. Baldwin, America's leading authority on desertion and nonsupport laws, agreed with his peers in charity work that desertion was caused by the "serious moral defect" of delinquent husbands, not by their inability to find steady wage work. This "fact" alone, Baldwin explained, meant "the law has to deal rather with offenders than with unfortunates." But Baldwin insisted the true offense against the public – what made desertion a crime – was economic. "The interest of the public attaches by reason of the non-support rather than the absence in case[s] of family desertion," he explained. "The essence of the evil," Devine agreed, was nonsupport.[33]

By 1905, forty-four of America's fifty states and territories had enacted new statutes that made a husband's desertion or failure to support his wife or children a crime. Between 1905 and 1911, states passed over fifty more criminal statutes on the subject. And by 1916, every state in the union had made desertion or nonsupport (or both) a crime. The degree of the offense ranged from a misdemeanor to a felony, the maximum penalty from thirty days' imprisonment (Indiana) to

---

[32] Richmond in Colcord, *Broken Homes*, 2; Devine, *Practice of Charity*, 133. See Boyer, *Urban Masses*, 175–251; May, "'Problem of Duty,'" 7–11.

[33] Lilian Brandt, *Five Hundred and Seventy-Four Deserters and Their Families: A Descriptive Study of Their Characteristics and Circumstances* (New York, 1905), 7; Baldwin, *Family Desertion and Non-Support Laws*, 9, 10; Edward T. Devine, *The Principles of Relief* (1904; New York, 1914), 138.

three years (Rhode Island). Many statutes specified that the term be at hard labor, and some required that the family of the convicted husband receive a daily wage for this work. The measures probably would have been even tougher if lawmakers had not feared that stiffer fines and sentences would further impoverish offenders' families.[34]

The first step toward criminalization in Illinois was the passage of an 1887 statute that made it a felony for any parent, guardian, or custodian to abandon a child less than one year old. In 1903 the General Assembly enacted the Wife and Child Abandonment Act, which made it a misdemeanor for a husband "without good cause" to abandon his wife or children *and* to fail to provide for them; the statute applied also to mothers who deserted their children. The assembly enlarged the category of criminal nonsupport in 1905 by making it a misdemeanor for any person to contribute to the dependency, delinquency, or neglect of a minor. In 1915, several years after the Chicago Court of Domestic Relations opened, Municipal Court judges, charity officials, members of the Illinois Equal Suffrage Association, and women activists from Hull-House would persuade the legislature to pass a uniform Nonsupport Act. The statute made it a misdemeanor for a husband not to support adequately his wife or children – even if he continued to live with them under the same roof. The statute, which applied also to mothers who failed to support their children, carried a maximum penalty of a $600 fine and a year in jail. The act's author, Municipal Court Judge Charles Goodnow, promised it would "reach those men who either through laziness, gambling, drunkenness or pure cussedness remain at home and refuse to work, or when they do work spend all their wages in drinking and gambling."[35]

---

[34] Baldwin, *Family Desertion and Non-Support Laws*, 13–14, 58–134; Baldwin, "Present Status of Family Desertion and Non-Support Laws," 1–3; Eubank, *Study of Family Desertion*, 6.

[35] Charles N. Goodnow, *A New Law Dealing with Wife and Child Abandonment* (Chicago, n.d.), 9; "An Act to prevent the abandonment of children," approved June 16, 1887, in *Illinois Revised Statutes*, 1911, ch. 38, sec. 42h; "An Act making it a misdemeanor to abandon or willfully neglect to provide for the support and maintenance by any person, of his wife, or of his or her minor children...," approved May 13, 1903 (hereafter cited as 1903 Abandonment Act), ibid., ch. 68, secs. 24–26; "An Act to provide for the punishment of persons responsible for or directly promoting, or contributing to, the conditions that render a child dependent, neglected or delinquent...," approved May 13, 1905, ibid., ch. 38, sec. 42hb. 1915 Act excerpted in Stelk, *1917 Report*, 77–79. See also *MCC* 7 (1913), 90; Louise de Koven Bowen, *Some Legislative Needs in Illinois* (Chicago, 1914), 9; "Society Women Talk Suffrage," *Chicago Tribune*, Jan. 9, 1912.

The novel array of penalties and disciplinary techniques contained in the nonsupport statutes show that the administrative style of modern welfare governance – its peculiar mix of provision and policing – has origins not only in the "protection" of mothers and children but also in the prosecution of delinquent husbands. The statutes assumed that local courts had the capacity to investigate defendants' employment histories, to administer a system of support payments, and to punish recalcitrant husbands with incarceration and fines. The Illinois Wife and Child Abandonment Act of 1903 set a maximum penalty of a $500 fine and a year in jail. That much would have been familiar to nineteenth-century ears. But the act also empowered judges to experiment with the new judicial technique of probation (eight years before Illinois enacted an adult probation law). The desertion act permitted trial courts to release a defendant on probation for one year, on the condition that he pay a weekly sum to his wife or to the court, which would then distribute it to his wife. In fixing this sum, the court would take notice of "the circumstances and financial ability of the defendant," and it could call the defendant back in at any time to readjust his payment schedule. Surveillance and administrative discretion were thus fixtures of breadwinner regulation nearly a decade before enactment of the first mothers' aid laws.[36]

Even though some states (including Illinois) had previously criminalized desertion in vagrancy or disorderly persons statutes, the new desertion and nonsupport statutes ratcheted up the state's power over wage-earning husbands. The power of the state – and the public at large – to police delinquent husbands grew, as lawmakers gave over this old area of equity and civil jurisdiction to the criminal law. Legal aid activists such as Reginald Heber Smith hailed the new statutes as "unpriced relief" for poor wives, who could now pursue legal action against their husbands by signing a criminal complaint. But though wives were the preferred complainant – because of their moral claim to support and because their testimony was vital to a successful prosecution – desertion and nonsupport was now a crime against the state. *Anyone* could set the prosecutorial machinery in action. In addition to neglected wives, charity workers, county welfare officials, police officers, neighbors, and relatives could demand the arrest of home slackers. Prosecutors, meanwhile, assumed a role previously performed mostly by private parties, the merchants who filed suits

---

[36] 1903 Abandonment Act, ch. 68, secs. 24–26. The 1915 nonsupport act worked in an identical fashion. The key changes were the enlarged category of the offense – it now included simple nonsupport – and the slightly higher fine.

to recover credit extended to wives for necessaries. Roscoe Pound explained that the desertion and nonsupport statutes expressed the new "social interest," secured by the state, in the family.[37]

As charity workers trumpeted the fiscal threat of delinquent husbands, appellate court judges, the guardians of the common law, redefined nonsupport as an offense against the public. The Kansas Supreme Court, for example, upheld that state's nonsupport statute as a reasonable exercise of police power to protect the public purse. "The essence of the act," the court declared, "is that a man shall not be allowed to shift the burden of supporting his wife and children upon others under no obligation to bear it, and possibly upon the state itself." Appellate courts found it reasonable for trial courts to look into husbands' earning power when fixing support payments and to compel them to work for wages. Significantly, the courts ruled that a wife's ability to support herself did not lighten her husband's legal burden. Neither the granting to married women of new rights to make contracts and own property during the nineteenth century nor the slowly rising economic independence of wage-earning women reduced a husband's duty to support his wife. In the face of these social and legal changes, the criminal statutes helped to keep alive the old common-law coupling of male protection and female dependence – only now with a stronger and more overtly class-specific element of public force.[38]

By 1911, when the Chicago Court of Domestic Relations opened for business, reformers and lawmakers had universally, if not uniformly, criminalized desertion and nonsupport in the United States. Local charity organizations, welfare officials, social workers, police, prosecutors, and wives were actively engaged in bringing home-slacking men to justice. Many private charities either required or strongly encouraged deserted wives applying for relief to seek warrants against their husbands. And in New York City, the National Conference of Jewish Charities – concerned about high rates of desertion among recent Jewish immigrants and the public image this problem fostered – opened the National Desertion Bureau, a legal aid office for deserted women that publicized, tracked down, and initiated prosecution against deserters in cities across America.[39]

---

37 Smith, *Justice and the Poor,* 76; Roscoe Pound, "Individual Interests in the Domestic Relations," *MLR,* 14 (1916), 195. See also Eubank, *Study of Family Desertion,* 52–53; Stelk, *1917 Report,* 28.

38 *State v. Waller,* 90 Kans. 829, in Stelk, *1917 Report,* 83. See also *Brandel v. State,* 161 Wisc. 532, in ibid., 81.

39 Reena Sigman Friedman, "'Send Me My Husband Who Is in New York City': Husband Desertion in the American Jewish Immigrant Community

The criminalization of desertion and nonsupport meshed surprisingly well with the masculine rhetoric of the American labor movement. In the late nineteenth century, skilled workingmen agitating for higher wages had stressed their duties as heads of republican households. In the new century, unskilled industrial workers, many of them recent immigrants from southern and eastern Europe, expanded this rhetoric of masculine citizenship. Workingmen in Chicago and other industrial communities took to the streets, demanding wages adequate to provide their families with an "American standard of living": a respectable home, with store-bought goods, no boarders, and, if possible, a "room where no one slept." "We cannot bring up our children as Americans on fifteen cents an hour and [no more than] forty hours a week," one Polish worker protested during Chicago's 1904 meat-packing strike. "We cannot live decently. Our wives, our children, our homes demand better wages."[40]

The grail of a family wage, as settlement activists and other middle-class friends of labor called this old ideal, was out of reach for most workers. A 1911 survey of Chicago's meat-packing district showed that on average husbands earned just over half their families' incomes; wives, children, and boarders brought in the rest. Four years later, the U.S. Commission on Industrial Relations reported that fully 79 percent of American fathers did not earn enough to support an average-sized family. Precisely what workingmen were struggling to establish as a *right* of masculine citizenship – the ability to support a family on their wages alone – the state was ever more vigorously enforcing as a *duty* through the criminal law.[41]

But the criminalization of nonsupport did not sound the death knell of family wage ideology. Far from it. Masculine responsibility was a core value and tenet of that ideology, and of the passel of public welfare initiatives it helped generate. The idea of a family wage for men was politically indefensible without the existence of a morally responsible, legally liable husband, who would earn that wage in the industrial workplace and bring it home to his dependents. It remains an open

1900–1926," *Jewish Social Studies*, 44 (1982), 1–18; Igra, "Other Men's Wives," 29–31, 159.

[40] Ron Rothbart, "'Homes Are What Any Strike Is About': Immigrant Labor and the Family Wage," *JSH*, 23 (1989), 267–84, esp. 270–71; "Stock Yards Workers Ask Bare Living Wage," *New Majority* (Chicago Federation of Labor), Jan. 4, 1919. See Lawrence B. Glickman, *A Living Wage: American Workers and the Making of Consumer Society* (Ithaca, N.Y., 1997).

[41] Barrett, *Work and Community*, 91, 90–107; Axinn and Levin, *Social Welfare*, 126.

question whether state lawmakers would have so quickly passed social insurance legislation for male industrial workers and especially pension legislation for single mothers without first enacting new criminal sanctions against delinquent husbands. But there is no question that these three distinct innovations of modern welfare governance grew out of the same progressive ideology of family preservation. In carrot-and-stick fashion, the criminal sanctions worked together with those later welfare initiatives to protect and police the "social unit."

While the desertion and nonsupport laws targeted wage-earning husbands who *would not* perform their manly duties as breadwinners, public concerns about husbands who *could not* shaped the most important welfare policy debates of the era. Campaigns for adult probation laws, enacted in thirty-four states between 1909 and 1915, stressed that incarceration made it impossible for men to feed their families. The figure of the worthy but incapacitated breadwinner, his body mangled by industrial machinery, provided persuasive imagery in the nation-wide campaign for employer-supported, state-administered workmen's compensation systems, which forty-two states established during the teens. The photographer Lewis Hine immortalized this figure in the heart-wrenching portraits he contributed to the feminist lawyer Crystal Eastman's influential reform tract, *Work-Accidents and the Law* (1910). One shot displays a disabled workman, his arm severed just below the shoulder, standing on a porch beside his wife and children. "ONE ARM AND FOUR CHILDREN," the caption reads. Another photo (not attributed to Hine) shows six young children, their backs to a soot-covered brick wall, gazing forlornly into the lens: "THE PROBLEM OF A RAILROAD WIDOW." The widow's problem, the reader understands, is soon to become the public's. The New York Employers' Liability Commission (1909–10) made the point more explicitly: "Through accidents of employment, thousands of workingmen's families are brought to extreme poverty and deprivation, the state suffers through the lowered standard of living of a vast number of its citizens, and the public is directly burdened with the maintenance of many who become destitute."[42]

The social cost of the deceased or disabled breadwinner also helped to justify the most revolutionary form of public assistance introduced in the early twentieth century: direct monetary aid to single mothers

[42] For the photos, see Crystal Eastman, *Work-Accidents and the Law* (New York, 1910), 156–57, 132–33; for the commission report, see 285; Theda Skocpol, *Protecting Soldiers and Mothers: The Political Origins of Social Policy in the United States* (Cambridge, Mass., 1992), 286, 285–302; Samuel Walker, *Popular Justice: A History of American Criminal Justice* (New York, 1980), 155.

to help them raise their children in their own homes. Between 1911 and 1919, the National Congress of Mothers and the Federation of Women's Clubs led a nationwide campaign that won mothers' pension laws in thirty-nine states. In theory, the statutes would replace the lost wages of a deceased or disabled breadwinner with a tightly regulated (and none too generous) government "pension." In a message to Congress in 1909, President Roosevelt had promised that pension programs would target "above all deserving mothers fairly well able to work but deprived of the support of the normal breadwinner." Mrs. G. Harris Robertson, president of the Tennessee Congress of Mothers, described the pensions in a 1911 speech as a necessary response to "a type of home which is a blot upon the name of civilization . . . a broken family circle, shattered by loss of father, the breadwinner – the home of the helpless widow burdened with little children."[43]

For all their moral freight, Roosevelt's and Robertson's words left open the possibility that states might choose to aid unmarried, divorced, or deserted mothers. But a chorus of charity workers and public officials warned that granting aid to deserted mothers would lighten the breadwinner's responsibility and reward desertion. With few exceptions, the new statutes withheld aid from unmarried mothers, and most excluded divorced or deserted mothers. Massachusetts, which did allow aid to deserted mothers, required them to first obtain a warrant against their husbands.[44]

Illinois provides a concrete example of the explicit policy linkages between mothers' pensions and breadwinner regulation. In 1911, Illinois enacted the nation's first, and one of its most inclusive, aid laws. The Funds to Parents Act specified no eligibility criteria whatsoever. In just two years the General Assembly replaced that law with one of the nation's strictest pension statutes. The Aid to Mothers and Children Act reserved aid for women whose husbands were dead or

---

[43] Roosevelt in Mimi Abramovitz, *Regulating the Lives of Women: Social Welfare Policy from Colonial Times to the Present* (Boston, 1988), 200; Robertson in Skocpol, *Protecting Soldiers*, 450, 424–79; Leff, "Consensus for Reform," 397–417; Barbara J. Nelson, "The Origins of the Two-Channel Welfare State: Workmen's Compensation and Mothers' Aid," in Gordon, ed., *Women, the State, and Welfare*, 123–51.

[44] Robertson herself urged that "provision include the deserted wife, and the mother who has never been a wife." Quoted in Skocpol, *Protecting Soldiers*, 451; see 467; Joanna Colcord, "Family Desertion and Non-Support," *Encyclopaedia of the Social Sciences*, 15 vols. (New York, 1930–35), 6: 80; Frank W. Goodhue, "Problems of Administration of Mothers' Aid: Discussion," *Proceedings of the National Conference of Social Work at the Forty-fifth Annual Session Held in Kansas City, Missouri, May 15–22, 1918* (Chicago, 1919), 366; Igra, "Other Men's Wives," 179.

permanently disabled. The disqualification of deserted mothers was a political response to public sentiment, which viewed giving cash to deserted women as an invitation to husbands to bolt. Judge Pinckney of the Juvenile Court, who drafted the 1913 act, warned that continuing to aid deserted mothers would unleash the "desertion microbe" of "indifferent men" and trigger "a migratory epidemic." Withholding aid from deserted families was thus a means of deterring shiftless breadwinners. Deserted wives who applied for pensions in Cook County were now redirected to the Chicago Court of Domestic Relations to seek their husbands' arrest. When Illinois finally reinstated pensions for deserted wives in 1923, it followed the long-standing practice of many private charities and made aid conditional upon wives' cooperating to prosecute their husbands.[45]

The pioneering welfare initiatives of the Progressive Era emerged piecemeal, not as a unified program. In the case of Illinois – which in a single year, 1911, introduced adult probation, workmen's compensation, mothers' pensions, and the Chicago Court of Domestic Relations – the temptation is perhaps all too great to see complete unity of purpose in those diverse innovations. Still, all of those initiatives were conceived in the same ideological milieu, and they attest to a common, gendered framework of expectations for progressive welfare policies. These polices all aimed to provide working people with a greater level of economic security, without threatening the family as an institution or allowing wage-earning husbands to shift their masculine responsibilities to the state. Few reformers (and still fewer politicians) would have favored family wage initiatives if the designated breadwinner had been free to shirk his duties. This was especially true for the private charity workers who joined the family wage cause in the 1910s after securing tighter legal sanctions for desertion and nonsupport a decade earlier. In Chicago, Jane Addams and other Hull-House activists were strong supporters of mothers' pensions and the family wage, even as they persuaded the judges of the Municipal Court to create a specialized criminal branch court for desertion and

---

45 Pinckney in David Spinoza Tanenhaus, "Policing the Child: Juvenile Justice in Chicago, 1870–1925," Ph.D. diss., University of Chicago, 1997, 2: 315, 320. See "All Charities Join," *Chicago Record-Herald*, Jan. 3, 1913; Eubank, *Study of Family Desertion*, 27, 61–62; Goodwin, *Politics of Welfare Reform*, 79–81, 128–29, 150; Joel DuBois Hunter, "Desertion and Non-Support by Fathers in Mothers' Aid Cases," *Proceedings of the National Conference of Social Work at the Forty-sixth Annual Session Held in Atlantic City, New Jersey, June 1–8, 1919* (Chicago, 1920), 308–9; Hugh Mann, "Mothers' Pension Law," *Chicago Socialist*, Oct. 16, 1911; "The Widows' Pension Law Again," *Chicago Inter Ocean*, Jan. 12, 1913.

nonsupport cases. Addams expressed optimism about the court's system for efficiently extracting support payments from delinquent workingmen like Frank Bumba. "Getting something from nothing," she called it.[46]

State lawmakers and local judges created socialized family courts in more than twenty-five cities and counties between 1910 and 1930. Buffalo established the first in 1910, followed later that year by New York City and then by Chicago. Cities borrowed each other's ideas. Bowen's 1910 visit to the New York court, for example, informed her vision for a Chicago tribunal. As in all matters of social regulation, however, federalism produced a multijurisdictional mosaic. Contemporaries used the term "domestic relations court" to identify those tribunals, such as Chicago's, that handled chiefly desertion and nonsupport. They used "family court" for institutions that also had a standard juvenile court jurisdiction over neglected, dependent, and delinquent children. A few family courts, such as those set up in Cincinnati (1914) and Honolulu (1921), also had civil jurisdiction over divorce. When talking of the entire class of tribunals, people used the generic term family court.[47]

The first annual report of the Chicago Court of Domestic Relations reads like a manifesto for the family court movement. High on every advocate's agenda was family preservation through tenacious judicial intervention. The report promised that channeling all domestic relations cases into a special tribunal would protect women and children from the "evil influences of a police court environment," facilitate individual "treatment" of offenders as judges became experts in home life, enable private social agencies to keep closer watch over families, and generate useful social knowledge – a "more intelligent understanding of conditions and environment surrounding each case and consequently a more just and sympathetic treatment of each offender." That knowledge could not be had by adjudicating conflicts as they landed on the court's threshold. Instead, the court would make a "vigorous reaching out for the causes of delinquency and dependency in children and by promptly checking the cause, lessen the effect." Roscoe Pound, whose writings were widely cited by welfare activists, applauded the socialized techniques of family courts. But even he was wary. "The powers of the court of Star Chamber were a bagatelle compared with

[46] Addams in Ida M. Tarbell, "A Court of Hope and Goodwill," *American Magazine*, Jan. 1914, p. 44; Stelk, *1917 Report*, 70–71. See Goodwin, *Politics of Welfare Reform*, 46, 102.
[47] Children's Bureau, *Child, the Family, and the Court*, esp. 65–67.

those of American Juvenile Courts and Courts of Domestic Relations,"
he exclaimed.[48]

The Court of Domestic Relations, Judge Uhlir observed, was "primarily a court for poor people and immigrants." In 1916, the University
of Chicago sociologist Earle Edward Eubank examined more than
300 case files. He found that the defendants were mostly "men of
humble occupations – wage-earners." More than half were unskilled
laborers. Eighteen nationalities were represented. Some 48 percent
of the men were Protestants, 41 percent Catholic, and 10 percent
Jewish (a few were unaffiliated). Although the public image of the
home slacker was a "white" immigrant workingman, desertion was already a serious problem in Chicago's African-American community.
African-Americans comprised only 2 percent of the city's population
in 1910, but 21 percent of the deserted families aided by the county
agent from 1909 to 1915 were black. African-American elites were far
more critical than white reformers of the racial inequities of the city's
criminal justice system. But they were no less willing to use that system to enforce marital bonds in workers' homes. Ida B. Wells-Barnett,
the famous antilynching activist, worked as a probation officer in the
Municipal Court during the 1910s. Wells-Barnett handled cases of
black men convicted of desertion or contributing to dependency,
and she filed some complaints herself. The *Chicago Defender*, the city's
leading African-American newspaper, was vigilant about the personal
comportment and morals – as well as the civil rights and material
well-being – of black laborers. The *Defender*'s "Legal Helps" advice column told neglected wives how to file nonsupport cases, and articles on
African-American women doing just that were common. In 1921, after
the wartime migration had swelled the African- American population
to 4 percent of Chicago's total, 16 percent of the Court of Domestic
Relations' defendants were black.[49]

Many were the pathways to socialized justice in the Court of Domestic
Relations, as the desertion and nonsupport statutes dispersed the

---

[48] *MCC* 5 (1911), 69; Roscoe Pound, "The Administration of Justice in the
Modern City," *HLR*, 26 (1913), 322.

[49] Uhlir in City of Chicago, Municipal Court, *Report of the Work of the Court of
Domestic Relations*, 1913–14 (n.p.), 3; Eubank, *Study of Family Desertion*, 17,
15, 16. See E. Franklin Frazier, *The Negro Family in Chicago* (Chicago, 1932),
147; Allan H. Spear, *Black Chicago: The Making of a Negro Ghetto, 1890–1920*
(Chicago, 1967), 12; "Defender's Legal Helps," *Chicago Defender*, May 16,
1914. See also "Pierson Must Pay," ibid., May 10, 1919; "Many Women Force
Men in Court; Non-Support," ibid., April 8, 1922. For cases involving Wells-
Barnett, see *People v. Willie Scott*, case 105630, March 20, 1914, MCCCR;
People v. William H. Rhoden, case 105634, March 26, 1914, ibid.

power to police men through the body politic. The range of public officials and private citizens who brought delinquent husbands to the attention of the police and the court shows how embedded the court was in Chicago's mixed economy of welfare provision. Wives were the most common complainants; theirs were acts of courage and desperation. But they did not always file complaints freely. Some private charities required deserted women to obtain warrants against their husbands in order to receive clothing, food, or fuel for their families. The United Charities apparently had no black-and-white policy, but its agents grew suspicious if a wife who claimed to be deserted did not seek a warrant, thinking she may be harboring a shiftless husband at home. Agents of the United Charities, the JPA, and other private agencies also filed many complaints in their own names. The growing public machinery of provision created a second pathway to the court. After deserted women lost eligibility for mothers' pensions in 1913, social workers and probation officers from the County Juvenile Court, which administered the pensions in Chicago, became familiar faces in the Court of Domestic Relations. In 1914, Margaret Grace of the Juvenile Court signed a complaint against Dennis Buckley, an American-born laborer who, according to his probation officer, spent his wages on whiskey and abused his family. Cases such as those were common enough that the Juvenile Court produced a standard form for requesting warrants from the Court of Domestic Relations. Relatives and neighbors also constituted a vast informal network of relief in working-class communities and a third pathway to judicial intervention. When cases of family neglect violated community standards, the task often fell to ordinary citizens to demand justice. In the winter of 1914, a neighbor filed a complaint against a hard-drinking teamster named Clarence McDougall for abandoning his wife, leaving her "very ill" and "paralyzed" and their child dependent on relatives.[50]

When a wife pursued legal action in the Court of Domestic Relations – and when her husband was hauled in on a warrant – they entered an institution defined by an explicitly gendered division of space, labor, and power. No socialized family court was complete without the teamwork of caring female social workers, who supervised the court's "social" functions, and a stern male judge, who maintained a firm hold on the law. "A confessional and a hand of authority," Ida M. Tarbell dubbed this arrangement in her glowing 1914 piece on the

---

[50] *People v. Dennis Buckley*, case 105591, March 16, 1914, MCCCR; *People v. Clarence McDougall*, case 105555, March 13, 1914, ibid. See also *People v. Henry Abbott*, case 105571, March 14, 1914, ibid.; *People v. Frank Beardsley*, case 413410, June 1, 1923, ibid.; Eubank, *Family Desertion*, 38, 61–62.

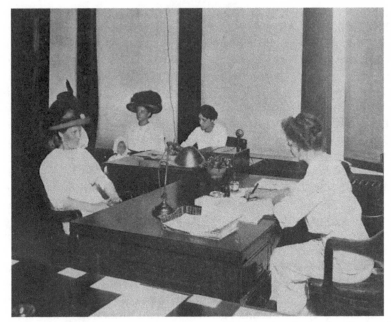

Wives seeking warrants against "home-slacker" husbands in the Court of
Domestic Relations first had to persuade social workers in the Social Service
Department that their cases merited legal action. Courtesy of the Chicago
Historical Society (ICHi-31058).

court for *American Magazine.* The court's first social service secretary,
Marie Leavitt, was a JPA officer. For the first seven months, Leavitt and
her "corps of investigators" were paid jointly by the JPA, the Catholic
Woman's Protectorate, and the Jewish Bureau of Personal Service –
three local associations led by women. The social workers then moved
onto the city payroll, continuing the JPA tradition of transferring its
initiatives to the public sector. By 1920, seven salaried social workers
staffed the Social Service Department.[51]

A wife seeking a warrant first had to make her case to one of those
women in the Social Service Department, across the hall from the
main courtroom. Many complainants arrived at the court half-starved

---

[51] Tarbell, "Court of Hope," 43–44. See "Domestic Tribunal Proves its Utility,"
Chicago Record-Herald, undated clipping, 1911, HODS, "Goodnow" file; JPA,
untitled annual report, 1910–11, 15; JPA, *Annual Report of the Juvenile Protective Association of Chicago,* 1913–14, pp. 13–14; Stelk, *1917 Report,* 70; MCC
12–14 (1918–20), 154, 156. See also Arthur J. Lacy, "What the Detroit
Court of Domestic Relations Accomplished," reprint from *American Legal
News,* Sept. 1914, unpaginated.

and disoriented, having walked from their neighborhoods through the frenetic business district of the Loop to seek justice. To them the department must have seemed an alien mix of the bureaucratic and the domestic. Housed in a converted courtroom, shades drawn to the public, the department was the domain of professional women who made a gendered claim to expertise in the social techniques of investigation and counseling. The layout conveyed the middle-class ideal of a well-ordered home life. Half the room served as the business area, where the social workers interviewed complainants amidst card catalogs brimming with social data. The other half was a waiting area, where an attaché, clad in governess's whites, watched over women and their children in a space done up like a parlor, with rocking chairs and a table filled with "proper reading matter." The waiting area was equipped with toys and blocks with which, Judge William Gemmill mused significantly, "the children could erect houses." Each year the staff set up a Christmas tree and handed out clothing, toys, and candy to the children of complainants. In 1920, the department reported, exactly 910 children had participated in that year's Yuletide festivities.[52]

The professional social worker and the working-class complainant met in an atmosphere of formal equality, seated across from each other at a desk. Tarbell believed sisterly understanding pervaded the process. "There are sides to [the complainant's] story which she could tell to no one but a woman.... It is her own story, told to one whom she instinctively knows can understand and sympathize, which determines whether a warrant shall be issued for the husband, or whether the woman shall be persuaded 'to try again.'" On a standard form, the social worker recorded the raw sociological facts of this domestic narrative: the age, race, nativity, occupation and wages, schooling, religious training, criminal records, children, and marital history of the woman and her husband. One section of the form consisted of a list of common causes of desertion for the investigator to check off when applicable: excessive drink, immorality, venereal disease, ill temper and abuse, interference of in-laws, the youth of the parties when married, illness, and, last on the list, the husband's "inability to support family." If the case came to trial, the judge would have this sheet of social facts before him on the bench.[53]

Given the alternatives – a male cop or court clerk – complainants may well have preferred to tell their stories to a social worker of their

[52] *MCC 6* (1912), 84–97, esp. 85; Gemmill, "Chicago Court," 122; *MCC 12–14* (1918–20), 162. See John Stelk to Harry Olson, Jan. 9, 1917, MCC, box 2, folder 32.

[53] Tarbell, "Court of Hope," 43–44; *MCC 5* (1911), 72; *MCC 6* (1912), 84–97.

TABLE 2: Court of Domestic Relations Caseload, 1912–1920

Year	Complaints filed	Warrants issued	Cases disposed of
1912	–[a]	–	3,386
1913	–	–	4,241
1914	10,765	4,413	3,961
1915	–	–	3,930
1916	9,895	3,521	2,914
1917	12,895	4,578	4,671
1918	14,217	4,221	2,806
1919	16,931	3,986	3,538
1920	38,441	3,342	3,165

[a] –: Data not available.
Source: Compiled from Municipal Court of Chicago annual reports.

own sex. But there was no mistaking the class difference between these women, no forgetting who controlled the process. The social workers were trained professionals, plainly but neatly clad, accustomed to working within institutions of middle-class, usually male, power: universities, charity organizations, and courts. They exercised wide discretion in vetting complaints to determine which cases made it to court. In "emergency cases," which exceeded some unwritten threshold of domestic violence or deprivation, the department requested an immediate warrant. In "non-emergency cases," social workers tried to reconcile husbands and wives with only the threat of punishment. Judges praised the social workers for their skill in calming down "hysterical" women, "convincing three-fourths of their callers that, instead of an arrest, the husbands are entitled to notification by mail." The social workers exercised wide discretion. In 1914, for example, only 4,413 of the 10,765 total complaints filed in the court resulted in a warrant issued. Over time, a diminishing percentage of complaints filed would make it to trial. The greatest gap came in 1920, when the post–World War I crisis of inflation and unemployment overwhelmed the department with more than 38,000 complaints, of which fewer than one-tenth generated a warrant. (See Table 2.)[54]

Husbands who fell under the scrutiny of the Social Service Department did not share reformers' enthusiasm for a domesticated judiciary. In 1915, Chief Justice Olson received an angry letter from a defendant

54 Stelk, *1917 Report*, 41; "The Court of Domestic Relations: A Branch of the Municipal Court of Chicago and Three Judges who made it famous...," unpaginated pamphlet dated Sept. 30, 1914, JHO, box 2.

named A. Welthony. Welthony had appeared twice in the Court of Domestic Relations, and he hit Olson with a litany of grievances. Welthony insisted he had left home because his "insane wife" had driven him out. Now that she had used the court to seize control of his household, her "sporty" relatives had made themselves at home. He also protested the court's "unreasonable" support orders – three-quarters of his twenty-dollar weekly wage in a hand laundry. But the defendant reserved his greatest ire for a social worker named Caroline Grimsby, a former JPA protective officer, who so impressed him that he mistook her for a judge. "I ask you to please help me as I have been driven beyond human endurance," he wrote. "Judge Grimsby will not listen to any man's complaint." Welthony concluded with a man-to-man plea to the chief justice. "As this court furnishes help and advice for women, please inform me on this subject. How can I end this trouble?"[55]

But the husband's real troubles were in the courtroom, the seat of legal authority, where the power of the state resided exclusively in men, from the judge on his elevated bench to the assistant state's attorney, assistant city prosecutor, bailiffs, and clerks below. The court was a public space with a seating capacity of 100 and a jury box as likely to be filled with visiting sociologists and students as with actual jurors. Unless a defendant requested a jury – fewer than 1 percent did – the judge had the final word on his case. Prosecutors presented cases in a perfunctory manner, allowing judges to pepper defendants with direct questions and challenges to their manhood. "What have you done that is noble in life?" Judge Stelk asked one defendant. For the court's many immigrant defendants, a day in the court must have felt like a crash course in the duties and prerogatives of American masculine citizenship. In one 1911 case, Judge Goodnow lectured a Russian immigrant baker, through an interpreter, on his "sacred duty" of support. "No man who deserts his family can ever be a good citizen." The judge had the final authority to arrange the contested claims of domestic conflict into an official narrative and to render judgment. The threat of incarceration backed their every word. Judge Gemmill warned reformers, "In advocating law reforms, in order to secure social justice, it is all-important to keep in mind the urgent need of keeping the law *strong and virile,* and in making the penalties for its violation real and substantial."[56]

[55] A. Welthony to Harry Olson, Aug. 4, 1915, MCC, box 4, folder 29. I have corrected punctuation and spelling.
[56] Joseph Dillabough, "A Day in Court with Judge Stelk," in Stelk, *1917 Report,* 165–66; ibid., 168; Goodnow in "Joy in Family Court"; Gemmill, "Chicago Court," 123, emphasis added. See Stelk to Olson, Jan. 9, 1917.

There was little question among reformers and commentators that the judge who would deploy the strong and virile law to usurp a workingman's right to govern his own household must be a man – a man of unimpeachable character, intelligence, and, by virtue of his occupation, an upstanding member of the middle class. Some judges assigned by Harry Olson to the Court of Domestic Relations had risen to political office from the same populations whose home lives the court policed. Joseph Uhlir was a Bohemian immigrant who grew up in what progressives called a broken home: His father died when he was only four. He had this in common with both Olson and Stelk, who lost their fathers during their teens, and later remembered being thrown at an early age into the role of breadwinners. Uhlir received his education in the Chicago public schools and his legal training in the way of immigrant lawyers, first as a law office grunt, then at night school. He served as a popular three-term Republican alderman from the Twelfth Ward – no mean achievement in Anton Cermak's Democratic stronghold – before his election to the municipal bench in 1908. He enjoyed the political support of women welfare activists, who praised his "deep sympathy with the poor and wonderful understanding of the home conditions among our immigrant population." Among his innovations was the small fund he created to provide emergency relief to starving families and milk for babies brought to court.[57]

Whether or not judges had actual life experience among the poor, many of them quickly assumed public personas as experts on home life. Many judges became respected spokesmen for greater state control of home life. Judge Goodnow was a popular speaker before civic groups. In 1912 he told the Illinois Congress of Mothers and Parent Teacher Associations, "The absolute ignorance of the masses in regard to the responsibilities, duties, rights, and privileges is appalling and the home should be subjected to the gravest criticism." Judge Gemmill, a Republican and nationally renowned criminologist, contributed articles to social science journals and law reviews under titles such as "Divorce as a Sign of Degeneracy or of Progress." (A bit of both, he concluded.) The enterprising Judge Sheridan Fry penned an advice column in the *Record-Herald*, serving up to a middle-class audience wisdom gleaned from policing working-class home life. Judge Stelk, a tough-minded Democrat, topped the public relations efforts of his brethren by compiling a 183-page report on the court, dedicating

---

[57] "Court of Domestic Relations: A Branch"; *Chicago City Manual* (1908), 179; *BOC* (1917), 1917, 687; *MCC 10–11* (1916–17), 8; Alfred H. Gross, "John Stelk," in Stelk, *1917 Report*, 130–31.

nearly half of those pages to his own social theories and boot-strap exhortations.[58]

When Roscoe Pound compared domestic relations courts to the Star Chamber, he might have had in mind the unusual discretion exerted by the new specialized judges. To get at the social facts behind cases, the judges discarded the procedural model of the common-law court, with its presumption of innocence and its image of the judge as an impartial referee who passed judgment on evidence presented to him, in an adversarial process, by prosecutors and defense attorneys. "Nearly all of the questions are put by the judge," Gemmill explained, "and are aimed to reach the heart of the trouble by the most direct route." Reaching the heart of the matter might involve dispatching a probation officer to interview the defendant's landlord, employer, neighbors, relatives, or pastor. It might entail sending the defendant – or complainant – to the Psychopathic Laboratory for a battery of mental tests.[59]

If the judge's inquisitorial powers were extraordinary by common-law standards, his powers of disposition were even more so. The desertion and nonsupport statutes armed the judge with the power to incarcerate, fine, and supervise men, and to do so continuously for a year. Because long-term incarceration of breadwinners defeated the purpose of family courts, lawmakers designed nonsupport statutes to be coercive rather than purely punitive. The typical convicted husband was put on probation with a one-year jail term hanging over his head, ordered to make regular support payments, and required to comply with a set of personalized conditions. Representative probation orders from 1914 include "Keep sober, work and support his family" and "work, stay home at nights and give money to wife." The court could order a husband to make payments directly to his wife, under the supervision of a probation officer, or to the court, which then paid the wife. The judge fixed support payments according to the husband's earning power, based upon inquiries made with his employer. (The court lacked authority to garnish wages.) And judges returned the favor, passing along social data to industrial employers in Chicago who requested it. In calibrating support payments, judges

---

[58] "Judge Blames Mothers for Domestic Troubles," *Chicago Tribune*, May 9, 1912; William N. Gemmill, "Divorce as a Sign of Degeneracy or of Progress," *ILR* 9 (1914), 32–34; Gemmill, "Chicago Court"; "Why Go to Court When the Judge Will Come to You?," *Chicago Record-Herald*, Nov. 15, 1914; Stelk, *1917 Report.*

[59] Gemmill, "Chicago Court," 121. See *People v. Joseph Marek*, June 5, 1923, case 413422, MCCCR; *People v. John Tobin*, May 10, 1923, case 413265, ibid.

also took notice of the expanding meaning of "necessaries" in America's consumer culture. Judge Gemmill recalled, "In many cases the court was called upon to determine how much a wife, whose husband earns from $15 to $20 per week, should pay for her spring or fall hat." In other cases, "the all-important question was how much the wife should allow her husband during the week for carfare, beer and cigars."[60]

It was a common and powerfully symbolic event for a defendant to experience the full wrath of the virile law. Accused home slackers were often arrested in front of other men, at their place of work or favorite saloon – which, in many cases, was their most reliable address. One baker was arrested at his union office. The arrest and trial of home slackers must have sent a message to working-class communities and the public at large that the manly prerogatives authorized by the breadwinner norm were contingent upon men fulfilling their legally assigned roles. Some defendants, such as a Polish laborer named Alexander Unisky, suffered the maximum penalty. Prosecuted for contributing to the dependency of his two children in 1914, Unisky spent a year in the House of Correction. Many more defendants, including Charles S., a twenty-eight-year-old unemployed butcher, served shorter terms, when judges thought a few weeks on the rock pile would steel them to perform their manly duties. Charles S. was committed to the House of Correction for a year, but after six weeks he was ordered back into court and placed on probation. Judge Stelk incarcerated one out of every six defendants who appeared before him. He arranged with the warden of the House of Correction to have home slackers assigned to the brickyard or quarry.[61]

As World War I heated up in 1917, Judge Stelk hit upon a new idea for reforming home slackers. He entered an order to have a group of

---

[60] Gemmill, "Chicago Court," 122. For typical orders, see *People v. Peter Krukowski*, case 105509, March 9, 1914, MCCCR; *People v. Austin Sutton*, case 105514, March 9, 1914, ibid.; *People v. Thomas Burke*, case 105535, March 11, 1914, ibid. For employer inquiries, see *People v. John Tobin*, case 413265, May 10, 1923, MCCCR; *People v. Marek*. See also Robert C. Brown, "The Duty of the Husband to Support the Wife," *VLR*, 18 (June 1932), 823–24; Stelk, *1917 Report*, 66; Tarbell, "Court of Hope," 44.

[61] "Joy in Family Court." *People v. Alexander Unisky*, case 105562, March 13, 1914, MCCCR; *People v. Charles S.* [last name illegible], case 105530, March 10, 1914, ibid.; *People v. John Ryan*, case 413448, June 6, 1923, ibid. The exact figure for those incarcerated is 630 of 3,958. Stelk also noted that hundreds of the men listed in his official report as "D.W.P." (dismissed for want of prosecution) had in fact been briefly incarcerated by him before being released. Stelk, *1917 Report*, 121, 18–19.

able-bodied men whom he had previously committed to the House of Correction brought back into the court. There he offered the prisoners a choice: join "the colors" or return to the workhouse. A number of the men agreed to take their chances on the battlefield. The judge had them escorted to an American recruiting office. An officer's refusal to induct the convicts into the U.S. armed services did not quell what Stelk described as his "desire to see them of service to world-democracy and freedom." So he sent the men who were not U.S. citizens to the British-Canadian Recruiting Mission. An officer there inducted the men, Stelk happily recalled, and "promised to look after their redemption, making men of them, it is to be hoped." In his determination to make men of home slackers, the judge seemed to forget that he was sending those men even further from their homes into a war from which they might never return.[62]

Even Stelk conceded that the traditional judicial power of assigning punishment was present in the court as the brawn behind a much more ambitious project of social governance. The court "is designed to be not only a judicial force, but to partake of the nature of a constructive social agency," he explained. Social workers supplied husbands and wives with budget books to help stretch their pay envelopes. Women who filed bastardy complainants had to undergo a physical exam by the court's nurse to prove they were pregnant. The nurse, Isabelle Carruthers, was placed in the court in 1913 by the Visiting Nurses' Association, an agency that made house calls to poor patients who did not live close to a hospital. She quickly made the city payroll. Each month, Carruthers visited dozens of homes, where she took complaints from women too sick to make the trip downtown and investigated complaints of husbands and neighbors about drunken wives. In a 1916 report, she recounted what happened when the Visiting Nurses' Association asked her to secure the return of a child to the Lincoln State School and Colony for the Feeble-Minded. The child's mother "was exhausted after five years' constant care of it," but the father "was not willing that the child should be given institutional care." This solitary agent of the court, entering a home in nurse's whites for an investigation, did what she believed was in the best interest of the child. "I made an investigation, signed the necessary papers, and had the child sent through the Psychopathic Hospital, to Lincoln."[63]

---

[62] Stelk, *1917 Report*, 20. See Julia McGuire, "The Girl the Solider Left Behind," in ibid., 50.

[63] Stelk, *1917 Report*, 24, 52; Isabelle Carruthers, "Report of the Deputy Bailiff and Visiting Nurse for April 1916," MCC, box 5, folder 31, unpaginated; *MCC* 7 (1913), 90.

Several of the court's judges gave their hearty endorsement to the Psychopathic Laboratory and its eugenics program. Judge Stelk called the laboratory "a very valuable adjunct to the court," which had given him new insight into the people who appeared in his court. "It is a soul-shaking experience to have seen the horrors of transmitted disease in many cases brought to my attention," he wrote. Because he knew the laboratory was "overtaxed," he referred only "such cases as, in my opinion, required commitment." Women who brought complaints to the court unknowingly risked being sent there – another way the aggrieved became the policed. In 1917, for example, Stelk and his social workers referred 145 women and 237 men to the laboratory, though 84 percent of the defendants that year were men.[64]

A legion of voluntary organizations helped the tribunal deliver social governance to the neighborhoods. "The court that you see sitting up there is merely the first factor," Harry Olson told an audience of San Francisco charity workers, "he is merely the one person who sets these various institutions in motion." In 1917 alone, the Social Service Department made nearly 3,000 referrals. Some went to public institutions, such as the Psychopathic Laboratory and the County Agent. But most were referred to private agencies, including the Illinois Humane Society (542 referrals), the JPA (476), the Jewish Bureau of Personal Service (196), the Legal Aid Society (184), the Visiting Nurses' Association (145), the United Charities (141), the Citizens' League (135), the Catholic Protectorate (134), and the Bohemian Charities (60). The services provided by these groups varied. The JPA investigated families. The Citizens' League prosecuted saloon-keepers for selling liquor to habitual drunkards. The United Charities provided relief to poor families and made home visits for the court. When a man named Frank Hammond asked the chief justice to be relieved from jury duty, Olson asked the United Charities to check up on him. A social worker visited Hammond at home, and sent the judge a detailed report on his wages, debts, and the health of his entire family. "They appeared to be very grateful for your interest and for the visit," she wrote.[65]

The overriding purpose of socialized family courts was to keep poor families such as the Bumbas and the Hammonds off the welfare rolls, and in this the Court of Domestic Relations appears to have enjoyed some success. In 1910, the year before the court's creation, the Municipal Court clerk had collected a total of $13,000 from men found

---

[64] Stelk, *1917 Report*, 22–23, 34, 121–22.
[65] Olson, "Municipal Court of Chicago: A Tribunal," 10; Stelk, *1917 Report*, 113; Elizabeth Dixon to Harry Olson, March 15, 1916, MCC, box 5, folder 30.

guilty of nonsupport in the thirteen criminal branches. In the Court of Domestic Relations's first year, 1911, that figure rose 51 percent to $19,618. During the postwar unemployment crisis of 1920, the Social Service Department processed more than 38,000 complaints, and the clerk of the Municipal Court cut support checks for wives and guardians totaling $342,000. By comparison, the Board of Cook County spent only $269,000 that same year on noncash relief for the entire county. The board paid out a comparable sum in mothers' pensions. The United Charities spent just $200,000 on relief. So the Court of Domestic Relations was a major player in welfare provision in America's second largest city. And all of the money it distributed came from delinquent husbands – not the public coffers.[66]

The workingmen policed by the new regime of breadwinner regulation during the Progressive Era did not let the courts' interference with their manly prerogatives go uncontested. Men from the Court of Domestic Relations were the county probation department's hardest cases. "The defendant usually leaves the Court swearing that he never will make the payments ordered," one officer explained. "Some of these people run away, and some give wrong addresses ... and very few pay what is ordered without a great deal of effort on the part of the officer." Some defendants vented their rage by beating and abusing their wives. The court's response in the Bumba case was representative of the way it handled many other reports from probation officers of domestic violence. The judge ordered Bumba hauled back into court but then only attached a new payment order to his probation regimen. In its determination to keep poor families intact and off the welfare rolls, the court sometimes forced wives back into the arms of abusive husbands. When violence erupted, judges too often looked the other way.[67]

---

[66] *MCC 12–14* (1918–20), 153–56, 160; Children's Bureau, *Administration of the Aid-to-Mothers Law*, 112. In 1920 Chicago had a population of 2,701,705, compared with 3,053,017 for all of Cook County; see U.S. Bureau of the Census, *Fourteenth Census of the United States, Taken in the Year 1920*, vol. 1: *Population 1920* (Washington, 1921), 394.

[67] *MCC 7* (1913), 110; *People v. Bumba*. See also *People v. William Nausieda*, case 105580, March 16, 1914, MCCCR; Cora M. Winchell, "A Study of the Court of Domestic Relations of the City of Chicago as an Agency in the Stabilization of the Home," M.A. thesis, University of Chicago, 1921, p. 38. For other reports of domestic violence, see *People v. Oscar Blottiaux*, case 105519, March 9, 1914, MCCCR; *People v. Gustav J. Brown*, case 105741, March 30, 1914, ibid.; *People v. Charles O'Malley*, case 105766, April 1, 1914, ibid. See Linda Gordon, *Heroes of Their Own Lives: The Politics and History of Family Violence: Boston 1880–1960* (New York, 1988).

For all of the contradictions of the Court of Domestic Relations, its steadily rising caseload attests to the power that poor women sought and sometimes found there. For poor women, the court provided a new and affordable legal means to force their husbands to keep their marital promises. Wives approached the court as complainants, and they asked the court to help them claim some control over the scarce financial resources that so often lay at the heart of domestic conflict. Intriguing anecdotal evidence suggests that many wives came to regard the payments they received at the office of the Municipal Court clerk as a form of *entitlement* secured by the state – even if they were ineligible to stand in the other line of women at the office of the County Agent and receive a mother's pension. Judge Stelk reported, "It causes confusion and disorder in the clerk's office to have so many women calling there, including a large number who complain loudly and long when disappointed."[68]

After World War I, the Social Service Department handled more and more cases without a trial. In 1920, when the department's business exploded to 38,441 complaints, the number of warrants issued actually declined from the previous year to 3,342. The following year, a court report explained that high inflation and a tight labor market were still "responsible for much misery. Men who have families and who are out of work and who find employment sometimes hard to obtain become not only discouraged but in many instances positively desperate. This state of mind of such men is manifested in many ways, according to their mental make-up, surroundings and habits." This shifting causal perspective on male irresponsibility was reflected in the diminishing proportion of warrants issued. "Our court has become much more a great social agency than a court," observed Judge Harry Fisher in 1921. "The judicial power is resorted to only where coercion is necessary." Trial and punishment remained a common event, thanks partly to the 1923 revision of the Illinois mother's pension law, which opened eligibility to deserted mothers who helped the state prosecute their husbands. In 1926, for example, the Social Service Department conducted 39,656 "interviews" (no longer called "complaints" in the department's reports), claimed credit for 2,822 reconciliations, and secured 5,161 warrants. But as those numbers suggest, for most women seeking legal action against their husbands in the 1920s, the department *was* the Court of Domestic Relations. (See Table 3.)[69]

[68] Stelk, *1917 Report*, 30.
[69] *MCC 15* (1921), 124; Harry Fisher quoted in Children's Bureau, *Child, the Family, and the Court*, 14; MCC 19–22 (1925–28), 107.

TABLE 3: Court of Domestic Relations Caseload, 1921–1930

Year	"Interviews"	Warrants issued	Cases disposed of
1921	39,136	3,663	3,359
1922	32,165	–[a]	6,768
1923	33,344	–	3,789
1924	34,517	–	3,255
1925	39,665	4,513	4,000
1926[b]	39,656	5,161	5,767
1927[b]	35,104	5,847	4,353
1928[b]	36,169	4,377	2,766
1929	–	–	2,549
1930	–	–	2,324

[a] –: Data not available.
[b] From 1926 to 1928, the Municipal Court had a short-lived branch for bastardy cases. The bastardy branch was effectively an adjunct to the Court of Domestic Relations. The Social Service Department served both courts. The two courts were reunited in 1929. The figures above for 1926–28 include both branches.
Source: Municipal Court of Chicago annual reports.

The partial, ambivalent retreat from punishing home slackers in Chicago reflected a broader shift in sentiments among American social workers and child welfare activists after the war. The shift was registered in a 1919 study of the "social treatment" of family desertion by Joanna C. Colcord, the superintendent of the New York Charity Organization Society, which had played such a leading role in the turn-of-the-century movement for criminal statutes. "Changes in the social worker's attitude toward treatment," she wrote, "have meant less emphasis on punitive and repressive measures, more consideration of the man's point of view." But criminal sanctions remained important. "If they were not there in the background, ready to be taken advantage of when all else fails, the social worker's hands would be tied, and the possibility of a rich and flexible treatment of desertion problems would be lost to her." Representations of home slackers and their crime remained full of dissonance. There was a growing reluctance to lay the blame for desertion and nonsupport entirely upon the husband, a somewhat greater willingness to see his delinquency in the context of social factors beyond his control. When a team from the Children's Bureau produced a detailed report on socialized family courts in 1929, they concluded that desertion and nonsupport were "rarely the result of a deliberate desire to violate either the law or the traditional obligations of the family. Rather they are caused by economic conditions, poverty, and physical and mental limitations." But the criminal law still had a valuable function. Despite its "inherent limitations," the law remained a useful force for "social engineering."[70]

The perpetuation of the progressive regime of breadwinner regulation attests to its central and enduring importance to the political development of the American welfare state. This court-based regime emerged alongside the first modern welfare policies. From the start, social insurance for workingmen and public assistance for single mothers strengthened the expectation that able-bodied husbands must fulfill their legal duties as breadwinners – even if the state had to make them. Since the passage of the first mothers' pension laws, state lawmakers had made public assistance to mothers contingent upon the policing of husbands. And since the early twentieth century, the specter of the criminally inadequate male provider has resurfaced whenever government officials have needed to defend the legitimacy of welfare. Not long after the federal government began providing public assistance to mother-headed families in the Social Security Act of 1935, effectively federalizing mothers' pensions, welfare agencies administering the program required deserted women seeking aid to prove their husbands could not be found. Nearly half a century later, the federal Family Support Act of 1988 mandated a more efficient system of child-support enforcement that included withholding men's wages. As the "war on poverty" has devolved into the "war on welfare," states have passed countless measures – including new criminal statutes – to extract support payments from "deadbeat dads," the home slackers of our own time.[71]

As Progressive Era family courts served the social interest in the working-class family, their practices of governance revealed the paradoxical yet always powerful nature of socialized law. We need not think of home slackers as victims in order to see that the cultural and legal norm of the male breadwinner asked the impossible of many of these men. Given cyclical unemployment and the other structural uncertainties of an industrial economy, it is understandable that the breadwinner norm, a touchstone of masculine identity and prerogative, took a

---

[70] Colcord, *Broken Homes*, 63–64, 54; Children's Bureau, *Child, the Family, and the Court*, 55, 21. See Ellen Cook, "Factors in Desertion," *CCR*, 4 (April 1920), 103–5.

[71] Grace Abbott, *The Child and the State*, vol. 2: *The Dependent Child and the Delinquent Child; The Child of Unmarried Parents* (Chicago, 1938), 2: 309–18; Igra, "Other Men's Wives," 193, 195; Michael B. Katz, *The Undeserving Poor: From the War on Poverty to the War on Welfare* (New York, 1989), 98.

psychological toll on men who failed to live up to its expectations. As workers' demands for an "American standard of living" and countless social surveys made clear, industrial employers in the early twentieth century paid few workers a "family wage." And yet to charity workers, settlement house activists, lawmakers, and judges, making nonsupport a crime seemed an eminently practical and moral solution to dependency. The criminalization of nonsupport and the creation of socialized family courts gave state agencies, private charities, and neglected wives a powerful – if ultimately disappointing – tool with which to punish the irresponsibility and challenge the dominance of married workingmen. But punishment was never the final objective in a socialized court. Using the case as a ticket of entry, the state stepped with new vigor across the threshold of the working-class home and attempted to bring *all* of its occupants under the discipline of social governance.[72]

[72] Lizabeth Cohen, *Making a New Deal: Industrial Workers in Chicago, 1919–1939* (New York, 1990), 246–49; Gordon, *Heroes of Their Own Lives*, 91.

6

"To Protect Her from the Greed as well as the Passions of Man": The Morals Court

> It would be interesting to know how much of the social conscience of our time had as its first insight the prostitute on the city pavement.
>
> – Walter Lippmann, 1914

Public conceptions of prostitution in early twentieth-century America reveal the ideology of social responsibility for crime at its most expansive. For the ranks of progressive moral reformers – clergymen and professors, settlement house activists and businessmen, judges and physicians – the brazen and increasingly well-organized illicit markets in women's bodies raised broad and unsettling questions of political economy and cultural politics. In the rhetoric of socialized law, progressives found the words to convert their sense of society's collective responsibility for "the social evil" into a comprehensive mandate for governance. They filled vice reports and legal briefs with "social facts" about the allegedly demoralizing working conditions of wage-earning women in the industrial city. They declared a capacious "social interest" in the health, good morals, and reproductive capacities of all women as "mothers of the race," which trumped the rights of employers to set wages and working hours as they saw fit. And they persuaded state lawmakers, local judges, and health officials to enact new legal sanctions and institutional strategies to protect and police working women.[1]

---

[1] VCC, *The Social Evil in Chicago: A Study of Existing Conditions* (Chicago, 1911); Theda Skocpol, *Protecting Soldiers and Mothers: The Political Origins of Social Policy in the United States* (Cambridge, Mass., 1992), 373–74. There is a large literature on prostitution in the Progressive Era. See Mark Thomas Connelly, *The Response to Prostitution in the Progressive Era* (Chapel Hill, 1980); Barbara Meil Hobson, *Uneasy Virtue: The Politics of Prostitution and the American Reform Tradition* (New York, 1987); Ruth Rosen, *The Lost Sisterhood: Prostitution in America, 1900–1918* (Baltimore, 1982). See generally Timothy J. Gilfoyle, "Prostitutes

If the home slacker was a hard case for social responsibility, next to the juvenile delinquent the common prostitute was the easiest. In the rich multicausal narratives that urban Americans created to understand and promote public solutions to the social evil, the prostitute herself remained a transparent figure, the quintessential victim of circumstances beyond her control. The moral rage of vice reform did not target her. Reformers perceived her as a walking hazard, because the infectious diseases she carried threatened the public health, and because, if one believed the eugenicists, the hereditary mental defects that enfeebled her brain would inevitably multiply in the racial "life stream." Neither body nor mind, however, were thought to lie entirely within the "fallen" woman's control. Free will seemed to have little to do with her crime. Indeed, a long Anglo-American legal tradition defined that crime as the *status* of being a common prostitute (and thus a disorderly person or vagrant at law) rather than the *act* of selling sex.[2]

Contemporary beliefs about natural differences between the sexes shaped perceptions of prostitution's social causes, but in a complex way. Two inherited western cultural traditions may have predisposed urban moralists to see the social evil in terms of powerful forces bearing down upon frail female purity: a Victorian bourgeois ideal of women as passive sexual objects, and an ancient binary in religion, art, and literature that represented women as either virgins or whores. "No student of modern industrial conditions," wrote Jane Addams in her 1912 book, *A New Conscience and an Ancient Evil*, "can possibly assert how far the superior chastity of women, so rigidly maintained during the centuries, has been the result of her domestic surroundings, and certainly no one knows under what degree of economic pressure the old restraints may give way." But (as the same passage shows) observers also understood fallen women's dependence on the "wages of sin" in relation to their historically specific status as working women in the industrial city. In a way that was unthinkable in the case of the male home slacker, reformers and officials presented the female figure of

in History: From Parables of Pornography to Metaphors of Modernity," *AHR*, 104 (1999), 117–41.
[2] Amy Dru Stanley, *From Bondage to Contract: Wage Labor, Marriage, and the Market in the Age of Slave Emancipation* (Cambridge, 1998), 219–20; Howard B. Woolston, *Prostitution in the United States: Prior to the Entrance of the United States into the World War* (New York, 1921), 25. See Jane Addams, *A New Conscience and an Ancient Evil* (New York, 1913); Ernest A. Bell, *Fighting the Traffic in Young Girls or War on the White Slave Trade* (n.p., 1910); *Prostitution in America, Three Investigations, 1902–1914* (New York, 1976); Walter C. Reckless, *Vice in Chicago* (Chicago, 1933); William I. Thomas, *The Unadjusted Girl: With Cases and Standpoint for Behavior Analysis* (Boston, 1923).

the prostitute on the city pavement as concrete evidence of the moral disaster of unregulated industrialism: the invasion of home life by the market. They presented her deflowered, diseased body as a graphic social fact – the public moral, as it were – of an inequitable market in wage labor and an uncontrolled new market in urban leisure. These markets threatened the health, virtue, and reproductive capacities of *all* working women.[3]

The legal response to prostitution in the Progressive Era was fraught with the characteristic progressive tensions between old and new, repression and regulation, exposure and suppression, individual treatment and social control. In the Chicago Vice Commission's influential 1911 report, *The Social Evil in Chicago*, the coalition of progressive citizens announced a bold-faced demand for law-and-order: "CONSTANT AND PERSISTENT REPRESSION OF PROSTITUTION THE IMMEDIATE METHOD: ABSOLUTE ANNIHILATION THE ULTIMATE IDEAL." But if one read on, the realization dawned that this was merely an angry outburst in a report brimming with diligent investigative research on the causes of vice and multifaceted proposals for public and private interventions to address them. Near the top of the long wish list of initiatives was a novel governmental entity – a "morals court."[4]

In March 1913, commission veteran Harry Olson announced the impending opening of the Municipal Court's Morals Branch, one of the first socialized courts in the nation to specialize in vice cases. The specialized jurisdiction of the Morals Court would also cover fornication, adultery, obscenity, and other breaches of the public morals. Olson made his announcement before a meeting of the Bankers' Club, as the pièce de résistance of a talk whose title he cribbed from Professor Pound, "The Administration of Justice in the Modern City." The year 1913 would go down as the one in which the Second City got serious about vice. After decades of mutually profitable accommodation between ward politicians, police, magistrates, and brothel-keepers, State's Attorney John E. W. Wayman officially shuttered the old red-light districts, including the renowned Levee. During explosive hearings in the elegant La Salle Hotel, the Illinois Senate Vice Committee publicly interrogated Chicago's captains of finance, industry, and retail and chastised them for their role in driving thousands of working women into prostitution. And from their Hull-House headquarters, the women activists of the JPA stepped up their publicity campaign

---

[3] Addams, *New Conscience,* 57; Joseph Valente, "'Neither Fish nor Flesh': The Conundrum of Manhood in James Joyce's *Ulysses,*" paper presented to Newberry Library Fellows Seminar, Chicago, May 2000, p. 2.
[4] VCC, *Social Evil,* 25.

against the popular dance halls, where working girls – hair cropped, faces painted, cigarettes aflame, and hems high – turkey-trotted a fine line between innocence and ruin. When the Morals Court opened on April 7, the JPA's "first officer," Gertrude Howe Britton, sat next to Judge Jacob H. Hopkins on the bench.[5]

To Harry Olson and the men he assigned to the Morals Court, its segregated caseload made possible a new and promising set of socialized legal strategies for attacking prostitution at its roots. Under the old JP regime and even in the criminal branches of the Municipal Court, judges could do little more with prostitutes than discharge or fine them, up to $200 – a penalty that, like throwing a delinquent husband in jail, now seemed only to worsen the underlying condition of dependency. (And unlike sending a home slacker to the rock pile, fining a prostitute – and thus filling public coffers with the wages of sin – did not have a positive symbolic effect for the state.) Municipal judges worked with reformers to secure new state legislation in 1915 that allowed them to place prostitutes on probation (or jail them), and they drew on their experience with the Court of Domestic Relations to develop a greater range of punitive and therapeutic techniques. In addition to probation, the Morals Court ordered prostitutes treated for venereal disease and tested for mental defects, helped them find legitimate jobs, referred them to private agencies and refuges, and culled from their cases scientific knowledge of the social evil. It was an ambitious undertaking for a criminal court. Of course, the judges' first duty was to administer swift justice in the thousands of cases that crossed their threshold each year. But they strived to turn their court into another experimental station for socialized law, a mode of judicial administration less concerned with the law's ancient powers to repress and annihilate than its modern capacities to create knowledge, treat individuals, and distribute governance more widely and intimately into everyday life.[6]

The legal response to prostitution in the Progressive Era had roots in the distinctive governmental tradition of police power regulation in

[5] *MCC* 7 (1913), 81, 93–97; Illinois General Assembly, Senate, *Report of the Senate Vice Committee* (Chicago, 1916), 28, 42; "Morals Court to Open War on Vice," *Chicago Tribune*, March 17, 1913. See "Morals Court Opens with a Motley Grist," *Chicago Post*, April 7, 1913; "Morals Court Unique," *Chicago Daily News*, March 17, 1913; "Olson Declares Court on Morals Means Vice End," *Chicago Record-Herald*, March 16, 1913.
[6] *MCC* 7 (1913), 94; *MCC* 10–11 (1916–17), 85–96; *MCC* 12–14 (1918–20), 148–52.

nineteenth-century America. In antebellum legislatures, courts, and local common councils across the republic, the authority of state and local governments to regulate and protect the public morals, public safety, public health, and general welfare trumped individual liberties and property rights. Outside the official corridors of public power, benevolent reformers and charity societies in American cities used quasipolice powers to regulate domestic life in the tenements. Respectable working-class city-dwellers abated the "common nuisances" of brothels by ripping them down and chasing the "public women" from their neighborhoods. In Chicago in 1857, the mayor himself joined in when citizen vigilantes set fire to a row of brothels. After the Civil War, feminists and social purity reformers in New York, Chicago, San Francisco, and other cities beat back the efforts of physicians and law enforcement officials to set up municipal licensing systems that would have made prostitution a regulated industry, complete with compulsory medical inspection and treatment of suspected prostitutes. The initiatives were modeled upon the Union Army's wartime experiments with regulation around Memphis and Nashville, as well as the English Contagious Diseases Acts and Continental European precedents. The 1871 effort to install a licensing system in Chicago failed in the face of strong opposition from clergymen and feminist activists. The feminists reasoned that the system would violate the liberties of all women in order to make the bodies of prostitutes safer commodities for men.[7]

What made progressive morals regulation new was not a public interest in morality, a claim embedded in that very old common-law phrase "public morals." The novelty was in the *expanded scope of state intervention* and *centralized administrative power* that progressivism brought to public morals. In dramatic public campaigns, long-tolerated red-light districts were abolished in one great city after another during the 1910s. Local, state, and federal legislators enacted a breathtaking array of measures to prevent and punish public immorality: laws forbidding the transportation of women across state lines for "immoral purposes," injunction and abatement acts to prevent landlords from

[7] Timothy J. Gilfoyle, *City of Eros: New York City, Prostitution, and the Commercialization of Sex, 1790–1920* (New York, 1992); Richard Hofstadter and Michael Wallace, eds., *American Violence: A Documentary History* (New York, 1970), 447–50; William J. Novak, *The People's Welfare: Law and Regulation in Nineteenth Century America* (Chapel Hill, 1996), 149–89; Rosen, *Lost Sisterhood*, 4; Stanley, *Bondage to Contract*, 249–56; Christine Stansell, *City of Women: Sex and Class in New York, 1789–1860* (Urbana, 1982), 63–75, 171–216; Marilyn Wood Hill, *Their Sisters' Keepers: Prostitution in New York City, 1830–1870* (Berkeley, 1993).

renting their property to brothel-keepers, age-of-consent laws, and the creation of socialized morals courts, night courts, and women's courts in New York, Boston, Philadelphia, Chicago, and other cities.[8]

Local voluntary associations played a vital role in the legal assault on prostitution. In 1910 the Chicago Church Federation, an organization with 600 Protestant congregations behind it, persuaded Mayor Fred A. Busse to create America's first municipally funded vice commission. To the thirty-member commission, Mayor Busse appointed Protestant, Catholic, and Jewish religious leaders; the University of Chicago sociologist William I. Thomas; Graham Taylor of the Chicago Commons settlement; Sears, Roebuck and Company president Julius Rosenwald; and Chief Justice Olson. Only two women made the team: Ellen Henrotin of the Federation of Women's Clubs and Dr. Anna Dwyer, who would later become the physician of the Morals Court. To lead the investigation, the commission hired George J. Kneeland, a social worker who had earned his antivice stripes working with New York's Committee of Fourteen. The Chicago commission held ninety-eight public meetings, while Kneeland's investigative team plumbed the depths of the vice industry.[9]

The Social Evil in Chicago, a hybrid of a nineteenth-century social purity tract and a twentieth-century sociological legal brief, became an instant classic. According to the 400-page report, 5,000 prostitutes sold their bodies in the streets, brothels, saloons, and other "vicious" spaces of the city's commercialized "underworld." The commissioners enumerated a long list of root causes: immoral home lives, substandard education, feeblemindedness, and, especially, the long hours and low wages of working women. All but a dozen of the report's ninety-seven recommendations demanded governmental action: the establishment of Federal Bureau of Immigration offices in "great distributive centers" such as Chicago "to provide for the safe conduct of immigrants from ports of entry to their destination," "constant prosecution" by the State's Attorney's Office "of all keepers and inmates of existing houses of prostitution," a ban on unescorted women in saloons, the creation of "properly policed" municipal dance halls, public health

---

[8] George E. Worthington and Ruth Topping, *Specialized Courts Dealing with Sex Delinquency: A Study of the Procedure in Chicago, Boston, Philadelphia and New York* (1925; Montclair, 1969). See Connelly, *Response to Prostitution,* 24, 49–60; Lawrence M. Friedman, *Crime and Punishment in American History* (New York, 1993), 324–335; David J. Langum, *Crossing over the Line: Legislating Morality and the Mann Act* (Chicago, 1994).

[9] VCC, *Social Evil,* 1–10.

investigations of venereal disease and midwifery, and, not least, a Morals Court.[10]

The most astute critic of the report was Walter Lippmann. A young New York intellectual of socialist leanings, Lippmann applauded the report's causal analysis but expressed serious reservations about the unprecedented state powers it demanded. "To abolish prostitution would involve a radical alteration of society," he acknowledged. "Who that has read the report itself and put himself into any imaginative understanding of conditions can escape seeing that prostitution to-day is organic to our industrial life, our marriage sanctions, and our social customs?" But as Lippmann saw it, the Vice Commission's proposals were incompatible with American republicanism. They would require "a tyranny, a powerful, centralized sovereignty which could command with majesty and silence the rebel," he wrote. "In our shirt-sleeved republic no such power exists." The decade was still young.[11]

Historians of early twentieth-century vice reform have emphasized its symbolic, irrational, even "hysterical" character. The era's prodigious literature on vice – white slavery tracts, grand jury hearings, sociological studies, psychiatric theories, novels, and muckrakers' accounts – does invite such analysis. Freighted with cultural anxieties, the literature laments changing mores, the usurpation of city governments by ethnic machines, the organized power of corporations (and their underworld counterparts, the "vice trusts"), the promiscuous mingling of "races," and the eugenic threat of feeblemindedness. It is a tribute to the imaginative capacities of the literature's authors that they could read so much into prostitution. By unpacking the symbolism of vice reform, historians have shown that for some moral reformers, the cause was more of a rearguard struggle to preserve an idealized patriarchal family than a progressive effort to alter industrial society. But this attention to the symbolic luster of antiprostitution rhetoric can all too easily obscure the progressives' specific criticisms of the situation of working women in industrial cities.[12]

The late nineteenth and early twentieth centuries witnessed a transformation in the social status, lived experience, and cultural representation of women in America. Driving this transformation was the historic move of women into workplaces outside the home. Between 1880 and 1930, the female work force in the United States grew from 2.6 million to 10.8 million, outpacing the adult female population. In Chicago during the same half-century, the female work force expanded

---

[10] Ibid., 55, 57, 59, 60, 61, 63.
[11] Walter Lippmann, *A Preface to Politics* (New York, 1913), 134-35, 146.
[12] Rosen, *Lost Sisterhood*, 39–68, esp. 38; Connelly, *Response to Prostitution*.

by more than 1,000 percent, from 35,600 to 408,600 (outstripping female population growth). The nature of women's work also changed. Proportionally fewer women worked as domestic servants, whose compensation had customarily included room and board under the watchful eyes of a surrogate family. In 1880, some 47 percent of the female work force served as domestics, compared with 33 percent in 1900 and 22 percent in 1930. More and more women worked for wages in factories, department stores, restaurants, offices, and laundries. The largest Chicago firms hired thousands of women during the 1910s. In 1913, Sears, Roebuck and Company employed 4,732 women and girls. Marshall Field and Company had 4,222 women working in retail. Nearly 700 women and girls cut meat and produced soap and "butterine" at Swift and Company.[13]

Progressive women activists and vice reformers insisted that women's wage work posed a serious threat to working-class home life. The market in female wage labor severed the personal bonds and moral restraints of the family, the reformers argued, and prevented women from performing their essential domestic functions as wives and mothers. Government studies showed that a large proportion of the nation's working women were in fact young and single, lived on their own in the furnished-room districts of the industrial cities, worked long hours that weakened them physically and morally, and earned wages they could not live on. The Chicago Vice Commission cited "the economic stress of industrial life" and its "enfeebling influences on the will power" as a leading cause of prostitution.[14]

The rapid spread of state laws limiting women's working hours manifested the growing willingness of lawmakers and appellate judges to see government intervene in the industrial workplace on behalf of women and in the name of the family. As Theda Skocpol has shown, statutes restricting women's working hours "came earlier, easier, and more steadily in the U.S. political system than any other category of social legislation for adult workers." In 1893, Illinois enacted the first enforceable eight-hour law for women, a pioneering statute championed by a cross-class and -gender coalition that included the Chicago and Illinois Federations of Labor, women's trade unionists, and Hull-House activists. Initially, the Illinois Supreme Court refused to accept such "class legislation" designed to protect working women. In *Ritchie v. People* (1895), the court struck down the hours statute as an unconstitutional interference with the liberty of workers and employers to

---

[13] Meyerowitz, *Women Adrift*, xvii, 5; Illinois Senate, *Report of the Senate Vice Committee*, 178, 206, 698–701.
[14] VCC, *Social Evil*, 45. See Meyerowitz, *Women Adrift*.

contract. The same court used common-sense claims about married women's natural and legal dependence on men to deny them the right to practice law in the state. But in this case it refused to notice any sex differences that might make women, as a class, less competent than men to make their own wage contracts without state protection. Despite the chilling effect of *Ritchie*, by 1908 eight more states had enacted women's hours statutes and five others bolstered existing laws.[15]

That year the U.S. Supreme Court settled the question in *Muller v. Oregon*, upholding Oregon's ten-hour law for women as a legitimate exercise of police power. A landmark in American constitutional history, *Muller* marks the emergence of sociological jurisprudence at the federal level. The famous "Brandeis Brief," prepared by Josephine Goldmark and Louis Brandeis on behalf of the National Consumers' League, helped establish a legitimate role for sociological data in legal argument and judicial decision making. Judges had always relied on their own intuitions and their sense of the "common knowledge of mankind" when assessing the reasonableness of state legislation. As American institutions elevated scientific expertise over general knowledge in many arenas, judges grew more willing to consider expertly gathered data, especially in cases such as *Muller*, where there seemed to be such an obvious gap between actual social conditions and the abstract formalism of legal doctrine. Social scientific knowledge began to take its place alongside the folk wisdom of judges in appellate court decisions, and many courts accepted an enlarged role for the state in governing the social and economic relations of modern life. This was precisely the reorientation of legal reasoning that Roscoe Pound and other exponents of sociological jurisprudence demanded.[16]

But what made the Brandeis–Goldmark brief so persuasive was not simply its mass of social scientific data, drawn from the reports of industrial commissions, but its gendered argument. The brief purported to show that the physical structure of women made them uniquely vulnerable to industrial labor, which threatened their morals and reproductive capacities. (This was much the same argument that urban vice reformers were making.) As Brandeis and Goldmark well knew, hours legislation for male workers had often fared poorly in state and federal courts, which closely scrutinized laws not limited to public employees or to specific hazardous occupations such as mining and smelting. Just

---

[15] Skocpol, *Protecting Soldiers*, 373–423, esp. 375; *Ritchie v. People*, 155 Ill. 98 (1895). See *Bradwell v. Illinois*, 16 Wall. 131 (1873).
[16] *Muller v. Oregon*, 208 U.S. 412 (1908).

three years earlier the Court had struck down New York's ten-hour law for bakers in *Lochner v. New York*, declaring that bakers had the same mental and physical capacities as "men in other trades" and thus could "assert their rights and care for themselves without the protective arm of the State." The gendered legal strategy of the National Consumers' League worked in *Muller*. Justice David Brewer nodded approvingly to the brief in his majority opinion, which anchored the constitutionality of protective legislation – and, by explicit association, of antiprostitution legislation as well – in the social facts of sex difference. The Court held that a woman's "physical structure and a proper discharge of her maternal functions – having in view not merely her own health, but the well-being of the race – justify legislation to protect her from the *greed* as well as the *passions* of man."[17]

During the decade after *Muller*, nineteen states plus the District of Columbia passed new women's hours statutes, and another twenty states improved existing laws. State appellate courts upheld the new statutes, declaring again and again that society's interest in women as "mothers of the race" justified special protections for the weaker sex. In 1909, the Illinois General Assembly enacted a new ten-hour law. The state supreme court upheld it in a decision that, like *Muller*, mixed a modern eugenics rationale with old-fashioned, manly common sense. "It is known to all men (and what we know as men we cannot profess to be ignorant of as judges)," the court opined, "that woman's physical structure and the performance of her maternal functions place her at a great disadvantage in the battle of life." The court concluded that "as weakly and sickly women cannot be the mothers of vigorous children, it is of the greatest importance to the public that the state take such measures as may be necessary to protect its women from the consequences induced by long, continuous manual labor."[18]

Even more than women's working hours, their wages implicated modern capitalism in the social evil. The most temperate progressives sounded like Clarence Darrow when they talked about the relationship between "wages and sin." Like their socialist contemporaries who denounced modern capitalists for making "a commodity out of a woman's virtue just as they have made a commodity out of a man's

---

[17] *Lochner v. New York*, 198 U.S. 45, 57 (1905); *Muller v. Oregon*, 208 U.S. 412, 422 (1908), emphasis added. See William E. Forbath, *Law and the Shaping of the American Labor Movement* (Cambridge, Mass., 1991), 37–58.
[18] *W. C. Ritchie & Co. v. Wayman*, 244 Ill. 509, 520–21 (1910); Forbath, *Law and the Shaping*, 43–45; Thomas R. Pegram, *Partisans and Progressives: Private Interest and Public Policy in Illinois, 1870–1922* (Urbana, 1992), 80–82; Skocpol, *Protecting Soldiers*, 373–74.

talent," progressives saw the urban prostitute as the product of an immoral market in wage labor that exploited men as well as women.[19]

In the winter of 1913, the Illinois Senate Vice Committee put the wage labor system on trial. The committee was created by Lt. Gov. Barratt O'Hara, a Spanish-American War veteran and former Chicago newspaperman. O'Hara's long experience writing copy for the Hearst papers prepared him well for his role as author of the committee's report. The incendiary document, published in 1916, ran in excess of 700 pages. The committee's original mandate was to investigate the "white slave" traffic, at a time when many Americans believed the United States had become enmeshed in a vast international network of trade in women. But under O'Hara's leadership the agenda quickly shifted to the more tangible local problem of women's wage work. As the committee held public hearings in Chicago, Peoria, and Springfield, the general assembly was debating a minimum wage bill for women. O'Hara urged lawmakers to attend his hearings and see for themselves the connection between low wages and prostitution. The testimony of prostitutes, panders (people who lived off the wages of prostitutes), sociologists, reformers, and employers made for one of the biggest stories of the decade in the Chicago press.[20]

The report painted a complex picture of the market's invasion of home life. According to the committee, the story of a young woman's descent into an immoral life often began when her father or husband became unwilling or unable to support his family, forcing his dependents to maintain themselves by working outside the home. On their own in the labor market, young women quickly discovered that employers (like the legal system) presumed female dependence on men: They set women's wages far lower than those for men, according to the self-serving calculus that women's wages properly supplemented those of their fathers and husbands. Although eight dollars was widely recognized by contemporaries as the subsistence-level weekly wage for working women, 50,000 women in Chicago earned $5 or less per week. Many got by with the help of family, friends, and private social agencies. But countless others – weakened physically and morally by long working hours, poor nutrition, and after-hours forays into "tough" dance halls – were eventually driven to sell their bodies to men. "Thousands of girls are driven into prostitution because of the sheer inability to keep body and soul together on the low wages received by them," the committee charged. Not surprisingly, most employers called before

---

[19] Phillips Russell, "Women for Sale," *ISR*, 12 (May 1912), 728; Clarence Darrow, "Crime and Economic Conditions," *ISR*, 17 (Oct., 1916), 219–22.

[20] *Report of the Senate Vice Committee*, 13–23, 225–26; *BOC* (1917), 512.

the committee denied any meaningful causal link between wages and prostitution. Even Julius Rosenwald, the philanthropist and Chicago Vice Commission veteran, insisted there was "no connection between the two." Rosenwald's own firm, Sears, Roebuck, paid nearly 1,500 women less than $8 a week.[21]

The committee joined moral reformers and women's organizations across the nation in demanding minimum wage legislation for women. "Plain justice," the committee called it, "the first duty of the state." In state-level campaigns for women's wage legislation, the wages-and-sin argument helped vice reformers reach a middle-class public of churches, women's groups, and temperance organizations. The wage bills ran into staunch opposition from manufacturers' associations and workingmen's unions; union leaders believed employers would use the legislation to keep wages *down*. Although Illinois never passed a statute, the national Progressive Party adopted a minimum wage for women as part of its 1912 platform, and fifteen states plus the District of Columbia passed laws between 1912 and 1923. Once again, the many state courts that upheld the laws declared that the physical structure and "maternal functions" of women created a reasonable state interest in their welfare. The U.S. Supreme Court, however, put a temporary end to the minimum wage movement in 1923 when it struck down the District of Columbia's statute in *Adkins v. Children's Hospital*. When the issue was state regulation of actual cash wages rather than working hours, the social interest in women did not so easily or uniformly outweigh contract liberty in the courts.[22]

As if protecting women from the demoralizing effects of the shop floor and the department store counter were not challenge enough, progressive moralists also attempted to impose new governmental controls on the market in leisure, a burgeoning sector of the urban economy that catered to young wage earners of both sexes. If the reformers aimed to instill in working-class youth a nineteenth-century ideal of "civilized morality" – an ideal of patriarchal family life and pure subordinated womanhood – there can be no doubt that the new "cheap amusements" did much to subvert that end. The urban entrepreneurs who profitably marketed affordable recreation to the urban millions provided quasipublic spaces – the deck of an excursion boat, the dark nickel theater, the smoke-filled dance hall – where working-class youths

---

[21] *Report of the Senate Vice Committee*, 24–28, 36–37, esp. 225, 28, 554, 464, 180, 178.

[22] *Report of the Senate Vice Committee*, 52; Kermit L. Hall, The *Magic Mirror: Law in American History* (New York, 1989), 242–43; Skocpol, *Protecting Soldiers*, 401–23, esp. 414.

could mingle in relative anonymity beyond the supervision of parents, employers, neighbors, and the police. Youth behavior in these spaces tended toward the "immoral," which in the rhetoric of progressive moralists covered everything from casual dating and treating to the explicit exchange of sex for money. The growth of commercialized leisure also created lucrative new jobs for young women willing to work at the border of the licit and illicit female labor markets, including chorus girls, taxi dancers, and masseuses.[23]

The JPA and vice reformers called upon their state and local governments to use both positive and repressive measures to better regulate the leisure market, by creating safe public alternatives such as municipal dance halls and enforcing existing laws that forbade the admission of minors to dance halls where liquor was sold. Middle-class reformers, of course, were not the only city-dwellers who worried that the leisure industry was leading the "straight girl" down "a crooked path." The many immigrant working-class parents who brought their daughters and their lovers before juvenile courts in American cities during the early twentieth century were no less alarmed by the time and money their children spent in dance halls, theaters, and cafés. Commercial recreation, like the wage-labor economy that bankrolled it, undermined parents' economic and moral control over their children. Parents increasingly asked urban courts to help them police the sexual practices of their own children.[24]

Progressive concerns about the wage dependency of women extended to those for whom the struggle against economic pressure and evil influences had already been lost. Vice investigators and women reformers proposed numerous solutions for breaking the prostitute's criminal dependence on the wages of sin. Most agreed that a necessary first step was to repair one odious feature of the criminal justice system itself: the practice of fining prostitutes. Until 1915, the police in Illinois arrested prostitutes under local ordinances or under the loose rubric of the state's disorderly conduct statute. The only punishment permitted was a fine. Taking up a long-standing concern of the women's reform organizations, the Illinois Senate Vice Committee protested that the "obnoxious fining system" returned women to the "sporting life" more dependent than ever on the madams or pimps

---

[23] On "civilized morality," see Connelly, *Response to Prostitution*; Kathy Peiss, *Cheap Amusements: Working Women and Leisure in Turn-of-the-Century New York* (Philadelphia, 1985); Meyerowitz, *Women Adrift*, 92–116, esp. 40.

[24] Louise de Koven Bowen, *The Straight Girl on the Crooked Path* (Chicago, 1916); Mary E. Odem, *Delinquent Daughters: Protecting and Policing Adolescent Female Sexuality in the United States, 1885–1920* (Chapel Hill, 1995), 157–84.

who paid their fines. Fining "adds a link in the chain that binds her
to an immoral life," declared the Vice Commission. The most sensible
way to handle a prostitute, the commissioners insisted, was to place her
on probation "under the care of intelligent and sympathetic women."
The corollary of eliminating the fine system was thus to give courts a
longer, more intensive period of intervention with offenders.[25]

The creation of the Morals Court only called greater public
attention to the unpopular fining system. Harry Olson and his peers
on the municipal bench worked with social activists to secure a new
state law, which the Illinois General Assembly enacted in June 1915.
The statute was nicknamed after Kate Adams, the superintendent
of Chicago's Coulter House for wayward girls, a private refuge that
regularly received young women on referral from the Morals Court.
The law made it a misdemeanor to be an "inmate" of a "house of
ill-fame or assignation" or to solicit "in any street, alley, park or other
place." Prostitution was no longer a vaguely defined status offense;
the actual act of selling sexual services for money was now a crime.
The effect of this shift in statutory semantics on police behavior is
not easy to gauge. But the real significance of the law lay elsewhere,
in the expanded powers it gave to the criminal courts. The statute
made the maximum penalty for prostitution a $200 fine or one year
in jail. On its face, this was a repressive measure that imposed harsh
new penalties on prostitutes. It did not even eliminate fining. (The
Woman's City Club would continue to agitate toward that goal for
many years to come.) In practice, however, the Kate Adams law placed
fining on a much broader continuum of punitive, coercive, and
therapeutic judicial techniques. By turning prostitution into a jailable
offense, the statute made prostitutes eligible for probation. This gave
courts a longer period of control over them and a much wider range
of options for governing them.[26]

Located on the eleventh floor of City Hall, two flights up from the
Domestic Relations Branch, the Morals Court gathered into one public space, before one judge and gallery, the full gamut of defendants

[25] *Illinois Revised Statutes*, 1913, ch. 38, sec. 55; *Report of the Senate Vice Committee*,
54; VCC, *Social Evil*, 46; Chicago, City Council, *Report of the City Council
Committee on Crime* (Chicago, 1915), 50.
[26] *Illinois Revised Statutes*, 1915–1916, ch. 38, sec. 57a-1; Worthington and
Topping, *Specialized Courts*, 37–43; Harry Olson to Judge John A. Swanson,
April 20, 1915, JHO, box 9; Harry Olson to Illinois General Assembly,
May 19, 1913, MCC, box 4, folder 24. See "A Vicious Circle – Shall Illinois
Help to Redraw It?" *Woman's City Club Bulletin*, Jan. 1919, p. 5.

charged with breaching the public morals in the nation's second largest city. The official personnel formed a crowd of their own. In addition to the judge appointed to the bench by Olson, there were an assistant city prosecutor, an assistant state's attorney, two clerks, two bailiffs, and three women personnel: a probation officer, a physician, and a matron to handle the women prisoners. As in the Court of Domestic Relations, men controlled the formal apparatus of law – arrest, prosecution, finding, and disposition – while women claimed authority over the "social aspects" of the process – medical inspection, personal interviews, and compilation of case histories. Also present were the agents of local charitable organizations, including the JPA and the Catholic House of the Good Shepherd, who awaited an assignment to investigate a defendant's personal history, find her a job, or place her in an institution for fallen women. Missing from this populous courtroom were twelve people an uninitiated defendant might expect to find there. Clerks encouraged defendants to waive their right to a jury trial; if they demanded one, their case moved to one of the Municipal Court's criminal jury branches. Few defendants availed themselves of the option, and the longer wait, of a jury trial. The socialized approach of the Morals Court depended on the unfettered discretion of the man on the bench.[27]

The organizing principle of the Morals Court bore a surprising affinity to that of the officially eradicated red-light districts: segregation. Judge Harry Fisher, a Jewish social reformer and JPA board member, embraced this irony as a sign of progress. "Chicago," he wrote, "may now boast of the fact that, instead of that segregated place where vice was cultivated and encouraged, girls and women degraded and despoiled, it has a place for the gathering up of the unfortunate offenders; where those who desire to do better find friendly aid and encouragement; where the sick are ministered to, the vicious prosecuted and punished and where all the vile influences of the underworld are exposed to view." The bureaucratic practice of segregation – channeling all morals offenders into a single court – made a substantive and procedural departure from the generalized practice of the old police courts and the criminal branches of the Municipal Court. The segregated caseload was an administrative strategy designed to organize institutional capacities, facilitate specialization, and elevate the public credibility of judges. Departing from the common-law tradition that conceived judges' role as that of interpreters, rather than makers, of law, Morals Court judges explained that their segregated caseload

[27] *MCC* 7 (1913), 93–97; "All Get Chance in Morals Court," *Chicago Tribune,* April 8, 1913.

enabled them to develop "consistent policy." "A trained judge," Fisher wrote, "becomes expert in determining what disposition should be made of each case in the light of all the bigger facts of which he becomes cognizant, which are necessary to a proper understanding of the problem, but are not presented to him from the witness stand." Just as essential as the witness stand were the probation officer's interview desk, the physician's table, the psychiatrist's laboratory. Rather than bring the experts to the defendants, scattered about the city in more than a dozen criminal branches, the Morals Court brought this class of defendants to the experts. And centralization enabled the court to exploit the resources of the many private social agencies involved in protecting the health and morals of young women.[28]

A final virtue of segregation, Chief Justice Olson noted, was that it increased the visibility, and thus the "conspicuous responsibility," of the criminal justice system itself. Progressives knew that corrupt police had long allowed vice to flourish: Even though the red-light districts were shuttered, no one expected the police and ward politicians to sever their lucrative ties with commercialized vice. Moving vice cases from the dispersed police station courtrooms to City Hall made it easier for newspapers and reform associations to police the police. Progressives also interpreted public immorality as partly a propaganda problem. Vice commissions intended their high-profile investigations to "arouse" the "public conscience" and thereby mobilize the citizens. Municipal judges similarly believed that the continuous exposure of the vice industry in the Morals Court – delivered to the public in the trial room itself as well as in the court's published reports, in social science studies, and in the dispatches of the daily press – would keep the issue alive. The judges, however, could not control the message that Chicago's many publics took away from the judicial arena.[29]

For all of its strategic virtues, segregation created unanticipated problems. One of the great ironies of the Morals Court was how quickly it became integrated into the prostitution subculture. In the post–red-light era, the tribunal was one of the few dependable sites on Chicago's ever-shifting vice map. Professional bondsmen and lawyers who made a specialty of vice cases set up shop at the court. Pimps stopped by looking for "girls" they had lost track of. The courtroom was often packed well beyond capacity. On "raid days," the crowd in the ninety-seat room sometimes topped 300. The reformer Kate Adams watched with dismay as discharged prostitutes made dates outside the courtroom with spectators aroused (or so Adams imagined) by the

[28] *MCC 10–11* (1916–17), 85–96, esp. 85, 86.
[29] *MCC 7* (1913), 88, 96–97.

TABLE 4: Cases Disposed of in the Morals
Court, 1913–1930

Year	Cases	Year	Cases
1913	5,005	1922	7,280
1914	12,645	1923	7,291
1915	12,343	1924	11,106
1916	6,581	1925	8,464
1917	7,271	1926	10,127
1918	5,822	1927	14,549
1919	4,510	1928	15,438
1920	4,678	1929	14,035
1921	6,471	1930	9,741

Source: MCC 24–25 (1930–31), 35.

proceedings. "Men and women panders, cadets, keepers, and general roustabouts of the underworld, idle men and students (not sociological) come in to look the girls over," Adams protested. "Degenerates in search of the salacious sit spellbound by the testimony which is often obscene." Judge Fisher worried that the unwholesome "spectacle" demoralized the "unfortunate girls" and the "respectable people" who passed by the court. He even proposed moving the court to a more remote site – a proposal Olson flatly rejected. The Morals Court's own morality problem got so bad that a staff member posted a copy of the Illinois vagrancy statute, which prohibited "lounging about any court room."[30]

What engaged the attention of this rowdy audience? Between 1913 and 1930, the Morals Court disposed of a caseload that ranged from a low of 4,510 cases in 1919 to a high of 15,438 cases in 1928. (See Table 4.) Felonies – including rape, abortion, bigamy, incest, and crimes against nature (sodomy) – constituted a tiny portion of the caseload: 53 of the 6,581 cases disposed of in 1916. (And, of course, in felony cases the court had only preliminary jurisdiction.) The workaday practice of the Morals Court consisted of common misdemeanors and ordinance violations (quasicrimes), including adultery and fornication (236 cases disposed of in 1916), seduction (4), pandering (25), keeping a disorderly house (2,585), night walking (579), and the ubiquitous disorderly conduct (2,459), which was commonly referred to in

[30] Adams in *MCC 19–22* (1925–28), 115; Fisher in Worthington and Topping, *Specialized Courts*, 9, 24–26. The contempt cases that dot the court's docket confirm that the judges' hopes for orderliness through segregation were never realized. See, e.g., *People v. Gus Livingston*, case 368237, Sept. 25, 1922, MCCCR.

the court's case records as simply "57a-1": short-hand for the section of the Criminal Code where a citizen could find the Kate Adams Law.[31]

A closer look at how the Morals Court handled three common kinds of cases – adultery and fornication, pandering, and prostitution – illuminates both the ambitious scope and the practical limits of morals policing in the early twentieth century. Each category of offense involves a different facet of morals policing. In adultery and fornication cases, the state policed the consensual heterosexual relations of adults not legitimated by marriage. Pandering cases brought the court face-to-face with the vilified figure of the (usually) male sexual exploiter, who through coercion, seduction, or persuasion caused the "ruin" of an "innocent" woman. Prostitution cases – solicitation in the streets or in a house of prostitution – expressed the state interest in the morality and, increasingly, in the bodies of young women who had "fallen" from legitimate female status as daughters, wives, or mothers.[32]

Adultery and fornication were routine matters of morals regulation during the Progressive Era. In 1914 alone, nearly 500 fornication and adultery cases were filed in the Morals Court, roughly 4 percent of

[31] *MCC 10–11* (1916–17), 94–96.
[32] I examined two runs of 500 consecutive cases from the Morals Court, cases 119001–119500, 1914–15, MCCCR, and cases 368001–368500, 1922–23, ibid. Within each run, I identified one string of consecutive cases for the following types of cases: adultery and fornication, pandering, and prostitution.

"Adultery and Fornication String I," 50 cases: Nov. 5, 1914, case 119001, to Dec. 28, 1914, case 119073. "Adultery and Fornication String II," 50 cases: Aug. 11, 1922, case 368005, to Oct. 25, 1922, case 368408.

"Pandering String I," 20 cases: March 20, 1915, case 119139, to Aug. 10, 1915, case 119292. "Pandering String II," nine cases: Aug. 18, 1922, case 368021, to Nov. 24, 1922, case 368493.

"Prostitution String I," 50 cases: July 30, 1915, case 119256, to Aug. 23, 1915, case 119328. "Prostitution String II," 50 cases: Aug. 10, 1922, case 368001, to Aug. 28, 1922, case 368070.

The case files contain the court's half-sheet (containing all orders pertaining to the case). Many of them also contain arrest slips (with data on occupation, age, race, nativity, and address), criminal informations (the formal complaint), capiases (warrants for arrest), mittimuses (disposition orders), and sometimes probation applications and reports. The files do not offer access to defendants' own voices. Even where trial transcripts exist (in files for cases that were appealed), the language is statutory boiler plate, not a verbatim account. I have located only one memoir of a former prostitute that describes her experience in the Morals Court. [Bertha Thompson] Ben L. Reitman, *Sister of the Road: The Autobiography of Box-Car Bertha* (New York, 1937), 182–91. I have also found newspaper accounts that describe court proceedings, including defendant's reported language, e.g., "All Get Chance in Morals Court," *Chicago Daily Tribune*, April 8, 1913.

the caseload. Unlike pandering or seduction, the law assumed adultery and fornication to be consensual offenses, though not exactly victimless: These were plausible offenses against the public morals. The Illinois Criminal Code defined adultery as the practice of a married person living "openly" with someone of the opposite sex other than his or her spouse. Fornication involved a single person "openly" cohabiting with anyone of the opposite sex. Each offense carried a maximum penalty of a $500 fine or one year in jail. For recalcitrant lovers, the law made a special threat: A second offense doubled the penalty, a third trebled it, and so on. As if the law's purpose might be lost on some people, the statute had an escape clause for fornicators: "it shall be in the power of the party or parties offending, to prevent or suspend the prosecution by their intermarriage."[33]

The statutory definitions of adultery and fornication made no explicit reference to sex, and unlike in bastardy cases the law did not require any evidence of sexual contact. The Morals Court's case files are similarly reticent. The case of an unmarried twenty-two-year-old man arrested on an autumn's eve in 1922 in the act of having "illicit intercourse" in the back of a taxicab with an unmarried woman was thus a rare exception on the docket. By contrast, the law defined homosexuals not by their living arrangements or by the openness of their relationships but by their specific sexual practices, the "infamous crime against nature." There were no such offenses as homosexual adultery or fornication. Sodomy was punishable by ten years in prison and, like all infamous crimes, a lifetime stripped of the basic rights of masculine citizenship: to vote, hold office, and serve on a jury.[34]

A diverse cross-section of humanity came before the Morals Court on charges of adultery and fornication. Defendants tended to be young – typically under thirty – although it was not unknown for a man in his fifties to find himself on trial for fornication. When police bothered to record defendants' race and nativity on their arrest slips, American-born whites predominated, though African-Americans and immigrants constituted nearly half the docket in a typical month.[35]

[33] *MCC* 8–9 (1914–15), 56–57; *Report of the Senate Vice Committee*, 65; Worthington and Topping, *Specialized Courts*, 9.

[34] *People v. Louis Cella*, Sept. 30, 1922, case 368259, MCCCR; VCC, *Social Evil*, 296; *Illinois Revised Statutes, 1911, ch. 38, sec. 47–48*. See William N. Eskridge, Jr., "Law and the Construction of the Closet: American Regulation of Same-Sex Intimacy, 1880–1946," *Iowa Law Review*, 82 (1997), 1007–136.

[35] In Adultery and Fornication String I, ages were provided for 34 defendants: 23 defendants were under 30; seven fell into the 30–39 age group; four were 40 or over. In 27 cases, information on nativity and race was provided. Defendants identified as "Americans" are assumed to be white

Defendants tended to be employed (or temporarily unemployed) as wage earners: teamsters and bartenders, factory workers and domestic servants, clerks and laborers. A few were comparatively prosperous. In reviewing the case of Stanley Butkas, a twenty-seven-year-old Lithuanian laborer charge with fornication in 1922, a probation officer noted approvingly that "judging by his apparel and his evidence of economy and prosperity," he was gainfully employed. "The neighbors seem to know little or nothing about him only as he comes into the stores to buy things and is steadily employed. They know that he bought the property and lives there. The home is well furnished, almost too heavily for the size of the place."[36] More typical was the case of Carolina Statmack, a nineteen-year-old American-born factory worker, who contributed $6 a week to her parents' support.[37] By definition, fornicators were single and adulterers married. But the impersonal statutory definitions obscured the fact that some defendants were widows and widowers, whose presumed commitment to legal marriage had been interrupted by forces beyond their control.[38]

Morals Court judges were not averse to fining or locking up men and women who sought sexual companionship outside the marriage contract. Among fifty consecutive adultery and fornication cases filed during November and December of 1914, for example, prosecutors won guilty verdicts for nineteen defendants. Nine of them received a

Americans, because police officers wrote "colored" on arrest slips when the defendant was African-American. There were 19 native-born Americans, two Bohemians and two "Colored" persons, and one each of Canadian, German, Irish, and Swedish. Nativity and race of defendants in Adultery and Fornication String II were as follows: 20 Americans; three "Colored" persons; two each of Italians, Lithuanians, and Russians; and one each of Austrian, Belgian, English, German, Greek, Irish, and Polish.

[36] *People v. Stanley Butkas*, Oct. 23, 1922, case 368394, MCCCR. In Adultery and Fornication String I, the occupational breakdown is as follows: 19 not identified/illegible, nine no occupation/unemployed, six laborers, three clerks and three house domestic workers, two bartenders and two teamsters, and one each of electrician, expressman, factory worker, laundress, optician, and salesman. In Adultery and Fornication String II, the occupational breakdown is: 14 not identified/illegible; six housewives; five no occupation/unemployed; five laborers; three houseworkers and three salespeople; two cooks, two painters, and two waiters; and one each of assembler, cashier, clerk, electrician, factory worker, softdrink parlor worker, tailor, and teamster.

[37] *People v. Carolina Statmack*, Nov. 16, 1914, case 119010, MCCCR.

[38] See *People v. Winifred Hitchman*, Sept. 9, 1922, case 368109, MCCCR; *People v. Mary Sakizewsky*, Oct. 11, 1922, case 368306, ibid.; *People v. Frank Oshinski*, Oct. 23, 1922, case 368399, ibid.

one-year term of probation, seven were sentenced to three months in
the County Jail (three of those were granted probation after some time
served), one was sentenced to six months in jail (granted probation after four months served), another to three months at labor in the House
of Correction, and one paid a $25 fine plus court costs of $8.50.[39]

Although adultery and fornication could be sternly enforced, judges
favored probation. Among the varied tasks assigned to probation officers, determining whether two people continued to live together in
violation of the law had to be one of the easiest. Even so, investigators could be remarkably thorough, interviewing relatives, neighbors,
teachers, and employers. When officers visited offenders' homes, they
recorded their impressions of the orderliness and respectability of
the dwellings: "neat and clean, and fairly furnished in a fair neighborhood," reads one 1922 report.[40] Such off-hand judgments were a
staple of the reports. After interviewing the family of a twenty-year-old
German woman accused of adultery, an officer writes, "Marriage does
not seem to mean much to these people.... This girl seems to be in
bad with her father, and her mother seconds his objections. No doubt
she has been wild and had the habit of running the streets nights. Her
father has used all the different varieties of names on her, accused her
of being a whore and would like to cast discredit on the girl[']s birth.
She certainly has had an unfair start in life and as already intimated I
should think her parents are to blame for a great deal of her trouble."[41]

As this passage suggests, neither the state nor middle-class reformers
had a monopoly on the will to police working-class sexuality. Among
the fifty consecutive adultery and fornication cases from 1914, at least
eight were brought by a family member of one of the defendants.
Nineteen of fifty consecutive cases in 1922 were initiated by relatives.
Ordinary people had many reasons to use the courts to rein in or punish peripatetic relatives. Within working-class families, fornication and
adultery were not merely distasteful matters of sexual transgression.
Immigrant parents, especially those who came from cultures where
arranged marriages were still common, might view their daughter's
extramarital relations as a threat to her chances for a socially and eco-
nomically favorable marriage. A workingman's infidelity might force
his wife to share his wages, as well as his affections, with another.[42]

[39] Adultery and Fornication String I.
[40] Filed with *People v. Harry Shenbrook*, Sept. 16, 1922, case 368168, MCCCR;
People v. Alice Bonner, Sept. 16, 1922, case 368169, ibid.
[41] *People v. Catherine Vogt*, Oct. 21, 1922, case 368389, MCCCR.
[42] A family relationship is assumed to exist in these cases when the surname of
the complainant matches that of either the defendant or his/her partner in

The role of parents and spouses (and perhaps siblings and children, too) in social policing, however, is easily exaggerated. The state's own law enforcement officials still played a larger and more decisive role in the process. Winifred Hitchman, a thirty-five-year-old widowed assembly worker, and Walter Meyer, her unemployed companion of the same age, discovered as much when Officer Patrick J. Ryan of the Detective Bureau came knocking on their West Monroe Street door early one September morning in 1922, probably striking fear into Hitchman's twelve-year-old daughter. The Morals Court found Hitchman and Meyer guilty of fornication. Hitchman received a one-year term of probation – "To give her a chance to reform under the supervision of an officer." The court sentenced Meyer to thirty days in the House of Correction. Police officers or probation officers initiated half of the fifty consecutive cases from 1914, and the police brought twenty-two of fifty cases from 1922.[43]

No matter who initiated a complaint, once it landed in the Morals Court, family members had little control over the judicial process. In one 1920 case, an Italian woman filed fornication complaints against her nineteen-year-old daughter and the man with whom she was living. Both defendants pled guilty. Disabled and on crutches, the man told the court he earned $12 a week doing housework and offered to marry his partner in crime. Her mother strongly opposed this proposal and apparently expected the court to separate the two. But the judge continued the case for a few minutes and dispatched the defendants to his chambers, where a woman bailiff interviewed them. Back in the courtroom, the bailiff told the judge she had found the daughter to be "normal mentally" and stated her approval of the marriage. The judge sent the defendants back into his chambers to be married by a Methodist minister who had been observing the court's proceedings from the gallery. The fact that a Methodist conducted the makeshift ceremony probably did little to ease a Catholic mother's grief. With the defendants' relationship legitimated by marriage, the judge promptly dismissed the case – and with it, one mother's attempt to use public force to control her daughter.[44]

In the eyes of some moral reformers, no exertion of state power could be excessive when it came to catching and punishing the pander. A pander was any person who, by coercion or persuasion, caused

the offense. Adultery and Fornication Strings I and II. See Odem, *Delinquent Daughters*, 157–84.
[43] *People v. Winifred Hitchman. People v. Walter Meyer*, Sept. 9, 1922, case 368110, MCCCR; Adultery and Fornication Strings I and II.
[44] Worthington and Topping, *Specialized Courts*, 23–24.

a woman to sell her body and profited from her wages of sin – a particularly perverse reversal of the normative domestic relation between men and women. Professional "pimps," "cadets," and "white slavers" all fit this description. From the incendiary rhetoric of the white slavery literature to the more reasoned arguments of social scientists, panders were universally denounced as a scourge on society. Edwin W. Sims, a U.S. District Attorney in Chicago who put many local panders behind bars under federal white slave laws, said, "There is no more depraved class of people in the world than those human vultures who fatten on the shame of innocent young girls."[45]

Ample evidence exists that pimping and other forms of pandering were, in fact, on the rise during the Progressive Era. According to some accounts, the closing of the red-light districts actually increased prostitutes' dependence on pimps for protection. One convicted pander told the Illinois Senate Vice Committee in 1913 that he believed 1,500 cadets and panders worked in Chicago alone. Several young women testified before the committee that they had been lured by young men to "sporting houses" with the promise of marriage or money. Perhaps some of those women were merely using the narrative conventions of the ubiquitous white slavery literature to win the sympathy of the male senators, but the details make their stories plausible. In contrast to the white slavery literature's trope of the helpless girl drugged or shackled by swarthy or "colored" pimps, most of these women said they simply walked out of the sporting house without serving any customers. But others testified that, penniless and abandoned in a strange city, they had unwillingly entered the "sporting life."[46]

Some of the Progressive Era's most dramatic new law enforcement measures targeted panders. The Congressional White Slave Traffic Act of 1910 – known as the Mann Act, after its sponsor, Representative James R. Mann of Illinois – called for a significant new federal incursion into law enforcement. The act made it a federal crime to transport a woman across a state line "for the purpose of prostitution or debauchery, or for any other immoral purpose." By 1916 more than 1,500 Americans had been convicted under the act, and almost every state in the union had enacted its own laws against white slavery, pandering, or living off the earnings of a prostitute. Illinois legislated so aggressively against vice that Howard Woolston, an expert on American vice laws, called it a "banner state." Its 1908 pandering statute defined

45 Sims, *Fighting the Traffic*, 16.
46 *Report of the Senate Vice Committee*, 135–36, 138, 139–40, 141, 150, 151–55; VCC, *Social Evil*, 176–85; Hobson, *Uneasy Virtue*, 143–45; Rosen, *Lost Sisterhood*, 33, 112–35.

a pander broadly as "any person who shall procure a female inmate for a house of prostitution or who, by promises, threats, violence or by any device or scheme, shall cause, induce, persuade or encourage a female person to become an inmate in a house of prostitution, or shall procure a place as inmate in a house of prostitution for a female person." A first offense was a misdemeanor punishable by six months to a year in jail plus a mandatory fine of $100 to $1,000. A second offense was a felony, punishable by one to ten years in prison.[47]

Prostitutes were common complainants in pandering cases. Although the statutory language required the women to represent themselves as powerless victims, the same legal category allowed them to exert the power of the state against people – mostly men – who had exerted power over them. Prostitutes were named as complainants in eleven of the twenty consecutive pandering cases brought into the court during the first six months of 1915. (It is impossible to tell from the files, but it's likely that the police pressured prostitutes to file at least some of these complaints.) In March, Francis Van der Hayden filed complaints against Fred Bromo and Elizabeth Caird, charging that they "did unlawfully induce, persuade or encourage" her "to become an inmate of a house of prostitution, at 421 Wabash Avenue." The court found Caird not guilty. But the judge sentenced Bromo to one year at labor in the House of Correction plus a $1,000 fine and $6.50 in costs. In September 1922, Doris Rogers won a guilty verdict against a thirty-two-year-old chef named Louis Rogers (the relationship is unclear) for taking $10 from her that she had earned from prostitution. The court sentenced him to six months in the House of Correction and fined him $300 plus $6.50 costs. When Rogers completed his term, the judge gave him a pauper's waiver on the fine, ruling that he had had grown too sick in jail to work it off.[48]

Policing unmarried lovers and punishing panders were sidelines to the main event of the Morals Court, the "treatment" of prostitutes. Unlike those other offenses, prostitution was a sex-specific offense. Although vice investigators in American cities turned up evidence of an illicit male trade in sex, policing urban gay subcultures and "sex perversion" was usually peripheral to the commissions' mandates.

---

[47] Mann Act in Friedman, *Crime and Punishment*, 327; Woolston, *Prostitution in the United States*, 31–32, 84, esp. 33; "An Act in relation to pandering," approved June 1, 1908, *Illinois Revised States*, 1913, ch. 38, sec. 57g.

[48] Pandering String I; *People v. Fred Bromo*, March 12, 1915, case 119134, MCCCR; *People v. Elizabeth Caird*, March 12, 1915, case 119135, ibid.; *People v. Louis Rogers*, Sept. 2, 1922, case 368100, MCCCR.

The Chicago Vice Commission confined its brief discussion of male prostitution to its final chapter on the "medical aspects" of the social evil. In their investigations of saloons and disorderly houses, investigators had repeatedly stumbled across a gay male subculture, whose boundaries blurred with those of the heterosexual underworld. "It appears that in this community," the commissioners reported, "there is a large number of men who are thoroughly gregarious in habit; who mostly affect the carriage, mannerisms, and speech of women; who are fond of many articles ordinarily dear to the feminine heart; who are often people of a good deal of talent; who lean on the fantastic in dress and other modes of expression, and who have a definite cult with regard to sexual life." Vaudeville-style female impersonators were an entertainment staple in some music halls and saloons, where the impersonators sat at tables between acts and solicited for drinks, sometimes inviting men to join them in rooms above the saloon. In the early years of the Morals Court, male inmates and solicitors were a fairly common presence. Eight men were defendants in fifty consecutive prosecutions under the Kate Adams Law from July and August 1915. Although patrons could be prosecuted as inmates, in some cases the men were specifically charged with soliciting. On August 16, police arrested Walter George, a twenty-five-year-old native-born bartender, and Jack Lewis, a twenty-one-year-old American-born performer, for soliciting. The court found both men guilty and sentenced them to thirty days in the House of Correction plus a $1 fine and $6.50 in costs.[49]

Male prostitutes elicited none of the public sympathy and moral outrage expressed for their female counterparts. Instead, they were treated as physiological or psychological misfits who fell properly within the jurisdiction of medicine. (Male prostitutes were assumed to serve only other men.) For a time, the Supreme Court of Illinois even managed to deny they existed. In 1917, the court filed an opinion in the appeal of Lewis Rice, who had been convicted in the Morals Court as an inmate. Taking notice of the expertise of "recognized lexicographers," the high court explained that in "the generally used and popular sense of the expression, an inmate of a house of ill-fame or assignation refers to a woman and not to a man." The court reversed the Morals Court, and Rice walked. In 1921, the General

[49] VCC, *Social Evil*, 297, 295–98; Prostitution String I; *People v. Walter George*, Aug. 16, 1915, case 119301, MCCCR; *People v. Jack Lewis*, Aug. 16, 1915, case 119302, ibid. See *People v. Charles Davis*, Aug. 8, 1915, case 119320, MCCCR. "Disorderly House Raided," *Chicago Defender*, April 7, 1917. See Chauncey, *Gay New York*, 131–329.

Assembly amended the Kate Adams Law to cover male inmates and solicitors.[50]

In the eyes of moral reformers and in the black letters of the law – if not always on the street or in the saloon – the face of the prostitute was that of a woman. And in no small measure, the face of the woman offender was that of a prostitute. Some 88 percent of women arrested in Chicago in 1913 were charged with disorderly conduct; more than a third of those women were arrested specifically for prostitution. Prostitutes in American cities were overwhelmingly "white," second-generation Americans, the daughters of immigrants. But African-Americans were disproportionately represented among arrested prostitutes and would grow much more so by the 1920s. Edith Abbott, an expert on criminal demographics who did some of her finest work debunking the cultural myth of immigrant criminality, studied Chicago's 1913 police reports. She found that although 43.7 percent of the city's female population aged fifteen and over were born abroad, only 30.1 percent of the women arrested and 23.5 percent of those convicted were immigrants. In contrast, white American-born women, who constituted 53.9 percent of the female population, accounted for 59.4 percent of the arrests and 53.9 percent of the convictions. African-American women made "the most unfavorable showing" in the police reports. Although they constituted only 2.4 percent of the female population, 14.8 percent of women arrested and 17.1 percent of those convicted were black. Abbott rejected the common racist presumptions of black moral inferiority. "This disproportionately large share of colored women offenders," she wrote, "may be attributed largely to the generally unfortunate position in which the whole colored race finds itself, the difficulty of securing and holding employment, the difficulty of finding suitable places to live, the proximity of segregated vice districts to colored residence districts, and the fact that because of the assumption that they belong to an inferior race, young colored women find themselves in a perpetually defenseless and unprotected position." Missing from Abbott's astute analysis was the racist structure of morals regulation itself. Not only did the police deliberately drive vice into black neighborhoods, but blacks were frequently harassed by police and sternly treated by Municipal Court judges.[51]

[50] *People v. Rice*, 277 Ill. 521, 522, 523 (1917); Stewart P. Moss, *Moss' Chicago Police Manual* (Chicago, 1923), 65. State supreme courts in Indiana and Iowa struck down statutes against patrons, ruling that men could not be convicted of prostitution. Hobson, *Uneasy Virtue*, 158.
[51] City Council, *Report of the City Council Committee on Crime*, 49–50, esp. 51; VCC, *Social Evil*, 38–39; Chicago Commission on Race Relations, *The Negro*

The governmental rationality of socialized law received a full public trial in the Morals Court during the 1910s. The state interest
in the morality and bodies of women, so forcefully asserted against
the contractual rights of employers in cases such as *Muller v.
Oregon,* was here more directly applied to women themselves. Accused prostitutes were subject not only to fines and incarceration but also to
probation, psychological testing, physical examination, and medical
confinement. Morals Court judges justified the tribunal's extraordinary powers by claiming that the operation of the law was fundamentally different in this space than in other criminal courts: Segregation facilitated judicial specialization, efficiency, and individual
treatment. The court would mete out a personalized disposition
to each offender based on the social knowledge collected by the
court's officers. And by continually accumulating social knowledge,
the court would bathe the city's underworld in the purifying light of
publicity.

In pursuing this ambitious agenda, though, the judges ran into a
snag. Probation did not work in this court. Prostitutes were simply too
uncooperative. Like their counterparts in women's courts and night
courts in some other cities, Morals Court judges soon grew disen-
chanted with probation in prostitution cases. In 1915, the very first
year that judges could use probation with prostitutes, a report of the
Cook County Adult Probation Office shows a rapid decline in the
number of prostitutes assigned to officers. "The natural inference,"
said the county's chief probation officer, "would be that Judges believe there is more chance of reforming persons convicted of larceny,
burglary, receiving stolen property, and violation of city ordinances,
than there is to mend the conduct of defendants in cases involving
domestic infelicity or sex offenses." The natural inference was only
partly correct. It wasn't so much judicial belief as the resistance and
recidivism of offenders that precipitated the swift decline in probation
in this court. Few convicted prostitutes even applied for probation.
Those who did commonly gave the court fake names and addresses
or failed to show up for meetings. In the case of professional prostitutes, Judge Fisher concluded that probation exerted "no restraining
influence whatsoever." To make matters worse, recidivists crowded the
Morals Court docket, and the Adult Probation Act applied only to first
offenders. Still, the Morals Court judges were resourceful men. They
found other ways to use the investigative powers of probation officers.
For Fisher, the real value of a probation investigation lay in whatever

in Chicago: A Study of Race Relations and a Race Riot (Chicago, 1922), 327–56.
See Hobson, *Uneasy Virtue,* 142.

personal information an officer might be able to gather for him about a defendant *before* he issued his order in a case. Morals Court judges routinely used "probation" in this way, rather than in its intended form of post-conviction surveillance.[52]

Perhaps owing partly to the recalcitrance of prostitutes, Morals Court judges had a special enthusiasm for the Psychopathic Laboratory. During the 1910s, American eugenicists claimed that at least half of the prostitutes in the United States suffered from hereditary mental defects, especially feeblemindedness, which rendered them vulnerable to evil influences and dangerous to society at large. Until the early 1920s, these claims had remarkable currency among urban vice investigators, law enforcement officials, institutional superintendents, and women reformers. Even before Olson established the Psychopathic Laboratory in 1914, the Morals Court had an informal practice of examining prostitutes for mental "subnormality." Dr. Anna Dwyer, the court's physician, sized up the mental fitness of the women referred to her by the court for medical exams; she claimed half of them were subnormal. Soon after the laboratory opened, its director, Dr. William J. Hickson, announced that nearly 90 percent of the women he examined from the Morals Court were subnormal. Although the women Hickson examined were not representative defendants – judges sent him only those women they already believed to be "defective" – the judges presented the information to the public as if they were. The Municipal Court judges, charity officials, and even the JPA used the specter of professionally promiscuous feebleminded women to lobby the General Assembly for a new commitment statute, which took effect in 1915. After that time, only the laboratory's own overtaxed resources prevented Morals Court judges from sending a flood of prostitutes there.[53]

---

[52] Chief Probation Officer John W. Houston quoted in Worthington and Topping, *Specialized Courts*, 42; Fisher in *MCC 10–11* (1916–17), 92; *MCC 7* (1913), 94. See *People v. Alice Hanson*, Aug. 21, 1922, case 368026, MCCCR; Reckless, *Vice in Chicago*, 64, 253–54; Reitman, *Sister of the Road*, 182–91.

[53] "An Act to Better Provide for the Care and Detention of Feeble-Minded Persons," *Illinois Revised Statutes*, 1925, ch. 23, sec. 346; Connelly, *Response to Prostitution*, 41; Almena Dawley, "A Study of the Social Effects of the Municipal Court of Chicago," M.A. thesis, University of Chicago, 1915, pp. 34–35; "Goodnow Tells Why Girls Fall," *Chicago Tribune*, Nov. 9, 1916; Harry Olson, "A Constructive Policy Whereby the Social Evil May Be Reduced," address to Seventh Annual International Purity Congress, Minneapolis, Nov. 9, 1913 (n.p.); John Edward Ransom, *A Study of Mentally Defective Children in Chicago, an Investigation Made by the Juvenile Protective Association* (Chicago, 1915); Worthington and Topping, *Specialized Courts*, 32.

Only a handful of American communities ever established a "Continental System" of regulation, in which prostitutes were licensed and subject to compulsory medical examination and treatment. From the social purity battles of the 1870s to the vice investigations of the 1910s, the opposition to such a system in Chicago was overwhelming. It's no small irony, then, that the Morals Court's greatest institutional achievement was to help police and public health authorities establish a routinized system of venereal disease treatment and medical incarceration in the city.

At the outset the system was voluntary, at least formally. The court's resident physician, Dr. Dwyer, gave physical exams to willing defendants referred to her by the judge. Between May 7 and December 1, 1913, for example, the doctor examined 639 women offenders and found that 108 of them had infectious venereal diseases; 315 others "showed signs of having had syphilis." In the early years, the court had no authority to commit infected women to a hospital; it could only offer them free hospital treatment. But Judge Hopkins found a way around this dilemma, as a reporter for the *Chicago Inter Ocean* discovered when she saw Hopkins give a prostitute a scandalously high $150 fine. A social worker explained the fine to the incredulous reporter. "The only thing that can be done when disease is discovered, and it is absolutely necessary that the victim not be at large," she said, "is to place so heavy a fine on the offense that the offender, the patient – whichever you want to call her – has to go to the bridewell. You know, don't you that we in Chicago have in our bridewell one of the best regulated hospitals for the treatment of such diseases in the country?" By the end of the decade, such judicial sleight-of-hand would no longer be necessary.[54]

The mobilization of Americans for World War I brought a dramatic escalation of government intervention to combat the social evil and a shift in the public image of the prostitute. No longer the helpless victim of the white slave literature and vice commission reports, no more the "prostitute on the city pavement" driven to "ruin" by "unscrupulous men," the prostitute was redrawn in War Department propaganda as a deadly threat to the virility and strength of the men in uniform. The war, Woolston wrote, "brought home to the American people as nothing in our previous history had ever done, the menace of prostitution and venereal diseases to the young manhood of our country." The federal government assumed enhanced powers to

54 Dawley, "Social Effects," 34; Ernestine Evans, "In Chicago's Morals Court," *Chicago Inter Ocean*, Nov. 23, 1913; [Herbert Harley], "Success of Organized Courts," *JAJS*, 1 (1918), 143–44.

police public morals and health during the war. Under the authority of the Selective Service Act of 1917, federal agents assisted local authorities in closing brothels and arresting prostitutes near military bases. The Chamberlain–Kahn Act of 1918 gave local health boards authority to detain any person *suspected* of carrying venereal disease for compulsory examination and quarantine. Of more than 15,000 women detained as suspected venereal disease carriers during World War I, nearly half were later released without an arrest record, let alone a court hearing. In the War Department's Committee on Training Camp Activities, women social reformers, including many from Chicago, joined in the federal effort to police immorality around army bases. As Barbara Meil Hobson has argued, these middle-class reformers gained public power only by compromising the civil liberties of the same young working-class women they aimed to protect.[55]

Building on the momentum of the wartime venereal disease measures, the Morals Court in 1919 set in place a new system to test virtually every woman arrested in Chicago on a morals charge. An Illinois statute authorized the program. The statute required local judges to send to a hospital, sanitarium, or clinic for an examination any defendant brought before them on a criminal charge who appeared "from the evidence or otherwise" to be "suffering from a communicable venereal disease." If a defendant tested positive, the law continued, "he or she may by order of the court be sent for treatment to a hospital, sanitarium or clinic... and if necessary, be segregated for such terms as the court may impose." It made no difference whether the defendant's criminal case was later dismissed. The law suspended due process rights in the interests of public health. Morals Court Judge Arnold Heap praised the testing policy as an "enlightened and systematic attempt on the part of the Court and city government to circumscribe and limit the inevitable results and effects of the indiscriminate intercourse of the sexes." The statute was gender-neutral. Its administration was not. An investigator from the New York–based Bureau of Social Hygiene who visited the Morals Court in 1920 found that with a single exception, "no evidence could be found of the examination, treatment or segregation of male defendants."[56]

Compulsory testing transformed the practice of justice in the Morals Court. In the early '20s, fining was still the preferred punishment.

---

[55] Woolston, *Prostitution in the United States*, 33. See Hobson, *Uneasy Virtue*, 165–82.
[56] Law quoted in Worthington and Topping, *Specialized Courts*, 11, 12; Heap in *MCC 12–14* (1918–20), 148.

Judges levied fines ranging from $1 to $50 on thirty-six out of the fifty women charged in consecutive prostitution cases between August 10 and August 28, 1922. Two others received probation. Three were sentenced to the House of Correction for terms ranging from five to thirty days. But the arrest slips from these cases, filled out by vice squad officers, reveal the routinization of venereal disease testing before trial. Virtually without exception the slips say: "Hosp and Morals Ct." The de facto system of vice regulation negotiated by Morals Court judges, vice squads, and public health officials did not follow the procedures set forth in the 1919 statute. When the police arrested women for prostitution, they brought them into the station on an open charge, which allowed them to be detained without bail until they could be examined. The next morning, the women were taken by patrol wagon to Iroquois Hospital, where a physician examined them. When a defendant finally appeared in the Morals Court, a bailiff or clerk presented the judges with the results of her v.d. test. If the defendant tested positive, the judge would simply continue her case and order her quarantined in Lawndale Hospital, a run-down facility operated by the Department of Public Health, until she was rendered noninfectious. Treatment could take weeks or even months. In 1926 alone, the Department of Health examined 10,668 "cases" from the Morals Court and sent 761 of them to hospitals for compulsory treatment.[57]

Judges recognized that treatment at Lawndale was a form of incarceration and were not inclined to punish women further after they had completed treatment. For professional prostitutes, medical incarceration was a greater worry than anything else a Morals Court judge might mete out. In her autobiography, the former Chicago prostitute Bertha Thompson recalled waiting with forty-five other "girls" at a city clinic to be tested before being taken to the Morals Court. "All of us were nervous and excited," she wrote.

> The pinch didn't seem to mean anything to the girls. The worst thing that could happen in the court was to get a ten or twenty-five dollar fine. It was only occasionally that a girl was sent to the House of Correction. But the thing that bothered most of them was the fear that they might be diseased. That would mean a month or six weeks in the hospital, and they all dreaded this.

The Catholic girls fingered their rosaries and prayed. After her examination by a doctor, whom she described as "courteous and kind,"

57 Prostitution String II; Worthington and Topping, *Specialized Courts*, 29–31; City of Chicago, Department of Health, *Report of the Department of Health of the City of Chicago for the Years 1926 to 1930 Inclusive* (Chicago, 1931), 192.

Thompson learned that she had syphilis and an active gonorrhea. In the patrol wagon to Lawndale, she was consoled by a friend from her brothel, who told Thompson that she had been to the hospital three times before. "We'll live through it," the friend told her. Thompson was detained for six weeks. To hear her tell it, women offenders turned Lawndale into a tolerably sociable setting. "We danced and played dominoes and checkers. There was plenty to smoke and every day large bundles of food were sent in to the girls. We were not allowed to have visitors, but all our pimps drove up in their cars and stood on the sidewalk and waved to us."[58]

Thompson was not a representative offender – she later became a social worker. But her story does illuminate both the coercive aspects of examination and quarantine and the real health dangers endemic to prostitution in the early twentieth century, dangers that prostitutes knew all too well. In the first six months of 1920 alone, 274 women from the Morals Court were treated for venereal disease at Lawndale. The system of examination and quarantine obviously helped some women and probably did prevent the spread of disease. But it was a coercive system based on a gender-biased conception of venereal disease that defined the female prostitute – not her patrons – as disease carriers. And lest one take Thompson's light-hearted account as the final word on Lawndale, another statistic from the first six months of 1920 demands our attention. During that period, twenty-five women escaped from Lawndale, taking their health back from the public.[59]

There is a palpable narrowing of focus in Morals Court propaganda in the 1920s, as the once capacious language of socialized law – which could justify both protective legislation to regulate the hours and wages of women workers and interventionist court policies to police their bodies and minds – yielded to a narrower public health interest in ridding the prostitute's body of communicable disease. The mobilization of men for the war had precipitated this shift in thinking, but it had other causes as well, and its effects on the public regulation of urban prostitution far outlasted the war itself. The heightened emphasis on treating prostitutes' bodies, rather than improving their social environments, reflected a broader decline in the sort of causal thinking about social responsibility that had energized progressive vice reform. In retrospect, the policing of venereal disease, which involved the court in a system of public health regulation not entirely unlike the

---

[58] Reitman, *Sister of the Road*, 188–91.
[59] Worthington and Topping, *Specialized Courts*, 30–31.

once vilified Continental System, was the singular administrative success of the Morals Court. Referrals to the Psychopathic Laboratory and the practice of having probation officers investigate the background of women offenders declined in the early '20s, while compulsory venereal disease testing became routine.

Judges began to shed the optimism in segregation and social expertise voiced in earlier years and to emphasize the limits of what a socialized morals court could accomplish. From the beginning, Municipal Court judges had described the Morals Court as an onerous assignment. "A permanent assignment would hardly be fair to the judge," Judge Fisher had written in 1917. "It would require a judge with angelic patience, a giant's constitution and a contentment to remain constantly in this atmosphere of the ugly." But Fisher, one of the few judges to sit on the Morals Court for more than six consecutive months, had voiced no doubts about the good the court could accomplish. By the mid-'20s, such doubts began to surface. "The whole duty and power of the court lies in determining the innocence or guilt of accused persons, and . . . imposing sentence upon the guilty," Judge Daniel Trude wrote in 1924. This statement would have been institutional heresy ten years earlier. Chief Justice Olson confided in a letter to Ethel Sturges Dummer of the JPA that the Morals Court had become "the most discouraging branch of our Court."[60]

This loss of faith had diverse sources. One was a growing recognition of the limited capacity of the court's probation apparatus and psychological testing facilities, and a realization that surveillance required the unlikely cooperation of the offenders. Nothing drove this point home like the problem of recidivist prostitutes. Judges saw a lot of familiar faces in the court. Each of these faces represented a failure for socialized law and a drain on the court's limited capacity to practice labor-intensive socialized law at all. It was not uncommon for a single case to come before several judges over a period of several weeks only to result in discharge or a $1 fine. By the late 1920s, it had become a cliché in writing about the court to present a case of a prostitute who had been through the court more than a hundred times at great public expense. Kate Adams herself pointed to the case of "M.H.," a prostitute who had been arrested 82 times, appeared in the court 113 times, and been treated at Lawndale Hospital eight times. This savvy defendant would demand a jury when she wanted to avoid a

---

[60] Fisher in *MCC 10–11* (1916–17), 86; Trude in *MCC 16–18* (1922–24), 89; Olson to Dummer, Dec. 31, 1923, Ethel Sturges Dummer Papers, Schlesinger Library, Radcliffe College, box 33, folder 694; Worthington and Topping, *Specialized Courts*, 76.

strict judge, then suddenly waive her right when a more lenient judge took the bench. Four years of prosecuting M.H. had resulted in $96 in fines and $59 in recovered costs for the court. The net cost to the city of enforcing the (Kate Adams) law against M.H., based on "a very conservative estimate" of $50 per arrest, amounted to $3,950.[61]

Another factor contributing to the demoralization of the Morals Court bench may have been the mounting public evidence that, like the police, the judges were involved in a racist system of law enforcement. For years, the *Chicago Defender* had regularly published articles charging discrimination in the Morals Court. The city's organ of respectable black opinion expressed no qualms about the vice laws on the books; but the paper did condemn the racist practices of the Chicago Police Department that, after the formal closure of the red-light districts in 1913, turned the Black Belt into the city's "dumping ground" for vice. Articles on the Morals Court charged judges with levying exceptionally harsh fines and jail terms on black men charged with fornication with white women and upon black women arrested for soliciting white men. Bailiffs reportedly handled black defendants roughly. Clerks assured that "cases involving Colored persons are always delayed until the last." This was not the sort of publicity function that Olson had in mind for the Morals Court. The *Defender* turned the specialized tribunal into a place to bear witness to the inequities of law enforcement and to the prejudice of judges and, in an inversion of white slavery narratives, to collect tales of colored girls "lured... with promises of gold and finery" into disorderly houses, where their young bodies and souls were sold to "white men and Chinamen."[62]

The 1920s witnessed a steep rise in the presence of black women in the court, which cannot be explained away by the influx of migrants from the south during the war. By 1924, African-Americans outnumbered American-born whites and immigrants combined in the Morals Court. By 1930, a staggering 70 percent of the prostitutes brought into the Morals Court were black. Judges made no formal statement about the police practices that had incorporated them into a racist system of public morals enforcement not contemplated in the rhetoric of

---

[61] MCC 19–22 (1925–28), 112–13. See "Committee on Courts," *Woman's City Club Bulletin,* May 1926, 26; Worthington and Topping, *Specialized Courts,* 20, 19–20. See also *People v. May Ryan,* Aug. 16, 1922, case 368011, MCCCR. The case involved seven judges before it resulted in a fine of $1 plus $1 costs.

[62] "The Dumping Ground," *Chicago Defender,* July 24, 1920; "The Municipal Court – Morals Branch," ibid., Aug. 5, 1916; "Police Start War on Vice," ibid., May 12, 1917. See also "Judge Cook Displays Rank Racial Prejudice in Court Decision," ibid., Nov. 9, 1918.

socialized law. But some evidence suggests that to the white judges, black women made less appealing subjects for reform than their lighter-skinned predecessors. In 1930, Judge Joseph Shulman called for establishing a fingerprinting system in the court, with the telling complaint that colored women now dominated his caseload, "thereby making it utterly impossible for us to distinguish between the faces."[63]

A final factor in the Morals Court's waning optimism was the changing moral climate of urban America in the jazz age. By the mid-'20s, the burst of moral reform that had produced the Morals Court and so many other interventionist laws and state institutions during the Progressive Era had faded. A telling sign of the shifting sexual norms is the precipitous decline in fornication and adultery prosecutions in the Morals Court. Once accounting for more than 4 percent of the court's caseload (484 of 11,229 cases in 1914), by 1928, fornication and adultery cases comprised only 0.5 percent of the court's work (96 of 17,146 cases). Police and families alike were making less of an effort to police consensual sex outside the legal sanctity of marriage.[64]

The prostitute on the city pavement – and her female peers in the factories, laundries, and department stores of industrializing America – no longer inspired either the broad questions about political economy and cultural politics or the demands for state intervention that they did in 1913. Americans had grown somewhat more accustomed to the presence of women in the industrial, mercantile, and corporate workplaces and in the public spaces of commercialized leisure. This sea-change in public morality can be partly attributed to the machinery of commercial culture that had so alarmed the progressive moralists. Observers of urban life in the '20s noted that young middle-class women increasingly were behaving more and more like their working-class counterparts, socializing in dance halls, drinking and dating, smoking and petting. The appearance of flappers – white middle-class women who wore the high hemlines, cropped hair, and rouged faces previously associated with prostitutes – symbolized the emergence of a new era of sexual experimentation, which the entrepreneurs of mass culture eagerly cultivated in magazines and movies.[65]

In 1933, the sociologist Walter Reckless revisited the old haunts of the social evil in Chicago and found a highly dispersed prostitution economy dramatically different from the one the Vice Commission

[63] *MCC 23 (1929)*, 42 (publication of this report was delayed until mid-1930); Reckless, *Vice in Chicago*, 27.
[64] *MCC 8–9* (1914–15), 57; MCC 19–22 (1925–28), 116B.
[65] See Hobson, *Uneasy Virtue*, 183–84; Meyerowitz, *Women Adrift*, 117–39.

had documented twenty years earlier. Good Chicago School sociologist that he was, Reckless attributed these changes in small part to law enforcement and in large part to broader social forces – "to modern urban trends and to underlying causes of modern city growth." And then there were the women themselves. Just as women, by their growing presence in the workplace and commercialized recreational spaces, had helped spark the moral crisis of the Progressive Era, in Reckless's account, the everyday behavior of women eventually helped defuse that crisis in the '20s and '30s. "Women of ill-fame no longer form a distinct caste readily distinguished from other women by dress, manners, and place of residence," Reckless observed. "The activities of modern women – slumming, night life, exaggerations in dress, an unchaperoned life outside the home, entrance into business and sports – have erased the outward distinction between the painted sport and the paler protected lady."[66]

[66] Reckless, *Vice in Chicago*, 58, 54–57.

7

"Upon the Threshold of Manhood":
The Boys' Court

For a period of eight months during 1920 and 1921, I presided over this court and day after day watched a never-ending procession of boys passing before me. There were boys charged with brutal or serious crimes; boys charged with lesser misdemeanors; boys intolerant of parental or public command; and boys adrift from home and friends – the flotsam of a great city. And often the question came to me: "Whose is the fault?"

— Judge Charles F. McKinley

In the vast literature of social reform that survives from Progressive Era Chicago, "the boy problem" is a ubiquitous phrase. The boy problem signified tens of thousands of young men, mostly the sons of immigrants, who seemed to run loose at all hours in the city – undisciplined by parents, church, school, or regular work – until they ran afoul of the law. Catholic, Jewish, and Protestant agencies mobilized scarce community resources to address the problem. The City of Chicago plowed millions of taxpayer dollars into new playgrounds for immigrant neighborhoods, so budding citizens would have a bucolic yet well-supervised outlet for their "primitive" energies. Boys' Clubs raced to transform immigrant gangs into lawful incubators of Americanization faster than ward bosses could turn them into politically aligned "athletic clubs." The YMCA offered shelter and wholesome recreations to lone Christian pilgrims from the hinterlands. Intrepid JPA protective officers policed the dance halls where, as Jane Addams put it, "respectable" boys received a schooling in vice from "young fellows of evil purpose." The *Chicago Defender* exhorted Black Belt social agencies to provide "watchful care" for the Great Migration's cohort of young men: "[P]oorly clad, illiterate and unaccustomed to city ways," they made easy recruits for the "corner gang." Despite the inroads made by private associational efforts, many progressives agreed with Addams that only an expansive program of local-state intervention, aimed at policing boys' delinquency and channeling their primitive sexual energies into wholesome endeavors, could reclaim the city's spirited youth and, through youth regenerated, redeem the city itself.[1]

City courts occupied a strategic position in this vigorous movement for "juvenile protection." The riddle of responsibility that exercised Judge McKinley's conscience as he sat in judgment on that "neverending procession of boys" had first troubled Catholic charity workers, clubwomen, and progressive lawyers in the late nineteenth century. When McKinley graduated from Chicago-Kent College of Law in 1894, children accused of crime still went to trial in seedy police courts and shared cells with "hardened" adult criminals. The creation of the world's first juvenile court in Chicago in 1899 had changed all of that. The General Assembly established this special chancery court for defendants under sixteen. In 1905, lawmakers raised the age limit to seventeen for boys and eighteen for girls. By the time McKinley took over the Boys' Court in 1920, the idea that young offenders were entitled to judicial paternalism and therapeutic intervention, rather than an adversarial trial and punishment, had won acceptance throughout America and was spreading across the globe.[2]

One of the great questions of criminal justice reform in Progressive Era America was how far the new model of the juvenile court – with its age-specific presumption of diminished criminal responsibility, subsidiary social staff, and therapeutic techniques – should be applied to

---

[1] Jane Addams, *The Spirit of Youth and the City Streets* (New York, 1909); "Cornering the Corner Gang," *Chicago Defender*, June 11, 1921; "Boy Problem Commission Appointed," ibid., Jan. 15, 1916. See Louise de Koven Bowen, *Safeguards for City Youth: At Work and at Play* (New York, 1914); Sophonisba P. Breckinridge and Edith Abbott, *The Delinquent Child and the Home: A Study of the Delinquent Wards of the Juvenile Court of Chicago* (New York, 1912); Paul Boyer, *Urban Masses and Moral Order in America, 1820–1920* (Cambridge, Mass., 1978), 108–20, 233–51, esp. 243; *Boyhood and Lawlessness* (New York, 1914); George Chauncey, *Gay New York: Gender, Urban Culture, and the Making of the Gay Male World, 1890–1940* (New York, 1994), 131–49; Frederic M. Thrasher, *The Gang: A Study of 1,313 Gangs in Chicago* (Chicago, 1927), 487–530.

[2] *BOC* (1931), 658; "An act to regulate the treatment and control of dependent, neglected and delinquent children" (1899), *Illinois Revised Statutes*, 1911, ch. 23, secs. 169–190; "An act relating to children who are now or may hereafter become dependent, neglected or delinquent" (1905), ibid., ch. 23, sec. 169. See Grace Abbott, "History of the Juvenile Court Movement throughout the World," in *The Child, the Clinic, and the Court* (New York, 1925), 267–73; David S. Tanenhaus, "Policing the Child: Juvenile Justice in Chicago, 1870–1925," Ph.D. diss., University of Chicago, 1997, 1: 6.

adult offenders. Some social scientists, reformers, and jurists looked forward to the day when the states would adopt this model for the scientific treatment of *all* offenders, regardless of their age, gender, or crime. In the 1910s, during the high tide of progressivism, almost anything seemed possible. Deterministic views saturated crime talk, expressing deep-seated doubts about the actual autonomy and responsibility of the individual self in an urban-industrial society. And the juvenile court, a powerful symbol of social responsibility, was in reformers' minds as they set up socialized criminal courts for women offenders, home-slackers, and their families, and as they instituted adult probation, social work, and psychiatric testing in municipal courts. But most lawyers and judges, and, one suspects, most Americans, still expected the courts to treat accused felons *as if* their crimes were the product of nothing more than "the inscrutable moral free will." This reflexive legal formalism was strongest when the case at hand was a serious felony crime committed (as virtually all such crimes were) by a man. Absent persuasive evidence of insanity or mental defect, adult male felons whose cases went to trial were still prosecuted on indictment, before a jury, in an old-fashioned criminal tribunal.[3]

The Chicago Boys' Court was thus a radical experiment. Created in 1914, it was the first and only socialized criminal court in America equipped with full power to try and sentence young men between seventeen and twenty-one. "Juvenile adults," as the sociologists called them, occupied a kind of legal limbo. They were too old for the "wise paternalism" of the juvenile court, yet too young to assume the full rights and obligations of adult male citizens. Boys' Court judges had full jurisdiction over juvenile adults charged with ordinance violations and state misdemeanors. They also conducted preliminary hearings in felony cases for all offenders of this class, and they routinely had charges reduced to misdemeanors in order to keep jurisdiction over defendants. As in the juvenile court, fines and imprisonment were a last resort – the last, regrettable options on a continuum of techniques of governance, to be meted out only after the intervention of social workers, probation officers, psychiatrists, charity workers, and the judge himself had failed. "In this age and era of specialization," wrote Judge Edgar A. Jonas, "if any one problem demands expert

---

[3] Thomas A. Green, "Freedom and Criminal Responsibility in the Age of Pound: An Essay on Criminal Justice," *MLR*, 93 (1995), 1956, see 1915–2053, esp. 1950; Arthur W. Towne, "Shall the Age Jurisdiction of Juvenile Courts be Increased?," *JAICLC*, 10 (1920), 493–515. Increasingly, defendants avoided trial by cutting plea bargains. George Fisher, "Plea Bargaining's Triumph," *YLJ*, 109 (2000), 857–1086.

administration, it is the study of plastic young violators of the law, boys upon the threshold of manhood, about to be charged with the responsibility of adult citizens shortly assigned to take their places in the community as the heads of our families." Confident this inquiry would yield more humane treatment for plastic young offenders, a lower recidivism rate, and more scientific social policies, the judges ratcheted up their discretionary authority over the accused and extended the Municipal Court's legal and disciplinary power still deeper into Chicago's social life.[4]

The peculiar jurisdiction of the Boys' Court, however, created two dilemmas for its judges and social personnel. Taking these dilemmas seriously reveals that the court's practices, which at first glance appear grossly arbitrary, were, in fact, patterned and purposeful. The first dilemma arose from the liminal nature of the juvenile adult as a juridical subject. The noun "boy" fit the typical defendant like a Sunday suit recently but irreversibly outgrown. Though no longer easily mistaken for children, juvenile adults still appeared less responsible and more reformable than older male offenders. The new social scientific literature on "adolescence," which judges and reformers cited as authority for their claims about delinquency, was similarly conflicted. Were adolescent boys endangered or simply dangerous? Were they "plastic" or predestined by environment and heredity to a "criminal career"? The second dilemma was one acutely familiar to other progressive criminal judges: The judges' socially interventionist ambitions exceeded their actual legal authority. The Boys' Court was not, strictly speaking, a juvenile court. The Municipal Court judges had no statutory authority to create a chancery court, where the ordinary rules of criminal procedure could be suspended in favor of flexible, continuous disciplinary

---

[4] Jonas in *MCC 16–18* (1922–24), 102; *MCC 8–9* (1914–15), 49–51. In addition to Municipal Court reports, judges' correspondence, and case files, key sources include Murray Howard Leiffer, "The Boys' Court of Chicago," M.A. thesis, University of Chicago, 1928; U.S. Department of Labor, Children's Bureau, *Youth and Crime: A Study of the Prevalence and Treatment of Delinquency among Boys over Juvenile-Court Age in Chicago*, by Dorothy Williams Burke (Washington, D.C., 1930). Leiffer visited the court and interviewed defendants in 1926. Burke conducted her investigation in the mid-1920s, too, but her study presents extensive data from 1914 to 1925. See Frank Orman Beck, "A Study of Boys in the Municipal Court of Chicago: With Emphasis on Recidivism," *Bulletin of the Department of Public Welfare: City of Chicago*, 2 (1919), 5–39; Evelina Belden, "The Boys' Court of Chicago: A Record of Six Months' Work, *AJS*, 20 (1915), 731–44; Claude Willard Sprouse, "The Boys' Court of Chicago," Bachelor's thesis, University of Chicago, 1916.

intervention. Boys' Court judges negotiated this constraint with great ingenuity, manipulating the most mundane elements of criminal procedure in order to introduce the disciplinary style of juvenile justice into the conventional legal setting of a criminal court.

The discovery of the juvenile adult was the high-water mark of a century-long trend toward special treatment of young offenders in which the question of age-specific freedoms and responsibilities was paramount. One need only recall that the common-law threshold of criminal responsibility was seven to appreciate the significance of this trend. From the creation of the first urban houses of refuge in the 1820s and 1830s to the invention of the juvenile court, special treatment for young offenders hinged on two increasingly plausible claims about the innate differences of youth: children were incapable of forming the intent necessary willfully to commit a crime, and children had better prospects for reform than adults. But the states that rushed to adopt the juvenile court in the two decades after 1899 (all but Wyoming and Maine) differed on when childhood ended and adulthood began. Roughly one-third of the states capped the juvenile court's jurisdiction at the sixteenth birthday, another third at seventeen, the rest at eighteen or older. In Nevada and California, juvenile courts had exclusive jurisdiction over defendants under eighteen and concurrent jurisdiction (with the criminal court's approval) over offenders under twenty-one. Massachusetts, Missouri, New Mexico, New York, and Pennsylvania provided for juvenile adults in domestic relations or morals courts. And not all states set the same limit for males and females.[5]

Instead of directly challenging common law and statutory standards of criminal responsibility, the makers of the juvenile court created an institution that was no criminal court at all. The tribunal operated as a chancery court, subject to the rules of equity. Equity had developed in England as a body of jurisprudence and mode of judicial practice alternative to the common law. Courts of equity (also known as chancery courts because of equity's origins in the office of the king's chancellor) aimed at a fairness of disposition ill-afforded by the rigid principles of the common law; to this end, equity gave judges greater discretion. The juvenile court also enjoyed doctrinal support in the common-law rationale of parens patriae, according to which the state acts as parent to individuals recognized as less than fully competent legal subjects.

---

[5] Children's Bureau, *Youth and Crime*, 18, 19–21; Abbott, "History of the Juvenile Court"; Leiffer, "Boys' Court," 1; Sanford J. Fox, "Juvenile Justice Reform: An Historical Perspective," *SLR*, 22 (1970), 1187–239.

The judge's own intuitions about the child's "best interests" guided their practice.[6]

Dramatic differences in procedure distinguished a juvenile court from a typical criminal court. "The [Illinois Juvenile Court] law was expressly framed to avoid treating a child as a criminal," recalled Timothy Hurley, the Catholic activist and former Chicago police magistrate who helped draft the legislation.

> The child was not to be arrested, but brought in by the parent or guardian, or by a probation officer. The bill expressly forbade keeping a child in a jail or enclosure where adults were confined.
>
> When the child was brought into court, the inquiry was with reference to the condition of the child: Was there a condition of dependency, delinquency, or truancy? Instead of a prosecutor there was to be a probation officer who was there not to convict the child, but to represent his interests.
>
> The child was not to be convicted, but was to be found dependent, delinquent or truant, or discharged. . . . All the proceedings were to be informal. The strict rules of evidence were not adhered to; the effort being, first, to find out what was the best thing to be done for the child, and secondly, if possible, to do it.

As David Tanenhaus has argued, promoters of the juvenile court tended to idealize the institution, as if it sprang fully formed from the 1899 statute. Activists and judges struggled for years, against significant opposition, to establish a wholly therapeutic institution. They never purged all elements of criminal procedure.[7]

Still, law writers and appellate judges soon accepted the idea that the guilt or innocence of the child was beside the point in a juvenile court. State appellate courts hearing constitutional challenges to juvenile court acts shored up the distinction between a juvenile court and a regular criminal court. As the high courts shielded juvenile offenders from the common law's presumptions of criminal responsibility, they stripped juveniles of due process protections guaranteed by the

---

[6] Julian W. Mack, "Chancery Procedure in the Juvenile Court," in *Child, the Clinic, and the Court,* 310–19. Douglas R. Rendleman, "Parens Patriae: From Chancery to the Juvenile Court," *South Carolina Law Review,* 23 (1971), 205–59.

[7] Timothy D. Hurley, "Origin of the Illinois Juvenile Court Law," in *Child, the Clinic, and the Court,* 327–28. David S. Tanenhaus, "The Evolution of Juvenile Courts in the Early Twentieth Century: Beyond the Myth of Immaculate Construction," in *A Century of Juvenile Justice,* ed. Margaret K. Rosenheim, Franklin E. Zimring, David S. Tanenhaus, and Bernardine Dohrn (Chicago, 2002).

common law and state constitutions. "The natural parent needs no process to temporarily deprive his child of its liberty by confining it in his own home, to save it and to shield it from the consequences of persistence in a career of waywardness," the Pennsylvania Supreme Court explained in 1905; "nor is the state, when compelled, as *parens patriae*, to take the place of the father for the same purpose, required to adopt any process as a means of placing its hands upon the child to lead it into one of its courts."[8]

Cultural conceptions of youth were in a state of historic transformation during the Progressive Era. Advocates of compulsory education, child labor legislation, municipal playgrounds, and juvenile justice argued that childhood was a sacred stage of life that ought to be legally protected by the state as a period of nurturing and education. Childhood was a time to be "spent neither in idleness nor in labor," declared Julia Lathrop, the Hull-House veteran and first chief of the U.S. Children's Bureau. In 1904, the psychologist G. Stanley Hall lay the scientific foundation for the idea of adolescence in 1904 with his enormously influential study, *Adolescence: Its Psychology and Its Relation to Physiology, Anthropology, Sociology, Sex, Crime, Religion, and Education.* Hall called the attention of reformers and policy makers to the late teen years, when the child developed into an adult and, in the process, recapitulated the evolution of the race from savagery to civilization. For Hall, adolescence was a distinct phase of human development, replete with potentialities and dangers. Adolescents needed special protection from the rigors and freedoms of adulthood. Parents and educators, Hall advised, should sublimate youths' primal sexual urges by channeling them into wholesome activities such as sports, music, and religion. Jane Addams took up Hall's theme in *The Spirit of Youth and the City Streets* (1909). She chastised short-sighted city governments, such as Chicago's, which failed to provide young people with well-supervised places of recreation, thus allowing the proprietors of dance halls to cull profits from the sexually charged spirit of youth.[9]

[8] *Commonwealth v. Fisher*, 213 Pa. 48 (1905) in Frances Bowes Sayre, *A Selection of Cases on Criminal Law* (Rochester, 1927), 469–73, esp. 471; Joel Prentiss Bishop, *Bishop on Criminal Law*, ed. John M. Zane and Carl Zollmann (Chicago, 1923), 1: 264.
[9] Julia C. Lathrop, "The Background of the Juvenile Court in Illinois," in *Child, Clinic, and the Court*, 290; Addams, *Spirit of Youth*, esp. 3–8. See G. Stanley Hall, *Adolescence: Its Psychology and Its Relation to Physiology, Anthropology, Sociology, Sex, Crime, Religion and Education* (New York, 1904); David J. Rothman, *Conscience and Convenience: The Asylum and Its Alternatives in Progressive America* (Boston, 1980), 210–11.

Criminologists invested adolescence with enormous importance, warning that young men who became hardened adult offenders first took up their "criminal careers" during this turbulent age. "The greatest interest for all students of criminology," the progressive psychiatrist William Healy wrote in his monumental 1915 treatise, *The Individual Delinquent*, "centers about the fact that most frequently the career of the confirmed criminal begins during adolescence." By the 1920s, this stock cultural script of adolescent offenders as "criminals in the making" had become conventional wisdom in academic social science. Chicago School sociologist Frederic Thrasher plotted out the progressive "demoralization" that awaited the unsupervised youth of the "disorganized" immigrant "slum." "Beginning as a truant, he becomes in turn a minor delinquent, a hoodlum, a reckless young sport or a daredevil, an occasional criminal, and finally, if nothing intervenes, he develops into a seasoned gangster or a professional criminal."[10]

This view of adolescent male offenders as criminals-in-chrysalis led criminologists down two quite different roads, each with different policy implications. Reformers and judges unquestioningly followed the experts down both roads, without making the difficult choice between them. The first road led to the hopeful conclusion that since adolescents were still developing, expert individual treatment in specialized courts could remake budding criminals into lawful citizens, workers, and breadwinners. "When they are young they are plastic, divinely plastic," gushed Judge Ben Lindsey of the Denver juvenile court, which had jurisdiction over minors up to twenty-one. "They bend without breaking; they mend with miraculous vitality; and about them still float those trailing clouds of glory, tenuous yet indestructible, which are the heritage of childhood – and, let us hope, the ultimate inheritance of the human race." Lindsey's exuberant reference to racial inheritance hinted at the second road. Perhaps some, or even most, of these criminals-in-the-making were not plastic at all. Perhaps the die was cast before they were born. Reformers and judges learned from criminologists that adolescence was the transitional age when many boys predisposed to deviancy by hereditary "mental defect" embarked upon their criminal careers.[11]

As social scientists raised the stakes of adolescence, reformers in Chicago discovered the "juvenile adult," a term they borrowed from

[10] William Healy, *The Individual Delinquent: A Text-Book of Diagnosis and Prognosis for All Concerned in Understanding Offenders* (Boston, 1915), 713; *MCC 12–14* (1918–20), 114; Thrasher, *The Gang*, 37–38, esp. 369.
[11] Ben B. Lindsey and Wainwright Evans, *The Revolt of Modern Youth* (New York, 1925), 14.

British criminal justice policy makers. For years, the JPA leadership had questioned the "narrow line between the boy who has reached the maximum age for treatment in the Juvenile Court and the boy who, because he has already passed his seventeenth birthday is regarded as a criminal." In the face of the growing scientific literature on adolescence, that line seemed dangerously arbitrary. The JPA had several reasons for focusing on the problem of young *male* offenders "unprotected" by the juvenile court. The police arrested roughly nine men for every woman. The local jail population was even more skewed: In 1911, the County Jail held 1,389 minors above juvenile-court age; all but 61 were male. Furthermore, the juvenile court's age limit was already one year higher (eighteen) for girls. Finally, since the vast majority of women arrested in Chicago were charged with morals offenses, most juvenile-adult women already had their cases tried in a socialized tribunal, the Morals Court.[12]

The JPA's case for a specialized boys' court emphasized the disastrous social consequences of exposing impressionable young men to the Chicago jails. Police station lockups, the dank basement cell areas where defendants who could not make bail waited for their arraignments, were a long-standing public outrage. One sociologist described the lockups as "unbelievably filthy and unsanitary, a menace not only to the little decency of those locked up there, but to the health of the city as well." According to a JPA investigator, "unscrupulous bondsmen and shyster lawyers" hung around the police stations and preyed upon the boys and their "ignorant or foreign parents." Jailers handed out rough treatment to young and old alike. Impressionable first offenders shared cells with "hardened" men who corrupted them sexually. At Cook County Jail, where boys were held during continuances in Municipal Court trials, the warden tried to appease reformers by designating a separate tier of cells for juvenile adult boys. The JPA argued that many boys spent more time waiting for their trials behind bars than they would have if speedily convicted and sentenced. A specialized judge, "in full possession of all the facts and extenuating circumstances," the JPA investigator concluded, could have "settled" most of these cases in the Municipal Court.[13]

---

[12] Bowen, *Safeguards for City Youth*, 104, 112; A. P. Drucker, "A Study of One Hundrer [*sic*] Juvenile-Adult Offenders in the Cook County Jail," *JAICLC*, 4 (1913), 47; Edith Abbott, "Statistics Relating to Crime in Chicago," in City of Chicago, City Council, *Report of the City Council Committee on Crime* (Chicago, 1915), 46–49.

[13] Drucker, "Juvenile-Adult Offenders," 47–57, esp. 53; Belden, "Boys' Court," 732. See Louise de Koven Bowen, "Boys and Lock-Ups," *Survey*, Dec. 7, 1912,

The JPA's shocking investigations of the lockups and jail persuaded Chief Justice Harry Olson, who was by this time a JPA board member. With Louise de Koven Bowen looking on, Olson announced his plan to establish a new Boys' Court at a meeting of suffragists in Washington.[14]

Olson waited to sign the necessary paperwork until he could secure funds from the City Council to set up a psychiatric clinic for criminal defendants in the Municipal Court. To keep his institution on the cutting edge of legal socialization, Olson knew the Boys' Court would need access to a criminological clinic, an innovation first introduced in 1909 at the Cook County Juvenile Court. The council made the appropriation, and Olson signed the order. The Boys' Court opened on March 20, 1914, to the usual fanfare in the press. The headline in the *Chicago Tribune* drew upon Christian imagery, rather than the social scientific argot that Olson probably would have preferred, to tout the new tribunal: "Mercy Opens Boys' Court."[15]

To Harry Olson's mind, increasingly engaged with the exciting new racial science of eugenics, the socialized branches and the laboratory were now a seamless whole: a unified system for expert investigation and policing of the deviant family, which he had come to see as the wellspring of criminality. "It will be observed," the chief justice later reflected, "that the father and mother appear in the Court of Domestic Relations; the boy in the Boys' Court, and the girl in the Morals Court. Often one family is represented in all three courts. These courts are held in the City Hall near each other, and near to the Psychopathic Laboratory, and thus afford a great opportunity for the intensive study of those who conflict with the law."[16]

The records of the Boys' Court support reformers' claims that juvenile-adult crime originated less in individual moral failings than in the social conditions of the industrial city. Data collected from the court in 1924 and 1925 by the U.S. Children's Bureau provide a demographic snapshot of the policed population. Then, as now, African-Americans

pp. 304, 306; Louise de Koven Bowen, *Boys in the County Jail: Their Needs* (Chicago, 1913).

[14] Louise de Koven Bowen, *Growing Up with a City* (New York, 1926), 128–29.

[15] Olson, "The Municipal Court of Chicago, a Tribunal of Procedural Reform and Social Service," reprint from *San Francisco Recorder*, May 12, 1916, 10; Municipal Court of Chicago General Order No. 285, March 16, 1914, General Order Book, vol. 15, 1907–21, Cook County Circuit Court Archives. "Mercy Opens Boys' Court," *Chicago Tribune*, March 19, 1914.

[16] Harry Olson, "The Municipal Court of Chicago – Its Organization and Administration," *CLJ*, 92 (1921), 88.

---

were overrepresented in urban criminal courts. More than 13 percent of defendants in the Boys' Court were "colored," compared with 4 percent of the juvenile-adult age group in Chicago. Among "white" defendants, only 8 percent were foreign-born, compared with 15 percent of Chicago boys in their age group. But 57 percent of the boys' fathers were foreign-born, hailing predominantly from Poland, Russia, Italy, and Ireland. Only a third of the boys had completed eighth grade. Half were unemployed. Some 42 percent of the boys had been arrested before. And one-quarter of the boys had records for delinquency in the Cook County Juvenile Court – old-timers in the criminal justice system by the time they graduated to the Boys' Court.[17]

Many defendants were members of gangs, the ubiquitous male institutions that Frederic Thrasher believed sprang spontaneously from the social disorganization of the immigrant slums. In his exhaustive reportorial research for *The Gang* (1927), a classic of urban sociology, Thrasher identified no fewer than 1,313 gangs with 25,000 members inhabiting the interstices of Chicago's social, economic, and moral geographies. "The characteristic habitat of Chicago's numerous gangs is that broad twilight zone of railroads and factories, of deteriorating neighborhoods and shifting populations, which borders the city's central business district." For boys negotiating adolescence amidst the poverty and neglect of "the slum," gangs offered masculine sociability and collective power. Some gangs prided themselves on their quick resort to violence, a quality prized by ward politicians. The politically connected Ragen's Colts – an Irish athletic club from the Back-of-the-Yards area whose motto was "hit me and you hit two thousand" – provided strongarm services to their Democratic party patrons at the polls on election day. The Colts terrorized African-Americans who entered "their" territory, and the *Defender* implicated them for starting the murderous Chicago race riots of 1919.[18]

[17] Children's Bureau, *Youth and Crime*, 87–102. See Beck, "Study of Boys," 20; Chicago Commission on Race Relations, *The Negro in Chicago: A Study of Race Relations and a Race Riot* (Chicago, 1922), 330–56; Leiffer, "Boys' Court," 105–9; *MCC 16–18* (1922–24), 104. Boys' Court judges had to bind over defendants with Juvenile Court records to that tribunal, which had jurisdiction over its wards until they turned twenty-one. But recidivist boys learned to escape the juvenile court's grasp (and the prospect of a lengthy institutionalization) by disavowing their juvenile records in the Boys' Court. Albert Lepawsky, *The Judicial System of Metropolitan Chicago* (Chicago, 1932), 84–85.
[18] Thrasher, *The Gang*, 47, 53, 201–3, 228, 472, esp. 3. William M. Tuttle, Jr., *Race Riot: Chicago in the Red Summer of 1919* (New York, 1970), 199. "Ragan's [sic] Colts Start Riot," *Chicago Defender*, June 28, 1919.

The police arrested juvenile-adult males for the most brutal crimes on the statute books, including rape, murder, and assault with intent to kill. But the vast majority of juvenile-adult crimes were property offenses and breaches of public order. Crimes of acquisition – burglary, larceny, robbery (also by definition a violent crime), and receiving stolen property – constituted the bulk of felony cases handled by the Boys' Court, more than 85 percent in 1914. That same year the single crime of larceny accounted for 56 percent of the court's misdemeanor caseload, which also included assault and battery, vagrancy, and malicious mischief. Sundry minor property crimes loomed large among the thousands of city ordinance violations handled annually by the court.[19]

The actual acts covered by these statutory genera ranged from armed robbery and auto theft to the theft of piping and construction materials from vacant homes and lots. Chickens, loaves of bread, coffee, cigars, and bottles of beer were also common targets of petty larceny. The railroad lines running through poor neighborhoods laid out a veritable banquet for young thieves, who pilfered merchandise from railroad cars and picked up the coal and potatoes that fell onto the tracks. Scavenging on the tracks and even plundering train cars enjoyed the general sanction of some immigrant communities. "Boys and girls, men and women engage in robbing cars and many of them seem to think that there is nothing wrong about stealing from corporations," the German-American Municipal Court Judge Michael Frances Girten told a newspaper in 1907. "Children are sometimes sent out to steal grain, coal and lumber, by their parents." Social investigators attributed this community lawlessness to Continental "habits of thought and life" that clashed with American notions of private property. Sophonisba Breckinridge and Edith Abbott traced such property crimes to the common practice in peasant communities of collecting vegetables and grain dropped by wagons as they traveled along public ways to market. "No trespass is committed by one who goes along and picks them up." But the railroad corporations did not share this Old World view of the tracks as a common way. They demanded enforcement by the police and hired their own officers and detectives to patrol the yards. Still the practice did not abate. "Whole neighborhoods sometimes engage in stealing from the tracks," Thrasher reported in 1927.[20]

[19] *MCC 8–9* (1914–15), 52–54.
[20] Unidentified clipping attached to letter from Harry Olson to Michael F. Girten, Jan. 14, 1907, MCC, box 1, folder 2; Breckinridge and Abbott, *Delinquent Child*, 68; Thrasher, *The Gang*, 148–58, esp. 155. See Beck, "Study of Boys," 9–10; Belden, "Boys' Court of Chicago," 738; Drucker, "Juvenile-Adult Offenders," 48.

The largest single category of offenses in the Boys' Court during its early years was the quasicrime of disorderly conduct, more than half of the tribunal's burden in 1914. Into this roomy legal rubric, the City Council corralled almost every breach of public order imaginable. The police made good use of it to discipline young men. When a University of Chicago divinity student sorted through 562 disorderly conduct cases from the Boys' Court in 1916, he found that more than a quarter consisted of quarreling and fighting. Fifty-six boys had been arrested for loafing on street corners, fifty-two for drinking, and forty for sleeping out at night in doorways, barns, and other popular flop spots. Other common infractions included shaking dice, loitering in poolrooms, playing ball in the street, "being in bad company," "refusing to work," swearing, and "flipping trains" (leaping onto moving cars). Somewhat less common were boxing in a poolroom, pulling an old man's beard, kissing a girl in public, singing on a park bridge, and sticking a tongue out at a police officer. Generational conflicts, especially common between immigrant parents and first-generation sons, also underlay many of the disorderly conduct cases. Each year, hundreds of working-class parents had their own boys arrested for being abusive, refusing to hand over their wages, or hanging out with a gang.[21]

The many Boys' Court defendants who had experience in the Juvenile Court would have been struck by the comparison. In both courts, the only grown adults the boys encountered were on the right side of the law; there were no hardened adult offenders here. Juvenile Court veterans would also have been accustomed to the bustling presence of probation officers and social workers, representing the court and private social agencies, who peppered them with questions about their work histories, schooling, and families, dutifully recording their answers on data cards. As in the Juvenile Court, these officers needed sizing up and careful negotiation, because their advice could determine the outcome of the case.[22]

Defendants versed in the ways of the Juvenile Court, though, could not fail to notice the differences between it and the Boys' Court from the moment of their arrest. In the eyes of the police and in the language of the law, they were no longer children. Parents or guardians brought defendants into the Juvenile Court in response to a summons; when the court deemed it necessary, defendants were held in

[21] Sprouse, "Boys' Court," 7. See Belden, "Boys' Court," 733–35, 739; Children's Bureau, *Youth and Crime*, 41; Breckinridge and Abbott, *Delinquent Child*, 65–69; Leiffer, "Boys' Court," 47–48; Sprouse, "Boys' Court," 24.

[22] Children's Bureau, *Youth and Crime*, 17–23, 39–60; Leiffer, "Boys' Court," 27–69, 176–80.

a special juvenile detention home. Juvenile adults experienced arrest just as older offenders did: Police arrested them and hauled them into police stations. If they were charged with a quasicriminal offense and the desk sergeant knew them or their families, they were customarily released on their own recognizance. But defendants charged with misdemeanors or felonies who could not make cash bail or post a bond secured by property had to await arraignment with adult defendants in a police station lockup, where beatings and deprivation of food were a rite of passage. Juvenile adults learned that class discrimination was built into the system. Only poor boys who could muster neither bail nor bond had to await arraignment in the lockups or endure confinement in the County Jail during trial continuances. This was almost invariably the experience of black defendants.[23]

Whether a boy made bail or not also determined how he appeared in court. Boys who made bail entered the court from the front door and sat on benches alongside other spectators in the gallery as they waited for the bailiff to call their case. A photograph of the court from 1916 attests to the advantage these boys had over boys who had spent the night in a lockup or jail. The boys in the courtroom sported fresh hair cuts, clean clothes or suits, and many sat next to older women, presumably their mothers or guardians. Less fortunate defendants, whose presence is felt but not seen in the photograph, arrived in court wearing handcuffs, in the custody of a police officer. They awaited their case on hard wooden benches, often for hours, in the "bull pen," a small holding room off the main courtroom that reeked of disinfectant and harbored roaches and mice.[24]

From the dirty walls of the bull pen, the first offender learned that he had joined the ranks of a boisterous fraternity. The handiwork of penknives and pencils announced the street names and gang affiliations of Boys' Court alumni: "Radio Bill – 90 – days," "Two Gun man from the stock yards," "Jew Boy," "Ky Rambling Kids." One prisoner felt inspired to a flash of doggerel: "Kid Apes from 31st where [we] kic out windows, brake down doores, mistreat goodlooking women and trifling whores." The ethnic diversity of the prisoners impressed Murray Leiffer, a University of Chicago sociology student who hung out in the bull pen in the mid-1920s. "Boys are here from all the different neighborhoods of Chicago," Leiffer reported: "vagrants from west Madison and south State Streets, some colored boys brought in for making a

[23] Children's Bureau, *Youth and Crime*, 22–23, 46–47; JPA, untitled annual report, (Chicago, 1910), 10–11.
[24] "The 'Boy's [sic] Court' – It's [sic] Beneficent Work," *Public Safety*, Aug. 28, 1916, p. 3; Children's Bureau, *Youth and Crime*, 48.

disturbance at one o'clock in the morning on Grand Boulevard, two Polish boys arrested for stealing a car on Milwaukee Avenue, a few Italian boys from the near west side, charged with fighting, a neatly dressed bellboy from one of the fashionable hotels, accused of taking the overcoat of a guest. They are all here and many more: every nationality, every race, and charged with every offense." As the sociologist watched in amazement, the boys struck up acquaintances, swapped stories, chewed over each other's cases. Seasoned defendants offered up psychological profiles of the sitting judge. Judge Francis Allegretti always wore a flower in his buttonhole, and two boys engaged in a lively debate as to whether a yellow or red flower today would be most auspicious for their cases. Just as the creators of the Morals Court unintentionally opened up a gathering place for prostitutes, pimps, lawyers, bondsmen, reporters, vice cops, sociologists, and prurient observers in an era when Chicago's vice economy was increasingly dispersed, the Boys' Court's inventors unwittingly fostered a self-conscious subculture of masculine delinquency.[25]

The operations of the Boys' Court reflected the hybrid nature of its jurisdiction over the juvenile adult. The judges wanted their techniques to demonstrate their scientific knowledge of the late adolescent offender. "The application of the principles of criminal justice to delinquent youth of this class," Judge Allegretti explained, "requires special and peculiar consideration." But unlike their Juvenile Court counterparts, Boys' Court judges had no special statutory authority. They lacked the doctrinal rationale of parens patriae and the procedural latitude of a chancery court. Theirs was unmistakably a criminal court, formally governed by the criminal law's presumptions of innocence and age-specific criminal capacity, as well as the due process strictures of criminal procedure.[26]

This was a common problem in American criminal courts during the Progressive Era. The legal historian Thomas A. Green has argued that leading legal scholars and judges struggled to reconcile the deterministic implications of social science with the procedural restraints of a criminal court – and the cherished liberal ideals of individual liberty and responsibility from which those restraints derived. This was especially true in felony cases. Green suggests that by the 1920s American jurists reached a sort of compromise, which enabled them to defend political liberty and free will while extending some recognition to the social causes of crime. The compromise corresponded to the

[25] Leiffer, "Boys' Court," 32–37, 75.
[26] Allegretti in MCC 19–22 (1925–28), 109.

bifurcated structure of the criminal trial. During the guilt-assessment phase, the old common-law presumptions of free will and responsibility would remain undiluted. In the sentencing phase, judges could legitimately take notice of mitigating social facts, tailoring the sentence to their own subjective calculus of social versus individual responsibility in the case. Of course, progressive penal reforms had expanded the arsenal of sentencing options at judges' disposal. In short, judges held the unsettling ethical implications of social responsibility in abeyance during the trial, only to let them in the back door during sentencing.[27]

This intriguing model of a bifurcated judicial process may well have held true in old-fashioned felony tribunals such as the Cook County Criminal Court. But such courts occupied a relatively small realm within the universe of criminal justice administration. Inferior courts such as the Municipal Court of Chicago, which handled the vast majority of criminal and quasicriminal cases in America's great cities, evidently paid less respect to formal legal boundaries. This was especially true in socialized courts such as the Boys' Court, where an ethic of social responsibility of crime was supposed to govern every stage of the judicial process. So, how did Boys' Court judges reconcile social responsibility with the constraints of their institutional role? Animated by the notion that a wise judge could reform plastic male youths – even boys charged with felonies – judges used routine elements of legal procedure, at *all* stages of the judicial process, as techniques of individual treatment and social intervention.

Of course, the active presence of social personnel in itself did much to socialize court practice. Female social workers introduced a self-consciously maternalist commitment to social responsibility and therapeutic intervention. The court's Social Service Department was smaller than its counterpart in the Court of Domestic Relations – it never grew beyond three workers – but it served a similar purpose and shared a similar provenance in private initiative. When the Boys' Court opened in 1914, the JPA and the Protectorate of the Catholic Women's League each placed a woman social worker in the court to serve as a social secretary. Within seven months both women had joined the Municipal Court payroll as deputy clerks. Mary Regina Fugate, the Catholic social worker, served as head of the department through the 1910s and 1920s, developing a keen eye for recidivists. The JPA produced the standard forms on which the social secretaries recorded the "social data" of each defendant – his family background, work history, wages, education, personal character, and associations. The secretaries arranged examinations of boys in the Psychopathic Laboratory (at the judge's

[27] Green, "Freedom and Criminal Responsibility."

request) and referred boys to private social agencies and hospitals. They also vetted about fifty complaints each month from parents, most of them mothers, who requested the court's aid in controlling their "idle, unruly or untractable sons." The department did not let barriers of language or race limit its reach. In the 1920s, the department hired a woman who could interpret for boys and parents who spoke Slavic languages, and an African-American woman to work exclusively with black defendants. Judges also gave private social workers from religious organizations free rein to work with boys of their faith. Social workers representing the Jewish Social Service Bureau, the Catholic Holy Name Society, and the Protestant Federation of Churches interviewed defendants, visited their homes, advised judges to place defendants in various faith-based institutions, and openly proselytized to the boys.[28]

After negotiating the gauntlet of social personnel and volunteers, the defendant would eventually have his day – or, rather, his moment – in court. Nothing in the court's physical layout suggested that its purpose differed from the identical municipal courtrooms in City Hall. The Boys' Court had the same elevated bench, flanked by the same brass candelabras and clerk's desks, the same jury box (often occupied by police officers who smoked and dozed as they awaited their cases), and the same gallery filled with defendants, their families, spectators, and the press. Besides the presence of social workers leading boys to the back room for interviews, the official personages were no different, either. Unlike the Juvenile Court, where judges and probation officers ran the proceedings, the Boys' Court had public prosecutors: an assistant state's attorney, who handled felonies and misdemeanors, and an assistant city prosecutor, who dealt with the quasicrimes. Although it averaged about half the annual caseload of the Municipal Court's busiest outpost, Harrison Street Criminal Branch, the Boys' Court was still busier than most. In 1924 and 1925, for example, the judge heard an average of fifty cases every day – about half of them new. Despite this daily deluge, judges attempted to handle each case with the wisdom of both a father and an expert. The extent to which the practice of the Boys' Court actually differed from an ordinary criminal court depended in a large measure on the will and resourcefulness of the judge.[29]

[28] *MCC 10–11* (1916–17), 80; *MCC 12–14* (1918–20), 146–47. See Children's Bureau, *Youth and Crime*, 22, 40–44; JPA, *Annual Report of the Juvenile Protective Association of Chicago, 1913–1914* (Chicago, n.d.), 7–10; Leiffer, "Boys' Court," 43–46; Municipal Court of Chicago General Order No. 302, Oct. 14, 1914, General Order Book, vol. 15, 1917–21; *MCC 8–9* (1914–15), 50.

[29] In 1916, for example, when Harrison Street disposed of 12,595 cases, the Boys' Court disposed of 6,583 – more cases than thirteen of the seventeen other criminal branches disposed of that year. *MCC 24–25* (1930–31),

Like the Municipal Court judges as a whole, the Boys' Court judges were a diverse group. Harry P. Dolan, the court's second judge, was a Democrat who had spent his juvenile-adult years as a locomotive fireman and roundhouse foreman before studying law and becoming one of the Boys' Court's most popular judges. Dolan created a Public Defenders Association within the court, recruiting prominent members of the Chicago bar to spend a day in court and provide free counsel to defendants. Judge Daniel P. Trude, a Republican who served on the court in 1919, came of age in a prominent Chicago family – his father successfully prosecuted Patrick Eugene Prendergast for the murder of Mayor Carter H. Harrison in 1893 – and received his undergraduate education at Dartmouth College and the University of Chicago, before earning his LL.B. from Northwestern University. Most of the judges had humbler lineages than Trude. Several had grown up in the same immigrant neighborhoods on the West Side from which the court drew many of its defendants.[30]

Municipal Court judges viewed the Boys' Court as a plum assignment, in spite of the exceptionally long hours that came with the post. In the heyday of socialized law during the 1910s and 1920s, a handful of juvenile court judges attained a level of national prominence that must have mystified the typical city judge. No doubt, few of the municipal judges who approached Chief Justice Olson for an assignment to the Boys' Court aspired to the national visibility of Judge Lindsey of Denver, Judge Julian Mack of Chicago, or Referee Miriam Van Waters of Los Angeles, all public authorities on what Lindsey called the "revolt of modern youth." But service on the Boys' Court promised real perks: human interest press coverage, invitations to address civic associations, or an opportunity to mend fences with politically connected social agencies. And the court gave judges a chance to work with a seemingly more deserving and promising class of defendants than the typical criminal branch. Surely, it was the popularity of the post and not its purported hazards – insiders attributed Judge Dolan's tragic suicide to the rigors of the job – that motivated Olson to keep the post constantly in play. He assigned thirty-four different judges to the branch in just twelve years.[31]

34–35; Children's Bureau, *Youth and Crime*, 22, 49. Leiffer, "Boys' Court," 16–17.

[30] *BOC* (1917), 1917, 192, 683; *BOC* (1926), 880. See "'Boy's Court' – It's Beneficent Work," 3; Leiffer, "Boys' Court," 53–69, 131; Bessie Louise Pierce, *A History of Chicago*, vol. 3: *The Rise of a Modern City 1871–1893* (New York, 1957), 270, 386.

[31] Lindsey and Evans, *Revolt of Modern Youth*; Beck, "Study of Boys," 8; Children's Bureau, *Youth and Crime*, 22, 39; John Gutknecht, *The Chicago Boys'*

Brevity of tenure did not diminish the judges' perception of themselves as experts on juvenile-adult criminality. For the judges who contributed densely sociological entries to the Municipal Court's annual
reports, this self-image seems to have been the job's greatest reward.
It is notable how little space judges devoted to legal matters and how
much to their scientific findings. "The Court is really a Clinic, sepa-
rating the patients into various classes of mentality and criminality,"
wrote Judge Allegretti in 1928. "Every boy before it is an individual
problem and in its solution the judge must take into consideration
not only the law and the evidence, but also the defendant's mentality,
his health, his physical subnormalities and abnormalities, his environment, his education, his ancestry and his racial characteristics." The
judges uniformly praised the court's specialized structure, which facilitated "uniform and consistent policy," scientific record keeping, and
"closer supervision" of offenders placed on probation.[32]

In the courtroom, Boys' Court judges were guided, as were judges
in the other criminal branches, by procedural rules set down in the
common law, in the *Revised Statutes of Illinois,* and in the general rules of
practice established by the judges for the Municipal Court. But Boys'
Court judges did exercise exceptionally wide discretion. When a boy
first appeared in court, a clerk hurriedly placed before him a paper to
sign, usually with no explanation. First offenders and immigrants with
little knowledge of the American legal system were unlikely to realize
that they were signing away their constitutional right to have their
case decided by a panel of their peers. The defendant would want to
appear cooperative, an instinct his lawyer, if he had one, would have
reinforced. Veteran defendants who knew their rights usually signed
the waiver anyway, aware that if they did not their case would be transferred to an unspecialized jury branch, where judge and jury alike
might have less tolerance for the foibles of the adolescent male. Joseph
Dziupla, a second-generation Polish-American convicted of disorderly
conduct in 1925, explained this calculus to an investigator from the
Children's Bureau. "I have been in the boys' court seven times in a
year. . . . I got five breaks and got off light the other times, and I was
guilty every time and done lots worse than they caught me for." Judges
in the other branches "will sock you the limit of the law every time."[33]

Court in 1933: A Report on its Organization, Procedure and Results, pamphlet
(n.p.), 22; Leiffer, "Boys' Court," 53–69, 176, esp. 27; Julian W. Mack, "The
Juvenile Court," *HLR,* 23 (1909), 104–22; Estelle B. Freedman, *Maternal
Justice: Miriam Van Waters and the Female Reform Tradition* (Chicago, 1996).
[32] Allegretti in MCC 19–22 (1925–28), 109–10; *MCC 15* (1921), 115.
[33] Children's Bureau, *Youth and Crime,* 49, esp. 196; *Illinois Revised Statutes,*
1911, ch. 38, secs. 294–470.

An official faith in the plasticity of boy offenders set the tone of proceedings. As a matter of routine, many judges requested that first offenders charged with felonies – besides murder, rape, and armed robbery – be rebooked and charged with misdemeanors or even quasicrimes. A vote of confidence from the judge, this judicial sleight-of-hand seriously reduced the potential punishment for many defendants. Felonious larceny, for example, involved the theft of property valued at more than $15; petty larceny, a misdemeanor, involved $15 or less. A one-cent divide carried a dramatic difference in penalty (at least on the books): one to ten years in the state penitentiary for the felon, compared with a maximum $100 fine and a year in the workhouse or jail for the misdemeanant. By reducing the charge from felony to petty larceny, judges gave defendants a break. (How often judges made charge reductions contingent on a guilty plea is not clear from the records.) But reducing the charge had another, more instrumental, purpose. It enabled the judge to keep jurisdiction over boys they would otherwise have been obliged to bind over to the grand jury.[34]

As in the other socialized branches of the Municipal Court, Boys' Court judges moderated the procedural formalism of the criminal law with a personalized inquisitorial style and purpose. In a standard criminal trial, prosecutors and defense counsel presented their evidence and arguments to the judge and jury. In the juryless Boys' Court trial, the judge typically asked the boy to approach the bench, creating some distance between them and the crowded gallery, as well as the prosecutor and counsel, so he could speak informally to the boy and ask him direct questions. The judge had before him the data card on the defendant filled out by the Social Service Department, and he would appeal to the boy's religious beliefs and his sentiments toward his family, all the while sizing up his prospects for reform. All of this had little to do with guilt or innocence, conventionally understood. But prosecutors accommodated judges, keeping their own motions and maneuvers to a minimum. "These officials are not in the Court merely to seek convictions," Leiffer observed; "frequently they even give suggestions to the defense." Judges tended to "disregard" defense attorneys, a Children's Bureau observer noted. "The boys frequently seemed handicapped rather than helped by them."[35]

Boys' Court judges made extensive use of the continuance to socialize court practice. A standard procedural device, the continuance

[34] Belden, "Boys' Court," 739; Children's Bureau, *Youth and Crime*, 50. *MCC 15* (1921), 116; Gutknecht, *Chicago Boys' Court in 1933*, 5; *Illinois Revised Statutes*, 1911, ch. 38, secs. 167–76.
[35] Leiffer, "Boys' Court," 178; Children's Bureau, *Youth and Crime*, 49.

allowed judges to give prosecutors and defense counsel additional time to gather evidence, track down witnesses, and firm up their cases. Defendants who lacked the resources to post a cash bail or a bond secured by property waited out the continuance in County Jail. Boys' Court judges routinely used continuances to scare defendants straight, ordering continuances in misdemeanor cases even when neither defense counsel nor prosecutors asked for one. This practice was noted with some alarm as early as 1915 by Evelina Belden, who had left her job as a social worker in the court for a position at the Children's Bureau. "The custom has grown of using a detention in jail *before trial* as a punishment," she reported. By the mid-1920s, nearly one-sixth of defendants spent from a few days to several months in jail awaiting trial. Judges defended their extravagant use of the continuance in scientific and humanitarian terms. "The outstanding points of this system," Judge John Gutknecht wrote in defense of the long-standing practice in the early 1930s, "[are] a touch of punishment in the form of jail for every defendant guilty of something more than mere disorderly conduct, and a period of supervision under the control of the court with a chance for every first offender to prove his worth without being blackened with a permanent record of conviction as a criminal." Gutknecht's choice of words is telling: None of these defendants had in fact been found guilty. They hadn't been tried at all. Boys' Court judges routinely disregarded the presumption of innocence in order to discipline boys.[36]

Judges' liberal use of the continuance may sometimes have had the desired effect. But its use as a technique of socialized law represents another of those unintended consequences that litter the byways of criminal justice history. A technique promoted as objective and scientific in fact had a glaring class bias built into it. Boys who made bail or bond – in other words, boys with exceptional resources and members of politically connected gangs – were untouchable by the technique. African-American defendants, who usually lacked easy access to cash or pull, were far more likely than white defendants to experience detention awaiting trail. Moreover, the vermin-ridden Cook County Jail was no place for *any* plastic young man; so said the JPA in the public investigations that led to the Boys' Court's creation. By all accounts, conditions in the jail only got worse until its eventual closure (and the opening of a new jail) in 1929. An investigation conducted by the Chicago Community Trust in 1922 found that new prisoners were beaten and robbed, drugs circulated freely between the cells, and the

---

[36] Belden, "Boys' Court," 742, emphasis added; Children's Bureau, *Youth and Crime*, 78; Gutknecht, *Chicago Boys' Court in 1933*, 22.

overcrowded cells were scenes of homosexual "corruption" for young boys. The Boys' Court contributed directly to the jail's overcrowding. More than 2,600 young men under twenty-one were confined there in 1924 alone. The goal of segregating "respectable" from "rough" and "plastic" from "hardened" offenders in the socialized court was undone by judges' attempt to find a therapeutic use for jail. Had JPA leaders paid more attention to their own creation, they might have wondered whether things were not back where they had started. [37]

The practices of the Boys' Court reflected the new scientific knowledge coming out of the Psychopathic Laboratory about the causes of juvenile adult criminality. Indeed, the socialized court and the laboratory together embodied the central contradiction in the social scientific category of the juvenile adult as alternately endangered and dangerous, plastic or predestined to a criminal career. The psychiatrist Olson hired to direct the laboratory, Dr. William J. Hickson, was an ardent eugenicist. Hickson believed hereditary mental defect was the primary cause of crime. As laboratory director, he routinely recommended that the defendants he examined be committed indefinitely to a state institution for the insane or feebleminded. Boys' Court judges routinely followed his advice. Although the judges professed a strong belief in the plasticity of most juvenile-adult offenders – and their judicial practice showed that this faith was sincere – their conception of themselves as social experts led them to embrace the laboratory's message that many defendants were hereditary criminals, fixed and hardened in nature, who ought to be removed permanently from the "life stream." Between May 1, 1914, and July 1, 1917, judges referred 10 percent of their defendants to the laboratory; in 1924 and 1925, the rate of referral climbed to nearly 17 percent. Judges made referrals at every stage of the process – before, during, and after trial.[38]

Boys' Court judges voiced the highest praise for the laboratory. Several judges described how its findings had changed the way they thought about the social causation of crime. "Until the facts revealed by the Psychopathic Laboratory were available it was a simple matter to shift all the blame on the environment, and let it go at that," Judge Trude observed. "Environment is [now] seen to be, not a cause, but a result, and merely a contributory factor in delinquency." Judge McKinley recalled that as a state prosecutor before his "elevation to the bench" he was "critical of the work of the Psychopathic Laboratory. . . . But my work upon the bench, most of that time spent in the criminal branches, has forced me to the conclusion that the work

[37] Children's Bureau, *Youth and Crime*, 63–66, 78–79, esp. 64.
[38] Ibid., 44–46.

and conclusions of the laboratory are sound in principle." He now understood that all "subnormals" were potential criminals, "powder, as it were, set down in the midst of the community." Even Catholic judges, members of a church staunchly opposed to state measures regulating reproduction, endorsed the laboratory's eugenicist policy prescriptions, quoting chapter and verse from eugenics propaganda. Judge Allegretti, an Italian-born Democrat who prided himself upon his work with delinquent boys as a Catholic "Big Brother," warned in a court report that "only in keeping pure the stream of posterity can our race and our civilization be perpetuated."[39]

For Roscoe Pound and other contemporary observers, the socialization of law signaled a historic transfer of social control functions from church to state. Time and again, however, the socialized courts of the Municipal Court of Chicago belied this theory, as socialization facilitated the rationalization and expansion of religious social service operations. The Boys' Court offers a telling illustration of this flexible fusion of two modes of governance that Michel Foucault called the "city game" (the policing of a collectivity of citizens through laws) and the pastoral or "shepherd game" (the religious practice of ministering to individual souls). Foucault argued that what made the governmental rationalities of modern liberal states so powerful and dangerous to individual freedom was the way they combined the city game and the shepherd game – secularized over the centuries by medicine, psychiatry, and other modern disciplines that studied and treated people as individual cases – into an all-seeing "secular political pastorate." The history of the Boys' Court, however, shows that much more of a give-and-take has existed between religious institutions and the modern liberal state in the field of social governance than either Pound or Foucault realized. Equally important, the subjects of social governance had a talent for playing church and state off one another in order to elude the control of both.[40]

[39] Trude in *MCC 12–14* (1918–20), 115; McKinley in *MCC 15* (1921), 120–21; Allegretti in MCC 19–22 (1925–28), 111. On Catholic opposition to eugenics, see Jeffrey P. Moran, "'Modernism Gone Mad': Sex Education Comes to Chicago, 1913," *JAH*, 83 (1996), 502–6.

[40] Foucault's student Colin Gordon coined the phrase "secular political pastorate." "City game" and "shepherd game" are Foucault's own terms. Gordon, "Governmental Rationality: An Introduction," in Graham Burchell, Colin Gordon, and Peter Miller, eds., *The Foucault Effect: Studies in Governmental Rationality* (Chicago, 1991), 1–51, esp. 8; Roscoe Pound, "Administration of Justice in the Modern City," *HLR*, 26 (1913), 302–28; Roscoe Pound, *Criminal Justice in America* (New York, 1930), 4–5.

From the court's founding in 1914, the (Jewish) Social Service Bureau, the (Protestant) Chicago Church Federation, and the (Catholic) Holy Name Society each had a representative in the Boys' Court every day to work with their coreligionists gone astray. This work might end with a single interview, or it could lead to home visits and extensive social work with the boys' families. Given the long history in Chicago of judges committing juvenile offenders to religious institutions operated by the offenders' coreligionists, the aggressive presence of religious agents in the bull pen, clerk's office, and gallery of the Boys' Court did not initially spark controversy. But complaints arose as it became apparent that Catholics had gained a particularly strong influence within the court.[41]

It was not just that so many judges and Boys' Court officials were Catholic – such were the demographics of Chicago politics in the early twentieth century. But a Catholic social worker, Mary Regina Fugate, ran the Social Service Department, and many observers believed she ran it in the interests of her church. More impressive was the aggressive way in which the Archdiocese of Chicago used the court as a kind of hub for its "Big Brothers" program, which aimed to reclaim delinquent boys "for God and country." The Big Brothers were a significant part of the rapid expansion of the archdiocese's social service programs during and after World War I, under the leadership of George William Cardinal Mundelein. During his tenure as Chicago's third archbishop from 1916 to 1939, Mundelein presided over precisely the sort of institutional transformation that Chicago court reformers had long dreamed of for the Municipal Court system. The archbishop consolidated an archdiocese famous for its ethnic particularism, centralized its leadership and financial administration, and fostered the growth of welfare services and social programs for juvenile delinquents. The Big Brothers program, which the archdiocese's Holy Name Society established in the Juvenile Court and the Boys' Court during Mundelein's first year in office, presaged a decade and a half of organization and socialization in the Chicago Catholic Church that would culminate in Mundelein's pragmatic alliance with President Franklin Delano Roosevelt and New Deal liberalism in the 1930s.[42]

---

[41] Beck, "Study of Boys," 6; Children's Bureau, *Youth and Crime*, 42–43.
[42] Cornelius G. Craine, "The Big Brothers of the Holy Name Society of Chicago and What They Have Accomplished during 1919 as Volunteer Workers," *CCR*, 4 (1920), 116. See Steven M. Avella, *This Confident Church: Catholic Leadership and Life in Chicago, 1940–1965* (Notre Dame, 1992); C. G. Craine, "Our Big Brothers," *(Chicago) New World*, May 13, 1921; Edward R. Kantowicz, *Corporation Sole: Cardinal Mundelein and Chicago Catholicism* (Notre Dame, Ind., 1983).

The Big Brothers had a representative in the Boys' Court every day. This representative worked with the agent of the Holy Name Society to assign every Catholic defendant to a volunteer Big Brother who lived in the boy's parish and spoke his parents' language. The Big Brother made visits to the boy's home and took note of his schooling, work history, and church attendance. According to the *Catholic Charities Review*, by 1921 the Holy Name Society had 190 branches in the city with 85,000 laymen volunteers engaged in "the greatest work in the world today, that of redeeming boys who have fallen by the wayside." In just four years, the Big Brothers had assisted more than 20,000 boys from the Boys' Court and Juvenile Court, conducted more than 10,000 interviews in court with parents and relatives of defendants, made more than 15,000 home visits, and found jobs for 3,500 boys. Catholic physicians and lawyers affiliated with the Holy Name Society provided free medical and legal aid to indigent defendants.[43]

The vital relationships that many archdiocese institutions forged with the Municipal Court during the early twentieth century raise an intriguing ideological issue. After all, the determinist ideas at the heart of the progressive concept of social responsibility for crime did not rest easy with the tenet of free will in Catholic theology. "One of our greatest dangers lies in accepting a criminal type, in looking upon pathological, environmental, and hereditary factors as the sole cause of crime," the Reverend M. J. Murphy, chaplain at the Massachusetts State Prison, explained in 1918. "Without doubt, they predispose, but do not necessarily lead to crime. In the vast majority of cases the cause is found in the choice of the individual free will." But Murphy's vision of what could be accomplished in the saving of criminals' souls had strong resonances with the progressive logic of individual treatment. "We must take into our fatherly hands the erring hearts of those committed to our care," he wrote, "we must bring out bright and clear the image of God stamped upon their souls, sanctify their intellects, strengthen their wills, mold them to God's service in this world and the next, fit them for their part in the battle of life." During the 1910s and 1920s, writers in the *Catholic Charities Review* increasingly called attention to the many ways in which social circumstances could impinge upon the individual's ability to exercise free will without utterly

---

[43] Cornelius G. Craine, "What the Archdiocesan Union of the Holy Name Society of Chicago and Its Big Brothers Have Done for the Church and the Adolescent Boy in Chicago, in the Past Four Years," *CCR*, 5 (1921), 230–32, esp. 230. See Avella, *This Confident Church*, 20–22; Children's Bureau, *Youth and Crime*, 43; Kantowicz, *Corporation Sole*, 18–19; Leiffer, "Boys' Court," 129; Thrasher, *The Gang*, 519.

overcoming free will and moral responsibility. Like other progressives, Catholic charity officials and social workers referenced the social factors of juvenile delinquency to call for a larger commitment of public and private institutions to building the moral character of plastic youths. As one Fordham University criminologist put it in 1924, "The social message on Delinquency is, therefore, that a clear spiritual call must summon the Church, the home, and the school – that great trinity upon which the hopes of civilization rest – co-operating with the psychologist and the social agency, to fulfill more effectually their high mission in building character." Institutions such as the Boys' Court did powerfully marry the city and shepherd games. But they did so in a way that expanded and strengthened (rather than supplanted) the social intervention of religious institutions.[44]

The growing Catholic presence in the Boys' Court did not go uncontested. In April 1917, for example, Olson received a letter from attorney Alfred Hulbert, who had recently appeared in the Boys' Court representing an eighteen-year-old chauffeur who had struck a pedestrian with his truck. The judge continued the case, and as Hulbert was leaving the court with his client, a Holy Name Society social worker approached them and asked if the boy was Catholic. Apparently the boy said "yes." Over Hulbert's objections, the social worker led the boy into a room and barraged him with questions about his ancestry, his parochial school education, his attendance at mass, and his membership in various Catholic organizations. "Some Irish Catholic Society in Chicago is conducting a campaign of open proselytizing in and about this courtroom, making records of the boys, and urging them to join organizations connected with the Catholic Church," Hulbert wrote. "Our federal and state constitutions and all our laws are drawn with a design to keep the Church and State apart." For Hulbert, Catholic social work in the court was "an insidious campaign" and "a clear evasion of the defendant's rights." Hulbert did not say whether his client objected to the intervention.[45]

In a curt reply, Olson defended the role of faith-based agencies in the Boys' Court, insisting that the agencies "are attempting to aid these boys in a material way." He informed the presiding judge, John A. Swanson, a Protestant, of Hulbert's complaint and asked that he instruct the social workers not to do anything that "might be interpreted as interfering with the religious belief of anybody." But the

[44] Rev. M. J. Murphy, "The Prison Chaplain and His Duties," *CCR*, 2 (1918), 11–12; Edwin J. Cooley, "The Prevention of Delinquency," *CCR*, 8 (1924), 312.
[45] Alfred Roy Hulbert to Harry Olson, April 24, 1917, MCC, box 5, folder 33.

reputation of the Boys' Court as a Catholic outpost did not abate. An anonymous letter to Olson later in 1917 threatened political reprisals if Fugate were "permitted to continue to run this court in the interest of her church." "The only thing to do is to get rid of her," the writer demanded. "If not, you may – figuratively speaking – expect a bomb in the City Hall before long." The "bomb" never blew, and the Catholic presence in the court never diminished. Seven years later, Olson received a distressed letter from the Chicago Church Federation, protesting that Catholic and Jewish social workers had ordered the Protestant representative in the court to keep his "hands off" their boys.[46]

There is merit to both Olson's view and that of the court's critics. Although the court did give religious agencies quasipolice powers to investigate and supervise defendants, the agencies in return did provide forms of assistance, as well as surveillance, that the court simply could not.

Seasoned defendants viewed the tribunal's religious dimension in pragmatic terms, yet another part of the socialized court to negotiate and manipulate. Defendants often lied to the social workers about their faith. Recidivists, in particular, saw the advantage in a quick change of affiliation. In a court with a rapid turnover of official personnel, the social workers served as repositories of institutional memory, and boys tried to avoid being recognized and reported as repeaters, which could lead to a stiffer penalty. Defendants also knew that winning the support of a social worker could not hurt their case. Such was the motivation perhaps for a defendant who appeared in court toting a copy of the "Gospel According to St. John." He told a skeptical social worker that he had been "converted" in the County Jail.[47]

Defendants also appreciated the specifically Catholic dimension of the Boys' Court. In the mid-1920s, a young African-American defendant appeared in court wearing a piece of rosary around his neck. Although there were enough black Catholics in Chicago to constitute a tiny parish on the South Side (until the church burned down in 1924 and its members joined a larger Irish parish), a black youth with a rosary was a rare enough sight to raise the eyebrows of a social worker. When she asked the defendant about it, he admitted that he was a Protestant and had found the rosary in his cell at the County Jail. He thought it might bring him "good luck" in the Boys Court, he said. Leiffer recorded the exchange in dialect.

---

[46] Harry Olson to Alfred Roy Hulbert, April 24, 1917, MCC, box 5, folder 33; anonymous to Olson, Aug. 14, 1917, MCC, box 5, folder 34; Thomas F. [illeg.] to Olson, May 11, 1924, MCC, box 6, folder 38.
[47] Leiffer, "Boys' Court," 82.

"Do you think it will help you when you get out in Court?" the social
worker asked.
"Yeah," the boy replied.
"Do think it's as good as a rabbit's foot?"
The boy laughed. "Yeah, Ah think it's a lot bettah."[48]

Despite the special fondness of Boys' Court judges for the continuance
and the threat to defendant's life chances posed by the judges' faith
in the Psychopathic Laboratory, many defendants thought the Boys'
Court was a good deal. Some veterans of the court even gave it credit
for setting them straight. "That boys' court is a real good place for a
boy to go to rather than other courts I have seen," Patrick M'Ginnis,
an Irish-American tried for disorderly conduct in 1924, told an investigator from the Children's Bureau. "I think Chicago ought to keep
it; it helped me, and I know other boys it has helped." Murray Leiffer
noted that the boys he met in the court did not distinguish "the law"
from the men who enforced it. The boys had a much higher regard
for Boys' Court judges, who they felt attempted to treat them fairly,
than for the police, who often beat them.[49]

Though obviously untrained in the law, the repeaters in the court
were anything but legal neophytes. They reflexively viewed the Boys'
Court in terms as skeptical and penetrating as anything the then-
emerging school of legal realists at Yale could have mustered. One
defendant from the mid-1920s made an off-the-cuff remark that stands
as an apt rejoinder to the dilatory sociological rhetoric of the judges.
As he waited for the bailiff to call his case, the boy sized up the judge.
"Hope he liked his ham and eggs for breakfast this morning," the
boy said, "so he's in a good humor." The remark anticipated by several years the statement that would make Jerome Frank infamous: that
what a judge ate for breakfast was a more telling predictor than legal
doctrine of how the case would turn out.[50]

In their unsparingly realistic analysis of the Boys' Court, several veteran defendants pointed to an environmental factor that never received consideration in the court's public reports: politics. Many of

---

[48] Ibid., 83–84; Avella, *Confident Church*, 252; James R. Grossman, *Land of Hope: Chicago, Black Southerners, and the Great Migration* (Chicago, 1989), 173–74.
[49] Children's Bureau, *Youth and Crime*, 192; Leiffer, "Boys' Court," 87.
[50] Leiffer, "Boys' Court," 74; Jerome Frank, *Law and the Modern Mind* (New York, 1930). See Morton J. Horwitz, *The Transformation of American Law, 1870–1960: The Crisis of Legal Orthodoxy* (New York, 1992), 169–92, esp. 176; Edward A. Purcell, Jr., *The Crisis of Democratic Theory: Scientific Naturalism and the Problem of Value* (Lexington, 1973), 74–94.

the "hard-boiled" defendants were members of politically connected gangs that had strong clientelist relationships with ward politicians. Boys boasted to interviewers that they would never spend more than twenty-four hours in jail before a politician secured their release. When Frederic Thrasher asked a fourteen-year-old gang member what he wanted to be when he grew up, the eighth-grader told him he aspired to be a criminal defense lawyer. His curiosity piqued, the sociologist then asked whether the boy would defend a man he knew had committed murder. The boy skipped over the ethical question of whether and jumped straight to how. "First, I'd go see who the judge is," he said; "to be a lawyer, you have to have a whole lot of political pull." There is no clear evidence of pull in the Boys' Court, but many boys clearly took the forces of political gravity in the institution for granted.[51]

With or without pull, defendants often told interviewers that they believed they stood a better chance of getting lenient treatment in the Boys' Court than in another criminal branch of the Municipal Court. This was certainly true in the court's first decade, when Boys' Court judges consistently discharged cases at a higher rate than did the criminal branches as a whole. (See Fig. 2.) In the court's inaugural year, Judges Scully and Dolan discharged a staggering 70 percent of the defendants who came before them; in the other branches the rate that year came to 43 percent.[52] The gap narrowed a bit after these pioneers stepped down, but until the mid-1920s defendants had appreciably better odds in the Boys' Court than in the other criminal branches. Then in 1925, the odds changed. In every year but one between 1925 and 1930, the defendant had a better shot in the other branches. In 1926, Boys' Court judges discharged only 26 percent of defendants, compared with a 51 percent discharge rate in the criminal branches as a whole. Something had happened. A change of heart? A change of policy?

Remarkably, the judges never mentioned this dramatic shift of treatment in their annual reports. One plumbs their baroque sociological essays in vain for signs of a change of heart or motive. But a likely explanation presents itself in the changing composition of the court's caseload after 1924. (See Fig. 3.). The total caseload of the Boys' Court peaked at 9,297 cases in 1919 (a "crime wave" year in Chicago). After another small spike in 1924, the caseload turned gradually downward until in 1930 it stood at just 6,400 cases – a significant decline from where the court started in 1914, despite a decade and a half of robust

---

[51] Thrasher, *The Gang*, 454; Leiffer, "Boys' Court," 70–91.
[52] These figures do *not* include the defendants dismissed or nolle prossed because of prosecutorial discretion.

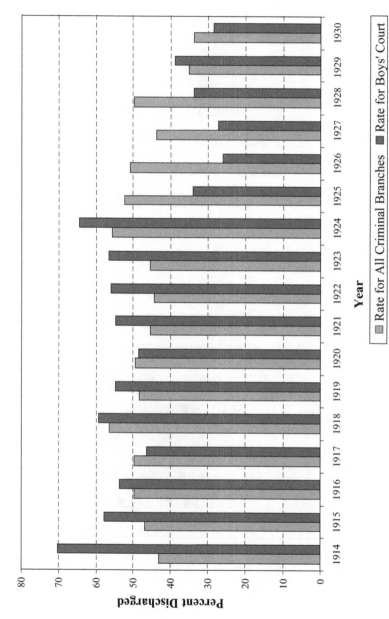

FIGURE 2. Discharge rates for the Boys' Court and all criminal branches, 1914–30. *Source:* Municipal Court of Chicago annual reports.

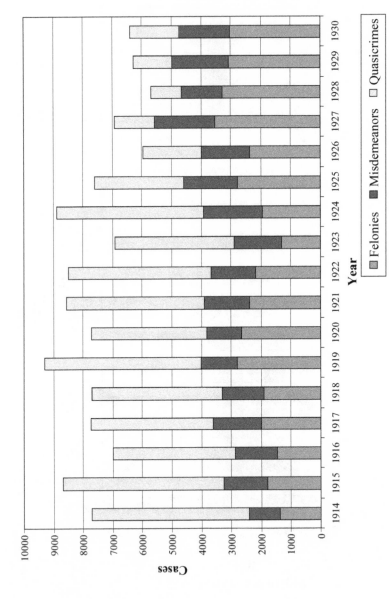

FIGURE 3. Cases disposed of in the Boys' Court, 1914–30. *Source:* Municipal Court of Chicago annual reports.

population growth in Chicago. The shrinking caseload itself would not explain a change of policy. But what well might is the much more precipitous drop in quasicrimes after 1925. Once the court's bread and butter – disorderly conduct cases alone had comprised half the caseload in 1914 – quasicrimes were withering in significance, if only temporarily. Whether the shift reflected an increasing severity of criminal practice or shifting strategies of policing (or, most likely, both), the Boys' Court had quietly been transformed into a felony tribunal. By 1927, the Boys' Court was leading the nineteen criminal branches in felony hearings, handling one out of every five felony cases heard in the court system. It was one thing to reduce a felony charge to a misdemeanor for a first offender; it was quite another matter to discharge the case completely.[53]

The boy problem had changed since the court's founding. The emblematic offender in the Boys' Court in the late 1920s was no longer a boy arrested for gathering coal from the railroad tracks or sleeping in a doorway. He was a bit more likely to be a robber or a car thief, a gangster or worse. The new predominance of felony offenders in the Boys' Court coincided with a shift in criminal justice reform from the broad-based emphasis on investigation and social policing characteristic of progressivism to the harder-edged ideology of deterrence and crime control that would set the tone of American criminal justice through the 1930s. The socialized style of judicial administration did not disappear, but specialized judges had to work in a political climate far less tolerant of social theories and judicial practices that lightened an offender's burden of criminal responsibility.

In the early 1930s, conservative critics such as the businessmen-reformers of the Chicago Crime Commission would assault the Boys' Court as an egregious example of the dangerous leniency that maudlin feminine sentimentality had brought to criminal justice during the Progressive Era. Socialized techniques, the Crime Commission argued, were totally inappropriate to the car thieves and other felony defendants who comprised one of the fast-growing segments of the court's caseload. For liberal critics, including investigators for an exhaustive 1930 study of the court issued by the U.S. Children's Bureau, the problem was exactly the reverse. From the bureau's perspective, the Boys' Court had never been socialized *enough.* Judges rotated on and off the court too frequently to develop consistent policies, the bureau charged. The court lacked sufficient social personnel necessary to conduct detailed investigation, examination, and supervision of the boys.

[53] Raymond Moley, "The Municipal Court of Chicago," in Illinois Association for Criminal Justice, *The Illinois Crime Survey* (Chicago, 1929), 396.

And the bureau objected that the courtroom itself was too crowded for judges to develop a style of procedure significantly "different from that usually characterizing inferior criminal courts."[54]

That was always the greatest challenge for the judges of the Boys' Court as they gazed down upon that never-ending procession of boys and asked, "Whose is the fault?" All in all, the judges did an impressive job with the materials at hand. The Boys' Court was in fact the single most daring effort in early twentieth-century America to test the temporal boundaries of juvenile justice and extend the socialized disciplinary techniques of the juvenile court to older male offenders. As the judges quickly discovered, it was no simple task to make the machinery of a criminal court run in the service of such interventionist ambitions or to reconcile an individualistic and adversarial tradition of criminal procedure to the modern ethic of social responsibility. And the unstable scientific conception of the juvenile adult as something of a split personality – a "plastic young violator" and yet a "criminal in the making" – made it difficult to shape a consistent socialized practice. Within those legal and cultural constraints, however, judges were surprisingly creative in their efforts to reform boys on the threshold of manhood. They staffed their court with social workers and probation officers. They mobilized the city's religious agencies to carry the court's work into the immigrant neighborhoods. They referred boys to the Psychopathic Laboratory, where their intelligence was tested, their family histories recorded, their emotions probed, and their personalities profiled according to radically new standards of mental defect. Finally, judges believed they had discovered a modern therapeutic use for the most unregenerate element of the criminal justice system, the county jail. In retrospect, the judicial practice that resulted from these interventionist aspirations, legal tethers, and imperfect social knowledge had an all too fitting resemblance to adolescence itself – it was fraught with awkwardness, ambivalence, and no small amount of recklessness. But in the eyes of a judge such as Edgar A. Jonas, the cause that set all of these institutions into motion every time a young defendant stepped before the bar could not have been plainer: "to save this boy for future citizenship."[55]

---

[54] Gutknecht, *The Chicago Boys' Court in 1933*; Children's Bureau, *Youth and Crime*, 24.

[55] *MCC 16–18* (1922–24), 102.

8

"Keep the Life Stream Pure": The Psychopathic Laboratory

Teeth and ears mark the criminal? Do they? And what about the law
that marks him still better ...?

– Joseph Conrad, 1907

The opening decades of the twentieth century, when the United States
emerged on the world stage as a major economic and military power,
were the heyday of eugenics in America. A potent mix of biological science, statistical method, and cultural assumptions, eugenics
won a large following of well-educated, well-off citizens from every
region: university professors, animal breeders, social workers, criminologists, psychiatrists, philanthropists, and activists spanning the political spectrum from socialists to white supremacists. Heirs to the Enlightenment pursuits of science, reason, and a rationally organized
state, eugenicists rejected the Enlightenment's egalitarian strain, insisting that hereditary endowment determined social structure. Fusing
Darwin's theory of evolution and Mendel's discoveries in plant heredity, eugenicist scientists claimed to find distinct genetic roots for the
many problems of personality and society that alarmed their contemporaries, from "feeblemindedness" to "hypersexuality." Within the
bright lines of a eugenic world view, poverty and crime were compre-
hended anew as the offspring of hereditary "mental defects," racial
"mongrelization," and sentimental charitable efforts that, in a vain attempt to reform deviant individuals, had only assured their survival
and reproduction. Propagandists for the science of "race betterment"
claimed that the nation's genetic stock – and thus the vitality of its
democratic social order – could be vastly improved, in a single generation of purposeful social intervention. They called for a combination of voluntary efforts to encourage "the fit" to procreate and

coercive state measures to prevent "the unfit" from reproducing "their kind."[1]

Eugenics owed its considerable political success to the same broad progressive reorientation of law, liberalism, and democratic practice that had enabled reformers to turn the criminal courts of the great cities into experimental stations of modern social governance. To be sure, a conservative politics of moral panic and racial fear gave eugenics much of its cultural appeal and authority. In an era of relative prosperity, many middle-class Americans were still deeply concerned about the labor struggles, rising ethnic heterogeneity, rapid urbanization, and upheaval of gender relations that were visibly remaking their society. But the most important sources of eugenics' institutional success lie elsewhere. Rather than a conservative aberration in the unfolding of American liberal democracy, institutionalized eugenics grew out of some of the era's most progressive trends in law, politics, and culture: legal socialization, the rise of new professional disciplines, the structural rationalization of courts, and, most paradoxically, the ideology of social responsibility itself.

The contemporary belief that crime was a scientifically knowable and preventable social problem enabled eugenics activists to transform their cause from a subject of specialized professional interest and popular curiosity into a mainstream force for institutional change. Unlike the laissez-faire Social Darwinists of the Gilded Age, eugenicists of the Progressive Era were eager to deploy the full range of state and local police powers to check the reproduction of criminality, deviancy, and dependency in the population. Although controversial in its own time, eugenics infused American public discourse on crime during the 1910s and 1920s, the critical years when law and order, historically a local matter, began to be redefined as a national issue. Newspapers and magazines lavished column inches on the link between crime and hereditary mental defects. Scholars debated the constitutionality and scientific validity of eugenic legislation in academic journals. Social reformers invoked the specter of the criminal mental defective to win support for compulsory sterilization laws, which thirty

---

[1] See Mark B. Adams, ed., *The Wellborn Science: Eugenics in Germany, France, Brazil, and Russia* (New York, 1990); Stephen Jay Gould, *The Mismeasure of Man* (New York, 1981); Mark H. Haller, *Eugenics: Hereditarian Attitudes in American Thought* (New Brunswick, 1963); Daniel J. Kevles, *In the Name of Eugenics: Genetics and the Uses of Human Heredity* (New York, 1985); Michael Willrich, "The Two Percent Solution: Eugenic Jurisprudence and the Socialization of American Law, 1900–1930," *LHR*, 16 (1998), 63–111. For fuller references to the relevant legal, sociological, and historical literatures, see ibid.

states enacted between 1907 and 1940. When the U.S. Supreme Court upheld the constitutionality of compulsory sterilization in *Buck v. Bell* (1927), disarming the hostile rulings of several state courts, Justice Oliver Wendell Holmes Jr.'s decision left no doubt that eugenics had reached the pinnacle of American jurisprudence. "It is better for all the world," the legendary champion of civil liberties declared, "if instead of waiting to execute degenerate offspring for crime, or to let them starve for their imbecility, society can prevent those who are manifestly unfit from continuing their kind." By 1964, more than 60,000 inmates of state institutions had been sterilized under state laws.[2]

The emergence of a court-based regime of social governance in American cities during the early twentieth century nurtured the rise of eugenic jurisprudence, the aggressive mobilization of law and legal institutions in pursuit of eugenic goals. Hereditarian penologists of the late nineteenth century had lamented that the American commitment to due process and equal protection of the laws stood in the way of any full-fledged scientific program to ferret out and incarcerate "presumptive criminals" *before* they committed crimes. In any event, routine mental testing in criminal courts would have been virtually impossible under the decentralized justice of the peace systems. But with the advent of socialized disciplinary techniques such as specialized courts, probation, and social work – all geared toward the "individual treatment" of offenders – local judges gained unprecedented discretionary powers. They solicited the professional expertise of the social workers and psychiatrists attached to the most innovative new municipal courts. In this way, psychological testing, including its prominent eugenicist variety, was integrated into the everyday practice of criminal courts, where the allegedly natural categories of eugenics – "feebleminded," "psychopathic," or simply "mental defective" – acquired unprecedented coercive power.[3]

---

[2] *Buck v. Bell*, 274 U.S. 200, 207 (1927); Donald T. Critchlow, "Keeping the Life Stream Pure," *RAH*, 20 (1992), 343; Gerald N. Grob, *Mental Illness and American Society, 1875–1940* (Princeton, 1983), 173. See J. H. Landman, "The History of Human Sterilization in the United States – Theory, Statute, Adjudication," *ILR*, 23 (1929), 463–80; Harry H. Laughlin, *The Legal Status of Eugenical Sterilization: History and Analysis of Litigation under the Virginia Sterilization Statute, Which Led to a Decision of the Supreme Court of the United States Upholding the Statute* (Chicago, 1930).

[3] Henry M. Boies, *The Science of Penology: The Defense of Society against Crime* (New York, 1901), 59–60, 91–92; City of Chicago, Municipal Court, *Report of the Psychopathic Laboratory of the Municipal Court of Chicago*, May 1, 1914–April 30, 1917 (Chicago, n.d.). See Collette Guillaumin, "Race and Nature:

The Workers' University Society

STUDEBAKER THEATRE

SUNDAY MORNING, DECEMBER 16th
ELEVEN O'CLOCK

Extra Special Lecture by

Chief Justice Harry Olson

On the Subject:

"Crime and Heredity"

Chairman: The Hon. L. A. Stebbins

Doors Open at 10:30   All Seats: Fifty Cents

COMING ! Sunday Morning, December 23rd, 11 o'Clock
GREAT DEBATE on "IS HUMAN PROGRESS AN ILLUSION?"
Between PERCY WARD and Attorney VICTOR S. YARROS.

Chief Justice Harry Olson

During the 1910s and 1920s, Chief Justice Harry Olson was much in demand
as a speaker on crime and eugenics. He traveled America, telling workers'
societies, middle-class women's organizations, and businessmen's clubs that
crime could be dramatically reduced by sterilization and other state measures to "keep the lifestream pure." Courtesy of the Northwestern University
Archives.

The Municipal Court of Chicago and its famous Psychopathic Laboratory demonstrated the stark human consequences of this marriage of scientific knowledge and juridical power. Using his judicial
post as a bully pulpit, Chief Justice Olson broadcast the dangers of
criminal mental defectives in the public reports of the Municipal
Court, in the pages of law journals, and in speeches before women's
clubs, bar associations, and welfare organizations across America.[4]
Between the laboratory's founding in 1914 and Olson's retirement
in 1930, municipal judges sent tens of thousands of criminal defendants – and even some complainants, witnesses, and family members not charged with any crime – to the laboratory. Using widely

The System of Marks: The Idea of a Natural Group and Social Relationships,"
Feminist Issues, 8 (1988), 25–43.
4 Harry Olson, "Disease and Crime – An Analogy," speech to State Conference
of Social Agencies, Los Angeles, May 2, 1916 (n.p.); [Harry Olson] "Report
of the Psychopathic Laboratory," in *MCC 10–11* (1916–17), 9–18; Harry
Olson, "The Psychopathic Laboratory of the Municipal Court of Chicago,"
CLJ, 92 (1921), 102–8; Harry Olson, "The Recent History of the Psychopathic
Laboratory of the Chicago Municipal Court," *CLJ*, 93 (1921), 132–40; Harry
Olson, "Crime and Heredity," in City of Chicago, Municipal Court, *Research
Studies of Crime as Related to Heredity* (Chicago, 1925), 13.

accepted psychological tests, laboratory director William J. Hickson routinely concluded that the individuals he examined were dangerous hereditary mental defectives. Heeding Dr. Hickson's advice, the judges committed, by Olson's estimates, 1,000 people each year to sexually segregated state institutions for the insane or feebleminded – regardless of whether the court found them guilty of breaking any law. "It cannot be doubted," Olson boasted in 1924, "that this practice... has been a very effective means for the preventing of crimes."[5]

We are accustomed to thinking of eugenics and environmentalism as ideological foes: the authoritarian racial science versus the enlightened liberal perspective that recognized crime as largely a product of social inequality. But during the early twentieth century, no such enmity existed. Eugenics and environmentalism were interdependent ideologies of progressive social governance. From 1900 through World War I, the ideological differences between an increasingly strident eugenicist such as Harry Olson and an environmentalist such as Louise de Koven Bowen of the Juvenile Protective Association did not prevent them from closely collaborating in the creation of a new kind of socially interventionist urban court system. Their ideological differences were tempered by the many interests and ideas they had in common: their mutual rejection of the nineteenth-century deterrence theory of punishment (and the ideal of the moral free agent on which that theory rested), their deep interest in root causes, and their joint commitment to two structural goals of socialized criminal justice: the individual treatment of offenders and the introduction of professional social experts into the judicial process. It was not until those goals had been achieved in most major urban centers in the mid-1920s that environmentalists joined the broad trend in psychiatry and social

---

[5] *MCC 16–18* (1922–24), 13. The court did not publish long-term commitment statistics. In 1924 Olson wrote, "Two or three years ago the commitments of such persons had reached a total of as high as one thousand per year. At the present time an even higher rate is reported." In the same report, Hickson claimed that the laboratory had made "over 40,000 complete examinations" since 1914, roughly 4,000 per year. He also noted that in a group of 1,002 consecutive cases sent from the nonspecialized criminal branches, 68.25 percent of the men and 87 percent of the women had been "committed to institutions as feebleminded or insane." These percentages suggest a much higher annual commitment rate than Olson claimed; ibid., 13, 182, 179, 181. See "Hickson Quits," *Chicago Tribune*, Sept. 14, 1929; H. Douglas Singer, "The Deranged or Defective Delinquent," Illinois Association for Criminal Justice, *The Illinois Crime Survey* (Chicago, 1929), 733–810.

science toward an explicit repudiation of eugenics and hereditarian beliefs.[6]

Criminological clinics proliferated during the 1910s and '20s, springing up in state reformatories and penitentiaries, local jails (including Chicago's House of Correction), police departments in big cities (including New York), and urban courts. The clinics were a logical outgrowth of socialized law and its rhetoric of scientific investigation and professional expertise. "Criminals must be classified as well as crimes," Roscoe Pound proclaimed. The wealthy Chicago feminist and JPA member Ethel Sturges Dummer founded the nation's first court-affiliated clinic in 1909 to study offenders in Cook County Juvenile Court. Called the Psychopathic Institute, it was officially incorporated into the Juvenile Court a few years later. Soon, court clinics appeared in Philadelphia, Boston, Detroit, and other major cities. V. V. Anderson, the director of the Municipal Court of Boston's Psychopathic Laboratory, called the new clinics "a forward step in socializing our courts," the product of "a growing tendency among criminal jurists toward individualization, and a handling of offenders *in the light of what they are,* rather than what they have done." The new clinics served a dual public function: to assist judges in devising a disposition, or "treatment," appropriate for each offender and to conduct policy-shaping clinical research into the origins of criminality. As Dr. William Healy, the founding director of the Juvenile Court's Psychopathic Institute, put it in a letter to Julia Lathrop of the JPA, "The fundamental question with regard to this whole matter is causation."[7]

Criminal classification and causation were the jurisdiction of criminology. For most of the nineteenth century, "classical" criminologists in Europe and America had conceived of criminals as free moral agents who chose to break the law. It followed from this premise that punishments should be calibrated to fit crimes in such a way as to deter potential lawbreakers by assuring that the punishment

---

[6] See Carl N. Degler, *In Search of Human Nature: The Decline and Revival of Darwinism in American Social Thought* (New York, 1991), 59–211.

[7] Pound in A. L. Jacoby, "The Psychopathic Clinic in a Criminal Court: Its Uses and Possibilities," *JAJS,* 7 (1923), 22; V. V. Anderson, "The Laboratory in the Study and Treatment of Crime," *JAICLC,* 5 (1915), 840–41, emphasis in original; Healy to Lathrop, April 4, 1908, Ethel Sturges Dummer Papers, Schlesinger Library, Radcliffe College, folder 578. See Herman M. Adler, "Organization of Psychopathic Work in the Criminal Courts," *JAICLC,* 8 (1917), 362–74; Louis E. Bisch, "A Police Psychopathic Laboratory," ibid., 7 (1916), 79–88; City of Chicago, House of Correction, Research Department, *Devoted to the Study and Treatment of Asocial Types* (Chicago, 1915).

outweighed their incentive to break the law. In the exceptional case of the insane or idiotic law-breaker, constitutionally incapable of distinguishing right from wrong, criminal responsibility was suspended. The so-called M'Naghten rule, as the right-and-wrong insanity standard was named after an 1843 English case, was adopted by virtually every American jurisdiction by 1880. An appealingly straightforward cognitive test, it rested solely on the defendant's ability to understand the illegality and consequences of his actions. It left unprotected a defendant who met that standard but suffered from paranoid delusions or an emotional disorder. In its clarity and formality, the M'Naghten standard was the exception that reinforced the rule of individual autonomy, free will, and criminal responsibility that governed criminal trials. In the irrelevance it accorded to factors external to the individual will and intellect, the rule comported well with the broader cultural conventions of causal attribution and moral responsibility in Victorian America.[8]

These strong individualistic notions of criminal responsibility and traditional morality withstood a highly public scientific assault in the trial of Charles Julius Guiteau, the deranged lawyer, sometime preacher, and disappointed office-seeker who assassinated President James A. Garfield in 1881. (Interestingly, Guiteau began his undistinguished legal career shortly after the Civil War in Chicago, where his practice consisted chiefly of bill collecting and petty criminal matters – specialties that should have made him a regular in the justice shops.) There was no doubt about Guiteau's guilt. The hapless assassin ran into the arms of a policeman while fleeing the murder scene. Guiteau quickly claimed credit for what he viewed as a righteous blow to save the Republican party from factionalism and the nation from another civil war. But the criminal responsibility of this strange man was a more contested matter. Guiteau understood the criminal nature of his actions. But he insisted that "the Deity" had inspired, indeed, compelled his act. "My free agency was destroyed," Guiteau declared at his trial. "I was overpowered." As the historian Charles E. Rosenberg explains, "Without free agency, there could be no criminal intent and no responsibility; God, in choosing him for this task, had stripped him of his moral faculty." Few Americans doubted that Guiteau was insane – his history of violent and bizarre behavior, his courtroom antics, and his grandiose letters to the press

---

[8] Harry E. Barnes, "Criminology," in *Encyclopaedia of the Social Sciences*, vol. 4, ed. Edwin R. A. Seligman (New York, 1931), 584–92. Charles E. Rosenberg, *The Trial of the Assassin Guiteau: Psychiatry and the Law in the Gilded Age* (Chicago, 1968), 53–60.

made that conclusion irresistible. But in a culture that still understood individual success and failure in terms of character, sin, habit,
and freely willed action, public sentiment demanded his conviction
and execution.[9]

Guiteau's dramatic public trial, in which the only issue was Guiteau's
insanity, turned into a culturally revealing contest between two competing professional positions on insanity and criminal responsibility. The
prosecution called upon leaders of the Association for Medical Superintendents of American Institutions for the Insane, the nearest thing
that the still inchoate discipline of psychiatry had to a professional
association. According to Rosenberg's definitive account of the trial,
these respectable men of medicine had a complex view of the causes
of insanity as a disease, conceding that "heredity and environment often conspired to impair free agency." But as champions of traditional
morality, the rule of law, and their own uncertain cultural authority,
they defended the M'Naghten rule. The prosecution witnesses testified that Guiteau "understood the nature and consequences of his
act, appeared to reason coherently, and hence, following the generally
accepted rule of law, was guilty."[10]

Guiteau's defense counsel appealed to a controversial new scientific
perspective on the etiology of mental disease that emphasized heredity.
The defense tried to persuade the court to loosen the M'Naghten standard and allow the jury to treat the question of Guiteau's sanity not as
a simple legal issue of criminal intent but as a broader question of fact:
Were there hereditary influences, beyond the defendant's control, that
compelled him to assassinate the president? The expert witnesses for
the defense represented a controversial new group of psychiatrists.
Young, European-trained, and outspokenly critical of M'Naghten, they
took a sharply determinist view of mental illness and criminal responsibility. Led by the German-trained American neuroanatomist Edward
Charles Spitzka, the defense witnesses testified that Guiteau "might
seem rational, even intelligent, and still not be responsible for his actions," Rosenberg writes. "The cause of an individual's criminality, they
were convinced, often lay in heredity, a congenital disposition toward
lack of moral perceptivity and control."[11]

In the end, the court upheld the M'Naghten rule. The jury convicted
Guiteau. The assassin was hanged. The old-guard institutional superintendents carried the day and defended their profession from public
scorn. But it was Spitka's determinism that represented the future.

[9] Rosenberg, *Trial of the Assassin*, 140, 201, 87, 26–27.
[10] Ibid., 66, xiv.
[11] Ibid., xiv.

Even as Guiteau stood trial in Washington, a new "positivist" criminology was building interest in the 1880s and 1890s, first in Europe, then in America, which fixed its gaze on the criminal instead of the crime. Under this gaze, heredity loomed large. Cesare Lombroso of Italy, the period's most influential criminologist, proclaimed the existence of "born criminals" – "atavistic" creatures whose criminality was inscribed in bodily "stigmata," including "enormous jaws" and "handle-shaped ears." Enrico Ferri, Lombroso's successor, made heredity central to his intricate classification scheme. American criminology at the century's turn was a diverse field, but a general consensus existed that criminals were an abnormal type, largely determined in the crucible of heredity.[12]

Hereditarian criminology – or "criminal anthropology," as it came to be known in the United States – found a receptive audience among American officials and reformers concerned with prisons and state institutions for the insane or feebleminded. In their conferences and journals, welfare reformers and caretakers expressed increasing interest in the link between heredity, feeblemindedness, and criminality. New York merchant Richard Dugdale composed the seminal work in the reform literature on crime and heredity. His 1877 book, *The Jukes*, traced the genealogy of an upstate New York clan whose lineage amounted to seven generations of deviants, prostitutes, and criminals – at a cost to the state of $1,308,000 in prison expenses, relief, and medical care. Although Dugdale implicated both environmental and hereditary factors in the making of the Jukes, hardline hereditarians brandished his work as evidence of the pervasive menace and immense public expense of hereditary defectives.[13]

It is important to note the distinction between the hereditarianism of Dugdale's generation and that of eugenicists in Olson's day. In the 1880s and 1890s, the widespread acceptance of Lamarck's theory of acquired characteristics gave a hopeful premise to hereditarianism and to the burgeoning public institutions for the insane and feebleminded: Under the disciplinary regime of the asylum, deviants could be reformed into sober, law-abiding citizens – characteristics their children would inherit. But by 1900, German embryologist August Weismann had exploded Lamarckianism. Together with

[12] Lombroso in Gould, *Mismeasure of Man*, 124, 122–45; Barnes, "Criminology"; Nicole Hahn Rafter, *Creating Born Criminals* (Urbana, 1997).
[13] Richard L. Dugdale, *The Jukes: A Study in Crime, Pauperism, Disease, and Heredity* (New York, 1877); Haller, *Eugenics*, 21–25; Kevles, *In the Name of Eugenics*, 70–84. See James W. Trent, Jr., *Inventing the Feeble Mind: A History of Mental Retardation in the United States* (Berkeley, 1994), 131–224.

the rediscovery of Mendel's pea studies in that year, Weismann's writings on the continuity of the "germ plasm" gave hereditarianism a harsher edge: heredity as destiny. The message of criminal anthropology meshed well with the new hereditarianism, and during the next two decades criminal mental defectives became a fixture of public discourse on welfare and corrections. Walter Fernald, superintendent of the Massachusetts School for the Feeble-Minded, expressed a view common among his peers when he wrote, in 1908, that "every imbecile...is a potential criminal, needing only the proper environment and opportunity for the development and expression of criminal tendencies."[14]

For eugenicists, hereditarian criminology resolved ideological problems and provided a wedge for a broader political program. Since Francis Galton first coined the term "eugenics" in 1883, eugenicists in Europe and America had proposed two quite different public strategies to "keep the life stream pure." Some eugenicists were content to launch public campaigns to encourage the fit to propagate (so-called positive eugenics). Others agitated for state programs to sterilize or sexually segregate the unfit (negative eugenics). The question of fitness exposed the most glaring normative assumptions of the eugenicists, and their answers were inflected with class, gender, and racial biases. Politically diverse as eugenicists were, they often quarreled over the criteria of social desirability. But few doubted who constituted the undesirable: Criminals, the insane, and the feebleminded topped every list. Harry Olson noted this strategic point in a speech to the national Eugenics Research Association. "Being most readily discovered, and most universally abhorred, crime control becomes the first step in the eugenics programme."[15]

Despite the prominence of hereditarianism, American criminology in the early twentieth century was a field diverse in its professional makeup and ideological possibilities. Professional criminologists variously attributed crime to poverty and socioeconomic influences, to political factors such as police corruption, or to a range of mental abnormalities caused by heredity or environment. In 1910, Olson served with Dr. Healy and the sociologist Edward A. Ross on a committee of the American Institute of Criminal Law and Criminology at Northwestern. The committee's purpose was to develop a scientific system for recording criminal data. The experts consulted by the committee suggest the extraordinary range of contemporaries interested in criminology: The

[14] Fernald quoted in Trent, *Inventing the Feeble Mind*, 161; Degler, *In Search of Human Nature*, 3–55.
[15] Olson, "Crime and Heredity," 11–12; Herbert S. Jennings, "Eugenics," in *Encylopaedia of the Social Sciences*, 5: 620–21.

philosopher Josiah Royce, the anthropologist Franz Boas, and the psychologist G. Stanley Hall shared the roster with lesser-known caretakers and professional experts. The proposed recording system, drafted primarily by Healy, gave equal attention to heredity and environment. It called for a medical exam, psychological tests, and even psychoanalysis. In retrospect, the system seems naive: Proper administration would have required a costly team of physicians, psychiatrists, psychologists, and social workers. Still, it suggests the depth of its authors' interest in root causes, experimentation, and fact gathering and their desire to enlarge the role of personal problems experts in the courts. The system also plainly conveys the permeability of hereditarianism and environmentalism in 1910. For Olson, however, the committee appears to have been a turning point, when his longstanding curiosity about the hereditary factor in criminality, first piqued during his years as a county prosecutor, began to crystallize into a personal belief system.[16]

Specialists in the emerging professions of psychiatry and psychology were leaders in early twentieth-century criminology. For psychiatrists, socialized courts, like the new psychopathic hospitals invented in the same period, provided an opportunity to extend their cultural authority beyond the walls of the asylum and the jurisdictional confines of insanity. "Psychiatrists could no longer limit their activities and responsibilities to the institutionalized mentally ill," historian Gerald Grob explains. "They had to lead the way in research and policy formulation, and to implement methods in such areas as mental hygiene, care of the feebleminded, eugenics, control of alcoholism, management of abnormal children, [and] treatment of criminals." As historian Elizabeth Lunbeck has argued, psychiatrists broadened their jurisdiction by claiming expertise on "normal" living and everyday human relations – the field of "the social," where "the issues of personal identity and gender relations with which contemporaries were so concerned could be legitimately addressed." In the process, psychiatrists inadvertently secured entry onto the same interpretive ground for specialists in the behavioral sciences of psychology and sociology. The psychologists' chief contribution to criminology was the intelligence test, a novel device that enabled criminologists to quantify, with apparent objectivity, the mental abnormality of offenders.[17]

---

[16] Herbert Harley, *A Modern Experiment in Judicial Administration: The Municipal Court of Chicago*, speech to Louisiana Bar Association, May 8, 1915 (Chicago, n.p.), 22; [William Healy], "A System for Recording Data Concerning Criminals," *JAICLC*, 1 (1910), 84–97.
[17] Grob, *Mental Illness*, 145; Elizabeth Lunbeck, *The Psychiatric Persuasion: Knowledge, Gender, and Power in Modern America* (Princeton), 23.

Following their higher-status peers in medicine, psychiatrists in the Progressive Era shifted their attention from the study of symptoms to etiology, the contested terrain of causation. Despite a general interest in heredity, psychiatrists remained divided over the causes of mental illness. The practices of many institutions, including the celebrated Boston Psychopathic Hospital, were dominated by the classification schemes of Emil Kraepelin and the German "organicists," who treated psychiatric problems as disease entities that corresponded to brain lesions. Although lesions might be caused by injury, the organicists' materialist perspective made them particularly receptive to hereditarian findings. After 1915, the organicists increasingly came under attack from the "dynamicists," including Adolph Meyer and William Healy, who stressed the interdependence of biology, physiology, and social experience. For the pragmatically inclined dynamicists, rigidly hereditarian etiology – and especially its eugenicist variety – became increasingly untenable.[18]

Professional disagreement among psychiatrists was no novelty in American courts, where (long before Guiteau shot Garfield) dueling alienists had been a familiar feature of trials that involved an insanity defense. Throughout the early twentieth century, leading psychiatrists would continue to try, with limited success, to persuade legislatures to abandon the nineteenth-century right-or-wrong standard for a broader inquiry into the defendant's mental makeup. Still, the organicism-dynamicism debate, which echoed the larger debate between hereditarianism and environmentalism, would shape the practices of socialized courts in ways far more subtle and powerful than a simple clash of views. Nowhere were the lines of this disciplinary debate so clearly drawn as in Chicago, which in the 1910s emerged as America's center of court psychiatry. Striking differences in outlook and practice developed between the dynamicist Dr. Healy at the Juvenile Court's Psychopathic Institute and the organicist Dr. Hickson at the Municipal Court's Psychopathic Laboratory. The different approaches of these two court psychiatrists show how individual actors, working in different institutional and urban contexts, could produce wide variations in the forms of socialized justice.[19]

Contemporaries and historians alike have celebrated Healy as the chief innovator of a new style of criminal psychiatry that rejected hereditarianism and advanced a "therapeutic" agenda. But Healy came only gradually to a therapeutic approach. In 1912, he served on the

---

[18] Grob, *Mental Illness*, 120, 108–78; Lunbeck, *Psychiatric Persuasion*, 117–20.
[19] Sheldon Glueck, "Psychiatry and the Criminal Law," *VLR*, 14 (1928), 155–81.

Eugenics Committee of the Illinois State Conference of Charities and Corrections, which passed resolutions favoring marriage restrictions for the feebleminded, alcoholics, and people with tuberculosis. But the open-minded Healy embraced dynamic psychiatry, and his application of it in his analysis of young offenders at the Psychopathic Institute gradually led him to conclude that environmental factors were the chief cause of delinquency. The doctor adopted a therapeutic approach that aimed to normalize delinquents – not to quarantine them from society. "We have not the slightest inclination to place delinquents as such in a list of abnormal individuals," he wrote in his influential 1915 treatise on juvenile delinquency, *The Individual Delinquent.* "In view of the immense complexity of human nature in relation to complex environmental conditions it is little to us even if no set theory of crime can ever be successfully maintained."[20]

Chief Justice Olson had postponed the opening of the Boys' Court until he could secure funding for a criminological laboratory from the City Council. He received hearty support from the *Chicago Tribune.* The newspaper urged that despite Chicago's "financial straits" in 1913 (the nation as a whole was then edging toward a depression), the project merited public funding. "What civilized peoples are coming to realize," the paper explained, "is that crime has sources in disease, and that the study of the heredity and environment of offenders is of paramount importance." The following year, the City Council approved an appropriation for the laboratory that was just large enough to cover the installation and maintenance expenses of a small laboratory and the salary of a qualified psychiatrist. To staff the laboratory, the municipal judges, with the cooperation of its chief bailiff and chief clerk, would later authorize the psychiatrist to hire a few psychologists as assistants.[21]

---

[20] William Healy, *The Individual Delinquent: A Text-Book of Diagnosis and Prognosis for All Concerned in Understanding Offenders* (Boston, 1915), 4, 781. See Barnes, "Criminology"; Patrick Almond Curtis, "Eugenic Reformers, Cultural Perceptions of Dependent Populations, and the Care of the Feebleminded in Illinois, 1909–1920," Ph.D. diss., University of Illinois at Chicago, 1983, p. 79; David J. Rothman, *Conscience and Convenience: The Asylum and Its Alternatives in Progressive America* (Boston, 1980), 54–56.

[21] "A Laboratory for Crime," *Chicago Tribune,* March 9, 1913, p. 4; "Fire and Police Bonds Favored By Committee," unidentified newspaper clipping, HODS, box 1, "Political 1914" file. The laboratory operated on an annual appropriation from the City Council; by 1921, it had reached $15,000. Harry Olson to Alroy S. Phillips, Jan. 21, 1921, JHO, box 5. Judges' orders authorizing personnel changes and salary increases can be found in *Municipal*

An ardent eugenicist, Dr. William J. Hickson served as director of the Municipal Court of Chicago's Psychopathic Laboratory from its founding in 1914 until 1929. Courtesy of the Chicago Historical Society (ICHi-34918).

In his search for a suitable psychiatrist to direct the laboratory, Chief Justice Olson naturally consulted Healy. But Olson, who had already begun to write favorably on eugenics, took the advice of Princeton psychiatrist Stewart Paton and recruited a psychiatrist with impeccable organicist credentials. Dr. William James Hickson, an American neurologist, had studied in some of Europe's most famous psychiatric centers: the clinics of Emil Kraepelin in Munich, Eugen Bleuler in Zurich, and Theodor Ziehen in Berlin. When Olson spotted him, Hickson was working under psychologist Henry H. Goddard at the Training School for Feeble-Minded Boys and Girls in Vineland, New Jersey, the premier American center for psychological testing. At the time, Goddard was a committed eugenicist and the leading

Court of Chicago General Orders, vols. 15 and 16 (1907–21 and 1921–30), Cook County Circuit Court Archives.

exponent of theories linking mental deficiency and crime. As director of the Psychopathic Laboratory from 1914 to 1929, Hickson would conduct a fascinating synthesis of organic psychiatry and eugenic criminology.[22]

In founding the Psychopathic Laboratory on eugenic principles, Harry Olson could count on the support of a broad and varied eugenics constituency in Illinois, where eugenics had gained a following of social workers, psychiatrists, superintendents, and welfare reformers. Hereditarianism justified the burgeoning populations within state institutions for the insane or feebleminded, which by 1914 housed 20,000 residents. *Institution Quarterly*, the organ of the State Board of Administration, frequently published favorable articles on eugenics. Although most caretakers considered sterilization too extreme, many commended the sex-segregated housing at their institutions, which functioned as a compulsory sexual prophylaxis. Harry Hardt, superintendent of the Lincoln State School and Colony for the feebleminded, noted that his institution served as "an adjunct to nature in her selective power." It was precisely to such audiences that eugenicists directed their message about criminal mental defectives. "By segregation or sterilization," Goddard told the Illinois Conference of Charities and Corrections in 1913, "we could, in a generation or two, reduce the number of our dependent classes enormously and save from a fourth to a half of the expense of our criminals, our paupers, to say nothing of the moral degradation and disease engendered by our prostitutes."[23]

Like many other states during the 1910s, Illinois experienced a spreading panic over the "menace of the feebleminded." A capacious nineteenth-century term, "feeblemindedness" was applied by

[22] Harry Olson, "A Constructive Policy Whereby the Social Evil May Be Reduced," speech to Seventh Annual International Purity Congress, Minneapolis, Nov. 9, 1913 (n.p.). Harry Olson, "Organization, Procedure, and the Psychopathic Laboratory," address to Iowa State Bar Association, June 25, 1920 (n.p.), 9–10. See Hamilton Cravens, "Applied Science and Public Policy: The Ohio Bureau of Juvenile Research and the Problem of Juvenile Delinquency, 1913–1930," in *Psychological Testing in American Society, 1890–1930*, ed. Michael M. Sokal (New Brunswick, 1987), 158–94; Henry H. Goddard, *The Kallikak Family: A Study in the Heredity of Feeble-Mindedness* (New York, 1912); Edward S. Scheffler, "The History of the Psychiatric Institute of the Municipal Court of Chicago," in *A Dynamic Era of Court Psychiatry, 1914–1944*, ed. Agnes Sharp (Chicago, 1944), 9.
[23] Hardt in Curtis, "Eugenic Reformers," 71; Goddard in Trent, *Inventing the Feeble Mind*, 165. See Curtis, "Eugenic Reformers," 90; Haller, *Eugenics*, 24–25.

professional experts and welfare workers to an array of mental deficiencies, including many today believed to be caused or exacerbated by poor nutrition and substandard education. By the 1910s, psychologists had subdivided the feebleminded into three categories: the "idiot," whom psychologists today might call "profoundly mentally handicapped"; the "imbecile," who might now be called "trainable mentally handicapped"; and the "moron," who matches today's profile of the "educable mentally handicapped." To welfare workers and professional experts, and to the public officials who heeded their alarmist message, the moron posed the greatest public threat. Intelligent enough to commit a crime and escape apprehension, the high-grade feebleminded person was, in the eyes of experts and laypeople alike, innately driven to criminal behavior.[24]

At the Vineland Training School for Feeble-Minded Boys and Girls, Goddard reified feeblemindedness as a unitary characteristic (like eye color) and amassed genealogical data to prove that the condition was hereditary. The feebleminded lacked sexual self-control and could not distinguish right from wrong, he argued. As psychological testing of prison populations began to suggest a high incidence of mental defect, Goddard and others publicized the link between criminality and feeblemindedness. By the mid-1910s, the discourse of the menace of the feebleminded had spilled over from welfare circles and professional journals into popular culture, popularized by the propaganda of the Carnegie Institution's Eugenics Record Office and a pulp heap of books on rural misfits. Legislatures responded to the panic by passing a wave of commitment and sterilization laws for the mentally defective.[25]

In 1914, A. A. McCormick, the progressive president of the Cook County Board of Commissioners, organized a group of Chicagoans to draft a bill for the involuntary commitment of the feebleminded. At that time, parents could remove their feebleminded children from state institutions, and adults could not be held against their will. Calling itself the Illinois Committee on Social Legislation, the group included Edward H. Ochsner, president of the State Charities Commission; a former psychologist at Lincoln; and Judge Olson. Correspondence between Ochsner and Olson shows that the judge played an instrumental role in the drafting and passage

[24] Steven Noll, *Feeble-Minded in Our Midst, Institutions for the Mentally Retarded in the South, 1900–1940* (Chapel Hill, 1995), 3.
[25] Curtis, "Eugenic Reformers," 112; Gould, *Mismeasure of Man*, 158–74; Haller, *Eugenics*, 125–43; Kevles, *In the Name of Eugenics*, 76–80; Trent, *Inventing the Feeble Mind*, 131–224.

of the 1915 commitment act. Olson proposed revisions, convened the Municipal Court's associate judges to assess the bill's legal merit, and even dispatched a judge to Springfield to lobby on its behalf.[26]

The act easily passed both houses of the General Assembly. It defined "feeble-minded person" broadly, as any "mentally defective" person "incapable of managing himself and his affairs or of being taught to do so, and requires supervision, control and care for his own welfare, or for the welfare of others, or for the welfare of the community." The act vested policing powers in the state's "reputable" citizenry. A commitment petition could be filed by "any relative, parent, guardian, conservator or friend of such supposed feeble-minded person, or any reputable citizen of the county in which such supposed feeble-minded person resides or is found." After a hearing, a commission composed of two physicians or one physician and one psychologist would examine the individual and make a recommendation. A circuit, county, or city court judge would review the commission's recommendations and make a final ruling to commit or discharge the individual. Olson contributed a crucial passage to the law: If a judge presiding over a misdemeanor or felony trial believed the defendant was feebleminded, the judge could continue the case and order the filing of a commitment petition.[27]

The cause of checking feeblemindedness in Illinois had support from reformers and organizations that historians have mistakenly remembered as single-minded environmentalists. The Juvenile Protective Association did promote a belief in the plasticity of human nature and an environmentalist view of crime. But the JPA's environmentalism was less a rigid ideological commitment than an informed sensibility, reinforced by the women's everyday encounters with poorly clad, malnourished, and uneducated youth offenders from the immigrant neighborhoods around Hull-House. Just as integral to the JPA members' world view was their faith in modern technique – experimentalism, empiricism, and expertise – which prevented them from closing their minds to the scientific claims and utopian promises

[26] Ochsner to Olson, March 29, 1915, MCC, folder 27; Ochsner to Olson, April 13, 1915, folder 28; Ochsner to Olson, April 19, 1915, folder 28; Olson to Ochsner, April 20, 1915, folder 28; Ochsner to Olson, May 6, 1915, folder 28; Harry Olson, "Objection to the So-Called Schofield Bill," folder 29; Curtis, "Eugenic Reformers," 146–58.
[27] "An Act to Better Provide for the Care and Detention of Feeble-Minded Persons," *Illinois Revised Statutes*, 1925, ch. 23, sec. 346; Curtis, "Eugenic Reformers," 155–58.

of eugenics. In her 1913 tract on prostitution, Jane Addams herself wrote hopefully of "the new science of eugenics with its university professors" and "organized societies."[28]

The JPA's public support for the 1915 Feebleminded Commitment Act demonstrates the power of state institutions to *shape* – rather than simply implement – progressive ideology. The evidence suggests that the Municipal Court's new Psychopathic Laboratory helped persuade the environmentalists to endorse a eugenic measure. In her 1914 book, *Safeguards for City Youth*, Louise Bowen described the group's stunned reaction to Hickson's first results with defendants from the Boys' Court. "While we all anticipated that a certain number of the boys would be sub-normal, we were hardly prepared for the first figures," she recalled. During the laboratory's first three weeks alone, ninety-five boys were found to be subnormal. Bowen was especially moved by the case of one "huge fellow" who had brutally slain his employer and his employer's family. According to Hickson's tests, he possessed a mental age of eight and a half. "Had his stature attained only the growth of his mind," Bowen wrote, "he would have lacked the strength to have accomplished a murder and his outbreak would have been regarded with the leniency we accord to the tantrums of a child." Taking Hickson's data at face value, she drew her prescriptive conclusion: "Is not society under obligations to place such a boy in a school fitted to his intelligence, to keep him there during his life, with a self-supporting occupation, that he may not be a source of danger to the community?" The following year, in a *Study of Mentally Defective Children in Chicago*, the JPA advocated a eugenic reform to protect society from feebleminded prostitutes. "Segregation of these women," the author declared, "at least during the childbearing period, would not only benefit public morals but would considerably lessen the number of the feeble-minded in the next generation."[29]

The 1915 Feebleminded Commitment Act revealed the breadth of support for eugenic jurisprudence in Illinois. And as the JPA's endorsement demonstrated, to support eugenics in 1915 did not require a hostility toward environmentalism. That same year, the City Council convened a much-touted Committee on Crime, chaired by Alderman Charles E. Merriam, the University of Chicago political scientist and a leading local progressive Republican. The laboratory had been open

---

[28] Jane Addams, *A New Conscience and an Ancient Evil* (New York, 1913), 130–31.
[29] Louise de Koven Bowen, *Safeguards for City Youth: At Work and at Play* (New York, 1914), 124–25; John E. Ransom, "A Study of Mentally Defective Children in Chicago," *Institution Quarterly*, 6 (1915), 49–50, quoted in Curtis, "Eugenic Reformers," 101.

for only a few months, but already the committee saw its promise. "The Psychopathic Laboratory renders indispensable service in diagnosing cases and indicating treatment for defective delinquents," the report announced. With that confidence in scientifically produced social knowledge so emblematic of Progressive Era political culture, the committee declared that the "chief causes of crime" were both "defective" physical and mental conditions *and* "defective environment." Modern judicial administration demanded the best that science had to offer. The committee urged that the laboratory be expanded.[30]

Occupying cramped quarters near the socialized branch courts in Chicago's City Hall, the Psychopathic Laboratory was no Pasteur Institute. The laboratory equipment consisted of little more than a handful of European visual memory tests, some of which Hickson revised to his own purposes. The tests were conducted by the doctor, his wife Marie, and one or two women psychologists. The doctor himself compiled the findings and drew astonishing conclusions from them.[31]

Hickson's writings, which Olson faithfully published in the Municipal Court's annual reports, were a mix of psychiatric theory and political economy that aimed as much to sell the laboratory as to explain it. Following the narrative conventions of eugenics propaganda (and of much progressive reform writing), Hickson weaved a Whiggish account of crime and punishment in the West: a long ascent from the maiming of the Middle Ages to the "cruel" solitary confinement of the Jacksonian penitentiary and, finally, in the bright light of modern science, to the applied theories of criminal psychiatry. Drawing an organicist analogy between criminality and disease, Hickson said the state imperative was clear: to "develop the scientific administration of the law as it is doing in medicine, to go to the root of things in order that intelligent treatment may be undertaken, looking for a successful solution to the problem."[32]

Synthesizing the insights of his European mentors with those of his former supervisor, Goddard, Hickson laid out his theory and methodology in a 400-page *Report of the Psychopathic Laboratory* in 1917. The jargon ran thick – one critic said it defied the comprehension of "ordinary people" – but Hickson's claims were quite straightforward. The psychiatrist, like many of his professional peers, believed in simple functional

[30] Chicago City Council, *Report of the City Council Committee on Crime* (Chicago, 1915), 12, 15.
[31] The definitive statement of Hickson's work is *Report of the Psychopathic Laboratory*.
[32] Ibid., 19–21.

locations of the brain: the upper brain was the seat of intelligence; the lower brain, the site of emotion or "affect." Whereas Goddard had linked criminality to a hereditary defect of intelligence (feeblemindedness), Hickson's chief innovation was his claim that "defective intelligence" posed a minor threat next to "affective defect." While he took complicating factors such as alcoholism and "sex perversions" into account, Hickson claimed that most criminality was caused by a single type of hereditary affective defect, dementia praecox. First developed by Kraepelin and Bleuler, the category covered a range of disorders that were part of the family, so to speak, of schizophrenia. Apathy and lack of remorse were characteristic; criminality, almost inevitable. "We see the determining role of dementia praecox as the great causative factor," Hickson observed, "the *leit motif* of crime."[33]

Although dementia praecox had become a routine diagnosis in American psychiatric institutions during the 1910s, the claim that a definite causal link existed between the disorder and criminality was controversial. Hickson discovered dementia praecox in 1,146 out of 3,259 individuals (35 percent) who crossed his threshold from 1914 to 1917. But William Healy and other dynamic psychiatrists viewed the matter more cautiously. "In some quarters it has been the tendency to over-estimate the percentage of cases belonging in the dementia praecox group which one meets with among young offenders," Healy wrote. "Certainly in not more than 25 cases in our 1000 young repeated offenders [2.5 percent] have the symptoms been interpretable as belonging in any way to dementia praecox." Of course, Healy was examining younger offenders than Hickson, which might have accounted for part of the discrepancy between their findings. But Hickson insisted that this "great causative factor" could be detected "even in the earliest years of childhood." This difference of professional opinion was anything but academic – it was political. Each position implied a different prescription for state action. Whereas Healy favored therapeutic treatments such as probation, Hickson viewed a diagnosis of dementia praecox as sufficient cause for indeterminate institutional commitment to prevent future criminal behavior – and future criminals.[34]

Hickson tested offenders for the presence of affective defect through a series of tests, including the Ziehen Memory Test and his

---

33 Hiram T. Gilbert, *The Municipal Court of Chicago*, 2d ed. (Chicago, 1928), 94–95; *Report of the Psychopathic Laboratory*, 31, 28–48; Curtis, "Eugenic Reformers," 126.

34 Singer, "Deranged or Defective Delinquent," 794–95; Healy, *Individual Delinquent*, 594; *Report of the Psychopathic Laboratory*, 31–32. See Lunbeck, *Psychiatric Persuasion*, 127–30.

own version of the Binet-Simon Intelligence Scale. The Binet-Simon test was ubiquitous in early twentieth-century America. A series of scaled tasks used to compare the test-taker's mental and chronological ages, it was the principal metric used by psychologists and psychiatrists in their aggressive pursuit of cultural authority through psychological testing, which culminated in the notorious "Alpha" and "Beta" tests of American servicemen during World War I. (According to the test results, the average white American adult possessed a mental age of thirteen or fourteen – hovering just above the intelligence level of a moron; eugenicists deployed the new data as further evidence of impending racial catastrophe.) Revised by Lewis M. Terman at Stanford University in 1916, the Binet-Simon scale served as the basis of American intelligence quotient (IQ) tests.[35]

Hickson's use of the Binet-Simon Intelligence Scale illustrates the dangerously slippery science of biological determinism. When the French psychologist Alfred Binet devised his test, he did not intend to provide an exact measure of human "intelligence." According to Stephen Jay Gould, Binet "greatly feared that his practical device, if reified as an entity, could be perverted and used as an indelible label, rather than as a guide for identifying children who needed help." Binet's fears proved prescient. Goddard, who first popularized the Binet scale in America, claimed it measured a unitary "intelligence." Hickson pushed the test further still. He used the test, he explained, "not only as [a] test for intelligence *per se* but also for primary disturbances of the intelligence function as found in paresis, senile dementia, narcotism, such as alcoholism, morphinism, cocainism, etc. We have also extended its use in an equally wide and important field in the psychoses, such as various forms of dementia praecox, manic-depressive insanity, hysteria, etc." In addition to pushing the Binet-Simon scale far beyond its creator's intentions, Hickson applied only part of it in his diagnoses: a visual memory test. It consisted of a series of drawings that the test-taker would briefly view and then attempt to duplicate. The memory test was the essence of Hickson's methodology, his caliper of "mental defect."[36]

Judge Olson incorporated eugenic jurisprudence into the workaday routine of the Municipal Court. He instructed judges in the criminal

[35] Gould, *Mismeasure of Man*, 146–233; Sokal, ed., *Psychological Testing and American Society*. See Walter Lippmann, "The Mental Age of Americans," *New Republic*, Oct. 25, 1922, in *The Bell Curve Debate: History, Documents, Opinions*, ed. Russell Jacoby and Naomi Glauberman (New York, 1995), 561–65.
[36] Gould, *Mismeasure of Man*, 151, 146–74; *Report of the Psychopathic Laboratory*, 170.

and socialized branches to be on the lookout for "defectives" among their defendants, plaintiffs, and even witnesses. Judges were expected to send suspected "defectives" to the laboratory for an exam. Though Hickson claimed to submit a full written report to the judge on each case, his diagnosis and recommendation were sometimes transmitted with a phone call. (Apparently, some judges violated the statutory requirement that commitment recommendations be made by a two-member commission.) The judge then enjoyed a range of options: He could commit the individual to a state institution for the insane or feebleminded, devise a probation regimen, or ignore Hickson's report completely.[37]

Olson liked to say that the laboratory's case pool was Chicago itself, a modern metropolis whose ability to centralize crime and vice seemed to rival its capacity to centralize the production, marketing, and distribution of every imaginable commodity. Although Cook County Criminal Court had final jurisdiction over felonies, the judge noted that all felonies committed in the city had a preliminary hearing in the Municipal Court. "The result is that our field affords ample material for the study of the more serious offenders, those who have committed homicide, robbery, rape and other felonies." Yet the overwhelming majority of the people examined in the laboratory were not such hardened criminals. They were sent by judges in the socialized courts. In a breakdown provided by Hickson of 4,447 cases examined in the laboratory during its first three years, 2,025 came from the Boys' Court, 1,236 from the Domestic Relations Court, 947 from the Morals Court, and only 329 from the other criminal branches. This disparity is particularly significant because, taken together, the other criminal branches handled a much larger caseload than the socialized branches. (In 1916, for example, the criminal branches disposed of more than 120,000 cases; the three socialized courts combined disposed of slightly more than 15,000 cases.)[38]

This disparity says something important about the relationship between the laboratory and the Municipal Court as a whole. When confronted with adult defendants accused of violent crimes or crimes against property, judges showed less interest in a psychiatric exam. They were far more likely to seek the laboratory's advice in adjudicating

---

[37] *Report of the Psychopathic Laboratory*, 13; Singer, "Deranged or Defective Delinquent," 797–98. In addition to the 1915 Feebleminded Commitment Act, judges could commit defendants under Illinois's 1893 "lunatic" act. See *Illinois Revised Statutes*, 1925, ch. 85, sec. 1–38.

[38] Olson in *Report of the Psychopathic Laboratory*, 9–10; *MCC 10–11* (1916–17), 46–51.

offenses committed in the morally ambiguous sphere of the social: vice, domestic disputes, and youth offenses. It was within this sphere of everyday life and domestic relations that eugenic jurisprudence had its greatest effect upon the life chances of defendants.[39]

Given the location of the Psychopathic Laboratory, at the heart of a municipal court system, it is no surprise that its subjects were mostly people employed (or unemployed) in working-class occupations. In a 1924 study entitled "Socio-Economics of Crime and Criminals," Hickson provided an occupational breakdown of 1,002 consecutive cases sent to the laboratory from the nonspecialized criminal branches. Of 825 males examined, fully 26 percent were laborers; 6 percent, clerks; 5 percent, factory hands; 4 percent, machinists; 4 percent, teamsters; 3 percent, painters and decorators; 3 percent, chauffeurs; 2.5 percent, mechanics; 2 percent, tailors; and 2 percent, janitors. Those were the top ten occupational classifications represented. From the professional categories, exactly two lawyers, two ministers, and nine "professions" made the list. Of 177 females, 33 percent were domestics; 12.5 percent, factory hands; 7.5 percent, waitresses; 6 percent, store clerks; 5 percent, tailors; 5 percent, housewives; 3.5 percent, laundry workers; 3.5 percent, telephone operators; 2 percent, farm workers; and 2 percent, dishwashers. Hickson claimed that "such data are indispensable to political economy and government." But he did not specify *how*. A similar occupational breakdown could be found in the court's statistics on men and women admitted to adult probation – a very different disposition than that which awaited mental defectives. Fully 68 percent of the men and a staggering 87 percent of the women in Hickson's sample were committed to state institutions for the insane or feebleminded.[40]

The largest pool of women came to the laboratory from the Morals Court on charges of prostitution or public immorality. Judge Olson and Dr. Hickson joined numerous other government officials, moral reformers, and psychiatrists in the Progressive Era in interpreting the contemporary upheaval of gender relations and sexual norms as evidence of an epidemic of feeblemindedness that only state action could eradicate. Like many of their peers, Olson and Hickson claimed that

[39] In the 1920s, the criminal branches accounted for a larger percentage of Hickson's caseload. Even then, most of the defendants examined in the laboratory had been charged with disorderly conduct and other minor offenses against public order; Singer, "Deranged or Defective Delinquent," 798–803.
[40] Hickson, "Socio-Economics of Crime and Criminals," in *MCC 16–18* (1922–24), 168–82, esp. 183; "Adult Probation," in ibid., 117.

at least half of the professional prostitutes working in American cities were feebleminded. The introduction of the Binet-Simon intelligence test in 1908 had coincided with the proliferation of urban vice commissions and foundation studies of women offenders, giving investigators a scientifically legitimate metric to assess the hereditary mental defect of "immoral women." The causal significance attributed to mental defect meshed well with the progressive moralists' view of prostitutes as helpless victims of industrialization, a vicious urban environment, and unscrupulous men. "The fact that so large a per cent[age] of the women engaged in public prostitution are mentally deficient removes the stigma of disgrace from womanhood," Olson claimed. The real effect of the discourse on women offenders' alleged mental subnormality was exactly the opposite: It gave their culturally determined moral stigma the scientific status of a biologically determined fact. And in a growth period for eugenics legislation across the United States, the search for mental defect among prostitutes could result in lifetime commitment and sterilization.[41]

For Hickson, women offenders were an easy case. "In the matter of recidivism, the Morals Court cases take the lead over all others, which is quite natural since the majority of these girls are too feebleminded or psychopathic to make a living legitimately," he wrote in 1917. Of 793 women defendants sent to the laboratory from the Morals Court between 1914 and 1917, Hickson found that 464 suffered from some sort of psychopathological condition, and he labeled 471 of the women "morons." The court's records provide no indication of what was done with these women, but the special enthusiasm of Morals Court judges for the laboratory in the 1910s suggests they did not fare well. Morals Court Judge Harry Fisher wrote in 1917 that Hickson's work had "brought a new vision" to the Morals Court. "A few months' experience in that court, aided by the advice of the laboratory's findings, enables the judge to detect these unfortunate creatures without much trouble." Fisher's confidence in his newfound ability to spot defectives from the bench was perfectly in keeping with the rhetoric of socialized law, which inspired confidence that rationally organized administrative courts could uncover the social facts underlying deviant behavior. Because judges were faced daily with recidivist prostitutes – whose repeated appearances in court reflected badly on judges' claims to social expertise – it is not hard to

---

[41] Olson, "Constructive Policy," 15. By the end of World War I, more than fifteen studies of American prostitutes had reported that 30 to 98 percent were feebleminded. Mark Thomas Connelly, *The Response to Prostitution in the Progressive Era* (Chapel Hill, 1980), 41.

imagine the appeal that mental defect might have for them as an explanation.[42]

Olson and Hickson clearly shared some of the racist assumptions of extreme American eugenicists. Eugenics is formally a racial theory, concerned as it is with matters of hereditary endowment and the bloodlines of allegedly natural social groups. In societies structured by racial conflict and oppression, the racialism of eugenics yielded virulent scientific racism. The racist strain of American eugenics provided a prominent argument for the immigration restriction acts of the 1920s; in Nazi Germany, eugenics laid the scientific foundation for mass racial extermination. Chief Justice Olson repeated the common claim that foreign nations were deliberately flooding the United States with mental defectives, and he lamented the "mongrelization of our people." The most blatant sort of racism surfaced in the 1922 treatise on sterilization legislation written by the Municipal Court's research associate, Harry H. Laughlin. The Zelig of the eugenics movement, Laughlin served at various times as assistant director of the Eugenics Record Office, "expert eugenical agent" of the House Committee on Immigration and Naturalization, and expert witness in *Buck v. Bell*. In the treatise, Laughlin cited the case of a white woman committed to the New Jersey State Village for Epileptics. To buttress his case that the woman should be sterilized, Laughlin noted that she had admitted having sex with a "colored" man. "This patient did not possess the normal aversions of a white girl to a colored man," he wrote, noting Smith's "hypersexuality which is common in defectiveness." That Olson would publish Laughlin's report – indeed, *applaud* it – suggests he found such views inoffensive. For eugenicists, as for white Americans generally, willful transgression of racial boundaries provided concrete evidence of deviance.[43]

More surprising than such scattered evidence of conventional racist beliefs, however, is the reticence of eugenicist jurists about race. Olson and Hickson made no effort at all to use eugenic jurisprudence to further criminalize African-Americans and immigrants as social groups. In the reports of the Municipal Court and the Psychopathic

---

[42] *Report of the Psychopathic Laboratory*, 92, 93–106; Fisher in *MCC 10–11* (1916–17), 90.
[43] Olson in *MCC 19–22* (1925–28), 17–18; Harry H. Laughlin, *Eugenical Sterilization in the United States: A Report of the Psychopathic Laboratory of the Municipal Court of Chicago* (Chicago, 1922), 296. See Garland E. Allen, "The Eugenics Record Office at Cold Spring Harbor, 1910–1940: An Essay in Institutional History," *Osiris*, 2d ser., 2 (1986), 225–64; Haller, *Eugenics*, 131–34, 138–39, 155–57; Olson, "Disease and Crime."

Laboratory – public documents published in a city where immigrants
(and increasingly blacks) held considerable political power – questions
of race and nationality were subsumed within the larger discussion of
mental defect. Race and nationality were often, but not always, mentioned in case histories published by the laboratory. Although commitment forms called for racial and ethnic data, no analysis of race
or nationality in the laboratory was ever published. The unsystematic
inclusion of ethnic and racial data suggests that Hickson and Olson
thought it relevant, but not essential, to their program. This helps
explain why Chicago's African-American elites – always quick to protest
racial inequities in the administration of criminal justice – did not see
eugenic jurisprudence as a threat to their community. The *Chicago
Defender* even alerted its readers to the dangerous mental defectives
"roaming about the city." "No matter how near or dear these people
are to us," the paper opined, "we owe it to the public, to the unfortunates and to ourselves, to throw every safeguard possible around them
to prevent their doing some crime for which we cannot hold them in
any way responsible."[44]

Eugenic jurisprudence conflated a host of social and health problems into a tableau of working-class pathology rooted in defective
genes. Hickson packed his reports with stark case histories, which he
used to establish the hereditary defectiveness of his examinees and
their relatives – and, no doubt, to strike terror in the reader. These
histories further illustrate the essentialist and value-laden assumptions
that underlay Hickson and Olson's "scientific" jurisprudence. The histories are litanies of addiction, alcoholism, incest, tuberculosis, domestic violence, illiteracy, illegitimacy, and desertion. Almost every individual has a relative described as "worthless." "There is a deadly monotony
in the sameness throughout all these cases," Hickson wrote, undermining his claim that the laboratory considered each case individually.
After 1917, Hickson's contributions to the court's annual reports diminished. "Results have been uniformly corroborative of the findings
first reported," Olson explained.[45]

44 "Demented People," *Chicago Defender*, Aug. 12, 1916. In a collection of
thirty-seven case histories of Boys' Court defendants, for example, twelve
were identified as children of immigrants, six as "American," and four as
"colored"; fifteen were not identified by nationality or race; *Report of the
Psychopathic Laboratory*, 367–80. The form Hickson filled out as a commissioner in feebleminded commitment cases asked him to identify the race
and nationality of defendants and their parents. Feeble-Minded Commitment Cases, Cook County Circuit Court Archives, box 1.
45 Hickson in *Report of the Psychopathic Laboratory*, 367; Olson in *MCC 16–18*
(1922–24), 14.

Although many court clinics in the Progressive Era experimented with eugenics, none committed itself more firmly than the Psychopathic Laboratory, and it could not have done so without the support of the Municipal Court's judges. The associate judges routinely signed orders authorizing pay increases and new staff for the laboratory, and judges of the socialized branches often adopted the laboratory's jargon as their own. Morals Court Judge Charles Goodnow held forth on the mental defectiveness of "delinquent girls" in public speeches and cited the laboratory's data in his campaign for marriage restriction laws, telling the Woman's City Club in 1916 that "the marriage license window is an open way to the destruction of the national health and morals, with the ultimate certainty of irreparable race degeneracy." More significant than judges' appropriation of Hickson's ideas was their routine approval of his recommendations for institutional commitment.[46]

In 1929, Chicago psychiatrist H. Douglas Singer compiled a report on "The Deranged or Defective Delinquent" for the influential *Illinois Crime Survey*. Singer traced the outcomes of 154 cases referred to the Psychopathic Laboratory from November to December, 1927. Hickson had recommended 111 (72 percent) for commitment in the Cook County Psychopathic Hospital and seven (4.5 percent) for commitment to the Lincoln State School and Colony for the feebleminded. The laboratory's propensity to recommend commitment, Singer observed, was "extremely high when compared with the recommendations from the Recorder's Court of Detroit (6 per cent), from the Municipal Court of Philadelphia (2 per cent) and from other clinics of this type."[47] Equally startling was Singer's discovery that the Municipal Court of Chicago judges had followed Hickson's recommendations for commitment in 105 of the 118 cases (89 percent). This proportion, too, was exceptionally high. At Boston's Judge Baker Foundation, judges followed clinic recommendations in only one of five cases (20 percent). Singer wryly noted the stunning significance of these figures: "The findings at the Chicago clinic indicate either: (1) that the selection of cases for examination is made with great accuracy and acumen, or (2) that the diagnoses and recommendations are very

[46] "Goodnow Urges Eugenics Law to Save Race," *Chicago Examiner*, June 23, 1916; "Goodnow Tells Why Girls Fall," *Chicago Tribune*, Nov. 9, 1916.
[47] Singer, "Deranged or Defective Delinquent," 801. Evidence from the feebleminded commitment case files supports this observation. In the thirty-four consecutive surviving cases from 1915 to 1917, all but six defendants were committed. Feebleminded Commitment Cases, box 1.

greatly colored by the personal views of the director as to the need for commitment."[48]

The laboratory's operations were a striking (if controversial) display of state power, but they were not always intrusive or unwelcome among the working-class families who comprised much of the laboratory's case pool. Feebleminded commitment case files from the Municipal Court reveal a pattern of family self-policing similar to that which historians have found in juvenile courts, where working-class parents called upon the state to help them regulate their unruly children. Petitioners in the surviving feebleminded cases were overwhelmingly parents or family members. They claimed before the court that they could no longer control or afford to keep their feebleminded and delinquent children at home.[49] One self-described "anxious mother" penned a letter to Olson in 1920, thanking him for his efforts to establish a state farm colony for feebleminded boys. "They are too good to be in Jail and not bad enough to be in an insane asylum," she wrote. "My Boy is almost 19 yrs old and it has been a case of Vigilance with me to keep him out of trouble." Although working-class parents had their own reasons for committing their children, their willing participation in the court's eugenics jurisprudence underscores Elizabeth Lunbeck's poignant insight about social policing. "Historically," writes Lunbeck, "it has proven far more palatable to blame the police for unjustly incarcerating the innocent than to imagine that the power that delivers them up to the authorities might be distributed throughout the social body, exercised by many and sustained by the troubled relations of everyday life."[50]

In some cases, however, parents and siblings did struggle with court officials to prevent the commitment of a loved one. Because of the youth of Boys' Court defendants, a feeble-minded commitment proceeding there could easily turn into a contest for authority between family members and the court-appointed commission of psychiatrists. Whenever possible, judges tried to persuade family members to sign the commitment papers themselves after hearing the doctors'

[48] Singer, "Deranged or Defective Delinquent," 801, 799–801.
[49] Feebleminded Commitment Case Files, boxes 1–10, 1915–19. Of 34 consecutive cases from 1915 to 1917, petitioners included 14 mothers, five fathers, five unrelated parties who identified themselves as interested in the defendant's welfare, three social workers, two aunts, and one each of brother-in-law, caretaker, court official, nurse, and police officer; box 1. See Mary E. Odem, *Delinquent Daughters: Protecting and Policing Adolescent Female Sexuality in the United States, 1885–1920* (Chapel Hill, 1995).
[50] "An anxious Mother" to Harry Olson, Feb. 2, 1920, JHO, box 3; Lunbeck, *Psychiatric Persuasion*, 83.

testimony. But when the relatives refused to comply, judges weighed the experts' claim to knowledge of the defendant against the intimate claims of the boy's own family. It was never a fair fight. The high stature of the Psychopathic Laboratory in the eyes of the judges gave the experts an undeniable edge. The family's case was also weakened by the unspoken subtext of these proceedings. According to the hereditarian logic of eugenics, the defendant's parents and siblings were automatically suspect as probable mental defectives.

One 1926 case before Judge Allegretti involved a boy who had already escaped from the Lincoln State School and Colony once. The boy had stolen some rings while hiding from the police. Dr. Hickson testified that the defendant had a mental age of ten and ought to be sent back to Lincoln. Hickson's fellow commissioner seconded the recommendation. At that point, the boy's brother and sister stepped forward. They flatly rejected the doctors' assessment and boldly insisted that their brother's confinement at Lincoln had done him more harm than good. They pleaded with the court to let them take care of the boy at home. Judge Allegretti tried to reason with the distraught siblings. "Don't you realize he's only ten years old as far as his mind is concerned and he doesn't understand the difference between right and wrong?" he asked. "Do you want him to go traveling in society, teaching other fellows to steal and get into trouble?" The brother tried a different tack. He asked Allegretti to sentence the boy to the House of Correction, at most a year's imprisonment, instead of returning him to Lincoln, where the doctors had the authority to hold him indefinitely. Allegretti was outraged. "I'm getting a little suspicious of you, too," he retorted. The sister's protests and tears were no more persuasive to the judge. "Lincoln, just the same," he ordered.[51]

And what of the alleged "mental defectives" themselves – these "unruly" youths, "hypersexual" women, and "worthless" men? It is a bitter irony that in the voluminous archival residue of this pioneering center of "individual treatment" the individuals so treated have no voice. Sheaves of visual memory tests record the scrawl of unsteady hands or inattentive minds – or unpromising artists. The salacious case histories published by the laboratory are boiler plate in their monotony and devoid of trustworthy personal detail. The words penned onto commitment petitions are copied from the commitment laws, set down by a court clerk as a routine matter. But if we can no longer hear the voices of the "defectives," if we lack a record of their thoughts on the merits or injustices of eugenic jurisprudence, we can at least infer something

[51] Murray Howard Leiffer, "The Boys' Court of Chicago," M.A. thesis, University of Chicago, 1928, pp. 169–72.

from their actions. For not all of the men and women committed by
the court acquiesced in their treatment. In the years following passage
of the 1915 Feebleminded Commitment Act, the population at the
Lincoln State School and Colony, increasingly made up of alleged
young lawbreakers and sex offenders, shook the institution's walls
with vandalism, riots, and assaults. Those committed by the Municipal
Court to the state's psychopathic hospitals were no more compliant:
During one year in the late 1920s, a quarter of them escaped. Acts of
personal liberation in the most literal sense, the escapes' political significance was not lost on well-placed critics of eugenic jurisprudence.
As Dr. Singer noted dryly in the *Illinois Crime Survey*, "These facts suggest that many of the persons who are committed as a result of recommendations from the laboratory of the Municipal Court cannot be
adequately cared for in the state hospitals." The rebellious acts of the
"defectives" undermined the legitimacy of eugenic jurisprudence at a
time when it was under attack from other quarters.[52]

Even at the height of their influence, American eugenicists – whether
in the courtroom or the statehouse, the university laboratory or on
the Chautauqua stage – faced charges that their scientific claims over-
reached their evidence and that their state programs trampled fundamental liberties. From the outset, Catholics protested eugenical
sterilization and marriage restriction laws as unconscionable state en-
croachments on the sacred terrain of reproduction. As early as 1905,
the Governor of Pennsylvania voiced widely shared humanistic doubts
about eugenics as he vetoed a sterilization bill: "Men of high scientific attainments are prone, in their love for technique, to lose sight of
broad principles outside of their domain of thought." And the strong
flavor of class legislation and arbitrary justice in eugenic statutes made
them sitting ducks for judicial review. During the World War I years,
state appellate courts scrapped half a dozen sterilization measures,
finding in them violations of the due process and equal protection
clauses of the state or federal constitutions. It is fitting that one of
the most acidic contemporary critiques of eugenics dripped from the
pen of Clarence Darrow, the fabled Chicago criminal defender and
counsel for John T. Scopes. Darrow himself often spoke of abnormal heredity and poverty in the same breath as the principal causes
of crime. But the class bias and authoritarian implications of eugenics disgusted him. "Amongst the schemes for remolding society," he
wrote in 1926, "this is the most senseless and impudent that has ever

---

[52] Curtis, "Eugenic Reformers," 160–61; Singer, "Deranged or Defective Delinquent," 802.

been put forward by irresponsible fanatics to plague a long-suffering race."[53]

In the mid-1920s, many American social workers, social scientists, and women reformers joined the rising tide of opposition to eugenics and began to distance themselves from hereditarianism. Major foundations, aware of geneticists' sharpening skepticism about eugenics, began to reject grant applications from eugenics organizations, deeming their work too unscientific or zealous. In academic social science, the anthropological concept of "culture," pioneered by Franz Boas, began to overtake evolution and heredity as the chief explanation of human behavior and social structure. In psychiatry, psychology, and social work, professionals increasingly spoke the therapeutic language of "adjustment" and "normal" living. The new idiom preserved the optimistic tenor of environmentalism while diverting attention from the socioeconomic root causes that had engaged progressive reformers; transforming the social environments that produced criminality, deviancy, and dependency now seemed less important than adjusting the individual deviant's "personality." New institutional practices accompanied this shift in discourse, as psychiatrists promoted outpatient services for the mentally ill and superintendents of institutions for the feebleminded redefined sterilization as a precondition for parole – not lifelong commitment. All of these changes were gradual and incomplete. But they spelled trouble for advocates of eugenic jurisprudence, making their demands for wider jurisdiction and increased state intervention more difficult to justify to politicians and the public.[54]

The significance of these changes for socialized criminal justice is evident in the increasingly critical stance taken by the JPA toward the Municipal Court of Chicago's eugenic jurisprudence. Convinced by William Healy's work in the Juvenile Court clinic and at the Judge Baker Foundation in Boston, the JPA embraced therapeutic psychiatry, an orientation better suited than eugenics to the group's hopes for reforming young lawbreakers. Rather than openly attack Judge Olson, JPA members tactfully urged their old ally to remain at the cutting edge of scientific jurisprudence by embracing the new theory of adjustment.

---

[53] Pennsylvania governor in Critchlow, "Keeping the Life Stream Pure," 348, 346; Clarence Darrow, "The Eugenics Cult," *American Mercury*, June 1926, p. 137.

[54] Critchlow, "Keeping the Life Stream Pure," 346; Degler, *In Search of Human Nature*, 59–211; Regina Kunzel, *Fallen Women, Problem Girls: Unmarried Mothers and the Professionalization of Social Work, 1890–1945* (New Haven, 1993), 44; Trent, *Inventing the Feeble Mind*, 198–206.

Ethel Sturges Dummer attempted to reeducate Olson in an illuminating series of letters. "Years ago you and Dr. Hickson took a long stride ahead in recognizing the need of psychiatry in the courts," she wrote in 1923. She noted the success of therapeutic methods in reformatories for delinquent girls. "Now, women who are not even psychologists are making cures which even the wisest of us have not solved, yet which we must accept. At least they are teaching us new possibilities . . . in the improvability of human beings." The diplomatic tone of Dummer's correspondence changed abruptly after she visited the Psychopathic Laboratory later that year. "I was considerably alarmed and surprised to find that Dr. Hickson not only gave no hope of improvement or correction after having come to an unfavorable decision in cases which reached his laboratory, but I found myself entirely out of sympathy with his open statement of this belief in the presence of patients." During this same period, Dr. Hickson adopted a more openly hostile stance toward environmentalism in his reports. "The environmentalists," he charged, "are to criminology what the anti-evolutionists are to science in general . . . pseudo-scientific meddlers, whose thinking is dominated by their feelings, wishes and prejudices."[55]

Dummer's criticisms, a dramatic departure from Louise Bowen's praise for the laboratory a decade earlier, were representative of the JPA membership and environmentalist social reformers generally in the 1920s. In 1925, the JPA and other advocates of socialized justice organized a conference to commemorate the twenty-fifth anniversary of the Cook County Juvenile Court and the fifteenth anniversary of its Psychopathic Institute. A showcase for the new environmentalism of therapeutic psychiatry, the conference made no mention of the JPA's former enthusiasm for eugenics. Dr. Healy, now residing at the Judge Baker Foundation, lectured on his dynamic psychiatry and therapeutic approach. Sessions emphasized the new work on "behavior adjustments" and the "preventive work" being conducted in the new child guidance clinics attached to public schools. Planning the event, Dummer had tentatively placed Olson on the program. The opposition was anything but tentative. Grace Abbott, the Hull-House veteran and chief of the federal Children's Bureau, told Dummer that "this would never do, that he was too unscientific." In more politic terms, Julia Lathrop agreed, but she proposed an interesting compromise. "The program might be so arranged that the contrast between what has been done under his supervision and that which seems scientifically sound to men

[55] Dummer to Olson, Dec. 11, 1923, Dummer Papers, folder 694; Dummer to Olson, Dec. 18, 1923, ibid., folder 694; Hickson, "Socio-Economics of Crime," 178.

in whom you have greater confidence could be set forth in a manner convincing to reasonable minds without too much offense." Like the delinquents themselves, Olson might prove capable of adjustment.[56] The reeducation plan failed. Olson remained an unregenerated exponent of eugenic jurisprudence. He trumpeted the cause of eugenical sterilization in speeches to state teachers' associations and Daughters of the American Republic chapters, businessmen's clubs, and law enforcement associations. As Justice Holmes's decision in *Buck v. Bell* suggests, the figure of the criminal mental defective still had plenty of life in American legal culture in the late 1920s. Laughlin's report, which included a model law for the sterilization of any individual who was a *potential* parent of an unfit offspring, aided the passage of new statutes in several states. The Municipal Court received hundreds of requests for the report from university libraries, law professors, sociologists, political scientists, zoologists, attorneys, judges, congressmen, school teachers, sanitarium superintendents, foundations, ministers, and, of course, committed eugenicists in the United States and Europe. Princeton biologist E. G. Conklin praised the volume in a letter to Olson, saying, "I am confident that it will be of the very greatest service in promoting eugenical education and practice in the United States." The cause proved unsuccessful in Olson's own state, however. Attempts to pass an Illinois sterilization law in 1925, 1927, 1929, and 1933 encountered overwhelming opposition from religious groups and the professional bar.[57]

A final demonstration of Olson's intransigence was his proposal for the creation of two "crime prevention bureaus" in Chicago, deputizing the local and state officials to police mental defectives. One

[56] Dummer to Julia Lathrop, Dec. 7, 1924, Dummer Papers, folder 636; Lathrop to Dummer, Dec. 13, 1924, ibid., folder 636. See *The Child, the Clinic and the Court* (New York, 1925).

[57] Olson to Dummer, Dec. 31, 1923; Olson to Dummer, Jan. 7, 1924; Dummer Papers, folder 694; Conklin to Olson, Jan. 27, 1923, JHO, box 8; *MCC 23 (1929)*, 14. See H.B. 231 (1925), *Journal of the House of Representatives of the General Assembly of the State of Illinois*, vol. 54 (Springfield, 1925), 115; H.B. 69 (1929), ibid., vol. 56, p. 141; H.B. 251 (1929), ibid., vol. 56, p. 208; H.B. 768 (1933), ibid., vol. 58, p. 738. In 1927, the Illinois Senate passed a sterilization bill, which was tabled in the House; S.B. 403 (1927), *Journal of the Senate of the General Assembly of the State of Illinois*, vol. 55 (Springfield, 1927), 845; Joan Gittens, *Poor Relations: The Children of the State in Illinois, 1818–1990* (Urbana, 1994), 189; Jeffrey P. Moran, "Modernism Gone Mad": Sex Education Comes to Chicago, 1913," *JAH*, 83 (1996), 502–6. Correspondence concerning Olson's speaking engagements can be found in MCC, folders 37–42; JHO, boxes 3, 4, and 6–8.

bureau, to be housed within the Department of Health, would treat
mental defect as a public health threat. "Give them the same right
summarily to pick up the insane, dementia praecox, paranoic, manic-
depressive and paretic as they now have to lay hands on the typhoid
carrier, smallpox sufferer, the syphilitic and other contagious cases,"
Olson urged in a court report. A second bureau in the Police Department would compile secret lists of local defectives, aided by the sharp
eyes of well-educated citizens, including teachers, physicians, police,
lawyers, and the courts. "Unless we invoke these methods the criminal conditions will grow and the mongrelization of our people will
progress."[58]

Olson presented his bureau scheme at a 1924 luncheon hosted by
the Chicago Crime Commission, but it was met with polite disinter-
est. A powerful coalition of businessmen, editors, and attorneys, the
commission represented a hard-line style of criminal justice reform
that was becoming increasingly dominant in America during the new
era of Prohibition and organized crime. The Crime Commission's deterrence perspective was closer to the classical criminologists of the
nineteenth century than to either the eugenicists or the environmentalists of their own day. Deterrence advocates rejected theories of crime
that emphasized sociological or psychological factors and thereby reduced an offender's responsibility. Never openly critical of Olson, who
shared their passion for efficient administration, the commissioners
declined to support Olson's eugenic jurisprudence at a time when it
badly need a political boost.[59]

In the late 1920s, Harry Olson began to lose authority over the
Municipal Court's system of eugenic jurisprudence. In 1925, the corporation counsel of Chicago rendered an opinion that shifted the
Psychopathic Laboratory to the Department of Public Health, depriving the chief justice of the power to designate the laboratory's director.
The opinion does not appear to have been an attack on eugenic jurisprudence; it was justified as a means of putting the laboratory on a
surer fiscal footing, and the health commissioner let Hickson stay on
as director until he resigned in 1929. Only then did the real consequences of the opinion for the Municipal Court's eugenics program
emerge. When the health commissioner searched for someone to replace Hickson, eugenicist psychiatrists were an increasingly rare and

[58] *MCC 19–22* (1925–28), 17–18.
[59] "In Crime Conference," *Bulletin of the Chicago Crime Commission*, Dec. 10,
     1924, pp. 1–20; Edwin W. Sims, "On Crime Conditions in Chicago," *JAICLC*,
     13 (1922), 105. See Walker, *Popular Justice*, 161–93.

disreputable species – by then even Henry Goddard had muffled his hereditarian rhetoric. The commissioner appointed Meyer Solomon, a Chicago doctor whose perspective on the relationship of crime to mental health was in tune with the psychiatry of adjustment.[60]

That same year, Olson released his final annual report. Solomon's contribution on the Psychopathic Laboratory mentioned heredity once – in passing. Solomon wrote compassionately of the "behavior problems" of his wards, their "chronic" addictions and "disorders of personality." "The object of the laboratory is to examine not merely committable mentally disordered and mentally retarded persons," he stressed, "but this other far larger group of cases." Like Hickson before him, Solomon included a few "illustrative cases." One man, whose wife had deserted him, developed "nervous and mental strain," took to moderate drinking, and forged a few checks; Solomon secured a probation order and sent him to a convalescent home "for a sufficient period of mental rest." The laboratory's procedure was still invasive: The staff compiled personal histories, interviewed family members, and charted the individual's habits and education, "his personal mental struggles and disappointments, his ideals and attitudes in life." Solomon left no mystery as to what became of the people he examined: After one year, 43 percent of them had been committed. A "therapeutic" approach to criminality had arrived in the Municipal Court.[61]

Chief Justice Olson buried Solomon's entry at the back of the annual report, loading the report's introduction with eugenics information and bookending Solomon's account with an essay on "Mental Defectives and the Criminal Law." Near the front of the report, Olson printed a full-page photograph of an Austrian statue of Mendel, proposing that one like it be built in Chicago. "The Municipal Court Laboratory has heretofore stressed the importance of heredity as a cause of crime and of much human misery and sorrow," Olson wrote. "Perhaps nowhere has the operation in the human of Mendel's law been demonstrated as it has been demonstrated in this laboratory." Eugenics would continue to spread in other American locales after 1929, and in Nazi Germany

---

[60] City of Chicago, Department of Public Health, *Report of the Department of Health of the City of Chicago for the Years 1926 to 1930 Inclusive* (Chicago, 1931), 345–57; Scheffler, "History of the Psychiatric Institute," 9–10; *MCC 23 (1929)*, 13. See Trent, *Inventing the Feeble Mind*, 166.

[61] Meyer Solomon, "Municipal Psychopathic Laboratory," in *MCC 23 (1929)*, 98, 96. See Andrew J. Polsky, *The Rise of the Therapeutic State* (Princeton, 1991).

the technology would soon be put to its most horrific test. But in Chicago, the era of eugenic jurisprudence had come to an end.[62]

In 1944, the Juvenile Protective Association hosted a fund-raising gala to celebrate the thirtieth anniversary of the Psychiatric Institute of the Municipal Court of Chicago. The laboratory's name had been changed in 1932, the commemorative literature gently noted, to alleviate the stigma attached to being examined there. The institute now aimed to "promote normal thought and action." Especially for the event, the court published a retrospective volume, entitled *A Dynamic Era of Court Psychiatry*. The authors took a harsh view of eugenic jurisprudence and suggested that a long battle with primitive ideas had been won when a therapeutic approach superseded eugenics. One contributor to the volume, a social worker, had dug up an annual report from the Olson era, which she described as "almost a violent reminder of the distance that has been traversed in the field of psychiatry since the early days." Briefly abandoning her Whiggish tone, the social worker made a candid observation about the relationship between environmentalists and the laboratory: "It was not necessary for the developing social work profession to agree with the Psychopathic Laboratory in its early years to recognize the great value of the establishment."[63]

Environmentalists and eugenicists had not been locked in a fierce battle for institutional hegemony in America's model socialized court; far from it. They had enjoyed a productive coexistence, as together they transformed the way criminal justice was done in America's second largest city. On the surface, environmentalism and eugenics seem irreconcilable. One located the roots of crime in the troubled social relations and urban culture of industrializing America, the other in biologically determined mental defect. But as idioms of reform and technologies of governance, both eugenics and environmentalism gave reformers the means to socialize the Chicago courts. The creation of socialized courts – state institutions that would police the intimate detail of everyday life – required political justification. So did the new powers of judges and the presence of psychiatrists, psychologists, and social workers in the courts. Eugenics and environmentalism provided convincing scientific rhetorics to support these developments. For eugenicists and environmentalists, as the alliance between Olson and the JPA clearly shows, a common commitment to socialized justice

---

[62] *MCC 23 (1929)*, 3; Dwight G. McCarty, "Mental Defectives and the Criminal Law," in ibid., 106–16; Curtis, "Eugenics Reformers," 129.

[63] Scheffler, "History of the Psychiatric Institute," 10; Sarah Schaar, "The Institute as I Know It," in Sharp, ed., *Dynamic Era*, 13, 15.

temporarily outweighed the fundamental differences in their conceptions of human nature.

By attempting to work out complex social problems through human individuals, both environmentalism and eugenics – indeed, the entire project of socialized criminal justice – circumscribed offenders' procedural rights and subjected the everyday lives of urban working-class populations to new levels of governmental intervention. This is the shared legacy of environmentalism and eugenics. But the ideological differences between eugenic jurisprudence and environmentalism were not empty formalisms. They had real consequences for the people policed in socialized courts. Eugenic jurisprudence and its techniques of institutional commitment and sterilization posed a much greater threat to defendants' civil liberties and life chances than environmentalist programs such as probation. Due process acquired a new shade of gray when judges heeded the eugenicist's motto: "keep the life stream pure."

Part III

Misgivings

9

America's First War on Crime

When there is a weed in your garden, and you cut it down, you
do not do this on any theory of the moral blame of the weed, but
simply on the theory that you are entitled to keep weeds out of your
garden.

— John Henry Wigmore, 1924

During the early 1920s, the tide of American progressivism, having
reached its highest level during the national mobilization for the Great
War, went slack and began to recede. The retreating tide did not carry
all away with it. Institutions, laws, professions, personal commitments,
public investments, scientific discoveries, distinctive ways of perceiv-
ing and representing everyday social life – the achievements of the diverse people who had called themselves and their times "progressive"
stubbornly persisted or only gradually drained away, like so many tide
pools awaiting the next surge of salt water. In those realms of public life
where the forces of historical change encounter the greatest inertia –
the law and governing institutions – progressive practices held on the
longest. But no longer embraced in a swelling sea of sentiment and
reform, much that was once novel and innovative gradually came to
be routine and entrenched. Thus was the fate of the progressive
regime of socialized urban judicial administration at the close of the
decade.[1]

For all of its Jazz Age improvisation, its cultural modernism, its sexual permissiveness, and its Prohibition lawlessness, the prosperous

---

[1] On the dynamic of change and persistence in American public life, see
Barry D. Karl, *The Uneasy State: The United States from 1915 to 1945* (Chicago,
1983); Morton Keller, *Regulating a New Society: Public Policy and Social Change
in America, 1900–1930* (Cambridge, Mass., 1994).

decade between the Great War and the Great Depression ushered in a conservative cultural reaction that challenged core tenets of American progressive ideology: the will to apply scientific knowledge and technique to social problems, the affinity for bureaucracy and administrative governance, the rejection of laissez-faire individualism, and the broad commitment to achieving greater social justice and control in an urban-industrial democracy through organized public and private action. In an era of heightened public fears of urban crime – fears grounded in an actual spike in reported crime in Chicago and other cities – the concepts of social responsibility for crime, socialized law, and individual treatment of criminals were particularly vulnerable to criticism.[2]

"Swift, implacable justice is the only remedy that will cure Chicago of its malady of crime," the Republican prosecutor Robert E. Crowe declared during his victorious 1920 campaign for State's Attorney of Cook County. Appropriating the progressive rhetoric of social diagnosis and treatment, Crowe turned it into a prescription for terror and deterrence. By the mid-1920s a new, self-consciously masculine type of urban businessman-activist – armed with slogans such as "swift and certain punishment," "deterrence," and "social defense" – had seized the initiative in criminal justice reform. Through well-financed organizations, such as the nationally renowned Chicago Crime Commission, the new citizen crime fighters worked with high-profile county prosecutors and a sympathetic mainstream press to restore the public values of individual moral responsibility and strict law enforcement. Unlike the social activists who had led urban criminal justice reform during the previous two decades, the big city crime-control activists were chiefly interested in felony crimes, the sort of serious offenses against property and persons that disrupted business, raised insurance rates, frightened customers, and tarnished the reputations of cities. Meanwhile in the state houses, politicians responded to the rising rage for crime control by imposing new restrictions on the indeterminate sentence, parole, and probation. By the end of the decade many states had enacted "habitual offender laws," mandating extended sentences for repeat offenders. "The new trends in criminology as interpreted by the state legislatures," one Chicago Crime Commission member observed in the *American Bar Association Journal* in 1927, "are clearly directed towards protection of society through more severe treatment of criminals, especially second termers, in contrast to the reforms of the past decades through which it was hoped to protect

---

[2] See John C. Burnham, *Bad Habits: Drinking, Smoking, Taking Drugs, Gambling, Sexual Misbehavior, and Swearing in American History* (New York, 1993).

society by the radical method of making criminals over into good citizens."[3]

The new rage for crime control, which dominated the politics of criminal justice in America from the mid-1920s through the 1930s, discouraged whatever "radical" ambitions social activists, women's organizations, and judges might have had to further expand the role of criminal courts as interventionist instruments of social governance in American cities. As the histories of the Municipal Court of Chicago's specialized criminal branches show, the changing public mood registered even in those local institutions where the practice of socialized criminal justice enjoyed its strongest support and achieved its fullest realization. In the Court of Domestic Relations, the commitment to enforcing male responsibility and serving the multifaceted social interest in the family remained strong. But in the Morals Court, the will to address the spectrum of prostitution's root causes – from the wages system to the market in working-class leisure – faded, as judges and court personnel came to see the coercive policy of venereal disease treatment as the one thing the court did undeniably well. The Boys' Court's commitment to individual treatment for juvenile adults weathered growing public criticism from the Crime Commission, which demanded that car thieves, young and old alike, bear the full brunt of the law. Even the Municipal Court's eugenic jurisprudence was visibly losing public support by 1925. Once-supportive social activists turned against eugenics, and the new crime-control advocates had little use for any determinist theory, hereditarian or environmentalist, that diminished individual responsibility and thereby distracted the public from the manly business of punishing crime. The Boys' Court and the Psychopathic Laboratory would continue to push the envelope of socialized law by trying to reach two kinds of defendants that had never been easily assimilated within the cultural category of the socially caused lawbreaker: young men and felony offenders. But the cultural atmosphere of the 1920s, which ushered in America's "first great war on crime," guaranteed that the jurisdiction of socialized

---

[3] Crowe quoted in Hal Higdon, *Leopold and Loeb: The Crime of the Century* (Urbana, 1999), 64; Joseph P. Chamberlin, "Punishment of Criminals," *ABAJ*, 13 (1927), 12; "For an Habitual Criminal Act," *Chicago Tribune*, Oct. 23, 1927; Joseph P. Murphy, "The Crime Wave and Probation," *CCR*, 6 (May 1922), 141–45. See Mark Haller, "Urban Crime and Criminal Justice: The Chicago Case," *JAH*, 57 (1970), 619–35; David E. Ruth, *Inventing the Public Enemy: The Gangster in American Culture, 1918–1934* (Chicago, 1996); Samuel Walker, *Popular Justice: A History of American Criminal Justice* (New York, 1980), 161–93.

judicial administration would not be further enlarged to include sane adults charged with the most serious crimes against persons and property.[4]

The cultural reaction against social responsibility, scientific determinism, and individual treatment of offenders coincided with a partial return to classical principles in American law. In the eyes of many old progressives and an emerging group of younger "realist" scholars, the Supreme Court under the conservative Republican Chief Justice William Howard Taft (1921–30) was fast returning to the old mechanical jurisprudence and reviving the formalistic doctrinal commitments to dual federalism, separation of powers, and liberty of contract that had brought the courts so much public criticism at the turn of the century. As early as 1921, Roscoe Pound had lamented this trend. That summer, the formidable dean of Harvard Law School delivered a series of lectures at Dartmouth College on "The Spirit of the Common Law." In his preface to the published lectures, Pound observed that a profound shift of sensibility and commitment had overtaken American legal thought since the war's end. In the early 1910s, when he had penned his prescriptive essays on the organization of courts and the socialization of law in the modern city, legal reformers had possessed a "faith in the efficacy of effort and [a] belief that the administration of justice may be improved by conscious intelligent action." Wistfully, Pound recalled the "decades of faith in progress" that had produced "the Municipal Court of Chicago and the modern city courts which have arisen in its image." But 1919 had brought a "recrudescence of juristic pessimism" and a withdrawal to narrow classical notions of law's social function. Once again, Pound sounded his old warning. If the common law continued its retreat – if the law failed to meet the needs of "the heterogeneous, urban, industrial America of today" – the march of administration would proceed without it. Tomorrow would belong to an administrative leviathan, "with loosely defined powers, unlimited discretion and inadequate judicial restraints."[5]

Pound's obituary for legal progressivism was premature. The dean himself would recoup some of his earlier optimism and continue for much of the decade to champion many of his old causes: the incorporation of the social sciences into law school teaching and scholarship

---

[4] Thomas A. Green, "Freedom and Criminal Responsibility in the Age of Pound: An Essay on Criminal Justice," *MLR*, 93 (1995), 2011–43, esp. 2011; Charles R. Holden, "Crime Roots Go Deep," *Bulletin of the Chicago Crime Commission*, Jan. 22, 1925, pp. 1–6.

[5] Roscoe Pound, *The Spirit of the Common Law* (Boston, 1921), xi–xiii.

(a cause that realist scholars at Yale and other elite law schools took up as their own); the administrative centralization and procedural reform of the local, state, and federal judiciaries; and the articulation of a set of principles of administrative law that could allow for the controlled growth of the administrative process. Pound saw the growth of the administrative state as inevitable. But he advocated measures to tether the discretion of agencies in procedural restraints, modeled on the common law, and to subject the actions of administrative officers to greater judicial review.[6]

For one cause in particular – the organization of courts – the 1920s were years of expansion. Building on the momentum of the municipal court movement, the American Judicature Society, with Harry Olson presiding as chairman of the board, worked to extend court consolidation and procedural reform to the state and federal levels. It is not surprising that progress continued in these areas. Those causes had always appealed not only to social activists concerned about the legal access of the poor but also to businessmen and elite lawyers, who might favor some moderate social reforms (if only as a means of quieting social unrest) but who had a clear economic interest in making the administration of justice more efficient, uniform, and predictable.[7]

Drawing upon the Municipal Court of Chicago as a model of top-down administration, many states during the 1910s and 1920s established "judicial councils." The councils imposed an unprecedented level of centralized coordination on state court systems by the innovation of collecting judicial statistics and assigning judges where they were most needed. Beginning in 1914, former president Taft led the charge for managerial reform of the federal courts – a cause he touted as "vindicated by the example of the Municipal Court of Chicago." For the next eight years, Congress resisted Taft's calls for a centrally coordinated federal judiciary by invoking the resilient political values of localism and judicial independence. By 1922, however, the federal trial courts were awash in Prohibition criminal cases and a surge of civil cases arising from wartime contracts. The mounting backlog created new interest in Taft's old cause. (Taft himself had recently taken

---

[6] Morton J. Horwitz, *The Transformation of American Law, 1870–1960: The Crisis of Legal Orthodoxy* (New York, 1992), 219; N. E. H. Hull, *Roscoe Pound and Karl Llewellyn, Searching for an American Jurisprudence* (Chicago, 1997), 126; John Henry Schlegel, *American Legal Realism and Empirical Social Science* (Chapel Hill, 1995), 82–98; 147–210.

[7] Michael R. Belknap, *To Improve the Administration of Justice: A History of the American Judicature Society* (Chicago, 1992); Eric H. Steele, "The Historical Context of Small Claims Courts," *ABFRJ*, 1981 (1981), 293–376.

over as chief justice of the Supreme Court and he continued to press
Congress with proposals for court reform.) In 1922, Congress gave
the chief justice authority to assign district judges as needed to any
district court in the nation. The same statute took the judicial council
scheme to the federal level, creating an annual Judicial Conference of
Senior Circuit Court Judges, which over the next few years would begin
to collect judicial statistics, craft new rules of federal procedure, and
cooperate with bar associations and the law school professoriate to improve the federal administration of justice. The impress of the Chicago
model on all of this was impossible to miss. As Felix Frankfurter and
James M. Landis noted with approval in their aptly titled 1927 study,
The Business of the Supreme Court, the managerial revolution in judicial administration begun in urban America at the century's turn had
finally percolated up to the national level. "The reorganization of the
local courts of Chicago into a unified municipal court was a concrete
demonstration of the part to be played by organization and administration in securing competence, dispatch and economy from courts,"
wrote these future champions of the New Deal administrative state.
"The success of this Chicago experiment gave the impetus of concrete
achievement to the new movement."[8]

The political support for administrative reform did not extend to
the social side of legal progressivism, however, and socialized justice
barely survived the reaction of the 1920s. As the crime-control activists
were quick to point out, the ethos of social responsibility had become
deeply rooted in the institutions of criminal justice, the professional
discourses of the social and behavioral sciences, the agendas of urban
religious and social agencies, the professional training of social workers, and popular cultural discourse on crime. But in the new era of
Prohibition, organized crime, and urban "crime waves," the old faith
in the ameliorative social power of an interventionist city judiciary withered. Nowhere was the ascendance of a crime control mentality more
visible than in America's Second City, where the progressive revolution
in judicial administration had opened just a few decades earlier.

America's war on crime began soon after its "war to make the world
safe for democracy" ended in Europe. With the signing of the Treaty

---

[8] Taft in Felix Frankfurter and James M. Landis, *The Business of the Supreme
Court: A Study in the Federal Judicial System* (New York, 1927), 229, 217–54,
esp. 226. See David S. Clark, "Adjudication to Administration: A Statistical Analysis of Federal District Courts in the Twentieth Century," *SCLR,* 55
(1981), 105–17; James Willard Hurst, *The Growth of American Law: The Law
Makers* (Boston, 1950), 113–14.

of Versailles, a storm cloud of violence and social disorder seemed to descend on the western world. In the United States, violent crime and public disorder exploded. Lynching escalated in the South, while race riots rocked northern cities in the "long hot summer" of 1919. The Chicago riot was the nation's most violent. Thirty-eight people died. More than 500 suffered injuries. In September, the nation's eyes turned to Boston, where 1,100 of the city's 1,500 police officers went on strike for better wages and the right to unionize. The thinning of Boston's blue line precipitated widespread vandalism, looting, and, in the headlines if not on the streets, a state of "anarchy." The same year witnessed the beginning of the Red Scare, which would culminate in January 1920 with the notorious Palmer Raids and the arrests of more than 5,000 alleged radicals and aliens in thirty-three cities across the nation. The Municipal Court of Chicago's caseload registered the postwar boom in violence and disorder. Although the total criminal caseload dipped slightly in 1919, the court conducted more preliminary hearings for felonies than ever before. Compared with 1918, murder cases rose by 71 percent (from 79 to 135); robberies by 56 percent (from 1,230 to 1,917); burglaries by 53 percent (from 1,129 to 1,728); assault to kill cases by 43 percent (from 234 to 334); and rape cases by 56 percent (from 138 to 216).[9]

Many factors contributed to the surge of serious crime in Chicago and other cities, including rising unemployment and skyrocketing inflation, the competition for jobs engendered by the wartime migration of African-American workers from the south into the industrial cities of the north, and the sudden return of hundreds of thousands of young men into the domestic population. Observers also blamed the spike in crime on the social-psychological environment created by the war. "Science and wealth and energy were everywhere called into the service of taking life and destroying property," Clarence Darrow recalled. "When day after day the world read of the deliberate slaying of one thousand, ten thousand, or twenty thousand men or more, killing soon became one of the commonplace events in every-day life." The *Chicago Defender*, its pages filled with grim reports of the heightened violence against African-Americans, arrived at the same conclusion. "Chicago, like other large cities, is having a reign of terror," the paper reported two months before the race riot. "This is a legacy of the

[9] *MCC 12–14* (1918–20), 56; "Riot Sweeps Chicago," *Chicago Defender*, Aug. 2, 1919; William M. Tuttle, Jr., *Race Riot: Chicago in the Red Summer of 1919* (New York, 1970), esp. 3–31; Richard Polenberg, *Fighting Faiths: The Abrams Case, the Supreme Court, and Free Speech* (New York, 1987); Walker, *Popular Justice*, 162–69.

late war, a legacy that borders on anarchism." The riots, too, were related, in a complicated way, to the war. In addition to the heightened competition between blacks and whites in Chicago for housing and work, the experience of military service in the name of freedom and democracy had fostered a strong rights consciousness among black veterans. "A Race that has furnished hundreds of thousands of the best soldiers that the world has ever seen is no longer content to turn the left cheek when smitten upon the right," the *Defender* proclaimed.[10]

Public fears that a crime wave had overtaken the nation's cities did not soon abate. When the Volstead Act went into effect in January 1920, those fears had a deadly new source. Prohibition gave birth to a new era of organized crime. In Chicago, ethnic entrepreneurs such as Johnny Torrio and Alphonse Capone rationalized the illicit manufacture, distribution, and sale of liquor into a big business. Widespread allegations that the second mayoral administration of William "Big Bill" Thompson (1919–23) eagerly abetted the bootleggers are supported by the records of the Municipal Court. Thompson's successor Mayor William Dever (1923–27) campaigned on a promise to clean up Chicago by enforcing the letter of the law, and he ordered his chief of police, Morgan A. Collins, to do so. During Dever's first year in office, state prohibition cases nearly doubled in the Municipal Court. When Thompson returned to power in 1927, they quickly plummeted again.[11]

Public fears centered less on actual violations of Prohibition – a law hated by ethnic workers and openly flaunted by the urban middle class – than on the rash of collateral crimes against property and persons associated with organized bootlegging. "Gangland" violence, though overdramatized in the media, was undeniably real. The Dever

---

[10] Clarence Darrow, *The Story of My Life* (New York, 1932), 334–35; "The Crime Wave," *Chicago Defender*, May 31, 1919; "Reaping the Whirlwind," Aug. 2, 1919.

[11] Prohibition violations disposed of in the Municipal Court rose from 3,646 in 1922 to 6,479 in 1923. In 1924, Dever's first full year in office, the court heard 8,837 prohibition cases. In 1928, Thompson's first full year back in office, prohibition cases dropped to 924. *MCC 24–25* (1930–31), 31. See Douglas Bukowski, "Big Bill Thompson: The 'Model' Politician," in *The Mayors: The Chicago Political Tradition*, ed. Paul M. Green and Melvin G. Holli, rev. ed. (Carbondale, 1995), 61–81; John Landesco, "Organized Crime in Chicago," in Illinois Association for Criminal Justice, *The Illinois Crime Survey* (Chicago, 1929), 815–1100; John R. Schmidt, *"The Mayor Who Cleaned Up Chicago": A Political Biography of William E. Dever* (DeKalb, 1989); Walker, *Popular Justice*, 180–82.

administration's crackdown tightened competition in the illicit liquor business, precipitating one of the bloodiest sprees in the city's history. Frederic Thrasher toted up the body count: "Between November, 1924, when Dion O'Banion was murdered in his florist's shop, and October 11, 1926, when Earl ('Hymie') Weiss was assassinated, more than one hundred and fifteen men had fallen in Chicago's gang wars." In the era's most famous episode, on Valentine's Day of 1929, gangsters hired by "Machine Gun" Jack McGurn, sporting police uniforms and badges, shot down seven members of George "Bugs" Moran's gang in a North Clark Street garage.[12]

Urban newspapers fanned the public fears and fascination with the gangster, while the burgeoning film industry appropriated the cultural figure of "the public enemy" from urban criminal justice reform. According to contemporary lore, the phrase was coined by Municipal Court Judge John H. Lyle, a publicity-grabbing Republican crime fighter who served on the Municipal Court's new Felony Branch. Olson created the branch in 1929 to conduct preliminary hearings in all felony cases originating in Chicago (not including cases from South Chicago and those involving boys under twenty-one). Filmmakers used the public enemy to address contemporary anxieties about the power of big business, the morality of mass consumption, the assimilation of immigrants, and the breakdown of traditional gender relations. In this sense, the conceptual capaciousness of Progressive Era crime talk survived. But the use of urban crime as a political proxy, rather than simply a cultural marker or signifier, for social problems like poverty and neglect, had lost much of its public salience.[13]

Everywhere in urban America during the 1920s were signs that a defensive crime wave mentality had taken hold. The Illinois Bankers' Association, hoping to check rising insurance premiums, offered a $2,500 reward to anyone who lawfully killed a "bandit" in the act of robbing a bank. The armored truck became a symbol of the new era. Banks and corporations used them for payroll deliveries. Armored U.S. Postal Service trucks wended their way through the streets of Chicago, bristling with riot guns. Gangland slayings and bootlegging rackets replaced the war as the obsession of banner headlines in the urban

---

[12] Frederic M. Thrasher, *The Gang: A Study of 1,313 Gangs in Chicago* (Chicago, 1927), 429.
[13] "A Record of Action," *Criminal Justice*, Dec. 1930, p. 2; John M. Allswang, *A House for All Peoples: Ethnic Politics in Chicago, 1890–1936* (Lexington, Ky., 1971), 171; Laurence Bergreen, *Capone: The Man and the Era* (New York, 1994), 304–14; *MCC 23 (1929)*, 12–13.

dailies. By mid-decade, Chicago had sealed its reputation as the world's "murder capital" – a reputation many local newspaper editors aimed to cultivate rather than contest. Veteran reporters for mass-market metropolitan newspapers, such as the *Chicago Daily News*'s Ben Hecht, the man who turned Chicago's Al Capone into Hollywood's *Scarface*, parlayed their urban knowledge and rat-a-tat-tat prose into lucrative careers as screenwriters for the gangster pictures. A few calmer souls tried without much success to deflate Chicago's reputation. "The so-called 'crime wave' is a state of mind," Thrasher wrote in 1927. "Crime is an ever-present reality. It is the attention and the interest of the public which moves in waves."[14]

There is solid evidence, however, that this ever-present reality became ever more present in Chicago. The agents of law and order, however compromised by official collusion with the bootleggers, were busier than ever. The criminal business of the Municipal Court outstripped population growth during the 1920s. Bootleggers and bank robbers, though, had relatively little to do with it. The vast majority of people arrested in the city were, as always, unorganized lawbreakers, ordinary people charged with the ordinary run of everyday crimes: misdemeanors and quasicrimes ranging from disorderly conduct (more than 100,000 cases in 1925 alone) to pickpocketing and other forms of petty larceny. The real growth area in everyday law-breaking was a distinctly middle-class phenomenon associated with the rapid spread of the automobile in an age of prosperity. Speeding and other quasi-criminal traffic infractions grew from 15,576 cases in 1921 to 89,524 cases in 1926, while misdemeanor automobile cases rose from 17,536 to 40,499 cases. (See Fig. 4.)[15]

Despite these statistical trends, the leading edge of criminal justice reform in the '20s belonged to organizations that concerned themselves almost exclusively with the policing, prosecution, and punishment of felonies. The Chicago Crime Commission represented the new era. Organized by the Chicago Association of Commerce in 1919, following the city's first daytime payroll heist, the commission was a businessmen's organization in the narrowest sense. The first commission of its kind, it served as the model for the similar organizations that appeared in many major cities during the '20s. From the start, the Crime Commission distanced itself from the social reform initiatives of the Progressive Era. "It is not a reform organization," the commission's

---

[14] Thrasher, *The Gang*, 414–51, esp. 448; Ruth, *Inventing the Public Enemy*, 6.
[15] *MCC* 24–25 (1930–31), 31–32; Lawrence M. Friedman, *Crime and Punishment in American History* (New York, 1993), 277–80; Hurst, *Growth of American Law*, 163–68.

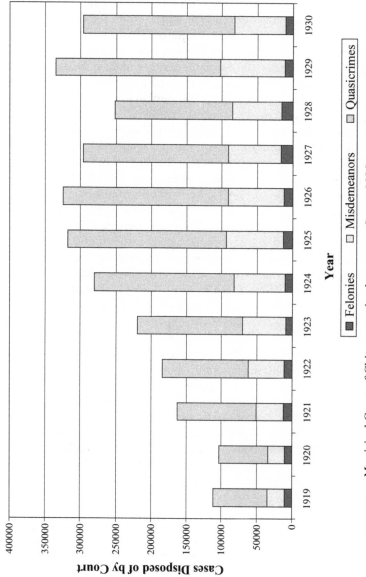

FIGURE 4. Municipal Court of Chicago caseload, 1919–30. *Source: MCC* 24–25 (1930–31), 35.

bulletin proclaimed in 1919. "It is not a debating society. It is a business proposition."[16]

The commission's leaders deliberately represented that proposition in gendered terms. The rhetoric of business that saturated public discourse in an era that offered little opportunity for women in management was itself a masculine language. The Crime Commissioners distinguished their manly professionalism, discipline, and tough-minded realism from the womanly sentimentalism of organizations such as the JPA. "The mawkish sympathy of good, but softheaded women with the most degraded and persistent criminals of the male sex is one of the signs of unhealthy public sentiment," the commission's operating director, Henry Barrett Chamberlin, declared. "The first duty of the community is to protect the law-abiding from the law-breaker, not to encourage murder, robbery and burglary by showing greater sympathy for the criminal than for his victim."[17]

The considerable success of the Crime Commission in seizing the public agenda and raising private funds during the '20s did not bode well for the JPA. The JPA was no longer the same well-funded, cutting-edge organization that had once brought together middle-class women reformers, sociologists, law professors, and judges at Hull-House. During the war, JPA president Louise de Koven Bowen had served as the only female member of the Illinois State Council of Defense, mobilizing Illinois women to fight vice, venereal disease, and poverty on the home front. After that heady experience, the postwar reaction blindsided her. Beginning in 1924, a defeatist attitude seeped into the JPA's annual reports. Bowen conceded a "feeling of profound discouragement" as she surveyed the organization's efforts over the past quarter-century. Pointing to the JPA's shrinking fund-raising base, she blamed the new rage for crime control and the declining interest in morals offenses and domestic problems. The *Chicago Tribune* had grown newly critical of the group's efforts to police cabarets, dance halls, and other morally suspect social spaces. By 1926, Bowen had descended still deeper into self-pity. "Our officers have more complaints than they can handle," she complained. "The evil conditions which

---

[16] Quoted in Andrew Wender Cohen, "The Chicago Crime Commission: Business Reform, Business Philanthropy and Social Science in the 1920s," unpublished paper, 1991, p. 7, in author's possession; Haller, "Urban Crime," 632–34; David R. Johnson, "Crime Fighting Reform in Chicago: An Analysis of Its Leadership, 1919–1927," M.A. thesis, University of Chicago, 1966; Walker, *Popular Justice*, 169–70.

[17] Henry Barrett Chamberlin, "Crime as a Business in Chicago," *Bulletin of the Chicago Crime Commission*, Oct. 1, 1919, pp. 3, 4.

they constantly encounter could be remedied if they had public opinion behind them but society is too busy or indifferent and it often seems as **if nobody cared.**"[18] Bowen may well have been right. The rise of the Crime Commission did coincide with a growing public distaste for moral policing in the age of Prohibition. But on a deeper level the commission represented a clear break with the organizational style and ideological commitments of progressive criminal justice reform. It is instructive to compare the Crime Commission with that paragon of progressive moral reform groups, the Chicago Vice Commission of 1910–11. Both organizations demonstrated a faith in the power of social knowledge, promoting expert investigation and public exposure as first steps toward attacking crime. Both commissions targeted governmental collusion with criminals. Finally, both groups lit up the front pages with a rhetoric of zero tolerance. "Constant and persistent repression of prostitution the immediate method: Absolute annihilation the ultimate ideal," trumpeted *The Social Evil in Chicago*, the Vice Commission's 1911 report. The Crime Commission had no less a flair for attention-grabbing histrionics. "This is no time for excuses," president Edwin W. Sims thundered in a 1922 meeting. "It is a time for action. The turning point has come. Decency wins or anarchy triumphs. There is no middle course."[19]

But there the similarities ended. The composition of the commissions differed dramatically. The Vice Commissioners, appointed by the mayor, included clergymen, doctors, judges, a psychiatrist, sociologists, a social settlement director, clubwomen, businessmen, and attorneys – a classic progressive lineup of the socially active middle class. The 100 self-appointed men of the Crime Commission were almost all leading businessmen and lawyers, with a handful of social scientists. This difference in organizational makeup influenced the way the groups posed and answered the questions that had been fundamental to crime policy since the Enlightenment: What is crime? What are its causes? and What should a rational government do about it?[20]

---

[18] JPA, *Annual Report of the Juvenile Protective Association of Chicago*, 1924 (Chicago, 1924), 9, 11; Louise de Koven Bowen, *Nobody Cared*, pamphlet (Chicago, 1926), 3, emphasis in original. See "Mrs. Bowen Heads State Union for Women's Service," *Chicago Tribune*, May 4, 1917.

[19] VCC, *The Social Evil in Chicago: A Study of Existing Conditions* (Chicago, 1911), 25; Edwin W. Sims, "On Crime Conditions in Chicago," *JAICLC*, 13 (1922), 105.

[20] Bertram J. Cahn, *The History of the Chicago Crime Commission* (Chicago, n.d.), 7; Haller, "Urban Crime," 626; VCC, *Social Evil*, 2.

The Vice Commission's *The Social Evil in Chicago* was a rich expression of the progressive social conception of crime. The report treated vice as a social phenomenon rooted not in individual moral failing but in the structure of the modern city. *The Social Evil* made causal connections between prostitution and housing, immigration, education, recreation, public health, feeblemindedness, industrial working conditions, and so on. The entire political economy and urban culture of Chicago fell under the commission's purview. The Crime Commission boasted that it took no interest at all in these matters. Crime was what the law said it was. Criminals were morally responsible free agents – rational economic actors like everyone else. "The Chicago Crime Commission has but one object – the minimizing of crime," Sims declared. "It cares not who commits the crime – the wealthy citizen or the ragged stranger. Time, place, social and financial ratings make no difference." Like the Vice Commission, the Crime Commission gathered reams of criminal statistics. But they detailed the machinery of law enforcement, not the social organization of criminality.[21]

These contrasting perspectives on crime yielded predictably divergent policy prescriptions. The Vice Commission report called for an aggressive mobilization of police power, broadly conceived, at the local, state, and even federal levels. Law enforcement was only part of a broader program that included the creation of municipal dance halls, expanded treatment of venereal disease, and new controls on child labor. The Crime Commission focused on making the criminal justice system itself more efficient and making punishment more certain, thereby deterring crime. A typical proposal was a state bureau to centralize criminal record keeping in Illinois. When the General Assembly balked, the commission established its own record system, indexing every robbery and burglary reported in Chicago and every homicide reported in Cook County.[22]

The Crime Commissioners did not deny that social causes of crime existed; instead, they sought to shift the terms of public discourse by denying that those causes had anything to do with the administration of justice, properly understood. Whatever social factors might influence an individual's deviant behavior, the criminal justice system should treat him *as if* he had complete control and bore complete responsibility for his actions. The Crime Commission's emphasis on moral free agency was not inspired by a civil libertarian desire to protect criminal defendants from excessive judicial discretion. The whole point was to

[21] VCC, *Social Evil*; Sims, "Crime Conditions," 105.
[22] Cahn, *Story of the Crime Commission*, 7–8; Haller, "Urban Crime," 632–33; VCC, *Social Evil*, 55–65.

make criminal justice swift, certain, and tough, and thus to deter or
incapacitate criminals.

The Crime Commission's position reflected a widening public debate on the causes and cure for crime. In the academic realm, the
mid-1920s brought a new burst of interest in criminal law, criminology,
and criminal justice administration. The bold interdisciplinary initiative launched by the American Institute of Criminal Law and Criminology at Northwestern in 1910 expanded. Legal scholars engaged
in heady conversations with social and behavioral scientists about the
relationship between law and science, criminal responsibility and mental illness, and the purposes of penal law. Many jurists taking on these
questions expressed serious concerns about the implications of scientific determinism for individual free will, responsibility, and political
liberty, on which they believed the penal law rested. But many scholars
insisted that only by adopting a modern determinist perspective on
human behavior could jurists and lawmakers liberate the law from its
old-fashioned prejudices. "The traditional views of human nature and
conduct in which all of the older and most of the younger men in the
legal profession were brought up have been seriously challenged for
the past thirty years and all but demolished during the past decade,"
wrote University of Buffalo social scientist Nathaniel Cantor in a 1930
article. "The advances in the neurological and physiological foundations of human behavior have invalidated the older views of 'knowing,'
'feeling' and 'willing.'" Cantor's essay ran in the *American Bar Association Journal* – hardly an organ of radical opinion.[23]

Beyond the campuses was another story. In the pages of daily newspapers and mass-market magazines, the once richly complicated and
protean progressive arguments for social responsibility were reduced
by their growing chorus of critics to a caricature: the monolithic, god-
less creed of determinism. During the early and mid-1920s, writes
historian David Ruth, "a contentious media debate about [the] apparently explosive growth in lawlessness centered on the issue of the
criminal's responsibility." The issue was joined between "determinist"
writers who promoted scientific theories of criminality (in some cases
basing their claims on the reports of Chicago's Psychopathic Laboratory) and "moralist" critics who sought to revive an old-fashioned,
pre-progressive view on crime, responsibility, and the law. By 1925,

---

[23] Green, "Freedom and Criminal Responsibility," 2012; Nathaniel Cantor,
"Law and the Social Sciences," *ABAJ*, 16 (1930), 387. See Clarence
M. Updegraff, "The Social Sciences and the Law Curriculum," *ILR*, 25
(1931), 743–58; William A. White, "Need for Cooperation between Lawyers
and Psychiatrists in Dealing with Crime," *ABAJ*, 13 (1927), 551–54.

The 1924 murder case of Leopold and Loeb put the progressive idea of social responsibility for crime itself on trial. From left: Nathan Leopold, Clarence Darrow, and Richard Loeb. Courtesy of the Chicago Historical Society (ICHi-31828); © *Chicago Tribune*.

the moralists had prevailed in the popular media. "Most mass media accounts . . . contended that criminals possessed free choice and the responsibility that accompanied it," Ruth writes. "However complicated society seemed to have become, and regardless of the experts' slick arguments, criminal behavior was easily understandable using long-established legal and moral principles." There was a savage tone to the whole debate. Writing in the *Saturday Evening Post* in 1925, Richard Washburn Child, a member of the new National Crime Commission, denounced determinists as "blithering sentimentalists . . . a lot of professors, social workers, amateur philosophers, ladies' sympathy circles and rescue leagues."[24]

For many Americans already wary of determinist theories, the turning point of the debate on criminal responsibility was the "Crime of the Century," the Leopold and Loeb case. Like the trial of presidential assassin Charles Guiteau four decades earlier, the 1924 trial of Nathan Leopold and Richard Loeb in Cook County Criminal Court for the murder of fourteen-year-old Robert "Bobby" Franks turned into a public debate on the nature of criminal responsibility. At first glance, Leopold and Loeb may have appeared ideal candidates for individual treatment. Only nineteen and eighteen years old, respectively, they were "juvenile adults," probably mentally unstable, and,

[24] Ruth, *Inventing the Public Enemy*, 9, 24; Child quoted on 24.

of special interest to the psychiatrists appointed by the defense, homosexual. But the defendants were also exceptionally intelligent university graduate students from affluent Jewish families – and they had confessed to cold-blooded murder. Leading the defense was a true believer in social responsibility, the sixty-seven-year-old Clarence Darrow. He was assisted by a seasoned Chicago defense attorney, Benjamin Bachrach, who had made his name representing aldermen and gangsters; Bachrach's younger brother, Walter, who had an interest in psychiatry, joined the team. Darrow assigned Walter to recruit expert witnesses for the defense. Leading the prosecution was none other than State's Attorney Robert E. Crowe. As in the Guiteau trial, the prosecution solicited the testimony of traditionalists within the psychiatric profession – including Psychopathic Laboratory critic Dr. H. Douglas Singer – who could be counted on to limit their testimony to the defendants' capacity to distinguish right from wrong. The defense selected three national leaders of psychiatric criminology: the dynamicist Dr. William Healy; Dr. Bernard Glueck, who had founded the famous psychiatric clinic at Sing Sing Prison; and William A. White, the superintendent of St. Elizabeth's Hospital in Washington and one of America's most outspoken determinists.[25]

Because the defendants had already pleaded guilty, the trial, in a packed county courtroom, was really an extended sentencing hearing. The question of the defendants' sanity and capacity for criminal responsibility was central. An estimated 600 reporters, representing newspapers from all over the country, appeared in court on the first day alone. The presiding judge, Chief Justice John Caverly of the Cook County Criminal Court, would alone decide whether the young defendants would hang or go to prison. Born in London, Caverly had immigrated with his parents in the 1860s to Chicago, where he "worked his way through school, carrying water in the steel mills." A Catholic and a minor figure in Democratic politics, Caverly had witnessed first-hand the dramatic transformation of the Chicago judiciary. It had cost him his first judicial office – as a Chicago JP and police magistrate from 1903 to 1906. In 1910 Caverly was one of the first former JPs to win election to the Municipal Court, and he remained on the bench until his election to the County Criminal Court in 1921. Unlike many of his fellow Municipal Court judges, Caverly had not cultivated a reputation as an expert of modern criminology. One of Nathan Leopold's professors at the University of Chicago Law School claimed that Caverly

---

[25] Higdon, *Leopold and Loeb*, esp. 7–8, 137. See Paula S. Fass, "Making and Remaking an Event: The Leopold and Loeb Case in American Culture," *JAH*, 80 (1993), 919–51.

"did not enjoy the highest of reputations, frankly, for his legal acumen and ability." But after nearly a dozen years working under Chief Justice Olson, Caverly must have had some familiarity with the sort of expert testimony that Darrow would present.[26]

In a joint report, the psychiatrists for the defense testified that the defendants' crimes were rooted in abnormal mental conditions. The report said Leopold was a "paranoid personality perhaps developing into a paranoid psychosis," Loeb the victim of "a 'disordered' or 'split' personality." In his own statements before the court, Darrow emphasized the youth of his clients, but he urged the court to take the scientific findings seriously. "Crime has its cause. Perhaps all crimes do not have the same cause, but they all have some cause," he told the court and the larger public watching the case unfold in the newspapers. "Scientists are studying it; criminologists are investigating it; but we lawyers go on, and on, and on, punishing and hanging and thinking that by general terror we can stamp out crime. It never occurs to the lawyer that crime has a cause as certainly as disease, and that the way to rationally treat any abnormal condition is to remove the cause."[27]

As if to prove Darrow's point, State's Attorney Crowe insisted the defendants were legally sane, fully responsible, and ought to hang for their crimes. The crime fighter mocked Darrow's theory of causation. With the same brush, he tarred the entire generation of activists who had worked to transform criminal courts into centers of individual treatment and social reform. "After the Bachrachs had completed my education in the psychopathical laboratories," said Crowe, sarcastically reviewing the defense case, "then my good friend Clarence Darrow took me on a Chautauqua trip with him, and visiting various towns, we would go to the social settlements such as the Hull House, and Clarence would expound his peculiar philosophy of life, and we would meet with Communists and anarchists, and Clarence would regale them with his philosophy of the law, which means there ought not to be any law, and there ought not to be any enforcement of the law!"[28]

Judge Caverly's decision, delivered to an expectant American public on September 10, 1924, sounded a note of caution and ambivalence. The judge seemed relieved to find enough room in the defendants' circumstances to let them live, without fully endorsing the psychiatric theories of the defense. He sentenced Leopold and Loeb to life in prison, resting his decision entirely upon their youth: "the court believes that

[26] Higdon, *Leopold and Loeb*, 8, 170, 171; *BOC* (1911), 126; *BOC* (1931), 177.
[27] Green, "Freedom and Criminal Responsibility," 2025; Higdon, *Leopold and Loeb*, 239.
[28] Higdon, *Leopold and Loeb*, 244.

it is within his province to decline to impose the sentence of death on persons who are not of full age." Caverly treated the report of the defense psychiatrists with a cautious respect. The defendants, he determined, were legally sane. "At the same time," he said,

> the court is willing to recognize that the careful analysis made of the life history of the defendants and of their present mental, emotional, and ethical condition has been of extreme interest and is a valuable contribution to criminology; and yet, the court feels strongly that similar analysis made of other persons accused of crime would reveal similar or different abnormalities.... The value of such tests seems to lie in their applicability to crime and criminals in general. Since they concern the broad questions of human responsibility and legal punishment, and are in no wise peculiar to these individual defendants, they may be deserving of legislative, but not of judicial consideration. For this reason the court is satisfied that his judgment in the present case cannot be affected thereby.

As Leopold later observed, "If Judge Caverly meant literally what he said in his opinion, the whole elaborate psychiatric defense presented in our behalf and the herculean efforts of our brilliant counsel were of no avail.... [W]e need only have introduced our birth certificates in evidence!"[29]

Perhaps Caverly lacked legal acumen and the respect of the elite bar. He was, like most Chicago judges of his day, a political animal: A workingman who, through service to the Democratic party, had risen from the steel mill floor to the county bench. But his decision struck a delicate balance. It spoke to the uneasiness that many judges of his day felt about the cultural authority of psychiatry, a sophisticated and at times stunningly arrogant young discipline, whose theories of human nature and society diverged so completely from the ancient legal doctrine of individual free will and responsibility. Caverly's upbringing, in a church whose teachings stressed free will as the foundation of a moral life, could only have strengthened his uneasiness. Jurists such as Harry Olson, who embraced psychiatry as a progressive discipline full of fresh answers to the complex problems of urban-industrial society, were perhaps too impatient with men such as Caverly, who were forced, in the bright public lights of the criminal courtroom, to reach a judgment on questions that still elude us. In a cautious endorsement of Darrow's claim that all "crime has its cause," the judge had acknowledged that routine psychiatric examination of criminal defendants would probably reveal that many (*most?* – Caverly seemed unsure) were mentally

[29] Ibid., 265–66.

abnormal. This was a major concession from the chief justice of the felony court of the nation's second largest city, an institution that tried and punished, with little pretense of "socialization," adults charged with murder, bank robbery, bootlegging, and so on. But Caverly went on to implicitly reject the premise of socialized criminal justice by saying that such questions still lay beyond the proper realm of judicial discretion in any court. Such questions of public policy properly rested with the legislature, he said. But what had the Municipal Court been doing all these years if not dealing with "broad questions of human responsibility and legal punishment," applying controversial tests and techniques to crime and criminals with the utmost judicial discretion? Psychiatric criminology was not some promising but untested new discipline. For decades it had shaped the everyday practice of criminal justice in courts, jails, prisons, state mental institutions, and even some big city police departments.

Caverly's balancing act may have eased his own conscience, but if he thought it would get him off the hook with the public he was wrong. The decision seemed to satisfy no one completely, except perhaps Darrow, a staunch opponent of the death penalty who, at a moment of peak anticrime sentiment in America, had just won a precedent against executing minors in Illinois. Many American newspapers treated the whole soul-searching discussion of responsibility as a farce, charging that Leopold and Loeb had been spared the noose because of neither their youth nor their mental states but their wealth and family connections. "The sentence shakes the faith of the people in the blind equality of justice," said the *New York Evening Sun*. "They will not believe that any poor man who committed the crime to which Loeb and Leopold pleaded guilty – or any crime approaching its diabolical brutality – would have escaped death." A week after the case ended, Harry Olson received an anxious letter from the secretary of the Citizen's League of Detroit, William P. Lovett. The reaction to the Leopold and Loeb case in Michigan was so strong that Lovett predicted "a general spasm of demand for restoration of capital punishment in Michigan." Lovett feared for the future of Detroit's own widely touted experiment in Chicago-style court reform, a fully centralized municipal court with a Psychopathic Clinic. "Our Municipal Court, organized as you know around the principle of psychiatry, has become so politicized that our town has nearly lost sight of the original intent of the program."[30]

For American jurists and judges, the case made clear, in an exceedingly public forum, just how indeterminate was the legal system's

---

[30] Ibid., 269; William P. Lovett to Harry Olson, Sept. 18, 1924, MCC, box 6, folder 39.

relationship to the social and behavioral sciences. As always, critics protested the use of psychiatrists as hired guns in the courtroom. And many observers were deeply troubled by the uncertain status of criminal responsibility in law *or* science. After all, the prosecution and the defense each had distinguished professional psychiatrists on its side. The defense counsel and the prosecution came at the question of the defendant's responsibility not just from different evidentiary bases but from visibly opposed ideological standpoints. The judge's decision seemed to decide nothing, other than to lighten the penalty of two privileged young men who had committed a heinous crime.[31]

In a symposium on the case published in the *Journal of the American Institute of Criminal Law and Criminology,* Chief Justice Olson protested that it was "most unfortunate for the administration of justice and the progress of modern psychiatry" that "omissions, half-truths, ignored facts and articles beclouded the real issues in the case." Neither the joint report of the defense psychiatrists nor Caverly's decision, in other words, had paid sufficient attention to the defendants' heredity. From his own reading of the report, the chief justice concluded that Leopold and Loeb both suffered from hereditary dementia praecox – Dr. Hickson's "*leit motif* of crime." What the defense psychiatrists had presented as "an environmental calamity," Olson announced, was in fact "a hereditary catastrophe!" In a private letter soon after the decision, Olson speculated that Caverly had ignored what was, to Olson, glaringly clear evidence of hereditary defect in order to protect the defendants' families, which he understood to "contain in both cases a bad heredity."[32]

In the same symposium, Dean John Henry Wigmore of Northwestern School of Law denounced Judge Caverly's sentence as an "astonishing" act that would "lessen the restraints on *the outside class of potential homiciders.*" Wigmore wrote that the report of the defense psychiatrists, "if given the influence which the defense asked, *would tend to undermine the whole penal law.*" This was the same Dean Wigmore who had brought Roscoe Pound to Chicago and who had made the American Institute of Criminal Law and Criminology into the nation's premier academic forum for the promotion of scientific study of the causes and treatment of crime. The psychiatrists' arguments were "sheer Determinism," Wigmore protested. By denying human choice, their theory eliminated "moral blame" and "penal consequences." Society had a

---

[31] John H. Wigmore, "To Abolish Partisanship of Expert Witnesses as Illustrated in the Loeb-Leopold Case," *JAICLC,* 15 (1924), 341–43.

[32] "Symposium on the Loeb-Leopold Case," *JAICLC,* 15 (1924), 395, 98; Harry Olson to Edward McCracken, Sept. 16, 1924, MCC, box 6, folder 39.

"right of self-defense." Deterrence theory – not retribution, not rehabilitation, and certainly not prevention – was "the kingpin of the
criminal law." "The fear of being overtaken by the law's penalties is,
next to morality, what keeps most of us from being offenders," he
claimed. "For the professional or habitual criminals...it is the only
thing." Wigmore's angry statement echoed, across more than half a
century, the sentiment of the nineteenth-century American jurist Joel
Bishop. It was Bishop who had written in 1865, without a hint of doubt
or disagreement, that "law, without punishment for its violation, is in
the nature of things impossible." Making much the same point in 1924,
Wigmore heralded a reactionary turn in American criminal justice.[33]

The law-and-order agenda of the Chicago Crime Commission was elaborated across the nation in the famous local, state, and federal "crime
surveys" of the 1920s. Unlike the social surveys of the Progressive Era,
the new crime surveys made little effort to map the complex social
landscapes of industrial cities. Instead, they focused on urban criminal justice as a functional institutional "system" fraught with internal inefficiencies. On their face, the surveys simply expanded the old
progressive arguments for the consolidation of criminal courts, the
modernization of common-law procedure, and the introduction of
administrative efficiency and caseload statistics. But on closer examination, the surveys reflected a change of tone and emphasis – from
optimism to skepticism, from a call for broad social intervention to a
narrower demand to root out partisan politics and official corruption.
The Cleveland Crime Survey of 1922, directed by Felix Frankfurter and
Roscoe Pound, was the first investigation of an entire criminal justice
system. Funded by the Cleveland Foundation, the survey's thirty-five-
member staff of legal experts and social scientists produced a massive
scholarly report that reflected Pound's longstanding concern for organization in judicial administration but little of his interest in the
socialization of law. The major discovery of this nationally publicized
study was the extent of plea bargaining and the other forms of unregulated official discretion and hidden administrative strategies that court
officials used to deal with an overwhelming criminal caseload. By carefully following the movement of criminal cases through the Cleveland
courts, the surveyors had learned that 60 percent of the felony cases
begun in 1919 had been discharged or reduced to less serious charges.
In other words, the public image of the criminal justice process – the

---

[33] "Symposium on the Loeb-Leopold Case," 400–404 passim; Joel Prentiss
Bishop, *Bishop on Criminal Law*, 9th ed., ed. John M. Zane and Carl
Zollmann, 2 vols. (Chicago, 1923), 1: 3.

adversarial trial before a judge and jury – was beginning to diverge from the actual administrative handling of criminal cases in American cities.[34]

Following on the heels of the Cleveland study came the *Missouri Crime Survey* of 1926 and the *Illinois Crime Survey* of 1929. Like their predecessor, these studies were funded largely by private business interests or community foundations and conducted by social scientists and legal experts. They emphasized issues of systemic efficiency in the policing, prosecution, and punishment of felony crimes. Causes of inefficiency – not causes of crime – were the target of expert inquiry. "The causes of crime are doubtless manifold," declared the chairman of the Missouri survey. "A number could be mentioned and with profit be discussed, though their relative importance would remain matters of dispute. But all agree that one of the most important of these matters is the criminal's lack of fear of the law, and that this is due to deficiencies in the law and in its administration." The *Illinois Crime Survey* took a somewhat broader focus than the others by including criminologist John Landesco's remarkable investigation of the practice of organized crime in Chicago.[35]

Along with stoking the deepening public dissatisfaction with Prohibition, the crime surveys encouraged the emergence of crime as a national problem that demanded a federal response. Congress had already taken major steps in this direction with the passage of the Mann Act in 1911, the Volstead Act in 1919, and the creation of the Bureau of Investigation two years later. Prior to the 1920s, however, no American president had seen fit to discuss crime in an inaugural address. By the time of Herbert Hoover's inauguration in 1929, a president would have been remiss not to. "Crime is increasing," the new president declared in his address, and he proposed a very Hoover-like solution: a national commission of experts to study the problem. The National Commission on Law Observance and Enforcement, chaired by former attorney general George W. Wickersham, took the systems analysis approach of the crime surveys to the national level.[36]

[34] Roscoe Pound and Felix Frankfurter, eds., *Criminal Justice in Cleveland* (Cleveland, 1922); Reginald Heber Smith, "Cleveland's Crime Survey," *JAJS*, 5 (1921), 68–83; Walker, *Popular Justice*, 170–72.

[35] Guy A. Thompson, "The Missouri Crime Survey," *ABAJ*, 12 (1926), 626; "Illinois Association for Criminal Justice Completes Crime Survey," *ABAJ*, 15 (1929), 426–28; *Illinois Crime Survey*. Missouri Association for Criminal Justice, *The Missouri Crime Survey* (New York, 1926).

[36] "Reports of the National Commission on Law Observance and Enforcement," *MLR*, 30 (1931), 1–132; Friedman, *Crime and Punishment*, 273; Walker, *Popular Justice*, 172–75.

The ascendance of the crime control perspective in criminal justice reform had serious implications for socialized law. Like the Chicago Crime Commission, the crime surveys took an uncompromising deterrence stance, espousing a universal conception of crime and a limited vision of the courts' proper role in addressing social conditions. Moreover, the crime surveys demonstrated intense interest in the causal potency of an environmental factor that the advocates of socialized criminal justice had generally left out of their analysis: partisan politics. The crime surveys unsettled municipal judges' claims to social expertise by calling into question their experience, judicial competence, and political impartiality.

The politics of judicial appointment had boiled the blood of businessmen reformers and bar association attorneys since well before the invention of the Municipal Court of Chicago. Since the 1880s, the Chicago Bar Association had been attempting, with limited success, to influence the outcomes of judicial elections in Chicago by recommending their own slates of "fit" and "competent" men for the bench. As early as 1914, bar association lawyers and law professors in Chicago had attempted to expose the democratic selection of judges in the city as an empty ritual. Antidemocratic though their motives may have been, they had a point. Municipal judges were elected in the general elections in November, when a dizzying number of candidates and an atmosphere of intense national partisanship overwhelmed the voters. Experts claimed, quite plausibly, that the real election took place far from the polling places, in the backroom ticket-forming negotiations of the major party factions. Participatory democracy versus judicial independence: It was a debate the federalists and antifederalists of the late eighteenth century knew well. But in the big cities of the early twentieth century, where hundreds of patronage jobs as well as powerful judicial seats were at stake in these elections, the problem had assumed unprecedented proportions. In 1914 Albert M. Kales, a professor of law at Northwestern University, proposed that the Municipal Court Act be revised to transfer the power of judicial appointment to the chief justice. Under Kales's scheme, only the chief justice would be elected, and he would appoint his associates. Kales's plan never came to pass, but similar proposals for removing the selection of city judges from the electoral process control were put forth in the 1920s. These failed, too. As late as 1936 the president of the Chicago Bar Association was still inveighing against "the vicious imperfections of the present method of selecting the judiciary."[37]

---

[37] Herbert M. Lautmann, "Preface," in Edward M. Martin, *The Role of the Bar in Electing the Bench in Chicago* (Chicago, 1936), v; Albert M. Kales, "Proposed

Despite the dead-on-arrival character of proposals for electoral reform, the allegations of judicial incompetence and political corruption
shaped the rhetoric and priorities of criminal justice reform. There was
ample evidence that the problem was indeed growing as the municipal courts of America's major cities grew into massive bureaucracies.
In the 1929 *Illinois Crime Survey*, Columbia University law professor
Raymond Moley, soon to be a member of President Franklin Delano
Roosevelt's inner circle, compared the judicial mettle of the judges
elected in the Municipal Court's first decade to judges elected in the
second decade and found the latter cohort a distinct disappointment.
On average the later judges were younger, had less education and
professional experience, and received far lower bar association ratings than their predecessors. The newer judges were exceedingly well-
educated in local politics, having risen up in the ranks of their parties
through faithful service as precinct captains, ward bosses, aldermen,
and prosecutors. "The court is full of incompetence, of political influences, of lamentable laxness in meeting an unprecedented tide of
crime," Moley wrote. "In the hands of such a staff the court, techni-
cally well organized and full of possibilities for good, yields a sorry
product." The only judge to escape the professor's condemnation was
Harry Olson, whom Moley praised for his "high standards and vigilant
watchfulness."[38]

Allegations of political influence in the Municipal Court carried
particularly disturbing implications because of the coziness of politics
and crime in the city. Some Municipal Court judges seemed to go out
of their way to reaffirm these fears. Imagine the euphoria on the faces
of the crime reporters as they reported these stories from Chicago's
gangland: the service of several municipal judges as honorary pallbear-
ers at the funeral of gangster Anthony Andrea in 1921, the presence
of five municipal judges at the wake of Dion O'Banion in 1924, and
the appearance of four judges at the christening of "Diamond Joe"
Esposito's son in 1925. It was hard to say exactly what such displays
of respect for one's supposed enemies meant for the administration
of justice in Chicago, but it couldn't be good. "In the hour of death,"

Amendments to the Municipal Court Act Relating to the Selection and
Retirement of the Judges of That Court," *ILR*, 9 (1914), 319–37; "Judges
Demand Better Men for Municipal Court," *Chicago Tribune*, Feb. 13, 1924;
"Selecting Judges in Large Cities: Ignorant and Misfit Judges Clearly Prove
That Method of Selection Is at Fault – Proposal That Candidates Be Re-
quired to Pass Examinations," *JAJS*, 14 (1931), 155–58.
[38] Raymond Moley, "The Municipal Court of Chicago," *Illinois Crime Survey*,
393, 397–98, 400–404; Martin, *Role of the Bar*, 252.

Landesco observed solemnly, "personal ties are disclosed, which in life were concealed."[39]

The reformers' exposure of political influence within Chicago's criminal justice system extended to its still burgeoning social staff. Chief Justice Olson came to view politics as the most serious threat to his ambitions for the Municipal Court as an experimental station. The *Illinois Crime Survey* revealed the "political domination" of the state parole board and the political distribution of the jobs of probation officers and parole officers throughout the state. After elections, the victorious party organizations raided the Chicago courts for the jobs of clerks, bailiffs, and probation officers. Women reformers voiced serious concerns about the fitness of the Municipal Court's politically appointed social personnel. Reflecting on the high hopes she had once held for the treatment of juvenile adults in the Boys' Court, Bowen noted, "These hopes have not always been realized because political appointments among the social workers in this and in other courts have not added to its efficiency." In a study of Chicago politics in the 1920s, Sonya Forthall described an "elaborate organization concerned with humanizing the law." She was not talking about social workers and probation officers. She meant the precinct captains, local party officers, and other political fixers who "humanized" the law by fixing traffic tickets, furnishing bail, and securing protection in the courts for bootleggers. The close relationship between the judiciary and politics would continue to flourish as Chicago's Democratic machine emerged during the Great Depression and World War II under Mayors Anton Cermak and Edward J. Kelly.[40]

Despite growing reservations and criticisms – despite calls for reforming judicial elections and demands for stricter vetting of social personnel – socialized criminal justice survived the onslaught of the '20s. The *Illinois Crime Survey* came out firmly in support of individual treatment – indeterminate sentencing, probation, parole, and court-based psychiatric testing – but it did so in terms starkly different from the expansive rhetoric of socialized law. "The strongest argument for the indeterminate sentence and parole consists in the protection for

[39] Landesco, "Organized Crime," 1039, 1025–39; Martin, *Role of the Bar,* 279–80.
[40] Louise de Koven Bowen, *Growing up with a City* (New York, 1926), 129; Andrew A. Bruce, E. W. Burgess, and Albert J. Harno, "The Probation and Parole System," *Illinois Crime Survey,* 451–452, 570; Martin, *Role of the Bar,* 283; Sonya Forthall, *Cogwheels of Democracy: A Study of the Precinct Captain* (1946; Westport, Conn., 1972), 67–78, esp. 68. See Rose Goodkind to Harry Olson, May 24, 1924, MCC, box 5, folder 38.

society it affords, not only through the opportunity for reformation of the criminal under supervision, but through its use as an instrument to return the parole violator to the penitentiary without the delays and technicalities of court procedure," a survey report declared. The authors pointed as well to the salutary effect of parole in reducing the need for costly new prisons. The Wickersham Commission also endorsed individual treatment. "Individualization is the root of adequate penal treatment," a commission report declared.[41]

In the Municipal Court itself, the crime control mood acquired its own institutional footholds without abolishing the old strongholds of socialization. During the late 1920s and early 1930s, new specialized branches opened. In 1929 the municipal judges added the Felony Court and the Racket Court (for Prohibition violations and cases "involving intimidation of employes, or employers, destruction of property by bombing or otherwise and various other so-called rackets"). By 1933, all gun law violations went to a single branch. And in 1934, Chief Justice Olson's successor created an Automobile Theft Court, in order to appease the Crime Commission, which had long complained that the Boys' Court coddled car thieves. All defendants charged with auto theft, including juvenile adults, would have their cases heard in the new branch. A few years later, a Municipal Court report touted the success of the Automobile Theft Court in terms the commission surely would have applauded: Auto theft insurance premiums had declined 60 percent since the court's creation.[42]

Harry Olson never won his grail of a fully unified Municipal Court with final jurisdiction over felonies. As early as 1917, Olson had written, "One of the things insistently required before Chicago can consider that it is in a fair way to grapple with its crime situation is the unification of all its various courts into a single system, with complete correlation of all the criminal branches.... Then, and only then, will the [Psychopathic] laboratory be able to render its fullest measure of service." Despite the longstanding support of the American Bar Association, the old progressive call for "one great court" – a completely centralized system in which all courts were departments under central control – was rarely realized in any American city or state. In fact, when

---

[41] Bruce et al., "Probation and Parole," 565, 566. Commission report quoted in Walker, *Popular Justice*, 176.

[42] *MCC 23 (1929)*, 17–18; *MCC 26–27 (1932–33)*, 5; *MCC 28–30 (1934–36)*, 5; John Gutknecht, *The Chicago Boys' Court in 1933: A Report on its Organization, Procedure and Results* (n. p.); Statement of Hon. John J. Sonsteby, in United States Senate, Committee on Commerce, *Investigation of So-Called "Rackets"*... (Washington, 1934), vol. 1, pt. 3: 406.

President Lyndon Johnson's Crime Commission produced its agenda-setting liberal report entitled *The Challenge of Crime in a Free Society* in 1967, the unification of urban criminal court systems still stood atop the unfinished agenda of progressive reform. Olson and his allies had no success persuading the Illinois General Assembly to give the Municipal Court complete jurisdiction over felonies in Chicago. Indeed, in 1929 the Crime Commission put forth an (equally unsalable) proposal for stripping the Municipal Court of its power to conduct preliminary examinations in felony cases. Olson may have been deeply disappointed by his failure to fully realize his ambitions to make the Municipal Court, as he called it, a perfectly unified "tribunal of procedural reform and social service." But it is remarkable that one city judge achieved all that he did.[43]

It took the city-wide Democratic sweep in the November elections of 1930 to finally remove Chief Justice Harry Olson from the office he had held continuously for a quarter-century. In an election that the *Chicago Daily News* called a "staggering Democratic landslide," Olson lost by only a "slight margin" to John J. Sonsteby, a Democratic lawyer and Cermak ally who had no previous judicial experience. According to the *Daily News*, "Close friends of the former chief justice said that his defeat was the most unexpected and inexplicable event of his life." This son of immigrants, this former small-town Kansas grade school teacher, had made himself a presence in Chicago politics for thirty-five years, first as an ambitious county prosecutor, then as the head of the nation's model municipal court. With his three-part gospel of court organization, procedural reform, and scientific criminology, Olson had taken up Governor Deneen's challenge to make the new Municipal Court "a great experimental station in regard to the practice of the law." Working with social activists, judges, lawmakers, and professors, this two-time mayoral contender had extended the power of the Municipal Court deep into the everyday life of the Second City, with decidedly mixed consequences for the people whose lives the court sought to regulate. After his defeat, Olson returned to private law practice. He did not attempt a political comeback. On August 1, 1935,

---

43 Harry Olson in City of Chicago, Municipal Court, *Report of the Psychopathic Laboratory of the Municipal Court of Chicago*, May 1, 1914–April 30, 1917 (Chicago, n.d.), 9; Harry Olson, "The Municipal Court of Chicago: A Tribunal of Procedural Reform and Social Service," speech to Associated Charities of San Francisco, May 10, 1916, reprinted from *San Francisco Recorder*, May 12, 1916; Henry Barrett Chamberlin, "Review Work under Loesch Leadership," *Criminal Justice*, March 1929, 4; United States, President's Commission on Law Enforcement and Administration of Justice, *The Challenge of Crime in a Free Society* (Washington, 1967), 129.

Harry Olson died of a heart attack in his Oak Park, Illinois, home, after working in his downtown Chicago law office until 9:30 the previous night. He was sixty-seven.[44]

The Municipal Court that Olson left behind, as the Great Depression engulfed Chicago and the nation, was, in the words of University of Chicago political scientist Albert Lepawsky, "a veritable adjudicating giant": a politicized big city bureaucracy that disposed of half a million civil and criminal cases each year. Thirty-seven elected judges were assisted by a staff of more than 800 court officers. The court's "mass of work" tested Lepawsky's powers of description. But what most impressed Lepawsky was not the 3,000 patrolmen "unearthing offenses and complaints which are poured upon the dockets" or the traffic policemen with their "staccato whistles" who served tickets on careless drivers. For Lepawsky, the "vortex" of this judicial machine was the Office of the Court Clerk on the eighth floor of City Hall, where civil cases were filed and criminal cases processed:

> Before a dozen windows and cages, queues of law clerks and lawyers are restlessly waiting their turn to have the seal of the clerk of the municipal court imprinted on the papers that are to be filed – as though the ten or fifteen minutes spent in line will add much time to the months or years that are likely to elapse before the case is disposed of. Screeching baskets overhead dart back and forth from cashier's cage to filing windows. Attending at these windows are busy filing clerks whose moods shift from familiarity to brusqueness as an antidote to the monotony of their duties. Behind them, scores of other clerks with pens and rubber stamps are working over stacks of "half sheets," or records of the cases, which are classified and assigned to the various branch courts on the floors above. Similar scenes are enacted in the bailiff's office a [city] block distant across the hall on the same floor, where arrangements are made for the service of writs. And in the courtrooms, as the cases are being forced through the mill, the routine is only occasionally tempered by an inexperienced attorney who makes a ridiculous plea.

If such Kafkaesque scenes inspired anyone to pine for the old days of the justice shops – when each JP dispensed his own brand of rough justice for a fee out of his own small office or police station courtroom – there was, to be certain, no going back.[45]

[44] "Former Judge Harry Olson, Municipal Court Chief, Dies," *Chicago Daily News*, Aug. 1, 1935, p. 1; "Harry Olson, Former Chief Justice, Dies," *Chicago Tribune*, Aug. 2, 1935, p. 18.

[45] Albert Lepawsky, *The Judicial System of Metropolitan Chicago* (Chicago, 1932), 26, 108, 167, esp. 3–4.

Chief Justice John Sonsteby's vision of what a modern municipal court could try to accomplish was cobbled together from old and familiar sources – part crime prevention, part social investigation, part crime control, and part bureaucratic imperative. Olson's successor saw the Municipal Court for the sprawling bureaucracy and political machine that it had become. A longtime member of the National Conference of Social Workers, Sonsteby believed that well-run local schools and social agencies could help prevent crime. Like Olson, he extolled the virtues of judicial specialization, but chiefly as a means to more efficiently process the relentless legal disputes and criminal cases of a diverse urban population nudging up against the three and a half million mark. Under Sonsteby, the court's annual reports were reduced to paper-thin shadows of their fat former selves: Gone were the miniature sociological treatises of the Boys' Court judges and the dispatches charting the progress of sterilization legislation in the states. Sonsteby took it for granted that the everyday practice of criminal justice in the Municipal Court would involve some measure of social work, probation, psychiatric evaluation, and coordination with private social agencies. Indeed, in a phenomenon that Lepawsky colorfully called "the pinch of the public expert," "the legal duties and practical powers of the social and legal expert" had continued to expand "at the expense of the functions exercised by the judge." This was especially evident in the Court of Domestic Relations, where Lepawsky noted that only two of the twenty-two employees worked "on the legal files and records of the traditional court, while the rest are concerned with the detailed investigation of cases." But for Sonsteby and many of his contemporaries, the languages of individual treatment and crime control were both thoroughly integrated and subordinated to the mass bureaucratic management of civil and criminal cases.[46]

Across the nation in the New Deal era, the rhetorics and institutions of crime control and socialization settled into a belligerent coexistence. The rhetoric of crime control and the nationalization of crime as a public problem legitimated an ever-increasing state and federal presence in crime fighting. The creation of a slew of new federal criminal offenses by Congress in 1934 eased the Federal Bureau of Investigation's rise from a minor entity to the nation's top law enforcement agency under the irrepressible crime fighter J. Edgar Hoover.[47]

[46] Lepawsky, *Judicial System of Metropolitan Chicago*, 113. "Statement of Hon. John J. Sonsteby," 395–411; *BOC* (1936), 948; Martin, *Role of the Bar,* 275.
[47] Friedman, *Crime and Punishment*, 269–72. See Mary M. Stolberg, *Fighting Organized Crime: Politics, Justice, and the Legacy of Thomas E. Dewey* (Boston, 1995).

But even in the crime control heyday of the 1930s, the crime fighters never managed to push socialization and socialized techniques from the criminal justice agenda. As Lepawsky's description of the Municipal Court suggests, social personnel and the logic of socialization were too firmly embedded in the political institutions of criminal justice, and their history was too intertwined with the rise of the welfare state in America, to permit their easy abolition. Addressing the Attorney General's Conference on Crime in 1934, President Roosevelt suggested that crime fighting and socialized justice were two sides of a coin. "Crime is a symptom of social disorder," he declared. "Widespread increase in the capacity to substitute order for disorder is the remedy. This can come only through the expert marshaling of the assets of home, school, church, community and other social agencies, to work in common purpose with our law enforcement agencies.... Scientific research, highly trained personnel, [and] expert service are just as necessary here as in any field of human endeavor."[48]

The ideology of social responsibility for crime found its way high onto the urban agenda of American liberal Democrats in the late 1960s. President Johnson's 1967 Crime Commission report was an impassioned, eloquent statement on the social causes and consequences of urban crime. It breathed new life into the old progressive vision of crime as a proxy for poverty and social inequality and called forth a burst of new social science studies of criminal justice. Since the "law and order" reaction of the late 1960s, however, civil libertarians of the political left and law-and-order conservatives of the right have steadily chipped away at socialized criminal justice. The U.S. Supreme Court reined in the procedural latitude of juvenile court judges, and many states, including Illinois, eventually did away with the indeterminate sentence altogether. But it was only in the late twentieth century, when the entire edifice of the American welfare state came under a devastating assault – and Pound's old notion of a "social interest in the individual life" had vanishing political currency – that juvenile courts and other socialized courts were seriously threatened with extinction.

At the turn of the twenty-first century, after decades of steadily intensifying punishment in America, the socialized criminal court has taken on a new life, this time as a partner in the War on Drugs. Seeking an alternative to the decades of senseless incarceration that have given the United States one of the largest imprisoned populations in the world, in recent years many states and cities have created hundreds

[48] Roosevelt quoted in Sarah B. Schaar, "Probation in the Municipal Court of Chicago," Jan. 2, 1936, MCC, box 6, folder 43.

of specialized "drug courts." In exchange for their partial freedom, and perhaps hoping for a new chance in life, drug offenders agree to participate in a highly discretionary and frankly coercive regime of personal surveillance, counseling, and compulsory drug treatment. And so the wheel of justice continues to turn, and once again there is hope that the power of a criminal court might be harnessed to serve a broader, more socially useful purpose than punishing criminals.[49]

[49] Friedman, *Crime and Punishment*, 305–9, 416–17; James L. Nolan, Jr., *Reinventing Justice: The American Drug Court Movement* (Princeton, 2001).

Afterword

We must remember this fact ... that "democracy" as such is opposed
to the "rule" of bureaucracy, in spite and perhaps because of its
unavoidable yet unintentional promotion of bureaucracy.

– Max Weber

The national crisis of the Great Depression exposed the practical
limits of urban social governance in criminal courts and other local
practices of welfare administration. After President Franklin Delano
Roosevelt took office in 1933, social workers, welfare activists, and
beleaguered local and state politicians prevailed upon his administration and Congress to federalize state-level programs created during the
Progressive Era, including mothers' pensions, breaking the poor law
tradition of local responsibility with an unprecedented national commitment to social welfare. The New Deal era accelerated the growth
of a centralized administrative welfare state in the United States, expanding the power of the state and federal governments to regulate
the economy and provide Americans with greater security against the
risks of modern life: permanent disability, child poverty, old age, unemployment. The innovative approaches to social management, policing,
and provision pioneered in urban socialized courts and welfare agencies during the Progressive Era remained a fund of experience as New
Deal policy makers, jurists, and judges dealt anew with the complex
and ever-shifting relationship of law, administrative power, and justice
in modern America.[1]

---

[1] Winifred Bell, *Aid to Dependent Children* (New York, 1965), 20–42. William R.
Brock, *Welfare, Democracy, and the New Deal* (Cambridge, 1988); Michael B.
Katz, *In the Shadow of the Poorhouse: A Social History of Welfare in America* (New
York, 1986), 206–47.

The great public controversies triggered by the emerging New Deal state must have evoked a sense of déjà vu for the many lawyers, social workers, and policy makers in Washington who had cut their teeth in progressive reform at the local and state levels. The national debates of the late 1930s – their high stakes made higher still by the collapse of constitutional regimes and the rise of totalitarianism in Europe – pitted "the rule of law" against "the administrative process," centralization against localism, and social responsibility against individual autonomy. Of course, powerful business interests and conservatives' self-interested fears of redistribution shaped these debates. But the fundamental questions raised in them had deep roots and a stubborn integrity of their own.

Suffice it to say that the New Deal put none of these issues to rest. Both the federal courts, retooled by the managerial and procedural reforms of the 1920s and '30s to behave a good deal more like agencies, and the suddenly plentiful administrative agencies, brought under heel by the Administrative Procedures Act of 1946 to behave a good deal more like courts, emerged from the era's battles stronger than ever: uneasy institutional partners in a modern liberal state that is distinctive in the world for its marriage of law, rights, and administrative power. Localism, too, proved a surprisingly resilient force in the face of massive centralization. The Economic Security Act of 1935 created a national welfare state in America, but one that depended heavily on state funds and left enormous discretion to local welfare officials to determine who got what and with what strings attached. Local and state officials drew on many of the familiar techniques of progressive social governance in determining the eligibility and policing the home lives of welfare recipients. In our own era of deregulation, devolution, and privatization, the courts, local governments, and private welfare agencies have once again been asked to shoulder enormous burdens of social and economic governance. At the same time, the popular conservative assault on social responsibility as a premise of liberal governance has reenthroned "personal responsibility," driving the progressive language of social interdependence and social responsibility into the shadows of mainstream political discourse. But there is no reason to think that the current ideological hegemony of personal responsibility and the market will be any more permanent than the reaction against social responsibility in the 1920s.[2]

---

[2] David S. Clark, "Adjudication to Administration: A Statistical Analysis of Federal District Courts in the Twentieth Century," *SCLR*, 55 (1981), 65–145; Morton J. Horwitz, *The Transformation of American Law, 1870–1960: The Crisis of Legal Orthodoxy* (New York, 1992), esp. 213–46; Michael B. Katz,

All of this, of course, lies beyond the scope of this story. Well, most of it.

The story of Roscoe Pound's thunderous assault on the New Deal state has oft been told, but always with a crucial piece missing. The familiar storyline is a narrative of betrayal, of one's own life's work and the people it inspired: Brilliant young iconoclast, the best legal mind of his progressive generation, stuns the legal world in 1906 by announcing – in a speech to the ossified American Bar Association, no less – that the individualistic justice of the common law has proved unsuited to urban-industrial society, creating widespread "popular dissatisfaction with the administration of justice." In the 1910s he launches a broad movement for sociological jurisprudence that transforms legal education, helps to elevate the weight of social interests in judicial decision making, and lays the intellectual foundation for legal realism and the administrative state. But just when those years of collective work were finally bearing fruit, in the New Deal and the Supreme Court's "Constitutional Revolution of 1937," the former progressive makes a stunning reversal and denounces the whole enterprise – *his* whole enterprise – as a dangerously relativist, absolutist, un-American nightmare. The denouement of this narrative echoes the legal realists' own professed shock at Pound's so-called about-face. "The reader of Pound's earlier writings," wrote Judge Jerome Frank, "rubs his eyes" and wonders, "Can this be the same man?"[3]

To be sure, Pound's politics, like those of his Republican party, had grown brittle and conservative by 1938. His best original work already lay well behind him (though he lived and continued to publish until 1964). An inveterate Germanophile, Pound had shocked his Harvard colleagues by accepting, in 1934, an honorary degree from the University of Berlin. His intemperate criticism of legal realism – "a cult of the ugly," he called it – and his vilification of the New Deal, for allegedly forsaking the rule of law for "administrative absolutism," did represent a retreat from his earlier, flexible, and painstakingly historicized understanding of administrative justice. And Pound's stand in 1938 gave

The Price of Citizenship: Redefining the American Welfare State (New York, 2001); Thomas J. Sugrue, "All Politics Is Local: The Persistence of Localism in Twentieth Century American Politics," in *Democracy in America: New Directions in American Political History*, ed. Meg Jacobs, William J. Novak, and Julian Zelizer (forthcoming).

[3] Frank in Horwitz, *Transformation*, 219. "No one in the history of American jurisprudence underwent such a remarkable volte-face as did Pound. He set the scene for a new, progressive perpective in jurisprudence, and then systematically and quite fanatically set about denouncing that perspective." Neil Duxbury, *Patterns of American Jurisprudence* (New York, 1995), 63.

rhetorical fuel to the conservative lawyers and business interests who opposed the New Deal, not only for its statism but for the redistribution of wealth and power that statism threatened.[4]

So there is much truth in the narrative of Pound's "about-face." But the story is much too neat. It can be told with such a tragic arc only by overlooking his enormously influential early writings on "the administration of justice in the modern city." These writings continued to shape the liberal agenda in criminal justice reform well into the era of the Great Society. This common oversight is understandable given Pound's vast corpus. But it reinforces an old habit among many historians and law scholars that Pound himself never fell into: the habit of seeing criminal justice as a peculiar backwater of social deviancy and institutionalized violence – a world apart from the main line of historical development in American law, constitutionalism, and liberalism. Nothing could be more mistaken. Like many urban social activists and judges in the progressive age of "city sense," Pound understood the riddle of judicial administration in the modern city as an extreme microcosm of the challenges that a pluralistic urban-industrial society posed for the tenets of late nineteenth-century liberalism: its emphasis on individual autonomy and responsibility, its antistatism, its ideal of a neutral and predictable rule of law that served as a *restraint* on state power – *not an instrument of it.* It was in those now largely ignored writings that the rising young progressive professor, who had witnessed Chicago's judicial revolution first-hand, articulated many of his early ideas about court organization and legal socialization as long-term legal solutions to the unprecedented challenges of modern social governance. Pound reprised this position in the 1922 Cleveland crime survey. "Undoubtedly one of the tasks of American law today is to work out an adequate system of administrative law," he wrote. "But there is no reason to suppose that judicial administration is not as adequate to this task as executive administration." For evidence of this, he pointed to the newly developed capacities of urban courts to collect statistics and "conduct psychological laboratories... for the study of criminals."[5]

4 Roscoe Pound, *Administrative Law: Its Growth, Procedure, and Significance* (Pittsburgh, 1942), 75, 131. See N. E. H. Hull, *Roscoe Pound and Karl Llewellyn: Searching for an American Jurisprudence* (Chicago, 1997).

5 Roscoe Pound, "Criminal Justice in the American City – A Summary," *Roscoe Pound and Criminal Justice*, ed. Sheldon Glueck (Dobbs Ferry, N.Y., 1965), 166. See United States, President's Commission on Law Enforcement and Administration of Justice, *The Challenge of Crime in a Free Society* (Washington, 1967).

By the late '30s, Pound had come to believe that, had court reform proceeded more rapidly along the lines he had suggested in the 1910s – organization of courts, streamlining of procedure, socialization of law – the incredible centralization and expansion of agency power during the New Deal might not have been necessary. During the 1910s Pound had often written about the administrative process – "justice without law," he called it – as a necessary supplement to legal rule. But he proposed Chicago-style court reform as a way to *save* the courts and the common law from the jurisdictional imperialism of the administrative state. Only by saving the courts could legal justice survive – and with it, its cherished protections for human freedom. Liberty itself, Pound recognized, could no longer be understood as some pure natural right distinct from the needs and interests of society at large. While he recognized that those needs and interests required some level of administrative agency growth, his long-term solution was to make the American courts more specialized, administrative, and penetrating instruments of social governance – thus meeting the demands for social justice and control without creating a dangerous and permanent system of justice without law. This was, in a far more flexible and nuanced rendering, much the same argument Pound later made against the New Deal state. In his infamous 1938 report on administrative law for the American Bar Association, Pound insisted that unless "the bar takes upon itself to act, there is nothing to check the tendency of administrative bureaus to extend the scope of their operations indefinitely even to the extent of supplanting our traditional judicial regime by an administrative regime." He warned against the dangers of "a highly centralized administration set up under complete control of the executive ... relieved of judicial review and making its own rules." And he charged that "[t]hose who would turn the administration of justice over to administrative absolutism" acted as if the rule of law was "illusory." "They expect law in this sense to disappear."[6]

Because we know what the New Deal state ultimately became, Pound's reaction to it may seem hysterical. But his concerns were not isolated. They resonated with the concerns of other former radical critics of the liberal rule of law ideal, including two brilliant German scholars of the famous neo-Marxist Institute for Social Research (the "Frankfurt School"), Franz Neumann and Otto Kirchheimer. Writing as the horrific implications of Nazi-style social law became clear in the 1930s, Neumann in particular developed a belated respect for the ideal of an impartial rule of law. Despite its bourgeois orientation,

[6] Pound quoted in Horwitz, *Transformation*, 219–20.

despite the ideological legitimation its individualistic categories had provided for monopoly capitalism, Neumann wrote, the rule of law ideal had also contained a genuine ethical commitment to personal and political freedom. One only fully appreciated that commitment when it had vanished.[7]

Neumann's point was echoed in the late twentieth century by the English social historian E. P. Thompson. Thompson's book, *Whigs and Hunters*, is a powerful Marxist critique of the classical liberal ideal of a rule of law and the ways it has often masked and legitimated real inequalities of power. But in the closing pages of this history of eighteenth-century England, Thompson looks forward to the twentieth century and arrives at a startling conclusion. "There is a difference between arbitrary power and the rule of law," he writes. "We ought to expose the shams and inequities which may be concealed beneath this law. But the rule of law itself, the imposing of effective inhibitions upon power and the defense of the citizen from power's all-intrusive claims, seems to me to be an unqualified human good. To deny or belittle this good is, in this dangerous century when the resources and pretensions of power continue to enlarge, a desperate error of intellectual abstraction." This passage contains an insightful bit of sociological jurisprudence. The old liberal ideal of the rule of law – which progressive jurists, including Pound, assailed as out of touch with the facts of modern social life – still has an ethical value that is irreducible to economic self-interest. The rule of law ideal withered – but it did not disappear – in twentieth-century America. It continued to provide a robust language of constitutional aspiration for the weak to challenge the powerful, and for the individual to contest arbitrary state power.[8]

But one question remains: Was Pound right? Did the fact that the progressive regime of urban social governance took root in criminal courts, rather than administrative agencies, make any difference? Did law act as a meaningful restraint upon administrative power? Or, by socializing the courts, did cities such as Chicago conscript the courts into the cause they were expected to guard against?

---

[7] Franz L. Neumann, "The Change in the Function of Law in Modern Society," in *The Rule of Law under Siege: Selected Essays of Franz L. Neumann and Otto Kirchheimer*, ed. William E. Scheuerman (Berkeley, 1996), 101–41, esp. 117–18.

[8] E. P. Thompson, *Whigs and Hunters: The Origin of the Black Act* (New York, 1975), 266. See Martin Luther King, Jr.'s meditation on "just" versus "unjust" laws in "Letter from Birmingham Jail," in Martin Luther King, Jr., *Why We Can't Wait* (New York, 1963), 76–95.

There is no easy answer, because in addressing the protean social conception of crime, progressive reformers and judges put the courts to so many paradoxical purposes: reconciling working-class families and referring them to social agencies, punishing "home-slacker" husbands, reclaiming juvenile adult males for future citizenship, helping women charged with prostitution to find jobs, subjecting those same women to compulsory medical inspection and treatment, delivering pensions to needy single mothers, dispatching social workers to make sure those mothers kept "suitable homes," identifying hereditary mental defectives and removing them from "the life stream."

The progressive approach to social governance through law is especially beguiling because of the way it opened up new possibilities for social justice, even as it produced powerful new forms of social policing. This is the paradoxical story that emerges when we shift our focus from the rise of national- and state-level economic intervention during the early twentieth century to the local realm of social governance. Both forms of intervention were justified by the new logic of socialized law, which conceived of judges not as discoverers of the timeless logic of the law but as managers of social life. But at the level of local governance, this legal revolution was decidedly double-edged. Despite the radical potential of progressive conceptions of crime and law – which seemed to demand a more equitable distribution of wealth and power – the new vision of urban courts, as social tribunals that would expose the root causes of criminality, bankrolled an unprecedented and often coercive extension of legal and disciplinary power into the social and domestic lives of working-class city-dwellers. The noble ideals of social justice expressed in progressive policies were undercut by the fact that the "social" sphere of everyday life that the new courts claimed as their own was partly constituted by the court officials themselves, informed by broader cultural assumptions about gender, age, race, and class. Legal socialization had the salutary effect of unsettling the individualistic tenets of criminal law and forcing judges and the public to consider more seriously the human costs of poverty, inadequate wages, and substandard education. But at the same time, socialization weakened the old protections of due process and civil liberties, which had been premised on formal liberal conceptions of individual agency and responsibility. Eugenic jurisprudence was the most extreme manifestation of this tendency.

From the late nineteenth century through World War I, a two-staged judicial revolution had made Chicago a veritable city of courts: an urban social world where "everyday rights and wrongs," and much else besides, were defined, governed, and policed by local legal institutions. From 1890 to 1905, businessmen, attorneys, and structural municipal reformers – men who shared the credentials and ethos of a rising professional class – had campaigned to rationalize judicial administration in Chicago. In an age of city sense, the invention of the Municipal Court embodied their admiration for the efficiency and administrative capacity of the modern business corporation, their fears of class conflict and social disorder in a cosmopolitan industrial city, and their determination to bring local judicial officers under the heel of centralized discipline. After 1910, this organizational framework was elaborated and "humanized" by judges, many of whom had come of age in poor immigrant neighborhoods, and social activists, many of them middle-class women. The judges and activists expressed deep compassion for the urban poor and a vision of law as an interventionist instrument of social justice – an instrument perhaps able to bring the treatment of law breakers into line with the protean social conception of crime. A common faith in professional expertise, specialized knowledge, and purposeful governmental intervention made for common cause among social reformers, court consolidators, and municipal judges. After 1919, the priorities of businessmen reformers and social reformers were no longer so easily reconciled, and legal socialization encountered its first serious wave of critique. But the institutions and governmental rationality of socialized law survived. By the start of the Great Depression, the Municipal Court of Chicago was an entrenched urban bureaucracy that inspired no one to grand visions of progressive social democracy.

The records of the Municipal Court of Chicago tell the forgotten local story of the transformation of American law in the late nineteenth and early twentieth centuries. The familiar achievements of progressive legal activists in the economic sphere – the invention of a "sociological jurisprudence" that legitimated the expanding reach of the modern liberal state into the corporate economy and the industrial workplace – were institutionally and imaginatively tied to a parallel burst of intervention in the social sphere: the terrain of everyday life, where the local state could define and address the volatile relations of gender and generation, race and class. Without discounting the meaningfulness and ethical claim of the progressives' expansive social conception of crime – which implicated the inequitable social relations of the modern industrial city as a major cause of crime – we can now see that, in those local institutions where the progressives put their ideas into practice, the result was often an intensified scrutiny and control of individual offenders and their families rather than the radical reconstruction of society that progressive ideology at times seemed to demand. Much of this outcome surely had to do with the fact that, in the absence of a more developed welfare state, progressives tried to enact so much of their social reform agenda through the machinery of criminal courts, where the lines between criminality and dependency, welfare and policing, vanished perhaps *too* easily. Even if we accept Clarence Darrow's now conventional claim that "crime has its cause" – that the forces of heredity and social circumstance overwhelm individual choice in the social production of what we call crime – the question of what to do with this knowledge remains stubbornly elusive. The history of one great city court that put the idea of social responsibility for crime to the ultimate test reveals the paradoxical human consequences that may arise from using urban crime control as a political justification for even the most progressive of purposes.

Appendix: Archival Sources from the Municipal Court of Chicago

The Municipal Court of Chicago was an object of great public fascination during its first quarter-century (1906–30), when it was America's most famous big city court. The footnotes reveal my debt to the reformers, social scientists, legal academics, journalists, government investigators, and university students who left behind an incomparable body of dissertations, government reports, newspaper and magazine articles, sociological studies, and personal correspondence about the court.

The Municipal Court's annual reports are held in toto at the University of Chicago's D'Angelo Law Library. These invaluable volumes include caseload statistics, rules of procedure, bits of official history, detailed reports on specific criminal branches, and lengthy policy statements by Chief Justice Harry Olson, Dr. William J. Hickson, and other judges. Several judges also discussed their judicial philosophies and practices in public speeches and articles for law reviews, social science journals, and newspapers.

Chief Justice Olson's administrative records and official correspondence survive in the Municipal Court of Chicago Collection, 1906–27 (MCC), at the Chicago Historical Society, and the Judge Harry Olson Papers (JHO) at the Northwestern University Archives. The collections contain extensive correspondence with fellow judges and court staff, officials of local and national reform associations, social scientists and jurists, as well as litigants, defendants, defendants' relatives, prisoners, and concerned citizens. The Chicago Historical Society also holds Harry Olson's Disassembled Scrapbooks (HODS), in which the chief justice faithfully preserved hundreds of newspaper and magazine articles dealing with the court and Chicago crime.

The Cook County Circuit Court Archives in Chicago holds the Municipal Court of Chicago Criminal Records, 1914–1924 (MCCCR), which are preserved on microfilm. This is not a complete run of cases from the decade. The collection contains more than 300,000 case files, but the court handled 193,000 criminal cases in 1920 alone. It is not clear why these particular files survived, though the most complete runs are from the criminal branches that were located in City Hall, including the socialized branches. (Fortunately, the annual reports contain comprehensive statistics.) Because of their incompleteness, the case records do not lend themselves to a quantitative study, and I have not attempted one. I have used the files to paint a more textured picture of the court in action and to gain a better sense of the people whose lives the court touched: complainants, defendants, and their families.

The case files are spare. Every file includes a half-sheet: a standardized form on which clerks recorded the defendant's name, the charges against her/him, and every order entered by every judge who handled the case. Municipal Court cases were prosecuted by information rather than indictment. Every file has a copy of the information, the formal statement of complaint set down by a clerk in boiler-plate statutory language; the information includes the name of the complainant. Many case files contain arrest slips, on which the arresting officers recorded the race, age, nativity, and occupation of the defendant. (This information is not always accurate or complete.) Applications for probation – two-page questionnaires regarding work history, family, and personal property – provide additional information about defendants. Many files also include reports of probation officers. Most are perfunctory, but some detail home conditions, family histories, and employment records. Case files from the Court of Domestic Relations are especially rich because they hold the sociological data forms filled out by the Social Service Department. Files of cases that were later appealed often contain an official transcript of the Municipal Court trial, but these transcripts are not verbatim.

The Circuit Court Archives also hold a small trove of the Municipal Court's Feebleminded Commitment Cases, 1915–36, as well as the Municipal Court's General Order Books, containing all orders signed by the Municipal Court judges for the general superintendence of the court.

Index

Abbott, Edith, 108, 135, 219
Abbott, Grace, and rejection of
eugenic jurisprudence, 272
Adams, Kate, 185, 187, 201
Addams, Jane, xxii, 154, 173, 208,
214; on social atomism, 83; and
Adult Probation Act, 91; and
founding of Domestic Relations
Court, 133–4, 136–7; on
eugenics, 258
Adkins v. Children's Hospital, and
minimum wages for women,
183
Adult Probation Act, 91–5
African-Americans: migration to
Chicago, xxx; as defendants in
Domestic Relations Court, 156;
and Morals Court, 190, 205; and
criminal demographics, 197; as
defendants in Boys' Court,
217–18, 221, 228; as social
workers in Boys' Court, 224; and
eugenic jurisprudence, 266;
postwar violence against, 287–8
Aid to Mothers and Children Act
(1913), 153–4
Alger, George W., 54
Allegretti, Francis, 222, 230
Altgeld, John Peter, 11, 76–8
American Institute of Criminal
Law and Criminology, 106, 107

American Judicature Society, 49,
107, 285

Barnes, Albert C., 80
Barnes, Harry Elmer, on
nineteenth-century penal
reforms, 75–6
Barrett, James R., 146
bastardy, 142
Beard, Charles, xxv
Beccaria, Cesare, 71
Belden, Evelina, criticism of use of
continuances, 228
Bentham, Jeremy, 71, 72
Binet-Simon Intelligence Scale,
261
Boas, Franz, 271
Boies, Henry M., 85
Bowen, Louise de Koven, 155, 292,
306; and Adult Probation Act,
91; and Boys' Court, 121, 217;
and founding of Domestic
Relations Court, 133–4, 135; as
environmentalist, 245; on
feeblemindedness, 258
Boys' Court, xxxiii, 121, 283;
jurisdiction of, 210–11; common
offenses in, 219–20; compared
with Juvenile Court, 220–1; class
discrimination in, 221;
defendants in, 221–2; individual

325

crime: social vs. individual responsibility for, xxi, xxii, 61, 67, 78–9, 85–7, 138–9; Cleland on, 65–6; and free will, 68–75; and interdependence of urban life, 84–5; individual responsibility for, 247–8, 282–3, 295–6, 314, 319; mental illness as cause of, 260; increase during World War I, 287; impact of Prohibition on, 288–93; media inflation of, 289–90; growing concern with felonies, 290; surveys of, 302–3; nationalization of responsibility for, 303, 310

criminology: history of, 246–9; and eugenics, 249–51; and hereditarianism versus environmentalism debate, 252–3

Crowe, Robert E., 282

Darrow, Clarence, 67, 68, 287; and critique of eugenics, 270; and Leopold and Loeb case, 297

Deneen, Charles S, and Harry Olson, 48–9

desertion and nonsupport: cases of in Domestic Relations Court, 128–32; in nineteenth-century law, 139–42; as challenge to gender norms, 139, 143–4, 145; criminalization of, 146–55; recognition of socioeconomic causes of, 169–70

Dever, William, and Prohibition-related crime, 288–9

Devine, Edward, 147

Dewey, John, 102

Dolan, Harry P., 225, 236

Domestic Relations Court, xxxiii, 120–1, 155; established by Olson and JPA, 133–7; defendants in,

156; complainants in, 156–8; Social Services Department, 158–61, 165–8; as source of empowerment for women, 168

drunkenness, as cause of desertion and nonsupport, 143

Duguit, Leon, and socialized law, 98

Dummer, Ethel Sturges, 201; and therapeutic psychiatry, 272

Dwyer, Anna, and Morals Court, 199

Economic Security Act (1935), 314

environmentalism, 245–6, 260, 276–7

eugenic jurisprudence, 242–3

eugenics, xxvii, xxxii, 138, 276–7; Olson as supporter of, 48; and hereditarian criminology, 85, 249–50; and prostitutes, 173, 199; defined, 241–2; and environmentalism, 245–6; support for, 255–9; critiques of, 270–3; replaced by therapeutic psychiatry, 271–7

family court, defined, 155

Family Support Act (1988), 170

family wage, 171; as answer to desertion and nonsupport, 143, 151–2, 154

Federal Bureau of Investigation, 303, 310

Feebleminded Commitment Act (1915), 258

feeblemindedness, and crime, 225–9

Fernald, Walter, 250

Ferri, Enrico, 249

Field, Stephen, 142

Fisher, Harry, 186, 188, 264

Forbath, William, 42

Forthall, Sonya, 306

Foucault, Michel, xxviii, 98n3, 230

199; impact of on Boys' Court proceedings, 229–30; role in socialized court system, 259–70
public health, 114; and prostitute as victim, 173; extension of government power to protect, 176

race and racism, in eugenics, 265–6. *See also* African-Americans
Reckless, Walter, 206
Rosenberg, Charles E., 247
Rosenwald, Mrs. Julius, 135
Ross, Edward A., 5, 108, 250; on social control, 83
Royce, Josiah, 251
Ruth, David, 295–6

Singer, H. Douglas, 267; and Leopold and Loeb case, 297
Skocpol, Theda, 179
Small, Albion, xxiii, 108
Smith, Reginald Heber, 129, 149
social control, xxviii, 60; court as instrument of, 72–3, 74–5; defined, 83
social justice: and socialized law, 98; results of progressive program of, 319
social responsibility for crime. *See* crime, social vs. individual responsibility for
Social Security Act (1935), 170
Social Services Department, of Domestic Relations Court, 158–61
social workers, in Boys' Court, 223
socialized law: defined, 98; significance of, 119–120; dualism in theory and practice of, 124–5; tensions and dualities in, 138–9; retreat from, 311–12

Solomon, Meyer, 275
Sonsteby, John J., 308; judicial philosophy of, 310
Spitzka, Edward Charles, 248
St. Valentine's Day Massacre, xxxiv
Stanley, Amy Dru, 143
state, as interventionist in socialized law, 112
state building: and interventionism, 59–60; and extension of powers to control vice, 176–7, 178
Stead, William T., 23, 34, 40
Steffens, Lincoln, 29
Stelk, John, 129, 164–5, 166
sterilization, laws on compulsory, 242–3

Taft, William H., 52; and reform of federal courts, 284, 285–6
Tanenhaus, David, 213
Tarbell, Ida M., 157–8
Taylor, Graham: on the justice of the peace system, 27; and Adult Probation Act, 91
temperance, and immigrant opposition to Chicago charter reform, 43–5
Thompson, Bertha, 202
Thompson, E. P., 318
Thrasher, Frederic, 215, 218, 219, 236, 289
Trude, Daniel, 204, 229

Uhlir, Joseph Z., 130, 132, 156
University of Chicago, as center of urban sociology, xxxii
urban life: dangers of, 82–4; interdependence of, 84–5

venereal diseases, 200–4. *See also* prostitution
Vice Committee, Illinois Senate, and women's wage work, 182–3
Volstead Act, 303

9 780521 794039